THE MODEL WORD BOOK, No. 2.

THE

MODEL ETYMOLOGY,

WITH

SENTENCES SHOWING THE CORRECT USE OF WORDS·

AND A

KEY,

GIVING THE PREFIX, ROOT, AND SUFFIX.

BY

A. C. WEBB,

AUTHOR OF "THE MANUAL OF ETYMOLOGY," "MODEL DEFINER,"
"HISTORICAL COMPANION," ETC.

Revised Edition.

NEW YORK   PHILADELPHIA

HINDS, HAYDEN & ELDREDGE, Inc.

PREFACE

THE favor with which the Model Etymology was received, has led to the issue of the present revised edition, more progressive and more comprehensive than the original work.

The Review of Prefixes and Suffixes is specially arranged for use in elementary classes.

The facts, contained in the illustrative sentences, are taken from reliable sources, and will be the means of imparting much useful information.

THE KEY

Is a valuable feature of the work. It analyzes every word about which a doubt could arise, and gives not only the prefix and root, but also that most difficult part, the suffix.

	PAGE
THE IMPORTANCE OF WORDS	5
AFFIXES	7
CLASSIFICATION OF THE ENGLISH LANGUAGE	9
ANGLO-SAXON	9
LATIN AND GREEK	11
LATIN PRONUNCIATION, BY W. G. RICHARDSON, M.A.	12
THE ROMAN METHOD OF PRONOUNCING LATIN	12
THE ENGLISH METHOD OF PRONOUNCING LATIN	15
THE CONTINENTAL METHOD OF PRONOUNCING LATIN	16
THE USE OF WORDS	17
AID TO COMPOSITION	18
DEFINITIONS	20
PREFIXES	20–27
REVIEW OF PREFIXES	27–39
ARRANGEMENT FOR WRITTEN EXERCISES	39
SUFFIXES	39–51
REVIEW OF SUFFIXES	51–60
ARRANGEMENT FOR WRITTEN EXERCISES — NOTE TO STUDENTS — ABBREVIATIONS	60
LATIN DERIVATIVES, WITH A SENTENCE SHOWING THE CORRECT USE OF EACH WORD	61–225
REVIEW OF ROOTS — WORDS SELECTED PROMISCUOUSLY FROM THE FIRST ROOT THROUGH EACH SUCCESSIVE TWENTY-FIVE OR FIFTY ROOTS	225–227
KEY	228–255

WORDS.

THE importance of WORDS, in all the processes of education, cannot be over-estimated.

Education depends on a knowledge of the meaning and application of WORDS.

Knowledge can be imparted and received only by the medium of WORDS correctly used and properly understood.

The basis of a good education must be laid with WORDS well chosen, properly arranged, and firmly implanted in the mind.

A complete Unabridged Dictionary of the English language contains one hundred and fourteen thousand words; yet it is possible for knowledge to be so contracted and thought so limited that one thousand words will supply every want. It is asserted that some of the English peasantry do not use more than three hundred words. In our own country, with all our boasted education, what poverty of language!—the same adjective describing qualities totally dissimilar; adverbs conjoined which actually contradict each other; stereotyped or even slang expressions betraying utter barrenness; generic terms where precision demands specific and, still more frequently, special and definite appellatives to express general ideas which can be conveyed only by generic terms. Many intelligent persons, moving in good society, cannot talk five minutes without betraying a lamentable ignorance of so-called synonyms, an utter lack of discrimination in the choice of words, a misapplication of terms and a poverty of speech, strangely contrasting with the material wealth of their surroundings.

No matter of whom, or of what, a man speaks, the one thing

that he reveals in speaking is — *himself*. Therefore the wise man showed a knowledge of human nature when he declared that "He that shutteth his lips is esteemed a man of understanding." A wiser than Solomon unfolds a still deeper truth in the declaration, "By thy WORDS thou shalt be justified, and by thy words thou shalt be condemned," for the words used by a speaker are a sure index of the depth of his knowledge, his acquaintance with literature, range of thought, mental discipline, habits of discrimination, and power of analysis.

Convinced, then, of the absolute importance of a thorough and familiar knowledge of our language, the question arises, "How is it to be taught?" Beside the ponderous Unabridged Dictionary, with its one hundred and fourteen thousand words, we lay the childish task in "definitions," acquired with painful effort, and frequently forgotten as soon as recited. One hundred and fourteen thousand words! The undertaking seems hopeless. But here Etymology, with its generalization and analysis, comes to our aid. It makes the impossible the possible. It takes the task out of the drudgery of mere abstract memorizing, and transforms it into a delightful pursuit. It awakens the perceptive faculties by presenting resemblances and differences; it strengthens the memory by calling reason and judgment to its aid. It invigorates all the powers of the mind, and enlarges its capacity by training it to accuracy and precision in the classification of words. The study of definitions is like the gathering of an armful of crooked and jagged sticks. Each gnarled and knotty limb lies apart from its fellow. The rough edges pierce the flesh; and in the attempt to add to our stock we lose those already acquired with such painful effort. But when we study the English language etymologically, we are as one who walks in a lovely garden, to cull its choicest flowers. Each step reveals new beauties. Fresh surprises await us on every hand. The senses are regaled and delighted. All the faculties of mind and body are stimulated and roused to active exercise. Attracted on every side, we go on, unweariedly, from flower-bed to flower-bed, gathering here a blossom and there a bud, constantly adding to our stock new treasures and new beauties. So with the student of Etymology. He is charmed with the novelty, delighted with fresh acquisitions of knowledge, and satisfied in the consciousness that faithful labor will be rewarded by a thorough knowledge of the language. While it is true that there are over one hundred thousand words, it is also true that the key to the meanings of a large portion of them is found in a few Root Words, not numbering probably one thousand.* Facio, factum, to make, to do, enters into the composition of six hundred words. By the aid of affixes, not less than three thousand words are derived from ten easy roots.

  Capio, I take.   Facio, I make.
  Grapho, I write.   Logos, reason, discourse, science.
  Mitto, I send.   Pono, I put, I place.
  Sedeo, I sit.   Sisto, I stand.
  Traho, I draw.   Verto, I turn.

A knowledge of the small number of Root Words gives us a conception of the wonderful formative and modifying power of affixes.

Affixes.

The richness and diversity of the English language result from causes which are organic. The language has reached its high rank by a steady growth; by development from within and not by accretions and additions from without. The words borrowed from foreign languages, and incorporated without change, in the English, do not number more than five per cent. Those who have given little attention to the subject, would be astonished at the number of words into which a single prefix or suffix enters. Take, for example, the prefix *un*, meaning in verbs, *to reverse the act of; to deprive of;* and in adjectives, *the reverse of; not*, and we shall find it probably in not less than seven thousand words. *Con*, with the various forms which it assumes, as, *co, col, com*, and its Greek equivalent, *syn*, probably enters into the composition of five thousand. We have no means of verifying these calculations, for even "Unabridged Dictionaries" do not attempt to give all the "compounds." Our purpose is to show the value of the study of Etymology to all classes of students — to those who are familiar with Latin and Greek, as well as to those whose only knowledge of these languages is their etymologic relation to the English. A careful investigation leads to the estimate, that

---

  * The whole number of Root Words is said to be less than five hundred, and philologists confidently expect, by continued research, to reduce the number to three hundred.

not less than twenty-five thousand words are formed by the use of ten prefixes, the same number of suffixes form or modify not less than sixteen thousand important words. By the small amount of study necessary to acquire the meanings of these thirty elements, we obtain a clew to the signification of each of the large number of words of which they are component parts; for there is no word whose meaning is not better understood by knowing the elements which compose it; while in a large number of derivatives, the etymologic is the only true meaning. The analysis of words reveals fine distinctions and subtle differences, never perceived by one ignorant of the roots from which they sprung. A homely, common flower, under the microscope of the botanist, discloses delicate tints and rare beauties never suspected by the careless observer; so a word, when seen through the glass of the etymologist, reveals beautiful analogies and remarkable differences; shows diverging and converging lines; calls up historic associations or national relations; tells of conquest, or commerce, or religious zeal, nay, ofttimes discloses in bold relief the very date when the stock, from which has sprung this beautiful flower, took root and became indigenous to our soil.

To the uneducated man, a large number of words have their synonyms. He is unable to detect any difference between the word and its meaning. Yet the number of words which appear exactly synonymous, might well be taken as a test of a man's knowledge of language. Generally, it will be in inverse ratio to the number of synonyms which exist in his mind. It is doubtful if, in the whole range of the English language, there are two words truly synonymous.

Instruction,	Education.
Demolition,	Destruction.
Eradicate,	Destroy.
Raze,	Pull down.
Dilapidation,	Ruin.
Dilation,	Expansion.

The ideas conveyed by these words, and many others which might be cited, serve as a gauge, a sure test of the mental status. To the child, first introduced to one of these words as a definition of the other, there is no difference between them — they are synonymous. To the grown-up children, whose minds have remained stationary while their bodies have grown to the normal size, these words present no differences. *To instruct* and *to educate* convey to such a mind but one idea. If asked whether he wishes his child *instructed* or *educated*, he would probably answer, "I do not care which, so that you make a man of him." He cannot conceive the idea, that merely to instruct a child will never make a man of him. The thing that is *pulled down*, is to him *demolished, destroyed, razed*, or *ruined*. All the words present precisely the same mental picture. Were you to tell him that the word "raze" depicted to your mind a *razor* and *the act of shaving*, he would have grave doubts of your sanity.

You tell your gardener to *eradicate* the wild carrot that disfigures the lawn. He thinks he is obeying your command when he mows them down with his scythe. You have to explain to him the fact that he has only *destroyed* them; that to *eradicate* a thing is to *take out the root*. (*E*, out; *radix, radicis*, a root; *ate*, to take.)

Classification of the English Language.

The words of the English language form three classes:
1. Anglo-Saxon words.
2. Words derived from Latin and Greek.
3. A comparatively small number of words borrowed, often without change, from other nations.

Anglo-Saxon.

The first of these, the Anglo-Saxon, is the framework of our speech. It is what we lovingly call our "mother-tongue." Three-fifths of the words of our every-day life are Saxon. It comes to us laden with the richest and dearest gifts — mother, father, husband, wife, brother, sister. It has inwoven itself into the warp and woof of our life. None but our dear mother-tongue, that we lisped in our childish days, tells us of the home, the hearth, the cradle, the thatch, and the roof-tree. Bread and broth, hay and harvest, wheat and oats, calf and cow and corn, the waving grass, the tall bending fir, the wide-spreading elm, the barley and the berry, the plow and the scythe, the open barn-door, with the chaff which the wind driveth away before the thresher's flail, all take us back to the happy household and well-tilled farm of a good, kind, well-to-do Anglo-Saxon before the Norman had stamped upon the Angle-Land his Norman-French. He needed not to go to the gay, sprightly Gaul, or the proud Roman of the olden time, to borrow the words in which to embody his choicest thoughts. The manliness of the son, the watchful care of the daughter, the cooing of the baby, the merry trill and laugh of little ones, who fill the house with joy, lose none of their loveliness by their home-made garb.

It is this dear mother-tongue that heaves up a heaven over our heads, that folds the tiny hands, and teaches the childish lips to say "Our Father which art in heaven."

So with all things around us in water and earth and sky. The day dawns with earliest blush of morn; the full moon and pale stars fade away in the west; the sun floods the round earth with his golden light; the dew sparkles in pearly drops on every leaflet; silvery clouds mingle with those of every hue, and sail on over stream and flood and sea; winter's cold and frost flee away at the breath of spring; in the summer's glare, the reaper hies him, for his noontide meal, to the purling brook, and cools his brow and slakes his thirst in its clear waters; thunders roll, lightnings flash, rain and storm, hail and ice and snow fill up the year, but none of these borrow aught of their worth from another tongue.

Thus it will be seen that the Saxon is the outcome of our every-day life. Saxon words are short. They do not change. They are understood by all, because they are needed by all. Both the old and the young, the good and the bad, the high and the low, *are*, and *do*, and *bear* in Saxon. We eat and drink, talk and laugh, come and go, get and give, love and hate, kill and make alive, buy and sell, chaffer and chew, blaze and blow, and ask help neither of Roman nor Greek, Frenchman nor Spaniard. We can send our ships over the sea, laden with the things that we have made, and then, weary with the long, busy day, at eventide we can sing our own songs, play our merriest games, read the best of books, and lie down to health-giving sleep, nor dream that there is lack or want in our dear old Saxon tongue.*

---

* It would be well for Teachers to call the attention of pupils to the difference in the style produced by the use of Anglo-Saxon words, or by Latin and Greek derivatives. Pupils will be interested in contrasting the small number of Latin and Greek derivatives in this article, compared to those employed in treating of the "Latin and Greek."

LATIN AND GREEK.

But with all our affection for the language of our infancy, we discover, as we advance towards adolescence, that it is totally inadequate to the exigencies of adult years. When we quit the paternal roof, and associate with strangers, novel objects present themselves, and old ones appear under varied and complex forms. Our range of vision enlarges itself. We attain to a more elevated plane, and our horizon is extended; imagination becomes more vivid; every faculty, whether mental or physical, is energized and invigorated. With everything new without and within, a new and totally different language is required. So, too, in the nation's life. As the English-speaking people developed into a manhood characterized by intellectual activity, profound research, and inventive genius, a new vocabulary was absolutely necessary. The ever-increasing circles of power and influence were constantly enclosing new words. As diplomatic, commercial, and scientific relations, united the English inseparably with the most cultured nations; as invention stimulated invention, and one wonderful discovery was but the incentive and prelude to another still more remarkable; as the products of their numerous factories were sent to every mart, there came back in exchange foreign names, terms, and modes of expression.

But the English language as it exists to-day, was not produced by simply borrowing words from other languages, and incorporating them without change in the vernacular. The transformation was a radical one — the grafting on the old, sturdy, Anglo-Saxon stock new buds, which have taken root, and have grown and blossomed, and fruited into the richest, most expressive, and most varied language of the living languages of the globe. This ingrafting has been principally from the Latin and Greek. The language of literary persons, and of authors - of non-scientific works, is composed of Saxon and Latin derivatives; while the Terminology of the whole range of Science, Art, and Mechanism is formed principally from the Greek. So small is the Greek element — not more than five per cent.— that the special advantages of the study of Etymology are:

First. In its application to that part of the language which is derived from the Latin.

Second. To that part derived from the Greek.

Third. To the Anglo-Saxon.

Latin Pronunciation.

There are three modes of pronouncing Latin:

1. The Latin; called also the Roman, and by some the Phonetic Method.
2. The Continental.
3. The English.

On the vexed question of the various modes, General Eaton, the Commissioner of Education, has been collecting facts from every part of the country. The information thus gathered is embodied and tabulated in a most interesting article from the pen of W. G. Richardson, M. A., Professor of Latin, Central University, Richmond, Ky. We think we shall confer a favor on the large number of educators who do not see the Report, by giving extracts from the article.

Professor Richardson says, "So far as I have been able to ascertain, the present prevailing pronunciation in England, namely, the English, does not go back two centuries. In the United States, till within the past twenty years, two systems have held nearly equal sway, the advantage being rather with the English system. But in the period named, the Latin method has made decided advances. At this time, usage is about equally shared among the three. The world over, nearly all the Latin grammarians and orthoepists of the last quarter of a century have urged a return to first principles. The Latin has rights of its own and a demonstrated pronunciation, which should be respected, as in the case of the sister tongue."

Speaking of the Bibliographical List for the Latin Pronunciation, Prof. Richardson says, "America may claim the credit of leading this reform, in the person of Prof. S. S. Haldeman, of the University of Pennsylvania. His admirable little treatise is entitled, Elements of Latin Pronunciation, for the use of students in language, law, medicine, zoölogy, botany, and the sciences generally in which Latin words are used."

The Roman Method of Pronouncing Latin

VOWELS.

Long and short vowels generally differ in quantity, not quality of sound.

$\bar{a}$ is sounded like our *a* in *father*.

LATIN PRONUNCIATION. 13

ĕ is French è, which Surenne properly represents as our e in *met*, very slightly prolonged. ē is same in quality, differing only in quantity.

ī as *i* in *machine;* ĭ as *i* in *purity*.

ō as *o* in *no*. For ŏ Roby gives *dot*.

ū like *oo* in *moon;* ŭ short, like *u* in *full*.

y intermediate between *i* and *u*.

A short vowel rendered long by position, as, for instance, *e* in *est* and *esse*, is still pronounced short.

Great care should be taken as to final short syllables; *e. g.*, essĕ, amatŭr, amatŭs. Distinguish fructŭs and fructūs.

DIPHTHONGS.

In all these each element is heard. Let the combination be rapid.

æ or *ai*, like *ay* (yes). In rapid utterance, it is nearly our personal pronoun of the first person. ī is a compound sound made up of *ah* and *ee*.

au like *ow* in *now*. The analysis is *ah-oo*. The rapid combination is *ow* in *now*.

ei as in *vein*, slightly drawled, and not like the English *i* in *time*.

eu as *eh-oo*, many give the sound of *eu* in *feud*.

œ or *oi* like *oi* in *oil*.

ui like French *oui;* very nearly our pronoun *we*.

CONSONANTS.

d, f, h, k, l, n, p, t, as in English.

bs like *ps*. Thus, *urbs, oorps*.

c hard like *k*.

g hard, as in *give*.

s always hissing, as in *this;* never like *z*.

ti with the pure sound of *t* always preserved; thus, *natio, nah-te-o,* and not *nā-she-o* or *nah-she-o*.

v is English *w*.

ps preserves the sound of both its elements, as in *psallo*.

As bearing upon the present situation of the controversy respecting Latin pronunciation, we give extracts from a paper read before the Massachusetts Association of Classical and High School Teachers, and printed in a recent number of the N. E. Journal of Education. The writer, E. R. Humphreys, LL.D., formerly of

Cambridge University, England, addressed letters of inquiry to various classical teachers, as to the methods of pronunciation used by them.

"I may at once say that the new system of pronunciation of Latin does not prevail at all in Oxford, i. e., is in no way publicly recognized, nor is it used by many, if indeed by any, of the tutors."

Rev. Mandell Creighton, A. M., recently for several years Dean and Tutor of Merton College, Oxford; now Vicar of Embleton, England.

"There is, I think, no great difference of opinion here in regard to the principles of Latin pronunciation; even the w sound of v is secure from ridicule."

Rev. John E. B. Mayor, M. A., Professor of Latin in the University of Cambridge, England.

REMARKS BY DR. HUMPHREYS.

"I BELIEVE that in most points the theory of Latin pronunciation associated with the name of Corssen in Germany, and Roby in England — most emphatically excepting, however, the weak Semitic sound of v as w — is correct. But even if I felt bound to assent to every one of the claims, made by these advocates of the so-called Roman pronunciation, I should still maintain that theory, based to some considerable extent on the law of probabilities, is one thing, and the altering by us of the mode of pronunciation of an ancient language, which enters so largely into the structure of our own English, a mode that has prevailed for so many centuries, is another and very different thing — a thing demanding very careful consideration. It has seemed to me, I confess, all along, that in thus too hastily undertaking to do justice to ancient Latin, we run the risk of doing great injustice, great injury, to our own modern English-American language, — into which the Latin has been constantly insinuating itself for the last three hundred years and more, ever in the garb of what is now termed the 'old-fashioned English' pronunciation.

. . . .

"But in Great Britain, as appears from this correspondence, there is no probability of the adoption of the new system to any material extent for a very long period of time, if ever. And in regard to the other countries of Europe, except, perhaps, some few of the German Universities, I do not hesitate a moment to say, that the Latin scholars of those countries would find it more difficult to understand an American or English Latinist speaking by this 'reformed' rule than ever they found it to be, even when listening to the old-fashioned English pronunciation. Italian scholars, especially, would deem this new method no less harsh than unintelligible.

"The most serious point, however, to my mind, is the confusion and injury which, as it seems to me, the sweeping change proposed is likely to produce in the pronunciation, and consequently in the intelligent study, of our own language, which surely deserves our first care and consideration. *The study of the Etymology of English I have always found to be a powerful and attractive means* of winning and leading on young minds and hearts, previously averse to learning, to an earnest study, first of their own language, and then of others which enter into its formation, especially the Latin. Hitherto, it has not been difficult to make clear to young and even dull children the close relationship of English and Latin; but if the hard pronunciation of *c* and *g*, and some of the other 'reforms,' be once generally accepted, the likeness and connection will only be patent to advanced Latin scholars.

"The appended tables indicate the usage in pronouncing Latin in the 237 Universities and Colleges and the 87 preparatory schools named, as reported by them to the United States Bureau of Education.

"Of the Universities and Colleges, 72 use the Latin or Roman method, 75 the Continental, and 90 the English.

"Of the preparatory schools, 25 use the Latin, 28 the Continental, and 34 the English."

THE ENGLISH METHOD OF PRONOUNCING LATIN.

1. EVERY word in Latin must have as many syllables as it has vowels and diphthongs; *viva voce, miles, male, fames, Ædes, dies, comes, ranceo,* pronounced *vī'va vo'cē; mī'lēs; mā'lē; fā'mēs; e'dēs; dī'ēs; cō'mēs; ran'cē-o.*

2. *C* is pronounced hard like *k* before *a, o, u*; and soft like *s* before *e, i, y, œ,* and *æ*; as *cado,* pronounced *ka'do; cælum,* pronounced *se'lum; cedo,* pronounced *se'do.*

3. *Ch* is pronounced like *k*; as, *chorus,* pronounced *ko'rus.*

4. *G* is pronounced hard before *a, o, u,* and soft like *j* before *e, i, y, æ, œ*; as, *gusto,* in which *g* is pronounced as in *Augusta; gero,* pronounced *je'ro.*

5. When a syllable ends in a consonant, the vowel has the short English sound; as, *bellum,* pronounced *bel'lum.*

6. Two consonants in the middle of a word, not proper to begin a word, must be divided; as, *mille,* pronounced *mil'le.*

7. The diphthongs *æ* and *œ* are sounded like *e*; as, *cædo,* pronounced *ce'do.*

Au is pronounced as in *author, aurum, plau'do.*

Eu is pronounced as in *neuter.*

8. Words of two syllables are accented on the first; as, *ager,* pronounced *a'jer.*

9. When a word of more than one syllable ends in *a,* the *a* should be sounded like *ah*; as, *musa,* pronounced *mu'sah.*

10. *Es,* at the end of a word, is pronounced like the English word *ease;* as, *miles,* pronounced *mi'les.*

11. *T, s,* and *c,* before *ia, ie, ii, io, iu,* and *eu,* preceded immediately by the accent, in Latin words, as in English, change into *sh* and *zh*; as, *fa'cio,* pronounced *fa'sheo; san'cio,* pronounced *san'sheo; spa'tium,* pronounced *spa'sheum; so'cius,* pronounced *sō'she-us.*

12. In final syllables ending in a vowel, the vowel is long; as, *glutio, sacri, servo, cornu,* pronounced *glū'she-ō, sā'krī, ser'vō, cor'nū.*

In final syllables ending in a consonant, the vowel is generally short; as, *ac'tŭm, nav'ĭs, no'mĕn.* In *pōst, rēs,* and some others, the vowel is long.

13. *S* is generally pronounced as in *sacred;* as, *sa'cer, sol, ser'vo;* but *s* final after *e, au, b, m, n, r,* is pronounced like *z*; as, *res, fraus, urbs, hi'ems, mens, fors.*

14. *X* has its regular English sound, like *ks*; as, *rex, lex.*

15. When two consonants, the sounds of which will not coalesce, commence a word, the first is generally silent; as, *Ptolemy,* pronounced *tol'e-me. Ch* before a mute consonant at the beginning of a word is silent; as, *Chthonia,* pronounced *Thonia.*

CONTINENTAL METHOD OF PRONOUNCING LATIN.

IN the Latin Grammar of Dr. Harkness, the Continental Method is dismissed (p. 7) with this remark: "The Continental Method, as adopted in this country, is almost identical with the Roman, except in the pronunciation of the consonants, in which it more nearly coincides with the English."

The Use of Words.

One of the problems in education, is to determine the method by which pupils are to be taught the correct use of words. From the richness of the English language, which gives many words to the same meaning, and many and diverse meanings to the same word, the proper *use* of a word cannot be deduced from its *meaning*. How, then, is the knowledge of the use of words to be imparted to children? Either by the teacher, or by conversation and reading. The knowledge acquired by conversation and reading is limited in extent; and, as it is entirely dependent on the power of observation, the impressions are faint and ill-defined, and the conclusions frequently incorrect.

No teacher would think of teaching Arithmetic by simply imparting the Rules, and then leaving to the child their correct application. Yet, the practice of Arithmetic might possibly be left to such teaching, inasmuch as Arithmetic is an exact science based on fixed principles, from which correct *reasoning* must deduce correct *results*. But no *reasoning* can show to the child, who has learned "*Deduce, to draw*," that he must not say, "I tried *to deduce* the horse from the stable;" or, "*Deciduous, falling*." "The boy *deciduous* from the window, was killed." The sympathizing teacher feels acute pain in witnessing the disappointment of the pupil, whose industrious and well-meant effort only provoked a laugh from idle scholars, who made no failure, because they made no attempt. Witness such failures as the following, taken from school exercises:

Incipient, commencing. We are *incipient* to draw.

Acute, sharp. The razor is *acute*.

Cogent, forcible. The boy gave a *cogent* blow, and the door flew open.

Aperture, opening. Mrs. A. will have her millinery *aperture* next week.

These are the errors of untrained children; but the laughable mistakes of intelligent foreigners, when they attempt to use words according to their meaning, is conclusive proof of the proposition that —

The only way by which the use of a word can be taught is to give a sentence in which the word is correctly used.

Even in his vernacular, an educated man would not use a word which he had neither seen in writing nor heard from the lips of a good speaker. Take, for instance, *Uncial*, relating to letters of a large size; *Intercalate*, to insert; *Fiduciary*, firm,—what intelligent man would *use* these words simply because he knew their meaning? How unjust and useless, then, to demand of an ignorant and untrained *child* that which no *adult* can give, namely, the *correct use* of a word derived from its *meaning* only.

Some teachers, convinced by experience of the necessity of illustrative sentences, require children to procure them at home. But the importance and difficulty of the work demand that it should not be left to the uncertainties of home teaching. The labor involved forbids that this essential part of education should be imposed on the parent. Like Arithmetic, or any other department of knowledge, it should be performed by the teacher in the time specially set apart for mental training.

The plan adopted in "The Model Word-Book Series," of giving illustrative sentences, is not new. All good *Dictionaries* illustrate the meaning by a *Model*. Just as the Patent-Office requires a "model" as well as a description, so a definition or explanation of a word is not complete without an illustrative sentence. To quote from a *good author* a sentence containing the word, as proof of its correct use, is the only authority acknowledged by literary men.

Aid to Composition.

TEACHERS will find the sentences a great assistance to pupils in that most difficult of all departments of education—composition. Where Teachers wish to make it an exercise in composition, they will find it of great advantage to require pupils to prepare sentences from the models given, excluding all derivatives except the word assigned.

Ex.: "Many who would not DEIGN to *notice* Columbus when he left Spain, except to *denounce* him as a *visionary* enthusiast, were willing to *ennoble* him on his return."

Many who would not DEIGN to speak to Columbus when he left Spain, paid him great attention on his return.

A simple trial of the work, either by requiring the pupil to form sentences similar to those given, or to memorize the sentences as models for future use, will convince any one of the following

ADVANTAGES TO BE DERIVED FROM THE "MODEL WORD-BOOK" SERIES.

1. Saving of time.
2. Increased knowledge of words.
3. Ease to teacher and scholar.
4. A knowledge of the correct use of words.
5. A knowledge of a large number of facts, commercial, historical, and scientific.
6. A great help in teaching Composition.

THE
MODEL ETYMOLOGY.

PART I.

DEFINITIONS.

Etymology is the science which treats of the origin and derivation of words.

A **Prefix** is a syllable placed *before* a root; as, **in,** meaning *not,* in**correct,** *not* correct; **con,** meaning *with* or *together,* **con**nect, to tie *together.*

A **Root** is the radical or essential part of a word; as, **act**-um in the word **act**-ion, **ann**-us in **ann**-als.

A **Suffix** is a syllable placed *after* a root; as, **ant,** meaning *one who,* ten**ant,** *one who* holds; **ize,** meaning *to make,* fertil**ize,** *to make* fertile.

I. PREFIXES
OF ANGLO-SAXON ORIGIN.

1. A signifies *on, in, to, at;* **a**field, *to* the field; **a**board, *on* board; **a**far, *at* a distance.

2. Be signifies *over, to cover with, about, upon;* **be**daub, to daub *over;* **be**mire, *to cover with* mire. In a preposition or a conjunction, **be** means *by;* **be**cause, *by* the cause.

3. En, with the form **em,** signifies *in, on, into, to make, to put into, to put in,* or *to put on;* enclose, to close *in;* endear, *to make* dear; embark, *to put into* a bark.

4. Fore signifies *before;* forenoon, the part of the day *before* noon; foretell, to tell *beforehand.* There is another **fore, for,** not related to the preceding, which has a *negative* meaning, or it shows that the action was done in a *bad* sense, as forswear, to swear *falsely;* forego, to give up, to resign.

5. In. Im. See **En, Em.** Imbitter, *to make* bitter.

6. Mis signifies *wrong, erroneous.* Misbelief, *erroneous* belief; miscall, to call *wrong.*

7. Out signifies *beyond, more than;* outbid, to bid *more than* (another); outlive, to live *beyond* (something specified).

8. Over signifies *too much, too great;* overburden, to burden *too much;* overload, *too great* a load.

9. Un signifies *to reverse the act of, to deprive of; the reverse of, not;* unbolt, *to reverse the act of* bolting; uncrown, *to deprive of* the crown; unclean, *not* clean; unjust, *the reverse of* just.

10. Under signifies *beneath, less than another;* under-sheriff, one *beneath* the sheriff; underbid, to bid *less than another.*

11. With signifies *from, against;* withdraw, to draw *from;* withstand, to stand *against.*

II. PREFIXES

OF LATIN ORIGIN.

1. Ab, with the forms* **a, abs,** signifies *from* or *away.*
AVERT', (verto, I turn,) to turn *away.*
ABSOLVE', (solvo, I loose,) to loose *from.*

---

* Teachers should give a great deal of practice in reciting the "Forms" of the prefixes, thus:
A, for **Ab,** signifies *from* or *away.*
A, for **Ad,** signifies *to.*
Cog, for **Con,** signifies *with* or *together.*

2. **Ad**, with the forms **a, ac, af, ag, al, am, an, ap, ar, as, at,** signifies *to*.
    Adhere', (hæreo, I stick,) to stick *to*.
    Accede', (cedo, I yield,) to yield *to*.
    Appear', (pareo, I am present,) to be present *to*.
    Attest', (testis, a witness,) to witness *to*.
    Attract', (traho, tractum, to draw,) to draw *to*.

3. **Am**, with the forms **amb, ambi,** signifies *round* or *about*.
    Am'putate, (puto, I think; I cut or prune,) to cut *round* or off.

4. **Ante**, with the forms **an, ant, ante,** signifies *before*.
    Antece'dent, (cedo, I yield, I go away,) going *before*.

5. **Circum**, with the form **circu,** signifies *around* or *about*.
    Circumvent', (venio, ventum, to come,) to come *around*.
    Circu'itous, (eo, itum, to go,) going *around*.
    Circumnaviga'tion, (navis, a ship; ago, I do, I perform,) going *around* in a ship.

6. **Cis** signifies *on this side*.
    Cis-Atlan'tic, *on this side* the Atlantic.

7. **Con**, with the forms **co, cog, col, com, cor,** signifies *with* or *together*.
    Compress', (premo, pressum, to press,) to press *together*.
    Convoke', (voco, I call,) to call *together*.
    Cohere', (hæreo, I stick,) to stick *together*.

8. **Contra**, with the forms **counter, contro,** signifies *against; contrary to*.
    Counteract', (ago, actum, to do, to perform,) to act *against*.
    Contradict', (dico, dictum, to say,) to speak *contrary to*.
    Countermand', (mando, mandatum, to command,) to command *contrary to*.

9. De signifies *down* or *from*.
DECLINE', (clino, I bend, I lie down,) to bend *down*.
DEPOSE', (pono, positum, to put, to place,) to put *down* or *from*.
DESCEND', (scando, I climb,) to climb *down*.
DESCRIBE', (scribo, I write,) to write *down*.

10. Demi signifies *half*.

11. Dis, with the forms **di, dif,** signifies *asunder, apart, away; not.*
DIVERGE', (vergo, I bend,) to bend or incline *apart*.
DISTRIB'UTE, (tribuo, tributum, to give,) to give *away*.
DISPEL', (pello, I drive,) to drive *away*.
DI'VERSE, (verto, versum, to turn,) turned *asunder*, various.

12. En signifies *in, on, into; not; to make.*
ENGRAVE', to grave *on*.
ENTOMB', to put *in* a tomb.
EN'EMY, (amicus, a friend,) *not* a friend.

13. Ex, with the forms **e, ec, ef,** signifies *out.*
EXCEED', (cedo, I yield, I go,) to go beyond or *out*.
EXPORT', (porto, I carry,) to carry *out*.
EXPEL', (pello, I drive,) to drive *out*.
EXPAND', (pando, I spread,) to spread *out*, to enlarge.
EMIT', (mitto, I send,) to send *out*.
ERASE', (rado, rasum, to shave, to scrape,) to scrape or rub *out*.

14. Extra signifies *beyond.*
EXTRAOR'DINARY, *beyond* ordinary.

15. In, with the forms **ig, il, im, ir, em, en,** signifies *in, on, into, not.*
INDUCE', (duco, I lead,) to lead *in*.
INHALE', (halo, I breathe,) to breathe *in*.
IMPORT', (porto, I carry,) to carry *in*.
IMPLANT', (planto, I plant,) to plant *in*.
INFUSE', (fundo, fusum, to pour,) to pour *into*.

IMPRESS', (premo, pressum, to press,) to press *upon*.
ILLU'MINATE, (lumen, luminis, light,) to put light *into*.
IMMATURE',* (maturus, ripe,) *not* ripe.

16. Inter, with the forms **enter, intel**, signifies *between, among*.
INTERCEDE', (cedo, I go,) to go *between*.
INTERPOSE', (pono, positum, to put, to place,) to place *between*.
INTERVENE', (venio, I come,) to come *between*.

17. Intra signifies *within*.
INTRAMU'RAL, (murus, a wall,) *within* the walls (of a city).

18. Intro signifies *within*.
INTRODUCE', (duco, I lead,) to lead *within*.

19. Juxta signifies *near to*.
JUXTAPOSI'TION, (pono, positum, to put, to place,) the state of being placed *near to* (anything).

20. Mis signifies *wrong, erroneous*.
MISCON'DUCT, (duco, ductum, to lead,) *wrong* conduct.

21. Neg for **nec** signifies *not*.
NEGLECT', (lego, lectum, to gather, to select, to read,) culpable omission.

22. Non signifies *not*.
NON'SENSE, (sentio, sensum, to feel, to think,) *not* sense.

23. Ob, with the forms **o, obs, oc, of, op, os,** signifies *in the way, against, out*.
OBSTRUCT', (struo, structum, to build, to construct,) to place something *in the way*.
OBTRUDE', (trudo, I thrust,) to thrust *in the way*.
OPPOSE', (pono, positum, to put, to place,) to place *against*.

24. Per, with the forms **pel, pil, pol, pur,** signifies *through, thoroughly*.

---

* The prefix **in**, with the forms **ig, il, im, ir,** in adjectives signifies *not*.

PREFIXES OF LATIN ORIGIN. 25

PERVADE', (vado, I go,) to go or spread *through*.
PERFORM', (forma, form, beauty,) to form *through*.
PURSUE', (sequor, secutus, to follow,) to follow (*through*).

25. Post signifies *after*.
POST'SCRIPT, (scribo, scriptum, to write,) something written *after* (the signature).

26. Pre signifies *before*.
PRECEDE', (cedo, I yield, I go,) to go *before*.
PREDICT', (dico, dictum, to say,) to say *before*.
PRE'FIX, (figo, fixum, to fix,) a syllable placed *before* a root.

27. Preter signifies *beyond*, or *more than*.
PRETERNAT'URAL, (nascor, natus, born,) *beyond* or *more than* what is natural.

28. Pro, with the forms **por, pur, pru**, signifies *for, forth, forward; out*.
PROCEED', (cedo, I yield, I go,) to go *forward*.
PROCLAIM', (clamo, I cry out, I shout,) to cry *out*.
PROLONG', (longus, long,) to lengthen *out*.
PRO'NOUN, (nomen, a name,) a word that stands *for* a noun.
PUR'POSE, (pono, positum, to put, to place,) to intend.

29. Re, with the forms **red, ren**, signifies *back; again, anew*.
RECEDE', (cedo, I yield, I go,) to go *back*.
RECLAIM', (clamo, I cry out,) to call *back*.
RECLINE', (clino, I bend,) to bend *back*.
REFORM', (forma, form, beauty,) to form *anew*.
REPEL', (pello, I drive,) to drive *back*.
RESPOND', (spondeo, I promise,) to answer *back*.
REVIVE', (vivo, I live,) to live *again*.
REVOKE', (voco, I call,) to repeal, to call *back*.

30. Retro signifies *backward*.
RET'ROGRADE, (gradior, I go step by step,) to go or move *backward*.

31. Se signifies *aside, apart.*
Secede', (cedo, I yield, I go,) to go *apart* (from a party or denomination).
Seclude', (claudo, or cludo, I shut,) to shut *apart.*

32. Semi signifies *half.*
Sem'i-circle, (circus, a circle,) *half* a circle.

33. Sine, with the forms **sim, sin,** signifies *without.*
Si'necure, (cura, care,) *without* care (a situation or office without employment).
Sim'ple, (plico, I fold,) without fold; artless.

34. Sub, with the forms **su, suc, suf, sug, sum, sup, sur, sus,** signifies *under.*
Subscribe', (scribo, I write,) to write (one's name) *under.*
Submit', (mitto, I send,) to send *under;* to yield.
Subvert', (verto, I turn,) to turn *under;* to overthrow.
Succumb', (cumbo, I lie down,) to lie down *under,* to sink *under* a difficulty.
Suf'fix, (figo, fixum, to fix, to fasten,) a syllable placed after a root.
Surrepti'tious, (raptum, to snatch,) without proper authority.
Suspend', (pendeo, I hang,) to hang (*under*).
Suspect', (specio, spectum, to look, to see,) to mistrust; to see *under* something.

35. Subter signifies *under.*
Sub'terfuge, (fugio, I flee,) an evasion; a fleeing *under.*

36. Super, with the form **sur,** signifies *above, over, more than enough.*
Supernat'ural, (nascor, natus, born,) *above* the natural.
Super'fluous, (fluo, I flow,) flowing *over;* unnecessary.
Supervise', (video, visum, to see,) to *over* see.

37. Trans, with the forms **tran, tra, tres,** signifies *over, through, beyond.*
Transact', (ago, actum, to do, to perform,) to do.

TRANSFER', (fero, I bear, I carry,) to bear *over* to another.
TRANSPORT', (porto, I carry,) to carry *beyond* (the sea).
TRES'PASS, (passus, a pace, a step,) to step *beyond*.

38. Ultra signifies *beyond*.
ULTRAMUN'DANE, (mundus, the world,) *beyond* the world.

Review of Prefixes.

[*This exercise is intended to familiarize pupils with the prefixes, and at the same time to teach a few of the more important roots. It can be omitted in advanced classes.*]
There is a great objection to the common practice of invariably giving the definition of a verb in the infinitive mood. Comparatively speaking, this form of the verb is rarely used; and the attempt to force it into sentences, in which the idea would be much more easily expressed by a finite verb, tends to produce a stiff and awkward style. Teachers will find it an excellent exercise to require the meaning both in the infinitive and in the mood and tense used in the sentence. This will aid pupils in giving the exact meaning of the verbs that occur in their reading, and will correct the pernicious habit of defining every verb in the infinitive, no matter what its mood may be.

1. *A'go,* I do, I perform. *Ac'tum,* to do, to perform.
 EXACT', *a.* accurate.
 TRANSACT', *v.* to perform.
  Be very *exact* when you are sent to *transact* any business.

2. *Ar'ma,* arms, weapons.
 DISARM', *v.* to take away the arms.
  When a rebel is taken prisoner, it is necessary to *disarm* him.

3. *Bel'lum,* war.
 REB'EL, *n.* one who revolts.
  When a *rebel* is taken prisoner, it is necessary to take away his gun, and other weapons.

4. *Bi'ni,* two by two.
 COMBINE', *v.* unite.
  A cipher has no value, *except* we *combine* it with a figure.

5. *Ca'pio,* I take. *Cap'tum,* to take.
 INTERCEPT', *v.* to seize by the way.
 EXCEPT', unless (4).*

---

* A number *after* a word, refers to the paragraph in which the sentence containing the word is found; thus, Except, unless (4). The word "Except" will be found in the sentence under Root 4.

General Gage found it difficult to *provide* for the army, as the Americans endeavored to **intercept** his supplies.

6. Ce'do, I yield, I go.   **Ces'sum,** to yield, to go.

ACCEDE', *v.* to agree.
CONCEDE', *v.* admit.
EXCEED', *v.* go beyond.
INTERCEDE', *v.* to request in behalf of another.
PRECEDE', *v.* to go before.
PROCEED', *v.* go forward.
RECEDE', *v.* to go back.

Columbus tried every means to *induce* Queen Isabella to **accede** to his request.

"I do not **concede** the point, that you have the right to tax us," said John Adams.

The cotton, wheat, wool, and oil that we *export*, **exceed** in value the silver that we *produce*.

When a person is convicted of crime, his friends are sometimes willing to **intercede** for his pardon.

The officer ordered the cavalry to **precede** the infantry.

To divide by a fraction, invert the divisor and **proceed** as in multiplication.

It is pleasant to stand on the shore and see the waves **recede.**

7. Ce'lo, I hide.

CONCEAL', *v.* to hide.

Columbus was not able to **conceal** the fact that there was danger in the voyage.

8. Cer'to, I contend, I vie.

CONCERT', *v.* to contrive together.

Washington held a council of his officers, in 1781, to **concert** a plan to capture Yorktown.

9. Ci'to, I rouse, I call forth.

EXCITE', *v.* stir up.

Harsh words **excite** angry passions and often *induce* persons to quarrel.

10. Cla'mo, I cry out, I shout.   **Clama'tum,** to cry out, to shout.

PROCLAIM', *v.* publish by authority.
RECLAIM', *v.* to reform.

The old bell in Independence Hall has engraved upon it, "*Pro-claim* liberty throughout all the land, unto all the inhabitants thereof."

Reformatory Homes are intended to *reclaim* and *reform* those who have bad habits.

11. *Clau'do,* I shut. *Clau'sum,* to shut.
CONCLUDE', *v.* decide.
PRECLUDE', *v.* prevent, shut out.

When you *perform* examples in Arithmetic, do not *conclude* too hastily that the answers are correct, but carefully *apply* the rule.

The Patent Laws *preclude* all persons, except the inventor, from taking out a patent.

12. *Cli'no,* I bend.
DECLINE', *v.* refuse.
RECLINE', *v.* to lie down.

When a person is called as a witness in court, he cannot *decline* to testify.

In ancient times it was customary to *recline* at meals.

13. *Cum'bo,* I lie down.
SUCCUMB', *v.* to yield.

The First Congress determined to *adopt* such resolutions as would show that they never intended to *succumb.*

14. *Cur'ro,* I run. *Cur'sum,* to run.
CONCUR', *v.* agree.
OCCUR', *v.* happen.

When Columbus explained his plans, the learned men of Spain and Portugal did not *concur.*

"No matter what difficulties *occur,*" said De Soto, "I intend to *traverse* the distance between the Atlantic Ocean and the Mississippi."

15. *Di'co,* I say. *Dic'tum,* to say.
PREDICT', *v.* foretell.

Many writers *predict* a time of peace on earth called the Millennium.

16. *Do'leo,* I grieve.
CONDOLE', *v.* to sympathize with another in his grief.

As far as circumstances *permit,* we ought to *condole* with those in affliction.

3*

17. Du'co, I lead. Duc'tum, to lead.
ADDUCE', v. bring forward.
CONDUCE', v. tend.
DEDUCE', v. to infer.
PRODUCE', v. manufacture or grow.
REDUCE', v. to make less.
INDUCE', v. persuade (9).

What fact can you *adduce* in proof that the earth is round?
Pure air, exercise, and cleanliness *conduce* to keep the body healthy
James Watt was able to *deduce* the principle of the steam-engine from the lifting of the kettle-lid by steam..
Every year we *produce* so many new articles, that we are able to *reduce* our imports.

18. Fa'cies, a face.
DEFACE', v. to disfigure.
EFFACE', v. to expunge.

It is easy to *deface* furniture by writing upon it; but it is not so easy to *efface* what you have written.

19. Fa'ma, fame.
DEFAME', v. to slander.

Washington had many enemies, who tried in every way to *defame* his character.

20. Fen'do, I strike. Fen'sum, to strike.
DEFEND', v. protect.
OFFEND', v. to annoy.

Nearly all animals will *defend* their young against those that *assail* them.
Those who wish to live peaceably with their neighbors are careful not to *offend* them.

21. Fe'ro, I bear, I carry. La'tum, to bear, to carry.
CONFER', v. to consult.
DEFER', v. put off.
OF'FER, n. proposal.
TRANSFER', v. to convey to another.

Penn was always ready to *confer* with the Indians and *explain* anything that seemed wrong.
Do not *defer* till to-morrow what ought to be done to-day.
England and America did not accept the *offer* of Russia to me diate in 1812.

"If you wish to *transfer* me to another department, I will not *oppose* it," said the General.

22. *Fi'do*, I trust.
CONFIDE', *v.* to impart.
A good child loves to *confide* his secrets to his mother.

23. *Fi'go*, I fix, I fasten.   *Fix'um*, to fix, to fasten.
PRE'FIX, *n.* a syllable placed before the root.
SUF'FIX, *n.* a syllable placed after the root.
The *prefix*, root, and *suffix* assist us very much in finding the meaning of a word.

24. *Fir'mus*, strong.
AFFIRM', *v.* to assert (without taking an oath).
CONFIRM', *v.* establish.
INFIRM', *a.* feeble.
A witness in Court is allowed to *affirm* if he prefers.
Historians do not *confirm* the story of George Washington and the hatchet.
John Adams, though very *infirm*, lived to see the fiftieth anniversary of American Independence.

25. *Flam'ma*, a flame.
INFLAME', *v.* irritate.
Angry words *inflame* the passions, but a soft answer turns away wrath.

26. *Flec'to*, I bend.   *Flex'um*, to bend.
REFLECT', *v.* to bend back.
To *reflect* the light of the sun, the moon must be opaque.

27. *Fli'go*, I beat, I dash.   *Flic'tum*, to beat, to dash.
AFFLICT', *v.* to distress.
Nothing in the Revolution seemed to *afflict* the patriots so much as the treason of Arnold.

28. *Flu'o*, I flow.   *Flux'um*, to flow.
IN'FLUX, *n.* a flowing in.
There was a great *influx* of visitors in Philadelphia to *attend* the "Centennial International Exhibition."

29. *For'ma*, form, beauty.
DEFORM', *v.* injure the shape of.
TRANSFORM', *v.* to change.

PERFORM', *v.* do (11).
REFORM', *v.* to reclaim (10).
> Stand erect, frequently *expand* the chest, and do not *deform* the body by stooping.
> Fairy stories pretend that a fairy has power to *transform* a pumpkin into a fine coach.

30. *Frons (fron'tis),* the forehead.
CONFRONT', *v.* to meet face to face.
> General Taylor determined not to *prolong* the Mexican War, but to *confront* Santa Anna at Buena Vista.

31. *Fun'do,* I pour. *Fu'sum,* to pour.
INFUSE', *v.* to instil.
> Washington tried to *infuse* fresh spirit and energy into his soldiers.

32. *Gra'dior,* I go step by step. *Gres'sus,* going step by step.
DEGRADE', *v.* to debase.
> The use of vulgar language is sure to *degrade* the character.

33. *Hæ'reo,* I stick. *Hæ'sum,* to stick.
ADHERE', *v.* to stick to.
COHERE', *v.* stick together.
> Glue causes smooth surfaces to *adhere* more easily than rough ones.
> In solid bodies, such as wood, iron, etc., the particles firmly *cohere.*

34. *Ha'lo,* I breathe.
INHALE', *v.* breathe in.
> We exhale and *inhale* many times in a minute.

35. *Hu'mus,* the ground.
EXHUME', *v.* to disinter.
> Charles the Second gave orders to *exhume* the body of Oliver Cromwell, who had been dead more than two years.

36. *Jun'go,* I join. *Junc'tum,* to join.
AD'JUNCTS, *n.* words joined.
> The relative, with its *adjuncts,* should be placed near its antecedent.

37. *Jus (ju'ris),* justice, law. *Jus'tus,* just.
ADJUST', *v.* set right.
> Each one must *adjust* the microscope to suit his own eye.

38. *Lon'gus*, long.
PROLONG', *v.* to lengthen out (80).

39. *Man'do*, I command. ***Manda'tum*,** to command.
COMMAND', *n.* injunction.
REMAND', *v.* to send back.
  If pupils desire to *acquire* a good education, they should cheerfully obey every *command* of the teacher.
  When William Penn was ordered to *appear* in court, he hoped to be set at liberty, but the Judge determined to *remand* him to prison.

40. *Matu'rus*, ripe.
IMMATURE', *a.* unripe.
PREMATURE', *a.* too hasty.
  Fruit is not wholesome when it is *immature* or unripe.
  When the rocks at Hurl Gate were to be blown up, great care was taken to *prevent* a *premature* explosion.

41. *Mer'go*, I dip. ***Mer'sum*,** to dip.
EMERGE', *v.* to rise out.
IMMERSE', *v.* to dip.
  Have you ever seen a diver *emerge* from the water?
  In bathing, it is necessary to *immerse* the whole body in water, especially the head.

42. *Mit'to*, I send. ***Mis'sum*,** to send.
EMIT', *v.* send out.
SUBMIT', *v.* to yield.
TRANSMIT', *v.* to deliver.
PERMIT', *v.* allow (16).
  Volcanoes are burning mountains which *emit* lava, ashes, stones, etc.
  If a student refuses to *submit* to the rules of the college, it is the duty of the president to *expel* him.
  The Constitution of the United States was formed to *transmit* the blessings of liberty to posterity, and to *promote* the general welfare.

43. *Mo'veo*, I move. ***Mo'tum*,** to move.
PROMOTE', *v.* to advance (42).

44. *Nec'to*, I tie, or bind. ***Nex'um*,** to tie, or bind.
CONNECT', *v.* to unite.
  A tunnel, under the Straits of Dover, is proposed to *connect* England and France.

C

45. Op'to, I wish. **Opta'tum,** to wish.
ADOPT', *v.* to take to one's self.
It was not unusual for an Indian chief to *adopt* a captive.

46. O'ro, I pray, I ask. **Ora'tum,** to pray, to ask.
ADORE', *v.* worship.
The heathen *adore* the thing that they themselves have made.

47. Pan'do, I lay open, I spread. **Pan'sum,** to lay open, to spread.
EXPAND', *v.* enlarge (29).

48. Par, equal, like.
COMPARE', *v.* examine with reference to likeness.
When we *compare* England and the United States, we find that England is a little larger than New York.

49. Pel'lo, I drive. **Pul'sum,** to drive.
IMPEL', *v.* to drive forward.
REPEL', *v.* to drive back.
EXPEL', *v.* to drive out (42).
We *consume* coal to *impel* cars, *compress* cotton, and *transport* goods to foreign countries.
In 1637, Massachusetts assisted Connecticut to *repel* the Pequods, who had attacked them.

50. Pen'deo, I hang. **Pen'sum,** to hang.
SUSPEND', *v.* to hang.
Formerly, it was the custom to *suspend* lamps by chains across the streets.

51. Plan'ta, a plant.
IMPLANT', *v.* to infuse.
SUPPLANT', *v.* to displace.
TRANSPLANT', *v.* to plant in another place.
When William Penn came to America, he told his wife to *implant* in the minds of their children the importance of truthfulness.
General Gates tried to *supplant* General Washington as Commander-in-chief.
Several authors *describe* a method by which it is possible to *transplant* large trees.

52. Pla'nus, plain.
EXPLAIN', *v.* to make clear (21).

REVIEW OF PREFIXES.

53. *Pli'co*, I fold. ***Plica'tum*,** to fold.
APPLY', *v.* fix closely (11).

54. *Plo'ro*, I cry, I bewail. ***Plora'tum*,** to cry, to bewail.
DEPLORE', *v.* regret.
War is so horrible that all good men *deplore* the necessity for it.

55. *Po'no*, I put or place. ***Pos'itum*,** to put or place.
DEPOSE', *v.* to put from (the throne).
INTERPOSE', *v.* interfere.
TRANSPOSE', *v.* to change the place of.
OPPOSE', *v.* resist (21).
Charles the First hoped, that if Parliament determined to *depose* him, the King of France would *interpose* and save him.
We are very apt to *transpose* the *e* and the *i* in such words as believe, siege, and liege.

56. *Por'to*, I carry.
IMPORT', *v.* to bring into a country.
EXPORT', *v.* to send out of a country.
TRANSPORT', *v.* to carry (49).
The United States used to *import* many articles which they now *export*.

57. *Pre'mo*, I press. ***Pres'sum*,** to press.
COMPRESS', *v.* to make smaller by pressure (49).

58. *Quæ'ro*, I seek, I ask. ***Quæsi'tum*,** to seek, to ask.
ACQUIRE', *v.* to obtain (39).

59. *Ra'do*, I shave. ***Ra'sum*,** to shave.
ERASE', *v.* to rub out.
To *erase* pencil-marks use India-rubber; acid will erase some kinds of ink.

60. *Ri'vus*, a stream, a river.
ARRIVE', *v.* come to.
DERIVE', *v.* deduce.
The Puritans did not *arrive* at Plymouth until December 21, 1620.
We *derive* a great many common words from the root, ago, I do, I perform.

61. Rup'tum, to break.
ABRUPT', *a.* unconnected.
George the Third, King of England, showed that he was *insane* by his *abrupt* answers.

62. Sa'lio, I leap, I spring. **Sal'tum,** to leap, to spring.
ASSAIL', *v.* attack (20).

63. Sa'nus, sound, healthy.
INSANE', *a.* deranged (61).

64. Scan'do, I climb. **Scan'sum,** to climb.
DESCEND', *v.* to go down.
Travellers find it as difficult to *descend,* as it is to ascend, the Alps

65. Scri'bo, I write. **Scrip'tum,** to write.
PRESCRIBE', *v.* give a rule of conduct.
SUBSCRIBE', *v.* to write one's name.
DESCRIBE', *v.* give an account of (51).
Both Houses of Congress *prescribe* the rules for the expulsion of a member.
To write one's name at the close of an article is to *subscribe* it.

66. Se'co, I cut. **Sec'tum,** to cut.
INTERSECT', *v.* cross each other.
In the upper part of New York, the streets *intersect* each other at right angles.

67. Sis'to or **Sto,** I stand, I set up.
RESIST', *v.* to withstand.
ASSIST', *v.* help (23).
Steel has power to *resist* a greater strain than iron.

68. Sol'vo, I loose. **Solu'tum,** to loose.
ABSOLVE', *v.* to loose from.
The effect of the Bankrupt Law, repealed in 1878, was to *absolve* the debtor from obligation to pay.

69. Spi'ro, I breathe. **Spira'tum,** to breathe.
CONSPIRE', *v.* plot.
INSPIRE', *v.* to infuse into the mind.
TRANSPIRE', *v.* to become known.
Columbus tried to *inspire* his men with hope, for he feared they would *conspire* to throw him overboard.

So many were in the Gunpowder Plot, that it was almost certain to *transpire* before the day fixed.

70. *Spon'deo*, I promise. *Spon'sum*, to promise.
RESPOND', v. to answer.
Arnold did not like to *advert* to his treason, and generally refused to *respond* if questioned on the subject.

71. *Stru'o*, I build, I construct. *Struc'tum*, to build, to construct.
OBSTRUCT', v. to block up.
No one is allowed to *obstruct* public roads, or the streets of a city.

72. *Su'mo*, I take. *Sump'tum*, to take.
CONSUME', v. use; burn (49).

73. *Ten'do*, I stretch. *Ten'sum*, to stretch.
ATTEND', v. to be present at (28).

74. *Tes'tis*, a witness.
ATTEST', v. to certify to.
In making a will, it is necessary to procure witnesses to *attest* the signature.

75. *Tol'lo*, I lift up.
EXTOL', v. praise highly.
Not only Americans, but foreigners *extol* the characters of Washington, Adams, Jay, and others, who formed the government in 1789.

76. *Tra'ho*, I draw. *Trac'tum*, to draw.
ATTRACT', v. draw.
All the planets, as they *revolve* in their orbits, *attract* the sun.

77. *Trib'uo*, I give. *Tribu'tum*, to give.
CONTRIB'UTE, v. to give in common with others.
DISTRIB'UTE, v. to dispense.
When there is great suffering, every one is glad to *contribute* something.
During the prevalence of the fever, it was necessary to *distribute* food and clothing to the sufferers.

78. *Tru'do*, I thrust. *Tru'sum*, to thrust.
OBTRUDE', v. thrust in.
Cuckoos will *obtrude* themselves wherever they can find a nest.

79. Va'do, I go. **Va'sum,** to go.
  EVADE', *v.* to elude.
  INVADE', *v.* to enter as an enemy.
  PERVADE', *v.* to spread through.
    Prince Charles, in order to *evade* his pursuers, hid himself in a large oak-tree.
    Montgomery and Arnold determined to *invade* Canada in the winter of 1775.
    The odor of some substances, such as musk, etc., will continue to *pervade* the air of a room for years.

80. Ve'nio, I come. **Ven'tum,** to come.
  CONVENE', *v.* to assemble.
  INTERVENE', *v.* come between.
  PREVENT', *v.* to hinder (40).
    President Van Buren, hoping to *avert* some evils, determined to *convene* Congress.
    More than three months *intervene* between the election and the inauguration of a President of the United States.

81. Ver'go, I bend.
  DIVERGE', *v.* tend away from each other.
    Lines, which *diverge* in one direction, converge in the opposite direction.

82. Ver'to, I turn. **Ver'sum,** to turn.
  CONVERT', *v.* to change from one state to another.
  DI'VERSE, *a.* various.
  PERVERT', *v.* to turn in the wrong direction.
  SUBVERT', *v.* to destroy.
  ADVERT', *v.* to turn the attention to (70).
  AVERT,' *v.* to turn away (80).
  TRAV'ERSE, *v.* to pass over (14).
    Many and *diverse* operations are needed to *convert* a piece of iron into a needle.
    On the trial of Aaron Burr for treason, it was evident that the witnesses did not *pervert* his words.
    Every one who breaks a law helps to *subvert* the government.

83. Vi'deo, I see. **Vi'sum,** to see.
  PROVIDE', *v.* to procure supplies (5).

SUFFIXES.

84. Vi'vo, I live. Vic'tum, to live.
REVIVE', v. come to life again.
Animals that lie dormant all winter *revive* in the spring

85. Vo'co, I call. Voca'tum, to call.
CONVOKE', v. to assemble.
REVOKE', v. to repeal.
If the state of the country demands it, Queen Victoria has power to *convoke* Parliament.
The President of the United States has no power to *revoke* a law, even though it is a bad one.

86. Vol'vo, I roll. Volu'tum, to roll.
REVOLVE', v. roll around (76).

ARRANGEMENT FOR WRITTEN EXERCISES.

1. ANNOUNCE', to give notice of. An for ad, to; nuncio, I announce. Washington sent a special messenger to Congress, to *announce* the surrender of Cornwallis in 1781.
2. APPEAR', to be present. Ap for ad, to; pareo, I am present. When William Penn was ordered to *appear* in court, he hoped to be set at liberty.

III. SUFFIXES.

ANGLO-SAXON AND LATIN.

1. Able, Ble, Ible, *that may be* or *that can be; worthy of; fit to be.*
AR'ABLE, (aro, I plough,) *that can be* ploughed or tilled.
AU'DIBLE, (audio, I hear,) *that can be* heard.
CU'RABLE, (cura, care,) *that may be* cured.
ED'IBLE, (edo, I eat,) *fit to be* eaten.
A'MIABLE, (amo, I love,) *worthy of* being loved.
LEG'IBLE, (lego, I gather, I select, I read,) *that may be* read
FLEX'IBLE, (flecto, flexum, to bend,) *that can be* bent.
VIS'IBLE, (video, visum, to see,) *that can be* seen.

2. Aceous, *of; consisting of; like* or *resembling; y.*
FOLIA'CEOUS, (folium, a leaf,) *consisting of* leaves.

3. Acious, *much; very; strongly; disposed to.*
Tena'cious, (teneo, I hold, I keep,) holding *strongly.*
Vera'cious, (verus, true,) *disposed to* telling the truth.
Contuma'cious, (tumeo, I swell,) swelling *greatly* with pride.
Pugna'cious, (pugna, a battle,) *disposed to* fight.

4. Acy, *state of being; quality of being; office of.*
Ac'curacy, (cura, care,) the *state of being* careful.
Mag'istracy, (magister, magistri, a magistrate,) the *office of* a magistrate.
Confed'eracy, (fœdus, fœderis, a league, a covenant,) the *state of being* leagued together.
Ad'equacy, (æquus, equal,) the *quality of being* equal to.

5. Age, *act of; a collection of; condition of; state of being; an allowance for.*
Fo'liage, (folium, a leaf,) *a collection of* leaves.
Peer'age, (par, equal, like,) the *condition of* a peer.
Por'terage, (porto, I carry,) *an allowance for* carrying.

6. Al, *act of; of; pertaining to; befitting; done by.*
Frater'nal, (frater, a brother,) *of* a brother; *pertaining to* a brother.
Fil'ial, (filius, a son;' filia, a daughter,) *befitting* a son or daughter.
Mater'nal, (mater, a mother,) *pertaining to* a mother.
Re'gal, (rego, I direct, I rule,) *of* a king; kingly.
Man'ual, (manus, the hand,) *done by* the hand.
Ru'ral, (rus, ruris, the country,) *pertaining to* the country.
So'cial, (socius, a companion,) *pertaining to* a companion.
Men'tal, (mens, mentis, the mind,) *of* the mind.

7. An, Ane, Ean, Ian, *one who or the person that; pertaining to.*
Ar'tisan, (ars, artis, art,) *one who* practises an art.
Vet'eran, (vetus, veteris, old,) *one who* is an old soldier.
Par'tisan, (pars, partis, a part,) *pertaining to* a party.
Hu'man, (homo, hominis, a man,) *pertaining to* man.
Humane', (homo, a man,) *pertaining to* man; benevolent.

MUN'DANE, (mundus, the earth, the world,) *pertaining to* the earth.

MERID'IAN, (medius, the middle; dies, a day,) *pertaining to* the middle of the day.

AGRA'RIAN, (ager, agri, a field,) *pertaining to* fields or land.

EUROPE'AN, *one who* lives in Europe; a native of Europe.

8. *Ance, Ancy, Ence, Ency,* *act of; state of being; quality of being; ing.*

ACCEPT'ANCE, (capio, captum, to take,) the *act of* taking.

AU'DIENCE, (audio, I hear,) a hear*ing*; an assembly of hearers.

CLEM'ENCY, (clemens, clementis, mild, merciful,) the *quality of being* merciful.

CRE'DENCE, (credo, I believe,) the *act of* believing.

CUR'RENCY, (curro, I run,) the *state of being* current.

FLU'ENCY, (fluo, I flow,) the *quality of* flowing.

CON'FLUENCE, (fluo, I flow,) the flow*ing* together.

CON'STANCY, (sisto or sto, I stand,) the *state* or *quality of being* constant.

9. *Ant, Ent,* *one who*, or the *person that; being; ing.*

DEFEND'ANT, (fendo, I keep off,) *one who* defends.

A'GENT, (ago, I do, I perform,) *one who* does.

RE'GENT, (rego, I direct, I rule,) *one who* rules (in place of the sovereign).

AR'DENT, (ardeo, I burn,) burn*ing*.

DOR'MANT, (dormio, I sleep,) sleep*ing*.

10. *Ar,* *one who*, or the *person that; like; of; belonging* or *pertaining to; having.*

LI'AR, *one who* lies.

BEG'GAR, *one who* begs.

AN'GULAR, (angulus, a corner,) *having* corners.

CIR'CULAR, (circulus, a little circle,) *like* a circle; *pertaining to* a circle.

LU'NAR, (luna, the moon,) *of* the moon; *pertaining to* the moon.

IN'SULAR, (insula, an island,) *belonging to* an island.

11. **Ard,** *one who,* or the *person that.*
   DRUNK'ARD, *one who* gets drunk.
   LAG'GARD, *one who* lags or is late.
   SLUG'GARD, *one who* is sluggish.

12. **Ary,** *one who,* or the *person that;* the *place where;* the *thing that; of; pertaining to.*
   AR'BITRARY, (arbiter, arbitri, a judge, an umpire,) *pertaining to* a judge; not governed by fixed rule.
   AUXIL'IARY, (auxilium, help, aid,) *pertaining to* help or aid; helping.
   DI'ARY, (dies, a day,) the *thing that* keeps an account of each day; a journal.
   GRAN'ARY, (granum, a grain of corn,) the *place where* grain is kept.
   LU'MINARY, (lumen, luminis, light,) the *thing that* gives light.
   HON'ORARY, (honor, honor,) *pertaining to* honor, conferring honor only.
   LI'BRARY, (liber, libri, a book,) the *place where* books are kept.
   MIL'ITARY, (miles, militis, a soldier,) *pertaining to* soldiers, or war.

13. **Ate,** *one who,* or the *person that; having; being; to make, to give, to put,* or *to take.*
   CU'RATE, (cura, care,) *one who* has the care of a parish.
   MAG'ISTRATE, (magister, a master,) *one who* acts as a master.
   AN'IMATE, (anima, the life, the vital air,) *to put* life into; to stimulate; to enliven.
   DEC'ORATE, (decor, grace,) *to give* grace or beauty; to adorn.
   LIB'ERATE, (liber, free,) *to make* free.
   AD'EQUATE, (æquus, equal,) *being* equal to.

14. **Ble, Able, Ible.** See *Able.*

15. **Cle, Cule, Ule,** *little, small.*
   ANIMAL'CULE, (anima, the life, the vital air,) a very *small* animal.

SUFFIXES.

CAN'TICLE, (canto, I sing,) a *short* song.
COR'PUSCLE, (corpus, a body,) a *minute* body.

16. Dom, *the place in which dominion is exercised; state of being; rank.*

DUKE'DOM, (duco, I lead,) *the place in which* a duke *exercises dominion;* the *rank* of a duke.
PRINCE'DOM, (primus, first; capio, I take,) *the place where* a prince *exercises dominion.*

17. Ean. See **An.**

18. Ee, *one who; one to whom.*
ABSENTEE', (ens, entis, being,) *one who* is absent.
ASSIGNEE', (signum, a sign, a seal,) *one to whom* an assignment is made.
REFUGEE', (fugio, I flee,) *one who* flees.

19. Eer, Ier, *one who,* or the *person that.*
MOUNTAINEER', (mons, montis, a high hill,) *one who* lives on a mountain.
AUCTIONEER', (augeo, I increase; auctum, to increase), *one who* sells by auction.

20. En, *made of; to make.*
WOOD'EN, *made of* wood.
SHORT'EN, *to make* short.

21. Ence, Ency. See **Ance.**

22. Ent. See **Ant.**

23. Er, *one who,* or the *person that; thing which; more.*
TEACH'ER, *one who* teaches.
ARCH'ER, (arcus, a bow,) *one who* shoots with bow and arrow.
FEND'ER, (fendo, I strike,) *that which* strikes off or defends from.
INQUI'RER, (quæro, I seek, I ask,) *one who* seeks or asks information.
ARTIF'ICER, (ars, artis, art, skill; facio, I do, I make,) *one who* is skilled in work; a workman.

24. Erly, Ern, *in the direction of.*
NORTH'ERLY, NORTH'ERN, *in the direction of* the north.

25. Ery, Ry, *state or quality of being; the practice of; the place where; things of a certain kind taken collectively.*
BRAV'ERY, *quality of being* brave.
SLAV'ERY, the *state of being* a slave.
PERFUM'ERY, (fumus, smoke), *articles* manufactured by perfumers *taken collectively; the practice of* a perfumer.
FER'RY, (fero, I carry,) the *place where* persons are carried over.
DISTILL'ERY, (stilla, a drop,) the *place where* distilling is carried on.

26. Escence, *state of growing or becoming.*
QUIES'CENCE, (quies, rest,) *state of growing* quiet.
ADOLES'CENCE, (oleo, I grow,) the *state of growing.*
CONVALES'CENCE, (valeo, I am strong,) *state of becoming* well or strong.
PUTRES'CENCE, (putris, rotten,) *state of becoming* rotten.

27. Escent, *growing or becoming.*
INCANDES'CENT, (candeo, I glow with heat,) *becoming* white with heat.
PUTRES'CENT, (putris, rotten,) *becoming* putrid.
CONVALES'CENT, (valeo, I am strong,) *growing* strong.

28. Esque, *like.*
PICTURESQUE', (pingo, I paint; pictum, to paint,) *like* a picture.

29. Et, Let, *little, small.*
CLOS'ET, (claudo, I shut; clausum, to shut,) a *small* private room.
RIV'ULET, (rivus, a stream,) a *small* stream.
CYG'NET, (cygnus, a swan,) a *young* swan.

30. Ety. See *Ity.*

31. Ful, *full of.*
CARE'FUL, (cura, care,) *full of* care.

SUFFIXES.

32. Fy, *to make.*
FOR'TIFY, (fortis, brave, strong,) *to make* strong.
DIG'NIFY, (dignus, worthy,) *to make* worthy; to advance to honor.
MAG'NIFY, (magnus, great,) *to make* great.
NUL'LIFY, (nullus, nothing,) *to make* to nothing.
CER'TIFY, (certus, certain,) *to make* certain.
REC'TIFY, (rectus, right,) *to make* right.

33. Hood, Head, *state of being; nature* or *distinguishing attributes of.*
CHILD'HOOD, *state of being* a child.
GOD'HEAD, the *nature* or *distinguishing attributes of* the Deity.

34. Ian. See **An.**

35. Ic, Ical, *pertaining to; like; made of.*
AQUAT'IC, (aqua, water,) *pertaining to* the water; living in the water.
LU'NATIC, (luna, the moon,) *pertaining to* the moon; a maniac.
MED'ICAL, (medeor, I heal,) *pertaining to* medicine.
NAU'TICAL, (nauta, a sailor,) *pertaining to* sailing or navigation.

36. Ice, the *thing that;* the *quality of* being.
MAL'ICE, (malus, evil, bad,) the *quality of* being evil or malicious.
JUS'TICE, (justus, just,) the *thing that* is right.
NO'TICE, (nota, a mark,) the *thing that* marks or makes known.

37. Ics, Ic, the *doctrine; science; art of.*
MU'SIC, (musa, a muse,) the *art of* singing or playing on musical instrument.

38. Id, *being; ing;* the *thing that.*
AC'RID, (acris, sharp,) *being* sharp.
FLU'ID, (fluo, I flow,) the *thing that* flows.
TIM'ID, (timeo, I fear,) *fearing.*
FER'VID, (ferveo, I boil, I am hot,) *being* hot.

39. Ier. See *Eer.*

40. Ile, *pertaining to; like; that may or can be easily.*
Hos'tile, (hostis, a foe,) *pertaining to* an enemy.
Ju'venile, (juvenis, young,) *pertaining to* youth.
Duc'tile, (duco, I lead; ductum, to lead,) that *can be easily* drawn out (as wire).
Feb'rile, (febris, a fever,) *pertaining to* a fever.
Doc'ile, (doceo, I teach,) that *can be easily* taught.

41. Ine, *of; pertaining to; like.*
Marine', (mare, the sea,) *of* the sea; *pertaining to* the sea.
Canine', (canis, a dog,) *like* dogs; *pertaining to* dogs.
Saline', (sal, salt,) *of* salt; *pertaining to* salt.

42. Ion, the *act of; being* or *state of being; ing; that which.*
Ces'sion, (cedo, I yield, I go; cessum, to yield, to go,) the *act of* yielding; yield*ing.*
Dona'tion, (do, I give; donum, a gift,) *that which* is given.
Fu'sion, (fundo, I melt, I pour; fusum, to melt, to pour,) the *state of being* melted.
Ses'sion, (sedeo, I sit; sessum, to sit,) a sit*ting* (as of Congress).

43. Ise, Ize, *to make; to give; to act like.*
Advertise', (verto, I turn,) *to make* one turn attention to a thing.
Au'thorize, (augeo, I increase,) *to give* authority to.
Le'galize, (lex, legis, law,) *to make* lawful.
Fer'tilize, (fero, I bear, I carry,) *to make* to bear; *to make* fertile.

44. Ish, *somewhat; belonging to; like; to make.*
Black'ish, *somewhat* black.
Span'ish, *belonging to* Spain.
Boy'ish, *like* a boy.
Pub'lish, (publico, I publish,) *to make* public.
Fin'ish, (finis, the end,) *to make* an end of.
Estab'lish, (sto, I stand, I set up; statum, to stand, to set up,) *to make* to stand; *to make* firm or stable.

SUFFIXES.

45. Ism, *state* or *quality of being; idiom; doctrine* or *doctrines of; ing.*
BAR'BARISM, (barbarus, rude, savage,) *state of being* savage.
AN'GLICISM, (Anglia, England,) an English idiom.
FANAT'ICISM, (fanum, a temple,) the *state of being* a fanatic.
CAL'VINISM, the *doctrines of* Calvin.

46. Ist, *one who,* or the *person that.*
NOV'ELIST, (novus, new,) *one who* writes novels.
FLO'RIST, (flos, floris, a flower,) *one who* cultivates flowers.
AR'TIST, (ars, artis, art, skill,) *one who* practices an art.

47. Ite, a *descendant of;* a *follower of;* a *sectarian* or *party leader.*
IS'RAELITE, a *descendant* of Israel.
HUSS'ITE, a *follower* of John Huss.

48. Ity, Ety, Ty, *state* or *quality of being; ness.*
AM'ITY, (amo, I love,) *state of being* friends.
ASPER'ITY, (asper, rough, harsh,) *state of being* harsh.
BREV'ITY, (brevis, short,) *quality of being* short.
CELEB'ITY, (celer, swift,) swift*ness.*
DEN'SITY, (densus, thick, close,) *the state of being* dense.
LIB'ERTY, (liber, free,) *state of being* free.

49. Ive, *one who,* or the *person that; that which; having power; ing.*
FU'GITIVE, (fugio, I flee; fugitum, to flee,) *one who* flees.
MO'TIVE, (moveo, I move; motum, to move,) *that which* moves.
RES'TIVE, (sisto or sto, I stand,) stand*ing* back; refusing to go forward.
PERSUA'SIVE, (suadeo, I persuade; suasum, to persuade,) *having power* to persuade.
FES'TIVE, (festum, a feast,) feast*ing.*

50. Ize. See *Ise.*

51. Kin, *little.*
LAMB'KIN, a *little* lamb.

52. Lent, Olent, Ulent, *full of.*

PES'TILENT, (pestis, the plague,) *full of* the infection of the plague; pestilential.

FRAUD'ULENT, (fraus, fraudis, deceit,) *full of* fraud.

COR'PULENT, (corpus, a body,) *full of* body or flesh; having a large body.

53. Less, *without.*

ART'LESS, (ars, artis, art,) *without* art.

POW'ERLESS, (posse, to be able; potui, I am able,) *without* power.

54. Let. See *Et.*

55. Like, *like or resembling.*

MAN'LIKE, *like* a man.

56. Ling, *little; young.*

DUCK'LING, a *little* or *young* duck.

LORD'LING, a *little* lord.

57. Ly, *like; in a manner.*

PRINCE'LY, (primus, first; capio, I take,) *like* a prince.

ABRUPT'LY, (ruptum, to break,) *in an* abrupt *manner.*

58. Ment, (see *Ure* and *Th*) *state of being; act of; the thing that; ing.*

AL'IMENT, (alo, I nourish; alitum, to nourish,) *that which* nourishes.

CONCEAL'MENT, (celo, I hide,) conceal*ing.*

ACCOM'PLISHMENT, (pleo, I fill,) *state of being* accomplished.

59. Mony, *state or quality of being; thing that.*

AC'RIMONY, (acris, sharp,) *quality of being* sharp.

TES'TIMONY, (testis, a witness,) *thing that* is offered by a witness.

60. Ness, *state or quality of being.*

ACUTE'NESS, (acuo, I sharpen; acutum, to sharpen,) *quality of being* acute.

REMOTE'NESS, (moveo, I move; motum, to move,) *state of being* remote.

SUFFIXES.

61. *Ock*, *little.*
HILL'OCK, a *little* hill.

62. *Olent.* See ***Lent.***

63. *Or*, *one who* or the *person that;* the *act of; sensation; that which causes; ness.*
AU'DITOR, (audio, I hear; auditum, to hear,) *one who* hears.
FA'VOR, (faveo, I befriend,) the *act of* favoring.
SPLEN'DOR, (splendeo, I shine,) bright*ness.*

64. *Ory*, the *place where;* the *thing that; pertaining to; ing.*
AR'MORY, (arma, arms,) the *place where* arms are kept.
DOR'MITORY, (dormio, I sleep; dormitum, to sleep,) a *place* for sleeping.
DEROG'ATORY, (rogo, I ask; rogatum, to ask,) lessen*ing* in value.
PRED'ATORY, (præda, prey, plunder,) *pertaining to* plunder; plunder*ing.*

65. *Ose*, *full of.*
JOCOSE', (jocus, a joke,) *full of* jokes.
VERBOSE', (verbum, a word,) *full of* words.

66. *Ous*, *full of; consisting; ing.*
POP'ULOUS, (populus, the people,) *full of* people.
FA'MOUS, (fama, fame,) *full of* fame; renowned.
FERO'CIOUS, (ferox, ferocis, fierce,) *full of* fierceness.
GRIEV'OUS, (gravis, heavy, grievous,) *full of* grief; causing grief.

67. *Ry.* See ***Ery.***

68. *Ship*, the *office;* the *state of.*
APPREN'TICE-SHIP, (prehendo, I seize,) the *state of* an apprentice.
PART'NER-SHIP, (pars, partis, a part,) the *state of* a partner.

69. *Some*, *full of; causing.*
WEA'RISOME, *causing* weariness.
FROL'ICSOME, *full of* frolic.

VENT'URESOME, (venio, I come; ventum, to come,) *full of* venture.

70. **Ster,** *one who,* or the *person that.*
SONG'STER, *one who* sings.
TEAM'STER, *one who* drives a team.

71. **T,** the *thing done; ing.*
DECEIT', (capio, I do, I perform,) deceiv*ing.*
GIFT, the *thing that* is given.
WEFT, the *thing that* is woven.

72. **Th,** (see **Ment** and **Ure,**) *state of being; act of;* the *thing that; ing.*
WEALTH, the *thing that* makes rich.
GROWTH, grow*ing.*

73. **Tude, Ude,** *being* or *state of being; ness.*
MUL'TITUDE, (multus, many,) *being* many; a large number
QUI'ETUDE, (quies, quietis, quiet,) quiet*ness.*
AL'TITUDE, (altus, high,) high*ness*; height.
AP'TITUDE, (aptus, fit, meet,) *being* apt.
SERV'ITUDE, (servio, I serve; servitum, to serve,) *state of being* a servant.

74. **Ty.** See **Ity.**

75. **Ude.** See **Tude.**

76. **Ule.** See **Cle.**

77. **Ulent.** See **Lent.**

78. **Ure,** (see **Ment** and **Th,**) *state of being; act of;* the *thing that; ing.*
CREAT'URE, (creo, I create; creatum, to create,) the *thing that* is created.
FRACT'URE, (frango, I break; fractum, to break,) break*ing.*
RUPT'URE, (ruptum, to break,) the *act of* breaking.
TEN'URE, (teneo, I hold,) a hold*ing.*
TEXT'URE, (textum, to weave,) *that which* is woven.
COMPOS'URE, (pono, I put, I place; positum, to put, to place,) the *state of being* composed; calmness.

79. Ward, Wards, *in the direction of.*
West′ward, *in the direction of* the west; towards the west.
Wind′ward, *in the direction* from which the wind blows.

80. Y, *the state of being; the quality of being; the faculty, full of; consisting of; covered with.*
In′famy, (fama, fame,) *state of being* infamous.
Mis′ery, (miser, wretched,) *state of being* wretched.
Mem′ory, (memor, mindful,) the *faculty* that is mindful.
Mod′esty, (modestus, modest,) the *quality of being* modest.
Health′y, *full of* health.
Flow′ery, (flos, floris, a flower,) *covered with* flowers.
Chalk′y, *consisting of* chalk.

Review of Suffixes.

1. A′g-o, I do, I perform. **Ac′t-um,** to do, to perform.
Act′ive, having power to act (56-4).*
A′gent, one who does the business of another (11-11).

2. A′l-o, I feed, I nourish. **Al′it-um,** to feed, to nourish.
Al′iment, nutriment (13-1).

3. Al′t-us (al′ti), high.
Al′titude, height (15-1).

4. A′m-o, I love. **Ami′c-us,** a friend.
A′miable, lovely (17-4).
Am′ity, friendship (17-1).

5. Am′pl-us, large.
Am′plify, to enlarge (18-2).

6. An′gul-us, an angle, a corner.
An′gular, having corners (20-3).

---

* The numbers in parentheses refer to Part II., Latin Roots. See the 4th sentence, under Root 56, Part II. By an unfortunate casualty in 1777, Arnold was unable to engage in any *active* pursuits.

7. **An'ima,** the life; the vital air.
An'im**a**te, to stimulate (21-4).

8. **Ap't-us,** fit, meet.
Apt'itude, fitness; disposition (26-2).

9. **A'qua,** water.
A'queous, watery (27-1).
Aquat'ic, living in the water (27-2).

10. **Ar'biter (ar'bitr-i),** a judge or umpire.
Ar'bitrary, not governed by any fixed rule (28-2).

11. **Ar'de-o,** I burn.
Ar'dent, passionate (31-1).

12. **Ar'm-a,** arms, weapons.
Ar'mory, the place where arms are kept (35-3).

13. **A'r-o,** I plough.
Ar'able, fit for tillage (36-1).

14. **Ars (ar'tis),** art, skill.
Ar'tisan, an artificer (35-6).

15. **As'per,** rough, harsh.
Asper'ity, harshness (39-1).

16. **Au'di-o,** I hear. **Audi't-um,** to hear.
Au'dible, that can be heard (42-2).
Au'dience, an assembly of hearers (38-1).
Au'ditory, an assembly of hearers (37-4).
Au'ditor, a hearer (91-2).

17. **Auxil't-um,** help, aid.
Auxil'iary, helping (43-5).

18. **Brev'-is,** short.
Brev'ity, shortness, conciseness (54-1).

19. **Ced-o,** I yield, I go. **Ces's-um,** to yield, to
Ces'sion, a giving up (377-5).

20. **Cel'ebr-is,** renowned, famous.
Cel'ebrate, to honor by ceremonies of joy and respect

REVIEW OF SUFFIXES.

21. *Ce'ler,* swift.
    CELER'ITY, swiftness (77-2).

22. *Cer't-us,* sure, certain.
    CER'TIFY, to make certain (87-1).

23. *Cir'cul-us,* a little circle.
    CIR'CULATE, to move in a circle (91-1).

24. *Cla'm-o,* I cry out, I shout.
    CLAIM'ANT, one who demands a right (93-1).

25. *Clé'mens (clemen't-is),* mild, merciful.
    CLEM'ENCY, mercy (30-3).

26. *Co'l-o,* I cultivate. *Cul't-um,* to cultivate.
    CUL'TIVATE, to till (103-1).

27. *Cor'p-us (cor'por-is),* a body.
    COR'PULENT, having a large body (112-5).

28. *Cre'd-o,* I believe.
    CRE'DENCE, belief (114-1).
    CRED'IBLE, worthy of belief (114-3).
    CRED'ULOUS, apt to believe (45-1).

29. *Cre'-o,* I create. *Crea't-um,* to create.
    CREA'TOR, God, the maker of all things (115-1).
    CREAT'URE, an animal (115-3).

30. *Cul'p-a,* a fault, blame.
    CUL'PABLE, blamable (122-2).

31. *Cu'r-a,* care.
    CU'RIOUS, rare, singular (124-2).
    CUR'ABLE, admitting of a remedy (124-4).
    CU'RATE, a clergyman hired to do the duties of another

32. *Cur'r-o,* I run.
    CUR'RENCY, money (125-1).

33. *Deb'e-o,* I owe. *Deb'it-um,* to owe.
    DEBT'OR, the person who owes (131-1).

5*

34. *De′cor*, grace.
Dec′orate, to adorn (133-3).

35. *Den′s-us*, thick, close.
Den′sity, compactness (135-1).

36. *Dex′ter*, pertaining to the right hand; expert.
Dexter′ity, expertness (138-1).

37. *Di′-es*, a day.
Merid′ian, (medius, the middle,) noon (141-2).
Di′ary, a journal (139-1).

38. *Dig′n-us*, worthy.
Dig′nify, to advance to honor (143-1).

39. *Do′n-um*, a gift.
Do′nor, giver (147-3).
Dona′tion, gift (36-1).

40. *Doc′-eo*, I teach.
Doc′ument, a paper containing evidence (11-5).

41. *Dor′m-io*, I sleep. ***Dormi′t-um*,** to sleep.
Dor′mant, insensible (152-1).
Dor′mitory, a place where persons sleep (72-1).

42. *E′d-o*, I eat.
Ed′ible, eatable (161-1).

43. *Æ′qu-us*, equal, just.
Eq′uity, *n.* justice (169-4).

44. *Er′r-o*, I wander. ***Erra′t-um*,** to wander.
Errat′ic, eccentric (170-1).

45. *Fa′ci-o*, I do or make. ***Fac′t-um*,** to do or m
Fac′tory, a place where things are manufactured (7

46. *Fa′m-a*, fame, renown.
Fa′mous, renowned (182-1).

47. *Fe′rox (fero′cis)*, fierce.
Fero′cious, savage (22-5).

48. *Fes't-um,* a feast.
   FES'TIVE, joyful (199-3).

49. *Fi'd-o,* I trust. *Fide'l-is,* faithful.
   FIDEL'ITY, *n.* faithfulness (63-1).

50. *Fil'i-us,* a son. *Fil'i-a,* a daughter.
   FIL'IAL, befitting a son or a daughter (42-3).

51. *Flec't-o,* I bend. *Flex'-um,* to bend.
   FLEX'IBLE, that can be bent (210-2).

52. *Flu'-o,* I flow. *Flux'-um,* to flow.
   FLU'ENCY, easy flow of speech (214-1).

53. *For't-is,* brave, strong.
   FOR'TIFY, to strengthen with forts, etc. (218-1).
   FOR'TITUDE, courage (42-3).

54. *Fran'g-o,* I break. *Frac't-um,* to break.
   FRACT'URE, a breaking (221-1).
   FRAG'MENT, a broken part (221-2).

55. *Fra'ter,* a brother.
   FRATER'NAL, brotherly (222-1).
   FRATER'NITY, brotherhood (222-2).

56. *Fraus (frau'd-is),* deceit.
   FRAUD'ULENT, deceitful, dishonest (122-2).

57. *Fu'g-io,* I flee. *Fu'git-um,* to flee.
   FU'GITIVE, one who flees (21-7).

58. *Fun'd-o,* I pour. *Fu's-um,* to pour.
   FU'SION, state of being melted (231-1).

59. *Gla'di-us,* a sword.
   GLAD'IATOR, one who fought in the arena for the ent ment of the Romans (242-1).

60. *Gra'n-um,* a grain.
   GRAN'ARY, a storehouse for grain (249-2).

61. *Gra't-us,* grateful, pleasing.
   GRAT'ITUDE, thankfulness (250-2).

THE MODEL ETYMOLOGY.

62. *Gra'v-is,* heavy, grievous.
    Griev'ous, mournful (251-1).

63. *Ho'm-o,* a man.
    Hu'man, belonging to mankind (27-3).

64. *Ho'nor,* respect, honor.
    Hon'orary, intended merely to convey honor (250-2).

65. *I'dem,* the same.
    Iden'tical, the same (134-2).

66. *In'sul-a,* an island.
    In'sular, belonging to an island (279-2).

67. *La't-us,* broad.
    Lat'itude, distance from the equator either north or south (107-1).

68. *Le'g-o,* I gather, I select, I read. *Lec't-um,* to gather, to select, to read.
    Le'gible, that can be read (302-1).

69. *Li'ber,* free.
    Lib'erate, to set free (15-2).
    Lib'erty, freedom (12-4).

70. *Li'ber (lib'r-i),* a book.
    Li'brary, a collection of books; the place where books are kept (147-3).

71. *Li'g-o,* I bind. *Liga't-um,* to bind.
    Lig'ament, a strong compact substance that binds one bone to another (310-2).

72. *Lit'er-a,* a letter.
    Lit'erary, relating to learning (11-2).

73. *Lo'c-us,* a place.
    Local'ity, place (56-3).

74. *Lon'g-us,* long.
    Lon'gitude, distance east or west from any established meridian (141-2).

REVIEW OF SUFFIXES.

75. *Lu'n-a*, the moon.
LU'NAR, pertaining to the moon (170-3)
LU'NATIC, an insane person (326-1).

76. *Lu'men (lu'min-is)*, light.
LU'MINARY, the sun; a body that gives light (206-1).

77. *Magis'ter (magis'tr-i)*, a master.
MAG'ISTRATE, a civil officer (328-3).

78. *Mag'n-us*, great. ***Ma'jor*,** greater.
MAG'NIFY, enlarge; to make great (329-2).
MAJOR'ITY, the greater number (97-3).

79. *Ma'n-us*, the hand.
MAN'UAL, performed by the hand (157-1).

80. *Ma'ter (mat'r-is)*, a mother.
MATER'NAL, pertaining to a mother (696-1).

81. *Matu'r-us*, ripe.
MATU'RITY, ripeness (119-1).

82. *Med'e-or*, I cure.
MED'ICAL, relating to healing (177-3).

83. *Me'mor*, mindful.
MEM'ORY, the faculty by which we remember (845-1)

84. *Mi'l-es (mil'it-is)*, a soldier.
MIL'ITARY, pertaining to soldiers (93-2).

85. *Mi'nor*, less.
MINOR'ITY, the smaller number (357-2).

86. *Mo'd-us*, a measure.
MOD'IFY, to change the form of (363-3).

87. *Mul't-us*, many.
MUL'TITUDE, a great number (359-3).

88. *Nau't-a*, a sailor.
NAU'TICAL, pertaining to sailing (385-1).

89. *Nos'c-o*, I know. ***No't-um*,** to know.
NO'TIFY, to make known (84-1).

90. *Nul'l-us,* no one.
NUL'LIFY, to make void (399-1).

91. *Nu'mer-us,* a number.
NUMER'ICAL, pertaining to numbers (75-12).

92. *Oc'ul-us,* the eye.
OC'ULAR, perceived by the eye (405-2).

93. *O'pus (o'per-is),* work.
OP'ERATE, to act (411-2).

94. *Or'n-o,* I ornament. *Orna't-um,* to ornament.
OR'NAMENT, adornment (89-1).

95. *O'r-o,* I pray, I ask. *Ora't-um,* to pray to ask.
OR'ATORY, eloquence (418-1).

96. *Pars (par't-is),* a part.
PAR'TISAN, an adherent of a party (394-2).

97. *Pen'd-o,* I weigh, I pay out. *Pen's-um,* to weigh, to pay out.
PEN'SION, stated allowance for past services (443-1).

98. *Pop'ul-us,* the people.
POP'ULAR, suitable to people in general (54-2).
POP'ULOUS, full of people (475-1).

99. *Por't-o,* I carry.
POR'TABLE, easily carried (477-1).

100. *Pro'b-o,* I approve, I try. *Proba't-um,* to approve, to try.
PROB'ITY, integrity (696-1).

101. *Qui'es (quie't-is),* rest.
QUI'ETUDE, tranquillity (510-5).

102. *Re'g-o,* I direct, I rule. *Rec't-um,* to direct, to rule.
RE'GAL, kingly (510-2).
RE'GENT, one who governs in place of the sovereign (826-1)
REC'TIFY, to correct (522-5).

103. **Rup′t-um,** to break.
RUPT′URE, open hostility (218-1).

104. **Rus (ru′r-is),** the country.
RU′RAL, belonging to the country (120-5).

105. **Se′c-o,** I cut. **Sec′t-um,** to cut.
SEC′TION, division (216-5).

106. **Sed′-eo,** I sit. **Ses′sum,** to sit.
SES′SION, a sitting (14-2).

107. **Se′men (sem′in-is),** a seed.
SEM′INARY, a school (558-2).

108. **Ser′vi-o,** I serve. **Servi′t-um,** to serve.
SERV′ANT, one who serves (68-2).
SERV′ITUDE, slavery (70-2).

109. **Sis′t-o,** or **St-o,** I stand, I set up.
REST′IVE, obstinate in refusing to move forward (576-5).

110. **So′ci-us,** a companion.
SO′CIABLE, companionable (286-2).
SO′CIAL, pertaining to society (139-2).

111. **So′l-us,** alone, only.
SOL′ITARY, living alone (20-3).
SOL′ITUDE, loneliness (222-2).

112. **Sol′v-o,** I loose. **Solu′t-um,** to loose.
SOLU′TION, the state of being diffused through a fluid (584-1).

113. **Ten′-eo,** I hold, I keep. **Ten′t-um,** to hold, to keep.
TEN′EMENT, a habitation (522-7).
TEN′URE, a holding (375-1).

114. **Ter′r-eo,** I fill with fear.
TER′RIBLE, fearful (20-3).
TER′RIFY, fill with fear (185-1).

115. **Tex′t-um,** to weave.
TEXT′URE, the manner in which anything is woven (178-1)

116. **Va′g-us,** wandering.
VA′GRANT, wandering (94-3).

117. **Ve'rax (vera'c-is),** veracious. **Ve'r-us,** true.
Verac'ity, truthfulness (422-2).
Ver'ify, to prove true (669-2).

118. **Ve'tus (vet'er-is),** old.
Vet'eran, an old soldier (550-1).

119. **Vid'e-o,** I see. **Vi's-um,** to see.
Vis'ible, that can be seen (428-1).
Vis'ion, sight (42-2).

120. **Vin'c-o,** I conquer. **Vic't-um,** to conquer.
Vic'tory, success over an enemy (821-2).

Arrangement for Written Exercises.

1. Majority, the greater number. Major, greater; ity, state or quality of being; ness. The House of Representatives elects the President, if no candidate has a *majority*.

2. Elevate, to raise. E for ex, out; levo, I raise; ate, one who or the person that; having; being; to make, to give, to put, or to take. The diffidence shown by Washington, when appointed Commander-in-chief, only served to *elevate* him in the estimation of the people.

Note to Students.

When English words are derived from Latin verbs, they are generally derived from the present Indicative; as, *agent*, from *ago*, I do, I perform; or from the supine of the verb; as, *actor*, from *actum*, to do, to perform.

When English words are derived from Latin nouns, they are generally derived from the Nominative case; as, *iterate*, from *iter*, a journey; or from the Genitive case; as, *itinerate*, from *itineris*, (of a journey,) the Genitive of *iter*.

The part of the Latin word not used in forming the English derivative is separated from the rest of the word by a hyphen; thus, the *o* in *ag-o*, *us* in *ann-us*, and *is* in *brev-is*, are not used in forming any English word.

Abbreviations.

n. stands for noun.	prep. stands for preposition.
v. " " verb.	A. S. " " Anglo-Saxon.
a. " " adjective.	L. " " Latin.
adv. " " adverb.	Gr. " " Greek.
part. " " participle.	Fr. " " French.

PART II.

Latin Derivatives,

WITH

A Sentence Showing the Correct Use of Each Word.

1. ***A'c-eo,*** to be sour or acid. ***Ace't-um,*** vinegar.

1. Acid'ity, *n.* sourness.
2. Acet'ic, *a.* sour (applied to certain acids).
3. Acetifica'tion, *n.* (tacio,) the act of making vinegar.
4. Ace'tous, } *a.* having a
4. Acetose', } sour taste.
5. Ac'id, *a.* sour.
6. Sub-ac'id, *a.* moderately sour.

  1. The ***acidity*** of limes, lemons, and other acid *fruits** is very refreshing in warm climates.
  2. Much vinegar is made from beer, but it lacks the agreeable flavor produced by the *presence* of ***acetic*** and other ethers.
  3. The ***acetification*** of many *articles* is promoted by the use of beech-shavings.
  4. Shavings *assist* in *clarifying* liquor, in which *state* it rapidly becomes ***acetous.***
  5. ***Acid*** substances are sometimes taken to prevent *corpulency;* if they *effect* the desired result, it is by weakening the *digestion.*
  6. ***Sub-acid*** fruits are doubtless *beneficial* to health, especially if they are taken without the *addition* of much *saccharine* matter.

2. ***Acer'b-us,*** bitter, severe.

1. Acerb'ity, *n.* bitterness, severity.

---

* Every italicized word is defined under its root. If the root is not known, consult the Key.

1. When General Lee was tried by *court-martial*, after the battle of Monmouth, in 1778, it was proved that Washington's *reprimand* was characterized neither by **acerbity** nor acrimony.

3. *Acid'ul-us,* slightly sour.

1. ACID'ULATE, *v.* to flavor with acid.

1. In tropical countries the lower classes use *vinegar* to **acidulate** many articles of food and drink.

4. *Ac'r-is,* sharp, harsh.

1. AC'RID, *a.* sharp, harsh. | AC'RIMONY, *n.* sharpness, harshness (2).

1. The **acrid** *nature* of pepper renders it very disagreeable in large quantities.

5. *A'cu-o,* I sharpen. *Acu't-um,* to sharpen.

1. ACUTE', *a.* sharp. | 2. ACU'MEN, *n.* intellectual sharpness.

1. James II. saw with **acute** pain the destruction of his troops at the Battle of the Boyne, 1690; historians *report* that he *exclaimed,* "O spare my English subjects."

2. John Adams, by his legal **acumen,** saved the life of Captain Preston, charged with *homicide* in the Boston Massacre, 1770.

6. *Adula't-um,* to fawn, to flatter.

1. ADULA'TION, *n.* servile flattery.

1. **Adulation** debases the character, both of those who *offer* it for their own *sordid* purposes, and of those who accept it as the *deserved* tribute to their worth.

7. *A'g-er (a'gri),* a field, land.

1. AGRICULT'URE, *n.* (colo,) the cultivation of fields.
2. AGRA'RIAN, *a.* favoring an equal division of land or property.
3. AGRA'RIANISM, *n.* an equal division of land or property.
4. PIL'GRIM, *n.* one who slowly and heavily treads his way, especially one who pays his devotion to a holy place.
5. PEREGRINA'TIONS, *n.* wanderings.

1. **Agriculture** was the *principal occupation* of the *antediluvians*. Is it *incorrect* to *attribute* their *longevity* to this cause?

2. With the name of **agrarian** law used to be associated the idea of the *abolition* of property in land.

3. It was the German scholars, Heyne (hī'neh), Savigny (sä-vēn-yē'),

LATIN DERIVATIVES.

and *especially* Niebuhr (nee′boor), who first explained that Roman *agrarianism* had reference only to public or State lands.

4. When books of travel were rare and newspapers a *novelty*, the *pilgrim* on his return was *doubly* welcome.

5. Travellers returning from their *peregrinations,* *represent* the scenery of the Yosemite (yo-sem′-i-te) Valley as very grand.

8. *Ag′ger,* a heap.

1. EXAG′GERATE, *v.* to increase, to magnify unduly.
2. EXAGGERA′TION, *n.* the act of increasing or of magnifying unduly.

1. The tendency at the present time to *exaggerate* in *conversation* is shown in the *frequent* use of the superlative, where the *positive* would be *preferable,* and of an *intensive adjective,* such as "awful," for the adverb "very."

2. Constant *exaggeration* *injures* the *moral* character by *habituating* the mind to untruthfulness; it blunts the *perceptive faculties* by placing in the same category things *radically different.*

9. *A′gil-is* (from *A′go),* swift, active.

1. AGIL′ITY, *n.* state of being active; activity.

1. Nature protects some *animals* by strength, some by *agility,* some by cunning, and others again by *repulsiveness.*

10. *A′git-o,* I drive, I move, I think of.

1. AG′ITATE, *v.* to put in motion.
2. AGITA′TION, *n.* the state of being moved (with irregular action).
3. COG′ITATE, *v.* to engage in continuous thought.

1. A very light wind is sufficient to *agitate* the surface of the ocean, and cause sea-sickness.

2. André's letter to Washington, beseeching that his *sentence* might be *commuted* to "a soldier's death," shows intense *agitation.*

3. Columbus, Galileo (gal-e-lee′-o), and all great discoverers of truth, *possessed* the power to *cogitate* deeply on a subject.

11. *A′g-o,* I do, I perform. *Ac′t-um,* to do, to perform.

1. ACT′UATED, *v.* incited to action.
2. ACT′UARY, *n.* clerk.
3. ACT′UAL, *a.* real.
4. CO′GENT, *a.* forcible.
5. ENACT′ED, *v.* decreed by authority.
5. TRANSACT′, *v.* to do.
6. EXACT′, *v.* to take by authority.

7. Ex'igency, *n.* pressing necessity.
8. Ambigu'ity, *n.* double meaning.
9. Coagula'tion, *n.* curdling.
10. Counteract', *v.* to hinder by counter-influence.
11. A'gent, *n.* one who does business for another.
    Act'ive, *a.* quick, busy (56-4).

Circumnaviga'tion, *n.* (navis,) sailing around (44-4).
Activ'ity, *n.* agility; quickness (435).
Exact', *a.* precise (20-2).
Naviga'tion, *n.* (navis,) the act of navigating (279-2).
Litig'ious, *a.* (lis,) fond of going to law (317-2).
Nav'igable, *a.* (navis,) passable by vessels (385).

1. Much blame has been cast upon Galileo (gal-e-lee'-o) for his *recantation;* but the *motive* which **actuated** him should be taken into consideration in judging of his *conduct.*

2. It is customary for the **actuary** of a *Literary Institute,* to *advertise* for the payment of the annual dues.

3. If the British had been *able* to *ascertain* the **actual** *condition* of the *soldiery* at Valley Forge, in 1777-78, they would have been *convinced* that they could never *subjugate* such a *people.*

4. The most **cogent** *argument* was not *sufficient* to *induce* Jackson to sign the bill *rechartering* the Bank of the United States in 1832.

5. In 1765, Parliament **enacted** a law that no *legal document* should be *valid* without a stamp. As no *merchant* could see the *propriety* of the Stamp Act, the whole mercantile *community* determined to **transact** no business requiring stamped paper.

6. One *cause* of the *Revolution* was the *attempt* of Great Britain to **exact** from the *colonies revenue,* to be applied to her own *benefit.*

7. In the latter part of 1776, *success* seemed to follow the British *arms;* New York had been taken, and Washington, closely *pursued* through New Jersey, had crossed the Delaware to Pennsylvania. In this **exigency,** Washington did not *succumb,* but, to the *surprise* of the British, recrossed the Delaware, and defeated the Hessians at Trenton.

8. The dullest *comprehension* in a besieged city could find no **ambiguity** in the usual demand of the Duke of Alva, for an *unconditional surrender.*

9. In making cheese, the **coagulation** of the milk, that is, the *separation* of the curd from the whey, is hastened by the use of rennet.

10. By *study,* a physician knows what substances **counteract** the effects of *deleterious* drugs.

11. A person is responsible for the acts of his **agent.**

LATIN DERIVATIVES.

12. A'li-us, or Alie'n-us, another, foreign.

1. AL'IENS, *n.* foreigners.
2. AL'IENATED, *v.* estranged.
3. ALIENA'TION, *n.* estrangement.
4. INAL'IENABLE, *a.* incapable of being transferred.
  A'LIAS, *adv.* otherwise (608-2).

1. In *reference to aliens,* the *Constitution* provides, that no *person except* a *natural* born *citizen* is *eligible* to the *Presidency*.

2. In 1779, Arnold's trial by court-martial *irritated* his *irascible* disposition, and *alienated* his *affection* from his country.

3. Arnold's *alienation* lasted till his *decease*, and it is not *strange* that he never wished even to *advert* to his country.

4. Life, *liberty*, and the *pursuit* of happiness, are the *inalienable* rights of every one in the United States.

13. A'l-o, I feed, I nourish. **Al'it-um,** to feed, to nourish.

1. AL'IMENT, *n.* nutriment.
2. COALI'TION, *n.* union.
3. COALESCE', *v.* to unite in one body.

1. The *commissary* endeavored *to provide* proper *aliment* for all the sick soldiers.

2. In 1643, Massachusetts, Connecticut, Plymouth, and New Haven, formed a *coalition* for mutual *protection* and defence.

3. Oil and water will not *coalesce;* oil, being lighter than water, rises to the top.

14. Al'ter, the other, another. **Alter'n-us,** one after the other; by turns.

1. ALTERCA'TION, *n.* angry dispute.
2. ALTER'NATELY, *adv.* by turns.
3. ALTERNA'TION, *n.* alternate action.
4. ALTER'NATIVE, *n.* a choice between two things.
  ADUL'TERATE, *v.* to corrupt by mixing baser materials (327-2).

1. The *constant altercation* between Mason and the people of New Hampshire was only settled by calling in an *arbitrator*.

2. The *Legislature* of Connecticut was formerly in *session alternately* at Hartford and New Haven.

3. The *alternation* of day and night is caused by the *rotation* of the earth upon its axis.

4. In 1776, it became evident that the only *alternative* was submission or a *declaration* of *independence.*

15. Al't-us (al'ti), high.

1. AL'TITUDE, *n.* height. | 2. EXALTA'TION, *n.* elevation.

1. The **altitude** of the highest *mountain* is found, by *accurate measurement*, to be 5¼ miles.

2. Sylla, the *Dictator*, determined to *liberate* 100,000 slaves, and *exempt* them from public service, that they might be made *subservient* to his own **exaltation.**

16. Am'bul-o, I walk.

1. PERAM'BULATE, *v.* to walk through. | 2. PRE'AMBLE, *n.* an introduction or preface.

1. Those who are able to **perambulate** a country, see much more than those who ride.

2. The **preamble** to the *Constitution* of the United States *asserts*, that the power of *government emanates* from the people.

17. A'm-o, I love. Ama't-um, to love. Ami'c-us, a friend.

1. AM'ICABLE, *a.* friendly. | 3. INIM'ICAL, *a.* unfriendly.
1. AM'ITY, *n.* friendship. | 4. A'MIABLE, *a.* lovely.
2. EN'MITY, *n.* hostility. | EN'EMY, *n.* a foe (75-5).

1. The most **amicable** relations *existed* between Massasoit and the Plymouth settlers in 1620, and a *treaty* of **amity** was made, which was not broken until King Philip became *hostile* in 1675.

2. Such was the **enmity** of the Indians to the colony of Virginia that *hostilities* commenced in 1609.

3. When Hull, in 1812, determined to *relinquish* the *territory* already acquired in Canada, he was considered **inimical** to the American cause.

4. The **amiable** disposition of Henry IV. of France caused him to be greatly beloved.

18. Am'pl-us, large.

1. AM'PLY, *adv.* abundantly. | 4. AMPLIFICA'TION, *n.* (facio,) the act of dilating upon all the particulars of a subject.
2. AM'PLIFY, *v.* to enlarge. |
3. AM'PLITUDE, *n.* extent. |

1. The Croton *aqueduct*, constructed for the purpose of *supplying* New York with water, was thought to be *capable* of *providing* **amply** for the wants of the whole city.

2. Nothing is more *tedious* in an *orator* than a *tendency* to **amplify** too much.

3. The **amplitude** of the *universe* may well *excite* wonder, even in the mind of a *scientific* man.

4. In his *preliminary* remarks, Webster's *argumentative* style is *terse* and *concise*, but his *amplification* is in the highest *degree* eloquent.

19. An'g-o, I vex.   Anx'i, I have vexed.

1. An'ger, *n.* resentment.
1. An'guish, *n.* extreme pain.
2. Anxi'ety, *n.* solicitude.
   An'gry, *a.* irritated (49-3).

1. When the White Ship, bearing the cherished son of Henry I. of England, *foundered* at sea, and all but one perished, no one was willing to carry the *intelligence* to the king, and to brave his *anger*. At last, a little child was *selected*. When the king understood the tidings, he fell to the ground in his *anguish*, and was never seen to smile afterwards.

2. Great *anxiety* was felt in 1807 for the four sailors of the Chesapeake seized as *deserters* from the British navy.

20. An'gul-us, a corner; an angle.

1. An'gle, *n.* a corner; the opening of two straight lines which meet in a point.
2. Equian'gular, *a.* (æquus,) having equal angles or corners.
2. Multan'gular, *a.* (multus,) having many angles or corners.
2. Rectan'gular, *a.* (rectus,) having right angles.
2. Trian'gle, *n.* (tria,) a figure having three angles.
3. An'gular, *a.* having corners.
4. Quad'rangle, *n.* (quadra,) a figure with four corners, or angles.

1. An *angle* is often denoted by one letter placed at the *vertex*.

2. The great advantages resulting from the study of Etymology are particularly seen in technical terms. The exact meaning of all these words can be known from their *derivation*; e. g. *multangular;* Multus, many; angulus, an angle; ar, having. Having many angles. The other words can be analyzed in the same way.

3. A *terrible desperado*, sentenced to *solitary confinement*, declared he would have been *insane* if his cell had been *circular* instead of *angular*.

4. Any figure having four angles is called a *quadrangle*, or quadrilateral.

21. An'im-a, the life, the breath.   An'im-us, the mind, the soul.

1. Animal'cule, *n.* a minute animal.
2. Anima'tion. *n.* liveliness.
2. Unanim'ity, *n.* (unus,) agreement of a number of persons in opinion.

3. Animadver'ted, v. (verto,) commented on by way of censure.
3. Animos'ity, n. violent hatred.
4. An'imate, v. to stimulate.
5. Magnanim'ity, n. (magnus,) greatness of mind.
6. Unan'imous, a. (unus,) of one mind.
7. Equanim'ity, n. (æquus,) evenness of mind.
An'imals, n. living beings (9).
Pusillan'imous, a. (pusillus,) of weak mind (509-4).

1. When we *magnify* a drop of water which is not pure, we find that it contains various species of *animalcule*.
2. Though the *discussion* on a declaration of independence was carried on with *animation*, yet the question was decided by the 56 signers, with perfect *unanimity*.
3. Hamilton *animadverted* *severely* upon the political course of the *Vice-President*, but *entirely* without *animosity*.
4. Before the battle of Trenton, Washington endeavored to *animate* the soldiers to renewed *effort*, by showing that the cause was not *desperate*, and by *promising* a *bounty* to all who would remain.
5. If Burr had had a *particle* of *magnanimity*, he would not have sought to *revenge* himself by taking the life of his *opponent*.
6. After the *evacuation* of Philadelphia, in 1778, it was decided, by a *unanimous* vote, to go to White Plains.
7. Washington bore with *equanimity* the *misfortune* of losing New York in 1776, and flying like a *fugitive* before Cornwallis.

22. *An'n-us,* a year.

1. An'nals, n. a series of historical events.
2. Septen'nial, a. (septem,) occurring every seven years.
2. Bien'nial, a. (bis,) occurring every two years.
3. Superan'nuated, a. impaired by old age and infirmity.
4. Peren'nial, a. lasting through the year.
5. Millen'nium, n. (mille,) a thousand years of peace.
6. Anniver'sary, n. (verto,) a day celebrated as it returns each year.
7. An'nual, a. yearly; lasting only a year.
Annu'ity, n. an annual allowance (443).
Centen'nial, a. (centum,) occurring every hundred years (76-1).
An'no Dom'ini, A.D. (dominus), the year of our Lord (25-1).

1. When Watson wrote his *"Annals* of Philadelphia," the *antiquated* house, occupied by William Penn was still standing.

2. The *Convocation* first made the meetings **septennial,** but *finally* *reversed* the *decision*, and made them **biennial.**

3. Had Gen. Prescott been **superannuated,** and *unable* to *resist* Col. Barton, his *capture* would still have been *ridiculous;* but we are scarcely able to *restrain* our *risible* faculties, at the thought of the *supercilious* General, accustomed to *domineer* over the *province* of Rhode Island, carried from his bed in almost a state of *nudity.*

4. A *plant* in which life will remain more than two years, is called **perennial.**

5 On *examining* the *Scriptures*, we find that several writers *predict* a time of *peace*, called the **millennium,** in which the most *ferocious* beasts will become harmless.

6. The *International Exposition* held in Philadelphia, to commemorate the one hundredth **anniversary** of the Nation's birth, was a great success.

7. The **annual** Report of the Commissioner of Education is very interesting.

23. *An'nul-us,* a ring.
1. An'nular, *a.* in the form of a ring.

 1. An **annular** eclipse is not a *common event*, as a *concurrence* of circumstances is necessary to *produce* the *result.*

24. *Antī'qu-us,* old, ancient.
1. An'tiquary, *n.* one who seeks ancient things.
1. Antique', *a.* old, ancient.
2. An'cient, *a.* primitive.

An'ciently, *adv.* in time long past (196-1).
An'tiquated, *a.* out of use (22-1).

 1. Nothing is more *precious* to the **antiquary** than some **antique** *relic* of *elaborate* workmanship.

 2. In the *inclement* season of the year, the **ancient** Scots found an *inexhaustible* fund of amusement in the *recital* of the *valiant* deeds of their brave ancestors.

25. *Ape'ri-o,* I open.   *Aper't-um,* to open.
1. Ap'erture, *n.* an opening.

 1. After the most *arduous* labors, some of the Roman soldiers gained access to Jerusalem by an **aperture** in the wall, A. D. 70.

26. *Ap't-us,* fit, meet.
1. Adapt', *v.* to fit. | 2. Apt'itude, *n.* disposition.

 1. The *preceptor* should endeavor to **adapt** his *instruction* to the *capacity* of each scholar.

 2. His **aptitude** for learning, and the *facility* with which he acquired a language, enabled him to obtain an *excellent* position.

27. A'qua, water.

1. A'QUEOUS, *a.* watery.
2. AQUA'RIUM, *n.* a globe or tank of glass, in which to keep aquatic animals.
3. AQUAT'IC, *a.* living in the water.
3. TERRA'QUEOUS, *a.* (terra,) consisting of land and water.
A'QUEDUCT, *n.* (duco,) an artificial channel for conveying water (18-1).

1. In a *corpuscle* of blood the *aqueous* portion is found to *predominate* over the *solid part*.
2. An *aquarium* is a convenient arrangement for *observing* the habits of *aquatic* animals.
3. This *terraqueous* globe is *admirably* adapted for the *habitation* of *human* beings.

28. Ar'biter (ar'bitr-i), a judge or umpire.

1. AR'BITRATE, *v.* to decide between opposing parties.
2. AR'BITRARY, *a.* not governed by fixed rule.
3. ARBIT'RAMENT, *n.* decision.
3. ARBITRA'TION, *n.* decision by arbitrators.
AR'BITRATOR, *n.* a judge appointed by parties to decide between them (14-1).

1. During the War of 1812, between the United States and England, Russia offered to *arbitrate*.
2. Both countries refusing to *accept* the *mediation* of Russia, England *continued* her *arbitrary* conduct.
3. Instead of submitting the question of *indemnification* for *damage* to our commerce to the *arbitrament* of war, both nations consented to *arbitration* at Geneva.

29. Ar'bor, a tree.

1. ARBORICULT'URE, *n.* (colo,) the management of forests.

1. *Arboriculture* in France and Germany consists almost entirely in the management of natural forests.

30. Ar'c-eo (in compounds, erceo), I restrain.

1. COERCE', *v.* compel by force.
2. COER'CION, *n.* force.
3. EX'ERCISE, *v.* to exert, as the body or the mind.

1. Washington had too much *discernment* to suppose that he could *coerce volunteers* to remain in the army.
2. Washington had no wish to *exasperate* the insurgents in the whiskey insurrection, but he determined to resort to *coercion,* rather than *permit* an *infringement* of the law.
3. Some of the most *celebrated* of the nobles, moved by the youth and *innocence* of Lady Jane Grey, besought the Queen to *exercise* her *clemency.*

LATIN DERIVATIVES.

31. *Ar'd-eo*, I burn, I desire earnestly. *Ar's-um*, to burn, to desire earnestly.

1. AR'DENT, *a.* passionate.
2. AR'DOR, *n.* earnestness.
3. AR'SON, *n.* setting fire to a dwelling.

1. The *ardent* desire of Wolfe to take Quebec was *gratified* in 1759.
2. The *ardor* of Wesley led him, whilst he was a *missionary* in Georgia, to perform almost *incredible* labors.
3. So dreadful are the consequences of *arson*, that no community should allow a person to *commit* the offence with *impunity*; in some countries it is common to *incarcerate* the *criminal*, in others to *decapitate* him.

32. *Ar'du-us*, steep, difficult.
AR'DUOUS, *a.* difficult (25).

33. *Argen't-um*, silver.

1. ARGENTIF'EROUS, *a.* (fero,) bearing or producing silver.

1. The wonderful *argentiferous* properties of the silver mines of the West have led to the formation of many companies, for the purpose of working them.

34. *Ar'gu-o*, I argue.

1. AR'GUE, *v.* to reason.
   AR'GUMENT, *n.* a reason offered (11-4).
   ARGUMENT'ATIVE, *a.* containing argument; inclined to argue (18-4).

1. Pocahontas, finding it useless to *argue* with the Indians, determined to *notify* the colonists of their danger.

35. *Ar'm-a*, arms, weapons.

1. AR'MISTICE, *n.* (sto,) a cessation of hostilities.
2. AR'MAMENT, *n.* a naval warlike force.
2. ARMA'DA, *n.* a naval warlike force.
3. AR'MORY, *n.* the place where arms are kept.
4. AR'MOR, *n.* defensive clothing.
5. AR'MY, *n.* a number of soldiers organized under officers.
6. AR'MORER, *n.* one who makes arms.
7. DISARM', *v.* to deprive of weapons.
8. ARM, *v.* to take arms or weapons.
   ARMS, *n.* weapons (11-7).

1. In 1847, Scott consented to an *armistice*, and our Government considering this an *auspicious* period, sent Nicholas P. Trist to *negotiate* peace.

2. Raleigh sent out his third *expedition* in 1587, but Spain having invaded England with a powerful *armament,* called the "Invincible *Armada,*" the colony failed for want of supplies.

3. On the first *appearance* of *defection* in Boston, Gage placed a strong guard around the ***armory.***

4. The wearing of ***armor*** has fallen into *disuse* since the *invention* of gunpowder.

5. The condition of the ***army*** in 1775, made it impossible for Washington to act on the *offensive.*

6. Every *artisan,* whether an ***armorer*** or not, was employed in the *manufacture* of arms and *ammunition.*

7. Nothing could be more *futile* than the attempt of George III. to ***disarm*** the colonists.

8. "I *deprecate* war," said John Adams; "but it is *inevitable,* and it is our duty to ***arm*** as *rapidly* as *possible.*"

36. A'r-o, I plough.

1. INAR'ABLE, *a.* not fit for tillage or ploughing.
1. AR'ABLE, *a.* fit for tillage or ploughing.

1. The first *donation* to Culpepper and Arlington, comprised only forests and ***inarable*** lands; but finally the colonists had to yield some of their best ***arable*** fields to the *rapacious* monarch.

37. Ars (ar't-is), art, skill.

1. AR'TIFICE, *n.* (facio,) stratagem.
2. ART'LESS, *a.* without fraud.
2. ARTIFI'CIAL, *a.* (facio,) made by art.
3. ART, *n.* skill.
4. INERT', *a.* destitute of the power of moving; sluggish.
5. INER'TIA, *n.* that property by which a body cannot put itself in motion when at rest, or come to rest when in motion.

AR'TISAN, *n.* artificer (35-6).
ARTIF'ICER, *n.* (facio,) artisan (35-6).

1. In 1775, General Gage resorted to every ***artifice,*** to *conceal* his *design* of seizing the stores at Concord.

2. An ***artless*** little girl, while walking in an *aviary,* delighted the artist by mistaking an ***artificial*** bird for a *real* one.

3. The painter, Reubens, *displayed* such ***art*** in the management of his *subject,* that it excited the *admiration* of every *spectator.*

4. An artful impostor tried to *obtain* money from his *auditory,* by *asserting* that he could move ***inert*** bodies by the mere force of his will.

5. A car, through its ***inertia,*** continues moving after the locomotive is detached.

38. *Artic'ul-us,* a joint or limb.

1. ARTICULA'TION, *n.* utterance of the elementary sounds.
2. INARTIC'ULATE, *a.* indistinct.
   AR'TICLES, *n.* substances (1-3).

1. Whitfield's *articulation* was so *distinct*, that he could preach to an *immense audience*.
2. Demosthenes, finding his speech very *inarticulate,* tried every *expedient* to improve it, and *labored* with the most *exemplary patience* and *perseverance* until he could speak *distinctly*.

39. *As'per,* rough, harsh.

1. ASPER'ITY, *n.* harshness; roughness.
   EXAS'PERATE, *v.* to enrage (30-2).

1. In 1781, the most *strenuous* efforts were made to *procure* a pardon for Isaac Hayne. Judge Balfour, however, was *inexorable,* and, with great *asperity* and bitter *invective*, subjected him to the *ignominy* of dying on a gibbet.

40. *At'rox (atro'c-is),* fierce, cruel.

1. ATROC'ITIES, *n.* savage cruelties.

1. The bare recital of the *atrocities* of the Wyoming massacre, was sufficient to *transfix* the listener with horror.

41. *Au'de-o,* I dare, I am bold.

1. AUDA'CIOUS, *a.* bold, daring.

1. For many years the Gulf of Mexico was infested with a band of pirates, who, with the most *audacious insolence*, would enter a town and carry off whatever they wanted.

42. *Au'di-o,* I hear. *Audi't-um,* to hear.

1. AU'DIT, *v.* to examine an account.
2. AU'DIBLE, *a.* that is heard.
3. OBE'DIENCE, *n.* performance of what is commanded.
   AU'DIENCE, *n.* an assembly of hearers (88-1).
   AU'DITORY, *n.* an assembly of hearers (37-4).
   AU'DITOR, *n.* a hearer (91-2).

1. When the *committee* came to *audit* the *accounts* of Arnold, they were astonished at the *enormity* of the *fraud*.
2. The ravishing *vision* of the *celestial host*, as they announced, with *audible* voice, the *incarnation*, filled the shepherds with joy.
3. Notwithstanding the *intercession* of the nobles, Queen Mary carried out her *sanguinary* purpose, and Lady Jane Grey met her *fate* with womanly *fortitude*, declaring that she suffered on account of her *filial obedience,* and not in consequence of *ambition*.

43. Au'g-eo, I increase. **Auc't-um,** to increase. **Auxil'i-um,** help, aid.

1. AUCTIONEER', *n.* one who holds an auction.
2. AUGMENT', *v.* to increase; to make or grow larger.
3. AU'THORIZED, *v.* empowered.
4. AUC'TION, *n.* a sale by bidding more and more.
5. AU'THOR, *n.* a writer of a book or other document.
6. AUXIL'IARY, *a.* helping.
7. AUTHOR'ITY, *n.* legal power.

1. In order to make such *vociferous* cries at a *vendue*, an *auctioneer* must *constantly expand* his lungs.

2. The wise and judicious *measures* of Hamilton to *augment* the funds in the Treasury, and to restore the *value* of the *depreciated* currency, placed the credit of the United States on a *firm* basis.

3. Charles II. *authorized* Culpepper and Arlington to sell the fertile lands of Virginia by *auction;* an act which greatly *incensed* the *occupants.*

4. Milton derived very little benefit from the *publication* of the works on *divorce,* of which he was the *author.*

5. Taylor's campaign in 1846 was *antecedent*, and *auxiliary* to the capture of Mexico by Scott.

6. The people of New Hampshire *contended* that Mason had no *authority* to exact rent for the land.

44. Au'gur, a soothsayer. **A'vi-s,** a bird.

1. AU'SPICES, *n.* (specio,) the omens of an undertaking.
1. AU'GUR, *v.* to predict; to foretell events.
2. INAU'GURATE, *v.* to invest with an office by solemn rites.
3. INAUSPI'CIOUS, *a.* (specio,) unfavorable.
4. AU'GURY, *n.* an omen.
AUSPI'CIOUS, *a.* (specio,) favorable (35-1).
A'VIARY, *n.* a place for keeping birds (37-2).

1. Columbus commenced his *voyage* under such favorable *auspices,* as led Isabella to *augur* success.

2. It is customary to *inaugurate* the *President* on the *portico* of the *Capitol,* with *appropriate ceremonies.*

3. *Inauspicious* as was the loss of Gilbert's expedition, it did not *deter* Elizabeth from making three attempts under Raleigh, all of which were *calamitous.*

4. When Magellan undertook the *circumnavigation* of the *globe,* he accepted as a favorable *augury,* the appearance of a beautiful dove flying over the vessel.

45. Au'r-um, gold.

1. AURIF'EROUS, a. (fero,) producing gold.

1. In 1609, the *credulous* settlers of Virginia, finding, as they supposed, *auriferous* clay, gave up everything to dig gold, and laughed at others for their *incredulity*.

46. Bar'bar-us, rude, savage, foreign.

1. BAR'BAROUS, a. savage; uncivilized.

1. De Soto, though often attacked by the *barbarous* tribes, pressed on *undauntedly* until he reached the Mississippi.

47. Bea't-us, happy, blessed.

1. BEAT'ITUDE, n. a blessing pronounced.
2. BEATIF'IC, a. (facio,) imparting bliss.

1. The *compassion* of the Saviour for the *suffering, incident to humanity,* is exhibited in each *beatitude*.

2. The story of the *beatific* vision, *announcing* the birth of Christ, is the delight of children all over Christendom.

48. Bel'l-um, war.

1. REBELL'ION, n. insurrection.
1. REB'EL, n. one who revolts.
2. BELLIG'ERENT, a. (gero,) waging war.

1. When the *rebellion* in Canada commenced, a *rebel* might have had a *transient* hope of ultimate success.

2. In the Russo-Turkish war, 1878, it was doubtful whether England would *adopt belligerent* measures.

49. Be'ne, good, well.

1. BENEF'ICENT, a. (facio,) kind, doing good.
2. BEN'EFICE, n. (facio,) a church living.
3. BENEDIC'TION, n. (dico,) a blessing.
3. BENEFAC'TION, n. (facio,) a benefit conferred.

BENEFI'CIAL, a. (facio,) advantageous (1-6).
BEN'EFIT, n. (facio,) advantage (11-6).
BENEV'OLENCE, n. (volo,) desire to do good (703-1).
BENEV'OLENT, a. (volo,) charitable (299).

1. In the *beneficent* character of Oglethorpe we *discern* a great *similarity* to that of William Penn.

2. In 1592, many a *doctor* of *divinity* resigned his *benefice* and became a *refugee*, rather than *submit* to the law of *Conformity*.

3. The father of William Penn was so angry at his son for what he deemed his *fanaticism*, that he refused him his *benediction*, and would have deprived him of the King's *benefaction*.

50. Benig'n-us, kind, liberal.

1. BENIGN', *a.* kind. | 2. BENIG'NITY, *n.* graciousness

1. Sir Harry Vane, a *compatriot* of Cromwell, was noted for his *benign* and *affable* manner.

2. The *benignity* and goodness of Henry the Fourth of France, made the *populace* almost *revere* him.

51. Bi'b-o, I drink.

1. IMBIBED', *v.* drank in.

1. Aaron Burr may not have been chargeable with *ebriety*, but that he *imbibed* spirituous *liquors* freely, at the time of his *duel* with Alexander Hamilton (1804), there can be no doubt.

52. Bis, twice.   Bi'n-i, two by two.

1. COMBINE', *v.* to unite; to link closely together.
2. BI'PED, *n.* (pes,) an animal having two feet.
3. BIS'CUIT, *n.* bread baked hard. (Fr. *cuit*, baked; literally, twice baked.)
BIEN'NIAL, *a.* (ánnus), happening every two years (22-2).

1. Hamilton was said to *combine* the finest *colloquial* powers with great *profundity* of learning.

2. Although a monkey can walk on two feet, he is not a *biped*, but a *quadrumane*.

3. Sailors assert that sea *biscuit* is the best *preventive* of sea-sickness.

53. Bo'n-us, good, bountiful.

BOUN'TY, *n.* premium (21-4).

54. Bre'v-is, short, brief.

1. BREV'ITY, *n.* conciseness. | 3. BRIEF, *a.* short, concise, in
2. ABBRE'VIATE, *v.* to shorten. | expression.

1. In the address of the first *Continental* Congress, the *introductory* remarks were written with great *brevity*, and with a simplicity and *candor* which forced *conviction* on the mind.

2. Before an article is *available* for *popular* reading, it is *frequently* necessary for an *editor* to *abbreviate* it.

3. Give a *brief* account of that *troublesome malcontent*, Clayborne, who kept Maryland in such a *turbulent* state.

55. *Bul'l-a,* a bubble in water. ***Bulli't-um,*** to bubble, to boil.

1. EBULLI'TION, *n.* a bubbling; a boiling.
2. BOIL, *v.* to rise in bubbles by the action of heat.

1. In a *vacuum*, *ebullition* can be produced with the heat of the hand.
2. Under ordinary circumstances, water will *boil* at 212° Fahrenheit's thermometer.

56. *Ca'd-o,* I fall. ***Ca's-um,*** to fall.

1. CA'DENCE, *n.* fall of the voice.
2. OCCA'SION, *n.* time of particular occurrence.
3. CAS'UAL, *a.* happening by chance.
4. CAS'UALTY, *n.* accident.
5. COINCI'DED, *v.* agreed.
6. COIN'CIDENCE, *n.* concurrence.
7. DECAY', *n.* gradual failure of soundness.
8. DECID'UOUS, *a.* falling, in autumn, as of leaves.

IN'CIDENT, *a.* apt to happen (47-1).

1. There was a sweet *cadence* in the tones of Mary Queen of Scots, and an *affability* of manner, which seemed to *inspire* her *attendants* with the most ardent affection.
2. Washington was the object of much *detraction* and *calumny*, and on no *occasion* was the *dignity* of his character more clearly exhibited, than in his *pertinacious adherence* to his *resolution* to take no notice of these slanders.
3. A *casual* remark betrayed the *precise locality* of Wayne, and enabled Grey to perform the *horrible* deed which has loaded his name with *infamy*.
4. By an *unfortunate casualty* in 1777, Arnold was unable to retain his command or to engage in any *active* pursuits.
5. To Washington, familiar with Indian warfare, the *fallacy* of Braddock's arguments was apparent, and in a modest manner he showed that the troops were in danger of total *destruction;* but as no *officer coincided* with Washington, Braddock considered his *advice impertinent*.
6. The decease of two ex-Presidents, Jefferson and Adams, on the fiftieth anniversary of our independence, is a remarkable *coincidence*.
7. Several authors *explain* the mode of *transplanting indigenous* trees so as to prevent the *decay* of the roots.
8. *Deciduous* trees and plants, such as the oak, rose-bush, and grape-*vine*, drop their leaves in the autumn.

57. Cæ′d-o, I cut, I kill.   **Cæ′s-um,** to cut, to kill.

1. Decide′, v. determine.
2. Excise′, n. a duty on manufactured goods.
2. Precis′ion, n. exactness.
3. Excis′ion, n. a cutting out.
4. Deci′sive, a. conclusive.
4. Infant′icide, n. (fari,) the killing of an infant.
4. Par′ricide, n. (pario,) the killing of a father or mother.
5. Incis′ion, n. a cut.
Concise′, a. brief (18-4).

Decis′ion, n. determination (22-2).
Frat′ricide, n. (frater,) the murder of a brother (222-3).
Hom′icide, n. (homo,) the murder of a man (5-2).
Mat′ricide, n. (mater,) the killing of a mother (338).
Su′icide, n. (sui,) **the killing** of one's self (321-4).
Precise′, a. exact; accurate; correct (56-3).

1. No *impartial* historian would *palliate* the *crime* of Dunmore, in burning Norfolk, but would **decide** that he was no better than an *incendiary*.

2. To *calculate* the **excise** with great **precision,** the *assessor* must visit each *manufactory*.

3. The **excision** Act, by which many a *curate* was compelled to practise *dissimulation*, or to *expatriate* himself, was passed in 1562.

4. Our *penal code* is **decisive** on the question that **infanticide** and **parricide** are *capital* crimes.

5. Portia resorted to no *supernatural* means to *defeat* Shylock, but with *feminine ingenuity*, required him to make an **incision** without drawing blood.

58. Calam′it-as, a misfortune.

1. Calam′ity, n. misfortune; such as fire, flood, etc.
Calam′itous, a. bringing great distress (44-3).

1. In 1665, London was visited by that terrible **calamity** the plague; and in 1666 by the Great Fire.

59. Cal′cul-us, a little pebble.
Cal′culate, v. to reckon (57-2).

60. Cal′e-o, I am warm or hot.   **Ca′lor,** heat.

1. Calor′ic, n. heat; the principle of heat.
2. Scald, v. to burn with a boiling fluid.

1. **Caloric** can be *generated* by chemical or mechanical action, and by electricity.

2. When the Romans were able to encircle Jerusalem, and *contract* their *lines* of *circumvallation* until they were in close *proximity* to the walls, the wretched inhabitants poured down boiling water to **scald** their besiegers.

LATIN DERIVATIVES.

61. Calum'ni-a, calumny; a false accusation.
CAL'UMNY, *n.* false accusation (56-2).

62. Can'd-eo, I glow with heat.
1. INCEN'TIVE, *n.* inducement.
2. CAN'DIDATE, *n.* one proposed for office.
3. CAN'DID, *a.* ingenuous.
   CAN'DOR, *n.* sincerity (54-1).
INCEN'DIARY, *n.* one who sets houses on fire (57-1).
INCENSED', *v.* irritated; inflamed to violent anger (43-3).

1. The *prospect* of a *remuneration* for labor was such an *incentive*, that large *numbers* were induced to *emigrate* to Virginia in the seventeenth *century*.

2. There is no *provision* in the Constitution that the *candidate* for Vice-President shall not be from the same State as the President.

3. Nathan Hale was a man of *rectitude*, and in the most *candid* manner acknowledged his *repugnance* to becoming a spy; but as it was *essential* to the success of the American cause, he consented, although he had a *presentiment* that he would never return.

63. Ca'n-is, a dog.
1. CANINE', *a.* pertaining to dogs.

1. The *fidelity* of the *canine* race, leads man to repose the greatest *confidence* in them.

64. Can't-o, I sing, I charm. **Canta't-um,** to sing, to charm.
1. CAN'TICLE, *n.* the song of Solomon.
2. INCANTA'TION, *n.* enchantment.
3. CHANT, *n.* a kind of sacred music.
3. DESCANT', *v.* discourse.
4. ENCHANTS', *v.* delights highly.
5. RECANT', *v.* to retract something previously asserted.
6. CHARMS, *n.* attractions.
   RECANTA'TION, *n.* retraction (11-1).

1. The *Canticle* and the prophecy of Isaiah *contain* some of the most beautiful *oriental imagery* to be found in the language.

2. The jugglers of the East practise their *incantation* upon snakes and many *species* of *vermin*.

3. Snake charmers in India sometimes lie *prostrate* before the snake, as if in *adoration*; sometimes they sing a low *chant,* and at others *descant* in a tedious *oration* on their power over evil *spirits*.

4. If the *effulgence* of the setting sun *enchants* the beholder, what must be the *rapture*, when the *glorious radiance* of heaven bursts upon the sight.

5. The enemies of John Huss persecuted him with such *malignity*, that they refused him an *advocate*. Huss evinced no *perturbation*, but in the most *placid* manner, announced his *irrevocable* determination never to *recant*.

6. Elizabeth, when *petulant* and *repulsive*, still expected her *imaginary charms* to captivate every beholder.

65. Ca'pi-o, I take. Capt'-um, to take.

1. CAPA'CIOUS, *a.* spacious.
2. CAPAC'ITATE, *v.* to enable.
3. CAP'TIOUS, *a.* cavilling.
4. ACCEP'TABLE, *a.* pleasing.
5. ANTICIPA'TION, *n.* expectation.
6. CONCEIVE', *v.* have an idea.
7. CONCEP'TION, *n.* idea.
8. INCIP'IENT, *a.* commencing; beginning.
9. UNPRIN'CIPLED, *a.* (primus,) profligate.
10. PARTIC'IPATE, *v.* (pars,) to share.
10. INTERCEPT', *v.* to seize by the way.
11. PERCEP'TIBLE, *a.* capable of being perceived.
12. PRIN'CIPLE, *n.* (primus,) fixed law.
13. RECEIVE', *v.* to take; to accept.
13. RECEIPT', *n.* acknowledgment for money paid.
14. RECEP'TACLE, *n.* that which receives or contains.
15. SUSCEP'TIBLE, *a.* capable of being affected.
15. REC'IPE, *n.* a medical prescription.
16. RECIP'IENT, *n.* one who takes.
ACCEPT', *v.* to receive (28-2).
ANTIC'IPATE, *v.* expect (125-4).
CA'PABLE, *a.* able (18-1).
CAPAC'ITY, *n.* ability (26-1).
CAP'TURE, *n.* seizure (22-3).
EXCEPT', *prep.* with exclusion of (12-1).
OCCUPA'TION, *n.* employment (7-1).
OC'CUPIED, *part.* inhabited (22-1).
OC'CUPANTS, *n.* persons in possession (43-3).
PERCEP'TIVE, *a.* having power to perceive (8-2).
PRECEP'TOR, *n.* a tutor (26-1).

1. A *capacious edifice* intended to *accommodate* a large *congregation* should be well supplied with means of ingress and egress.
2. To *capacitate* the mind to judge *correctly*, care must be taken to keep it free from prejudice.
3. Elizabeth of England was of a *captious* and *imperious* disposition.
4. How *acceptable* to the Americans, *exhausted* by forced marches,

LATIN DERIVATIVES. 81

in the retreat from Cowpens, must have been the *torrents* of rain which swelled the Catawba.

5. The **anticipation** of a speedy *cessation* of the war in 1776, induced Cornwallis to *reiterate* the statement that it was already ended.

6. Charles I. could not **conceive** that it was *prejudicial* to him to *detain* the Puritans in England.

7. How long did Newton ponder on the subject, before the **conception** of the *universality* of *gravitation* entered his mind?

8. The **incipient** measures for the *manumission* of the slaves in the West Indies were taken in 1834.

9. It was easy for Smith to predict the evils which would *ensue*, when the colony of Virginia was left under the *domination* of the **unprincipled** men who infested it.

10. As each soldier was to **participate** in the plunder, the greatest effort was made to **intercept** the supplies for General Hull.

11. An *eminent* astronomer saw that there was a **perceptible** *deviation* in the course of one of the planets.

12. As he could account for it on the **principle** of gravitation only, it was *conclusive* to his mind that another planet was near.

13. It is a good *rule* never to **receive** payment of a debt without giving a **receipt**.

14. The morgue is a **receptacle** for dead bodies, where they remain for friends to *identify* them.

15. Knowing that the *patient* was very **susceptible** to the *influence* of *medicine*, the **recipe** was written with great care.

16. Elizabeth, after her *accession*, showed great discrimination in making Lord Burleigh the **recipient** of the highest honors.

66. *Ca'p-ut (cap'it-is),* the head. *Capit'ul-um,* a little head, a chapter.

1. RECAPIT'ULATING, *part.* repeating again.
2. CAPITA'TION, *n.* counting by heads.
3. PRECIP'ITATELY, *adv.* hastily.
4. CAPIT'ULATE, *v.* to surrender on conditions.
5. PRECIP'ITATE, *a.* hasty.
6. PREC'IPICE, *n.* an abrupt declivity.

CAP'ITAL, *a.* punishable with death (57-4).
CAP'ITOL, *n.* the building in which Congress meets. (In some States the State House.) (44-2.)
CAP'TAIN, *n.* the head or chief of a company or ship, etc. (83-2).
DECAP'ITATE, *v.* to behead (31-3).

1. In a *lecture* on the *extensive migration* to the New World, John

Bright, **recapitulating** the causes of the miseries of Ireland, named as the most *prominent*, *extravagance*, oppression, and *extortion*.

2. Congress has no power to impose a **capitation** tax, except in *proportion* to a *census* taken every decade.

3. Lincoln, when attacked in 1780 by the *superior force* of Clinton, did not **precipitately** surrender Charleston.

4. Lincoln continued to *defend* Charleston until further *resistance* was useless, and he was obliged to **capitulate.**

5. The first Continental Congress, in 1774, made no **precipitate** declaration of war, but adopted *pacific* measures.

6. The *ascent* of the Alps can be *accomplished* with *proper precaution*, but the whole community must *deplore* the many *incautious* attempts of travellers, who have been dashed to pieces over the **precipice.**

67. *Car'cer,* a prison.
INCAR'CERATE, *v.* to imprison (31-3).

68. *Ca'ro (car'n-is),* flesh.

1. CAR'NAGE, *n.* slaughter.
1. CAR'CASS, *n.* a dead body.
2. INCAR'NATE, *a.* embodied in flesh.
3. CHAR'NEL-HOUSE, *n.* a place for depositing dead bodies.
4. CAR'NIVAL, *n.* (vale,) the festival preceding Lent.
   INCARNA'TION, *n.* the taking of a body of flesh (42-2).
   CARNIV'OROUS, *a.* (voro,) eating flesh (249-1).

1. Much *censure* was cast on Braddock for the fearful **carnage** in the expedition to Fort Du Quesne. Long after the defeat, the body of a soldier, or **carcass** of a noble horse, remained to shock the traveller.

2. The *Deity* became **incarnate,** not in the *similitude* of angels, but in the form of a *servant*.

3. A walk through the *subterranean* **charnel-house** of Paris is calculated to fill the beholder with *horror;* the *interminable* passages lined with the *corrupt* and ghastly remains, the walls *humid* with the *exhalations* of decaying bodies, the imaginary *movement* of a *pall* or limb, all *aggravate* the *emotion* experienced in this doleful abode.

4. The **carnival** is a *festival* observed in France, Spain, and Italy during the week preceding Lent.

69. *Ca'r-us,* dear, kind.
1. CARESS', *v.* to fondle. | 2. CHER'ISHED, *v.* fostered.

1. The *fierceness* of the lion has been so subdued, that his keeper has not feared to **caress** him.

2. Wolsey, for some time after his arrest, **cherished** the *fallacious* hope of *conciliating* the king.

70. *Casti'g-o,* I chastise.

1. CASTIGA'TION, *n.* punishment.
2. CAS'TIGATE, *v.* to punish by stripes.

1. The Israelites were forbidden to *inflict* a *severer* **castigation** than thirty-nine stripes.

2. To **castigate** those in *servitude* for trifling offences, only makes the character more *obdurate.*

71. *Cau's-a,* a cause. *Causa't-um,* to plead.

1. ACCUSA'TIONS, *n.* charges.
2. ACCUSED', *v.* charged with crime.

CAUSE, *n.* that which produces a result (11-6).
EXCUSE', *n.* apology (324).

1. When fortune forsook Wolsey, many **accusations** were brought against him, and by the King's order he was arrested.

2. Wolsey's *indomitable* will sustained him under every *mortification,* until the King **accused** him of *contumacy* and *duplicity.*

72. *Cau't-um,* to beware, to take care.

1. CAU'TION, *n.* prudence.
   INCAU'TIOUS, *a.* imprudent (66-6).

PRECAU'TION, *n.* previous care to prevent mischief or secure good (66-6).

1. By taking a *circuitous* route, and using great **caution,** Col. Barton captured Gen. Prescott in his *dormitory,* and transported him to the American lines before the guard could *interpose.*

73. *Cavil'l-a,* a cavil, a jest, a taunt.

1. CA'VIL, *n.* a frivolous objection.

1. Under every *discouragement,* Columbus never yielded to *despondency,* but to every **cavil,** replied, "Only give me the means to try."

74. *Ca'v-us,* hollow. *Caver'n-a,* a cavern.

1. EX'CAVATE, *v.* to hollow out.
1. CAV'ERN, *n.* a deep hollow place in the earth.

2. EXCAVA'TION, *n.* a hollow or cavity formed by removing the interior.

1. The workmen employed to **excavate** the ground for the *foundation* of a building in France, discovered in a **cavern** some arrow-heads, probably placed there at a *remote* period.

2. Such was the *hostility* of the Indians in 1644, that the Virginians were obliged to make a large **excavation** in the *declivity* of an *adjacent* hill, to which they could resort for *concealment.*

75. Cĕd'-o, I yield, I go. **Cĕs'ŝ-um,** to yield, to go. **Cessā't-um,** to leave off.

1. Success', *n.* favorable result.
2. Accede', *v.* to agree.
3. Acces'sory, *a.* rendering aid.
4. An'cestor, *n.* a person from whom one is distantly a descendant.
5. Concede', *v.* to admit.
6. Excess', *n.* more than enough.
7. Exces'sive, *a.* exceeding.
8. Inces'sant, *a.* without pause.
8. Succes'sion, *n.* series.
9. Predeces'sor, *n.* one who was in a place before another.
10. Prec'edent, *n.* an example.
11. Proce'dure, *n.* manner of proceeding.
12. Seces'sion, *n.* withdrawing.
13. Recede', *v.* to go back.
14. Cease'less, *a.* unending.
15. Succes'sive, *a.* following in order.
    Acces'sion, *n.* coming to the throne (65-16).
    Antece'dent, *a.* going before (43-5).
    Ces'sion, *n.* the act of ceding (377-5).
    Cessa'tion, *n.* discontinuance (65-5).
    Decease', *n.* death (12-3).
    Interces'sion, *n.* the act of interceding (42-3).
    Exceed' (see page 28).
    Intercede' (see page 28).
    Precede' (see page 28).
    Proceed' (see page 28).

1. When England adhered with such *pertinacity* to the "Right of Search," and refused to *adjust* the difficulty by *compromise*, Russia offered to *mediate*, but without **success**.

2. As the United States found it impossible to **accede** to the *proposals* of Great Britain, it was determined to *prosecute* the war with renewed *vigor*.

3. That Burr was guilty of *treason* may be *dubious;* but, unless the witnesses committed *perjury*, it is positive that he was **accessory** to some project of erecting an *empire* west of the Mississippi.

4. The *lineal descendants* of Henry VII. are found in the House of Tudor and House of Stuart; but no *sovereign* of the *lineage* of Stuart exhibits any of the qualities of his great **ancestor**.

5. The *Secretary* of State *positively* refuses to **concede** to a *neutral* power the right to supply the *enemy* with the *munitions* of war.

6. As the United States has a large **excess** of cereal productions, the merchant is able to *export grain*, and *import linen, linseed*, and other articles of *merchandise*.

7. The ***excessive*** use of ardent spirits induced Congress, in 1790, to lay a tax on every *distillery*, not so much to *promote sobriety* as to *increase* the *revenue*.

8. After the *conquest* of England, William hoped to pass his days in peace, but the ***incessant*** *quarrelling* of his sons for precedence, and a ***succession*** of *adverse* events, rendered the latter part of his life *miserable*.

9. Martin Van Buren considered the *suspension* of *specie* payments to be the natural *consequence* of a *series* of *injurious* measures, carried on during the *administration* of his ***predecessor***.

10. The *election* of a person to the Presidency for the third time is not *illegal;* but as Washington established the ***precedent*** of serving but twice, it has been thought best to follow his *example*.

11. Each House prescribes the mode of ***procedure*** for the *expulsion* of a member for a *transgression* of its rules.

12. The ***secession*** from the Church of England, of a few persons, regarded as *vulgar* and *fanatic*, has produced a *denomination* of great power and *numerical* strength.

13. Canute, in order to *reprove* his *obsequious* followers, issued his *mandate* to the wide *expanse* of ocean, and then waited for the waves to ***recede***.

14. As the *undulating* waters, disregarding the *command* of Canute, continued to advance, he reminded his followers that he was but an earthly *potentate*, and that none but the *omnipotent* God could stop its ***ceaseless*** flow.

15. In 1776, the American soldiers were reduced almost to *despair* by the news of each ***successive*** reverse.

76. *Cel'ebr-is,* renowned, famous.

1. CEL'EBRATE, *v.* to honor by ceremonies of joy and respect.
2. CELEBRA'TION, *n.* commemoration with appropriate ceremonies or solemn rites.
3. CELEB'RITY, *n.* fame.
CEL'EBRATED, *a.* famous (30-3).

1. It was determined to ***celebrate*** Washington's *centennial* birthday with *unexampled* pomp and *splendor*, in order to exhibit the *estimation* in which he was held, and the *prosperity* of the country.

2. A *discreet* ***celebration*** of the 4th of July is *salutary;* but the *deplorable* consequences attendant on the *conflagration* at Portland, ought to *admonish* us to select some more *rational* mode of showing our *approbation*.

3. William Pitt, Prime Minister, showed great *discretion* in *civil* affairs, but his ***celebrity*** is mainly *attributable* to his management of the war, by which Quebec — which, from its superior *fortification* and position, was considered *impregnable* — was captured in 1759, and in 1760 Montreal, thus completing the *subjugation* of Canada.

77. Cĕ'ler, swift, active, nimble.

1. ACCEL'ERATE, *v.* to hasten. | 2. CELER'ITY, *n.* swiftness.

 1. The British commander tried to ***accelerate*** the march from Concord, hoping to reach Boston before *excitement* should lead the *mob* to impede their *progress*.

 2. It is dangerous to jump from a car which is moving with great ***celerity***, on account of the *impetus* imparted by the motion of the car.

78. Cĕl'l-a, a cell, a cellar. **Cĕl'lul-a,** a little cell.

1. CEL'LAR, *n.* an underground room. | 2. CEL'LULAR, *a.* having cells; consisting of cells.

 1. Guy Fawkes hired a ***cellar***, with the *ostensible* object of storing coal; but his real *intention* was to *deposit* under the Parliament House a large quantity of *explosive material*, sufficient to *demolish* the whole *superstructure*.

 2. If we make a cut through the skin, we find a substance called "***cellular*** tissue."

79. Cĕl-o, I conceal.

CONCEAL', *v.* to hide; to keep from sight (37-1). | CONCEAL'MENT, *n.* the act of hiding (74-2).

80. Cĕl's-us, lofty, elevated, noble.

EX'CELLENT, *a.* of great worth (26-2).

81. Cœ'lum, the sky; the vault of heaven; heaven. **Cœles'tis,** heavenly.

CELES'TIAL, *a.* heavenly; of the visible heavens (42-2).

82. Cĕn's-eo, I judge, I blame, I think.

1. CEN'SOR, *n.* one who examines the works of authors before they are allowed to be published.
1. CEN'SURABLE, *a.* blameworthy. | 2. CENSO'RIOUS, *a.* judging severely.
 CEN'SUS, *n.* an official enumeration of the inhabitants of a country (66-2).
 CEN'SURE, *n.* blame (68-1).

 1. In *several* European countries there is a Government ***censor***, who has power to *condemn* a book. Before you are allowed to edit a paper, *permission* of this officer must be obtained, and if anything ***censurable*** appears, you must suffer the *penalty*.

 2. The ***censorious*** character of Gen. Henry Lee caused him to be generally despised and shunned.

LATIN DERIVATIVES.

83. Cen't-um, a hundred.

1. CENTENA'RIAN, *n.* a person who is a hundred years old.
2. CENTU'RION, *n.* an officer over a hundred men.
3. CEN'TIGRADE, *a.* (gradior,) divided into 100°.

CEN'TURY, *n.* a hundred years (62-1).
CENTEN'NIAL, *a.* relating to a hundred years (76-1).
CEN'TIPED, *n.* (pes,) an insect having many feet (556-1).

1. Rev. Daniel Waldo, when almost a ***centenarian,*** participated in the *obsequies* of Lincoln, having formerly been *intimate* with Washington.

2. The ***centurion*** in the Roman army commanded a company of infantry, *similar* to the company, commanded by a *captain,* in the American system.

3. A ***centigrade*** thermometer is one which has the zero, or 0, at the freezing-point, and the distance between that and the boiling-point of water divided into 100°.

84. Ceremo'ni-a, a rite or form.

1. CEREMO'NIOUS, *a.* consisting of outward forms and rites.

CER'EMONIES, *n.* forms prescribed (44-2).

1. Lord Beaconsfield (bec'-ons-field), on his return from Berlin in 1878, was received with ***ceremonious*** pomp and display.

85. Cer'n-o, I separate, I distinguish, I discern. Cre't-um, to separate, to distinguish, to discern.

1. CONCERN', *n.* anxiety.
2. DECREE', *n.* edict.
3. DECREE', *v.* to ordain.
3. DISCRIM'INATING, *a.* acute.
4. SECRETE', *v.* to hide.
   DISCERN', *v.* see (49-1).

DISCREET', *a.* prudent (76-2).
DISCERN'MENT, *n.* judgment (30-1).
DISCRE'TION, *n.* prudence (76-3)
SEC'RETARY, *n.* chief of a department of government (75-5).

1. Washington's great ***concern,*** when the war was likely to *terminate,* was to *secure* the *liberation* of the *prisoners.*

2. In 1598, Henry IV. of France issued a ***decree,*** allowing many *privileges* to *Protestants.*

3. The ***discriminating*** mind of William Penn led him to the conclusion, that to ***decree*** justice to every one, however *inferior* he may be, is the only safe *course* for a legislator.

4. After the battle of Worcester, in 1651, Prince Charles was obliged to ***secrete*** himself in an oak at Boscobel; several times, while in this *rustic* hiding-place, he thought himself on the *verge* of ruin.

86. *Cer't-o,* I contend; I vie.

1. Concert', *v.* to contrive together.
1. Disconcert', *v.* disturb.
2. Preconcert'ed, *a.* contrived or arranged together beforehand.

   1. Washington, in 1781, held a *council* of his officers, to **concert** a plan to invest Yorktown. Each officer was provided with a *succinct* statement of the details of the attack, and the most intense anxiety was felt, lest some *premature* movement should **disconcert** the plan.

   2. According to a **preconcerted** plan, André, the *emissary* of Clinton, met Arnold *clandestinely,* to *communicate* to him the amount of *recompense* offered by the British Government, as the *price* of his *perfidy;* namely, *promotion* to the rank of Brigadier-General, and £30,000.

87. *Cer't-us,* sure, certain.

1. Certif'icate, *n.* (facio,) a written declaration.
1. Cer'tify, *v.* to assure.
  Ascertain', *v.* to find out for a certainty (11-3).
  Cer'tain, *a.* sure (510-4).

   1. A **certificate** from a physician, to **certify** that a death was produced by natural means, is necessary before the body can be interred.

88. *Char'ta (kar'-ta),* paper.

1. Chart, *n.* a sheet of paper, or pasteboard, on which information is presented.
  Char'ter, *n.* an instrument from the sovereign power bestowing rights and privileges (112-3).
  Rechar'tering, *part.* granting again the rights and privileges (11-4).

   1. There was no map nor **chart** of America, in the sixteenth century, that was not full of errors.

89. *Cin'g-o,* I gird.   ***Cinc't-um,*** to gird.

1. Pre'cinct, *n.* limit. | Succinct', *a.* concise (86-1).

   1. In 1621, Massasoit, covered with a *profusion* of *ornament,* came within the **precinct** of the Plymouth Settlement to make a treaty of peace.

90. *Cin-is (cin'er-is),* ashes.

1. Incinera'tion, *n.* the act of burning to ashes.
2. Incin'erate, *v.* to reduce to ashes.

   1. It is easy to *distinguish* anthracite from bituminous coal, by the ashes which are produced by **incineration.**

   2. It is difficult to **incinerate** the slate that is found with coal.

LATIN DERIVATIVES.

91. *Cir'c-us,* a circle.   *Cir'cul-us,* a little circle.

1. CIR'CULATE, *v.* to move in a circle.
2. CIRCULA'TION, *n.* the act of moving in a circle.
   ENCIR'CLE, *v.* to form a circle about (60-2).
   CIR'CULAR, *a.* like a circle (20-3).

1. Fresh air and exercise cause the blood to *circulate* rapidly.
2. When Dr. Jenner attempted to convince any one that his theory of the *circulation* of the blood was correct, his *auditor* generally listened with an incredulous smile.

92. *Ci't-o,* I rouse, I call forth.   *Cita't-um,* to rouse, to call forth.

1. CI'TED, *pp.* summoned into court.
2. EXCIT'ABLE, *a.* easily stirred up.
3. RECITA'TION, *n.* rehearsal.
3. INCITE', *v.* to animate.
4. RESUS'CITATE, *v.* to enliven.
5. INCITE'MENT, *n.* impulse.
6. CITE, *v.* to quote.
7. CITA'TION, *n.* an official notice to appear in court.
8. RECITE', *v.* to repeat, to say, as a lesson.
   EXCITE', *v.* stir up (18-3).
   EXCITE'MENT, *n.* agitation (77-1).
   RECIT'AL, *n.* rehearsal (24-2).

1. When Parliament *cited* Charles to appear before them, he was a first *indignant* at the dishonor cast upon him; but, recovering his *composure*, he prepared for his journey.
2. When Charles I. appeared before the Parliament, everything was *portentous* of evil; the hope of *ultimately* obtaining his release was given up by his most *sanguine* friends, when they saw the *excitable* mob, *clamorous* for his death.
3. The *recitation* of deeds of *valor* by some *itinerant musician*, or wandering bard, was calculated to *incite* the Scots to the highest pitch of enthusiasm.
4. To *resuscitate* a drowned person, *remedial* measures should be applied *promptly* and without intermission.
5. To be able to *educate* their children according to the *dictates* of *conscience*, was all the *incitement* necessary to lead the Puritans to endure the hardships incident to *immigration*.
6. Aristotle, (ar'is-tòt-l,) the *disciple* of Plato, loved to *cite* the sayings of his master.
7. Between the *citation* and arraignment of Lord William Russell, for treason, and his *execution*, only eight days elapsed.
8. In oriental countries, all the pupils of a school are required to *recite*, or say over their lessons aloud, for the purpose of learning them.

93. Cĭv'ĭs, a citizen.

1. Cĭv'ic, *a.* relating to civil honors.
2. Cĭvĭl'ian, *n.* one versed in political affairs.
3. Cĭvĭlĭzā'tion, *n.* the state of a civilized people.
3. Cĭv'ĭlīze, *v.* to reclaim from a savage state.
   Cĭt'ĭzen, *n.* an inhabitant of a state or city (12-1).
   Cĭv'ĭl, *a.* relating to the community (76-3).

1. When the Duke of Monmouth was a *claimant* for the throne, several cities in the south of England loaded him with *civic* honors, doubtless expecting special favors should he become King.
2. The Secretary of State should not only be a *civilian,* but should be well *versed* in *military* affairs.
3. The *civilization* of the United States has never tended to *civilize* the Indians, but rather to *extirpate* them.

94. Cla'm-o, I cry out, I shout. **Clamā't-um,** to cry out, to shout.

1. Acclamā'tion, *n.* a shout expressive of assent.
2. Declamā'tion, *n.* exercise in public speaking.
3. Reclaim', *v.* to reform.
4. Proclamā'tion, *n.* publication by authority.
4. Disclaim', *v.* to deny the possession of any character.
   Claim'ant, *n.* one that demands a right (93-1).
   Clam'orous, *a.* loudly importunate, noisy (92-2).
   Claim, *n.* demand of a right (290-2).
   Exclaimed', *v.* uttered with earnestness (5-1).
   Proclaim', *v.* publish by authority (see page 28).

1. In a *convention* to *nominate* a candidate for the Presidency, the *nomination* is made either by *acclamation* or by balloting.
2. Demosthenes made such strenuous efforts to overcome the defect in his *vocal* organs, that he became a *model* in *declamation.*
3. Many of the Virginians had *previously* led *vagrant* lives, and Smith's efforts to *reclaim* them were useless.
4. The President, in his *proclamation,* was careful to *disclaim* any designs upon Mexico.

95. Clandestī'n-us, secret.

1. Clandes'tine, *a.* secret; underhand.
   Clandes'tinely, *adv.* secretly (86-2).

1. William Penn was charged with making *clandestine* visits to James II., who was living in *seclusion* in France.

LATIN DERIVATIVES.

96. *Cla′r-us*, clear, shrill.

1. CLAR′ION, *n.* a shrill trumpet.
CLAR′IFYING, *part.* rendering clear (1-4).

DECLARA′TION, *n.* a proclamation (14-4).
DECLARED′, *v.* asserted; proclaimed authority (180-9).

1. As the *clarion* announced the return of the British from Concord, the *militia* began to collect at Lexington, determined to throw every *impediment* in their way.

97. *Clas′s-is*, a class. *Clas′sici*, the first or highest class of Roman citizens.

1. CLAS′SIC, CLAS′SICAL, *a.* relating to authors of the highest rank, such as Virgil, Homer, and Milton.
2. CLAS′SIFY, *v.* to arrange in classes.
3. CLASSIFICA′TION, *n.* (facio,) arrangement in classes.

1. Milton must have been a *diligent student* of *classic* writers, as his *juvenile* pieces are *replete* with *allusions* to the Roman and Greek authors.
2. At the organization of the Government, it was necessary to *classify* the Senate, so that one-third *vacate* their seats every second year.
3. The *classification* of the Senate gives at all times a large majority *familiar* with the mode of transacting business.

98. *Clau′d-o*, or *clu′d-o*, I shut, I close. *Claus-cum*, or *clu′s-um*, to shut, to close.

1. SECLU1E′, *v.* to shut up apart.
1. CLOIS′1ER, *n.* a monastery.
2. PRECL′JDE′, *v.* to prevent.
3. CLAUSE, *n.* a separate portion of a written paper.
. SECLU′SION, *n.* retirement (95).

CONCLU′SIVE, *a.* decisive (65-12).
CONCLU′SION, *n.* final decision (85-3).
INCLUD′ED, *v.* comprehended (290-2).
CONCLUDE′, *v.* decide (see page 29).

1. In 1556, the *Emperor* Charles V. determined to *abdicate*, and *seclude* himself in a *cloister*, hoping to enjoy that *felicity* which the possession of *imperial power* was unable to *impart.*
2. In order to *preclude* the possibility of a Stuart coming to the throne, an act was passed settling the crown on Sophia. Henrietta, granddaughter of Charles I., determined to *protest* against the act of succession.
3. By a *clause* in the will of Henry VIII., a council of sixteen was appointed during the minority of Edward VI.

99. Cle'mens (clemen't-is), mild, merciful.

INCLEM'ENT, *a.* stormy (24-2). | CLEM'ENCY, *n.* mercy (30-3).

100. Cli'n-o, I bend, I lie down. **Clina't-um,** to bend, to lie down.

1. INCLINA'TION, *n.* propensity.
2. CLIN'ICAL, *a.* pertaining to a bed.
   DECLINA'TION, *n.* distance of the sun from the equator (169-9).
   DECLINE' (see page 29).
   RECLINE' (see page 29).

   1. "If my son shows any ***inclination*** to *dissent* from the Church of England," said Admiral Penn, "I will not *hesitate* to *disinherit* him."
   2. Medical students derive great benefit from ***clinical*** lectures at the hospitals.

101. Cli'v-us, an ascent, a hill.

1. PROCLIV'ITY, *n.* proneness.
2. ACCLIV'ITY, *n.* ascent.
   DECLIV'ITY, *n.* descent; a descending surface (74-2).

   1. The ***proclivity*** of the Indians to the use of ardent spirits, tends to *deteriorate* their character, and *reduce* them to the lowest rank in society.
   2. As the British ascended the ***acclivity,*** Prescott ordered his men to reserve their fire.

102. Co'dex (cod'ic-is), the trunk of a tree; a will.

1. COD'ICIL, *n.* a supplement to a will.
   CODE, *n.* a collection or digest of laws (57-4).

   1. King Richard's *procrastination* in altering his will endangered the succession; but on his death-bed he added a ***codicil,*** giving the kingdom to his brother.

103. Co'l-o, I cultivate. **Cul't-um,** to cultivate. **Colo'n-us,** a tiller, a husbandman.

1. CUL'TIVATE, *v.* to till.
2. COL'ONISTS, *n.* settlers in a colony.
   COL'ONIES, *n.* settlements abroad which are subject to the parent state (11-6).

   1. In the reign of Richard, a peasant employed by a baron to ***cultivate*** his land, found a *ponderous* chest filled with money.
   2. Had not Pocahontas given to one of the ***colonists*** an *intimation* of the *inhuman* plot to *exterminate* the white race in Virginia, it would have been entirely destroyed.

LATIN DERIVATIVES.

104. *Co'lor,* color, hue, tint.

1. COL'OR, *n.* hue, tint; that which gives color.
2. DISCOLORA'TION, *n.* alteration of hue or tint.

1. Black is the absence of *color,* and white the combination of all colors.
2. When the cuttle-fish is pursued, it throws out a brownish-black liquor; the *discoloration* of the water enables it to *elude observation.*

105. *Co'mes (com'it-is),* a companion. *Co'mis,* affable.

1. COM'ITY, *n.* kindness of manner.
2. CONCOM'ITANT, *a.* going with.
3. COUNT, *n.* a nobleman of the rank of an Earl.
   VIS'COUNT, *n.* a nobleman below an Earl (427-1).

1. The *comity* shown by Louis XIV. to the *destitute* James, would have been no *obstacle* to the continuance of peace, had not Louis induced James to *invade* Ireland.
2. The defeat at Long Island, with all the *concomitant* circumstances, was the cause of great *mental* distress to every *patriot.*
3. *Count* Andrassy represented Austria in the Berlin Congress, and Bismarck represented Germany.

106. *Concil'i-um,* an assembly; a council.

1. CONCIL'IATORY, *a.* fitted to allay angry feelings.
   CONCIL'IATING, *p.* winning to friendship (69-2).
   COUN'CIL, *n.* an assembly held for consultation (86-1).
   REC'ONCILE, *v.* to bring to acquiescence (241-1).

1. Many Tories, in 1775, fearing the *confiscation* of their *property* advocated *conciliatory* measures.

107. *Co'pi-a,* plenty.

1. CORNUCO'PIA, *n.* (cornu,) horn of plenty.

1. All the productions common to the *latitude* of Alabama, are found in such *abundance* in that State, that a *cornucopia* was placed on the coat of arms.

108. *Co'qu-o,* I boil. *Coc't-um,* to boil.

1. CONCOCT', *v.* to devise.
2. DECOC'TION, *n.* the act of boiling anything to extract its virtues.

1. In the war of 1812, Tecumseh went through the *frontiers* of Alabama and Georgia, to *concoct* a scheme for a general war.
2. Whether tea should be prepared by *infusion* or *decoction,* is a *disputed* point with housekeepers.

109. Cor (cor'd-is), the heart.

1. CONCORD'ANCE, n. an index of words contained in a book.
2. COR'DIAL, a. sincere.
3. COR'DIAL, n. anything that gladdens the heart.
3. DISCOUR'AGED, a. disheartened.
4. CORDIAL'ITY, n. sincerity.
4. ACCORD'ANCE, n. agreement.
DISCOUR'AGEMENT, n. that which deters (73).
COUR'AGE, n. boldness (509-4).
REC'ORD, n. register (558-3).

1. By referring to a **Concordance** of the Bible, it is easy to find any text.
2. William was received in the most **cordial** manner by the Parliament.
3. The best **cordial** that Columbus could *administer* to his *discouraged* men, was the cry of "Land ahead!"
4. William of Orange was received with great **cordiality** by the people of England, whose views were in **accordance** with his own.

110. Cor'nu, a horn, a trumpet.

1. COR'NET, n. a sort of trumpet.
CORNUCO'PIA, n. (copia,) horn of plenty (107).

1. When the immense *concourse* were gathered together to *dedicate* the *image* which Nebuchadnezzar had set up, a herald was heard to *iterate* the words, "At the *sound* of the **cornet**, &c., ye fall down and worship."

111. Coro'n-a, a crown.

1. CROWN, n. an ornament worn on the head by a sovereign.
1. CORONA'TION, n. the act of crowning.
2. COR'ONET, n. an inferior crown worn by the nobility.
3. COR'ONER, n. an officer to inquire into the cause of violent deaths.
CORO'NA, n. a luminous appearance which surrounds the dark body of the moon during a total eclipse (642).
COR'OLLARY, n. an inference (298-1).

1. The elegant **crown,** *resplendent* with jewels, which Victoria wore at her **coronation,** is kept in the Tower of London.
2. The **coronet** of a British *Duke* is adorned with strawberry leaves.
3. In large cities, the office of **Coroner** is no *sinecure.*

112. Cor'p-us (cor'por-is), a body.

1. COR'PORAL, n. the lowest officer over a body of soldiers.
2. COR'PORATE, a. united into one body.

LATIN DERIVATIVES.

3. Corpora'tion, *n.* a body politic.
4. Corpo'real, *a.* not immaterial.
5. Cor'pulent, *a.* bulky; very fleshy in proportion to the frame of the body.

Cor'puscle, *n.* a minute body (27-1).
Cor'pulency, *n.* excessive fatness (1-5).
Ha'beas-cor'pus, *n.* (habeo,) a writ to bring a person into court (307-2).

1. "A corporal's guard" is an *expression* used to denote a small body of soldiers which usually *accompany* a ***corporal***.
2. When an *association* desire to become a ***corporate*** body they apply to the Legislature or a court for a charter.
3. In 1629, the king granted a *charter* to the Plymouth Colony, and the ***corporation*** received the name of the "Governor and *Company* of the Massachusetts Bay in New England."
4. So *sanctimonious* was Becket, when he became Archbishop, that he appeared *unconscious* of the fact that he possessed a ***corporeal*** nature.
5. Henry VIII., towards the close of his life, became very ***corpulent***.

113. *Cras,* to-morrow.

1. Procras'tinate, *v.* to put off.

Procrastina'tion, *n.* deferring (102).

1. Lee intended to increase the guard, but, accustomed to *defer* and ***procrastinate,*** he *neglected* it; a long imprisonment was the result of his *delinquency*.

114. *Cre'd-o,* I believe.   *Cred'it-um,* to believe.

1. Cre'dence, *n.* belief.
2. Cred'it, *n.* trust.
3. Cred'ible, *a.* worthy of belief.
3. Creden'tials, *n.* those things which give title to belief.

Cred'ulous, *a.* apt to believe (45).
Incredu'lity, *n.* slowness of belief (45).
Incred'ible, *a.* not to be believed; not worthy of credit (31-2).

1. Arnold had appeared so *conscientious* in the discharge of his duty, and so energetic in the *defense* of Danbury, that few could give ***credence*** to the report of his treason.
2. Such was the *reputation* of Robert Morris, that, when Government ***credit*** was low, he could obtain on his own *security* a large amount of money.
3. It seemed scarcely ***credible,*** that one of the *legation* to France, possessing the proper ***credentials,*** should be rejected, while his colleague was received.

115. Cré'-o, I create. **Creat'-um,** to create.

1. Crea'tor, *n.* God, the maker of all things.
1. Crea'tion, *n.* the act of bringing into existence.
2. Recrea'tions, *n.* amusements.
3. Creat'ure, *n.* an animal; anything with life.

1. Dryden, in one of his poems, represents a *sapient deist* acknowledging God as the ***creator,*** but denying that he has given to man any *revelation* of the ***creation.***
2. Formerly, the higher classes in England devoted a great deal of time to ***recreations,*** calculated to *invigorate* the constitution.
3. There is scarcely any ***creature,*** whose habits are more interesting than those of the ant.

116. Crép-o, I sound, I rattle. **Crep'it-um,** to sound, to rattle.

1. Discrep'ancy, *n.* inconsistency.
2. Decrep'itude, *n.* feebleness produced by age.

1. There was a great ***discrepancy*** in the reports of the battle of Stillwater, as given by Gates and Arnold.
2. The *gradual* decay of the body, with the ***decrepitude*** which years produce, is beautifully described by Shakespeare.

117. Cres'c-o, I grow. **Cret'-um,** to grow.

1. Excres'cence, *n.* something growing unnaturally out of something else.
2. Cres'cent, *n.* a figure the shape of the new moon (used as the Turkish standard).
3. Accrues', *v.* arises.
   Increase', *v.* to augment (75-7).

1. A nutgall is an ***excrescence*** of the oak; a small quantity will give a black *tint.*
2. The ***Crescent*** has waved over Constantinople since 1453, when the city was taken by the Turks.
3. All the revenue which ***accrues*** from taxes, duties, imposts, and excises, goes into the treasury of the United States.

118. Crí'men (crim'in-is), a crime, an accusation.

1. Recrim'ination, *n.* return of one accusation with another.
2. Recrim'inate, *v.* to retort a charge.
   Crim'inal, *n.* an offender against law; a malefactor; a convict (31-3).
   Crime, *n.* a violation of the law (57-1).

LATIN DERIVATIVES.

1. The constant quarrelling and *recrimination* of Mason and the people of New Hampshire continued until 1686.

2. Commodore Barron's *impulsive* nature led him, when charged with cowardice, to *recriminate,* and from this and *subsequent* events there resulted a duel, in which Decatur received a *mortal* wound.

119. *Cru'd-us,* unripe, raw.   *Crude'l-is,* cruel.

1. CRUDE, *a.* unripe; not come to a perfect state.

   CRU'EL, *a.* causing unnecessary pain (216-3).

1. Fruit, which is wholesome in its *maturity*, will produce indigestion if taken when *immature*, or in a *crude* state.

120. *Crux (cru'c-is),* a cross.

1. CRU'CIAL, *a.* severe.
2. EXCRU'CIATING, *a.* extremely painful.
3. CRU'CIBLE, *n.* a chemical melting-pot.
8. CROSS, *n.* an instrument of torture.
4. CRU'CIFORM, *a.* (forma,) having the form of a cross.
5. CRUSADE', *n.* a hostile expedition undertaken for religious motives.
   EXCRU'CIATE, *v.* to put to severe pain (290-3).

1. To an ambitious man like Wolsey, the *crucial* trial was the *indignity* cast upon him *personally*.

2. The *Covenanters* of Scotland were subjected to the most *excruciating torture* to *extort* from them a *denial* of their faith.

3. Ancient alchemists, searching for the philosopher's stone, marked the *crucible* with a *cross*.

4. St. Mark's, at Venice, like most of the cathedrals, is *cruciform,* the transept and *nave* forming the Greek cross.

5. The desire to join the *Crusade* spread from the cities to the *rural* districts, and even *coy* and *timid* children started for the Holy Land.

121. *Cu'b-o,* or *cum'b-o,* I lie down.   *Cu'bit-um,* the elbow.

1. ENCUM'BER, *v.* to oppress with a burden.
2. INCUM'BENT, *a.* resting upon.
3. RECUM'BENT, *a.* lying.
4. ENCUM'BRANCE, *n.* a burden.
   SUCCUMB', *v.* sink under a difficulty (11-7).

1. The Navigation Laws of England seemed devised to *encumber* the colonies, and provoke them to act on the *defensive*.

2. It is *incumbent* on Congress so to *legislate*, that the laws shall tend to *establish* the *fundamental* principles of our government.

3. The *arrogant* Duke of Monmouth, after his defeat in 1685, was glad to *assume* a **recumbent** position in a ditch, where he had time to repent of his *presumption* and folly.

4. Those who contended in the Olympic Games, were careful to practise the *strictest temperance*, and to lay aside every **encumbrance** that might impede their progress.

122. *Cul'p-a*, a fault, blame.

1. EXCUL'PATE, *v.* to clear from blame.
2. CUL'PABLE, *a.* blamable; worthy of blame.

1. St. Clair hoped to *exculpate* himself, for the management of the expedition, which resulted in such a disastrous defeat.

2. The seizure of Osceola, under a flag of truce, was considered a most *culpable* and *fraudulent* act.

123. *Cu'mul-us*, a heap.

1. CU'MULATIVE, *a.* piled up; increasing by additions.
2. ACCU'MULATE, *v.* to heap up; to collect.

1. As the evidence against Arnold became more and more *cumulative*, no doubt existed that he would be convicted of *maladministration* of his office.

2. The desire of Henry VII. to *accumulate* wealth, led him to undertake an *enterprise* under the direction of John Cabot.

124. *Cu'ra*, care.

1. PROCURE'MENT, *n.* the act of procuring.
2. CU'RIOUS, *a.* rare.
3. CU'RABLE, *a.* admitting of a remedy.
   CARE'LESS, *a.* heedless; free from care.
   SI'NECURE, *n.* a position which gives income without care (111-3).

AC'CURATE, *a.* exact; free from error (15-1).
CU'RATE, *n.* a clergyman hired to do duty for another (57-3).
PROCURE', *v.* to obtain (39).
SECU'RITY, *n.* assurance (114-2).
SECURE', *v.* to make sure (85-1).

1. The *procurement* of a charter for Connecticut, from such a *volatile* and *voluptuous* monarch as Charles II., required great *tact*.

2. By a *fortuitous circumstance*, Winthrop had in his possession a *curious* ring, the gift of Charles I. The king at first ordered that the *application* should receive a *negative* answer, but, at sight of the ring, he was induced to *countermand* the *order*, and to grant the charter.

3. Smith, fearing that the *contusion*, from which he was suffering, would be no longer *curable*, returned to England.

125. *Cur'r-o*, I run. *Cur's-um*, to run.

1. CUR'RENT, *a.* passing.
1. CUR'RENCY, *n.* money.
2. PRECUR'SOR, *n.* forerunner.
3. CUR'SORY, *a.* hasty.
4. COU'RIER, *n.* messenger sent in haste.
5. DISCOURSE', *n.* speech.
5. DISCUR'SIVE, *a.* rambling.
6. RECOURSE', *n.* application for aid.
6. SUC'COR, *n.* help in distress.
6. INCUR'SION, *n.* invasion.
7. EXCUR'SION, *n.* expedition.
8. CAREER', *n.* course.
9. OCCUR'RENCE, *n.* event.
CONCUR'RENCE, *n.* combination of circumstances (23).
CAR'RIAGE, *n.* a vehicle.
IN'TERCOURSE, *n.* communication.
CON'COURSE, *n.* assembly of persons (110).
COURSE, *n.* policy (85-3).
CONCUR', *v.* agree (page 29).
OC'CUR, *v.* happen (page 29).

1. The debasing of the *current* coins, or the counterfeiting of the *currency* of a country, is a crime, punishable with imprisonment and *fine*.

2. John, the *precursor* of Christ, is thought by many to have baptized by *immersion*.

3. On a *cursory examination*, Columbus decided that the land he had discovered was the East Indies; it was impossible for him to *realize* the immense *extent* of ocean which lay between.

4. When the *courier* announced the surrender of Cornwallis, it was past midnight in Philadelphia, and the inhabitants, who did not *anticipate* such tidings, were astonished to hear the watchman calling "Past 12 o'clock, Cornwallis surrendered."

5. An *extemporaneous discourse* is generally more *discursive* than one delivered from *manuscript*.

6. The ancient Britons suffered so dreadfully from a *predatory incursion* of the *Picts* and Scots, that they had *recourse* to the Consul of Gaul, whom they *prayed*, in the most *abject* terms, to send them *succor*.

7. Queen Victoria has, for many years, made a summer *excursion* to Balmoral (bal-mŏ'-ral); the *salubrity* of the climate, and the *reverential* affection of the people, make these visits very agreeable to the royal *family*.

8. The *career* of Columbus is an excellent *exemplification* of the *transitory* nature of worldly honor.

9. The bursting of the Peace-maker, which resulted from some *error* in the construction, was a most *lamentable occurrence*.

126. *Cur'v-us,* crooked.

1. CURVE, *a.* bent without having any angles; crooked, curved.
2. CURVILIN'EAR, *a.* (linea,) consisting of curve lines.
3. INCURV'ATE, *v.* to bend.

1. Any part of the *curve* line, which forms a circle, is called an arc.
2. *Meridians* are *curvilinear,* although on the map they may be represented as straight.
3. Persons engaged in *sedentary* occupations, should be careful not to *incurvate* the spine, but to *maintain* an erect *posture.*

127. *Cus't-os* (*custo'd-is*), a keeper.

1. CUS'TODY, *n.* imprisonment.

1. In 1605, a *tremendous* excitement was produced in England by the discovery of a *conspiracy* to *destroy* both houses of Parliament, by an *explosion* of gunpowder. Guy Fawkes was taken into *custody,* and efforts were made to *implicate* a *peer* of the realm.

128. *Cur't-us,* short.

1. CURT, *a.* short, crusty.
1. CURT'NESS, *n.* shortness.

1. "What can I do for you?" said Alexander to Diogenes. "Stand from between me and the sunshine," was the *curt* reply. When asked "What can you do?" Diogenes replied, with *curtness,* "I can govern men; therefore sell me to some one who needs a *master.*"

129. *Cu't-is,* the skin.

1. CUTA'NEOUS, *a.* affecting the skin.

1. The Israelites, dreading the *contagion* of *cutaneous* diseases, were very careful not to *inhale* the breath of a leper, or come in *contact* with one in any way.

130. *Dam'n-um,* harm, loss.

1. INDEM'NIFY, *v.* to reimburse.
DAM'AGE, *n.* injury (28-3).
INDEMNIFICA'TION, *n.* (facio,) reimbursement of loss (28-3).
INDEM'NITY, *n.* compensation for loss (277).
CONDEMN', *v.* to give sentence against (82-1).
CONDEMNA'TION, *n.* act of condemning (181).

1. The *spoliation* bill paid by France in 1835, was intended to *indemnify* the United States for injury done to her *commerce* from 1794 to 1810.

131. Deb'-eo, I owe.   Deb'it-um, to owe.

1. DEBT'OR, *n.* the person who owes another.
2. DEB'IT, *v.* to charge with debt.

1. The *bankrupt* law, repealed in 1878, secured to the ***debtor*** an *absolute* release from his obligation to pay.

2. Edward III. determined to ***debit*** John of Gaunt with the expenses of the war in Castile.

132. Dec'-em, ten.

1. DECEN'NIAL, *a.* (annus,) happening every ten years.
   DEC'IMAL, *n.* a fraction proceeding by tens (492).

1. The ***decennial*** enumeration of our population, shows that the *immigrant* generally settles in the *interior*, rather than in the *maritime* portions of the country.

133. De'cen-s (decen't-is), becoming.   De'cor, grace.

1. DE'CENCY, *n.* propriety of conduct; quality of being suitable in behavior.
2. DECO'RUM, *n.* propriety of behavior.
3. DEC'ORATE, *v.* to adorn.

1. After the *deposition* of Edward II., his *treatment* showed a *total* want of kindness, or even ***decency***, and a determination to kill him by ill usage.

2. The attendants of Charles I. acted in his presence with the greatest ***decorum***.

3. To ***decorate*** St. Paul's, was the great delight of its architect, Sir Christopher Wren.

134. Dens (den't-is), a tooth.

1. INDENT'URE, *n.* a mutual agreement, a copy of which is held by each party.
2. DENT'IST, *n.* one who operates upon teeth.
3. INDENT', *v.* to cut into points or inequalities.
   DEN'TIFRICE, *n.* (frico, to rub,) a powder for cleaning the teeth (498-3).

1. In the reign of James I., the ***indenture*** of an apprentice usually contained an express *stipulation* of the quantity of beer allowed.

2. Formerly, the ***dentist*** and the barber were *identical*; the ability to *extract* a tooth, being the only dental knowledge necessary.

3. Anciently, it was customary to ***indent*** the paper on which the contract for an apprentice was written.

135. Den's-us, thick, close.

1. CONDENSA'TION, *n.* compression.
1. DEN'SITY, *n.* compactness.
2. CONDENSE', *v.* to compress.
DENSE, *a.* compact; opposed to rare (475-1).

  1. The application of cold, to *solidify* a fluid, usually produces *condensation;* but the *density* of ice is less than that of water.

  2. To write acceptably for the daily press, a person must be able to *condense,* and to seize on the *salient* points of a subject.

136. Dete'rior, worse.

1. DETERIORA'TION, *n.* the state of having grown worse.
DETE'RIORATE, *v.* to make worse (101-1).

  1. The *deterioration* of Spain as a nation is easily seen, if we *compare* its present and past condition.

137. De'-us, God.

DE'ITY, *n.* the Divine being. The nature and essence of God (68-2).
DE'IST, *n.* one who believes in God, but denies revelation (115-1).

138. Dex'ter, pertaining to the right hand, expert.

1. DEXTER'ITY, *n.* expertness.
2. DEX'TEROUS, *a.* expert; skilful and active.
3. AMBIDEX'TER, *n.* (ambo, both,) one who uses both hands with equal facility.

  1. The jugglers of India exhibit a *dexterity,* in every *manœuvre,* which is perfectly marvellous.

  2. Alexander, by a *dexterous* movement, seized the bridle of Bucephalus, and, by gentle treatment, soon made him *tractable.*

  3. It is *evident,* that for many kinds of work, it is necessary to have an *expert* workman, who is an *ambidexter.*

139. Di'c-o, I devote, I show. **Dica't-um,** to devote, to show.

1. IN'DICATE, *v.* to show.
2. INDICA'TION, *n.* token.
3. IN'DEX, *n.* a table of contents.
PRED'ICABLE, *a.* capable of being affirmed (231-4).
DED'ICATE, *v.* to consecrate (110).
AB'DICATE, *v.* to resign; to surrender formally, as a crown (98-1).

  1. "Everything," says John Robinson, in his *diary,* "seems to *indicate* that we must leave Holland."

  2. It is impossible to *surmount* the difficulties of our *social* position,

which tend to *demoralize* our children; every *indication* of Providence points to America as our refuge.

3. A scientific book is often much improved by the addition of an *index* and *vocabulary*.

140. *Di'c-o,* I say. *Dic't-um,* to say.

1. DIC'TION, *n.* style.
2. DICTATO'RIAL, *a.* overbearing.
3. CONTRADIC'TION, *n.* opposition; denial.
4. CONTRADIC'TORY, *a.* in opposition to.
5. INDICT', *v.* to charge by formal accusation.
6. MALEDIC'TION, *n.* (malus,) a curse.
7. E'DICT, *n.* proclamation of command or prohibition.
8. DIC'TUM, *n.* assertion.
9. IN'TERDICT, *n.* a prohibition of the Pope.
10. INDITE', *v.* to compose.
11. DIC'TIONARY, *n.* a vocabulary.
12. VER'DICT, *n.* (verus,) decision.

DIC'TATES, *n.* an authoritative rule (92-5).
DICTA'TOR, *n.* a Roman magistrate (15-2).
PREDICT', *v.* foretell (22-5).

1. To *acquire* a pure *diction,* read the works of the "Augustan Age."

2. The disposition of Henry VIII. was irascible, and his manner *dictatorial.*

3. When an invalid, Henry VIII. would not endure the slightest *contradiction.*

4. Catharine Parr, the last wife of Henry VIII., was generally able to *mollify* him; but one day she gave him an answer, which was *contradictory* to some of his opinions.

5. Excited by Bishop Gardiner's *insinuation* that it was *derogatory* to the *conjugal* relation, to allow such an act, Henry ordered the Chancellor to *indict* her.

6. The *prudent* and *sagacious* Catharine managed so adroitly, that the *malice* of the King was directed against the Bishop, on whom he pronounced a bitter *malediction.*

7. Every *avocation* in France suffered when Louis XIV. was induced to *revoke* the *edict* of Nantes.

8. "The proof of the *rotundity* of the earth," said Columbus, "does not rest on my *dictum,* but on three facts, *obvious* to all; *deride* as you please, but give me some ships, and I will *demonstrate* the truth of what I assert."

9. In the reign of King John, England was laid under an *Interdict.*

10. W. H. Prescott, notwithstanding his blindness, was able to *indite* such *erudite* works as the History of Mexico, etc.

11. A good *dictionary,* such as Webster's or Worcester's Unabridged, not only gives the meaning, but a sentence containing the word, as a model.

12. Sentence of death was pronounced on Charles I. the same day that the *verdict* was rendered.

141. *Di'-es,* a day.

1. Diur'nal, *a.* daily.
2. Di'al, *n.* face of a timepiece.
2. Merid'ian, *n.* (medius,) noon.

Di'ary, *n.* a journal (139-1).
Merid'ians, *n.* (medius,) great circles passing through the poles and cutting the equator at right angles (126-2).

1. The *diurnal* rotation of the earth upon its axis produces the change of day and night.

2. At all places between the *polar* circles, in the same *longitude,* the sun *dial* will indicate *meridian* at the same instant.

142. *Dig'it-us,* a finger; a finger's breadth.

1. Di'git, *n.* any one of the figures from 1 to 9.

1. Is the cipher to be considered a *digit?* No; there are but nine digits.

143. *Dig'n-us,* worthy. *Digna't-us,* thinking worthy.

1. Dig'nify, *v.* to advance to honor.
2. Condign', *a.* merited.
3. Deign, *v.* condescend.
4. Disdain', *v.* to contemn.

Dig'nity, *n.* nobleness (56-2).
Indig'nity, *n.* injury accompanied by insult (120-1).
Indig'nant, *a.* angry and disgusted (92-1).

1. The Queen determined to *dignify* the architect of the Crystal Palace by making him a Baronet.

2. On the arrest of André, a *conference* was held, and it was decided that *condign* punishment must be visited on all concerned.

3. Many, who would not *deign* to *notice* Columbus when he left Spain, were willing to *ennoble* him on his return.

4. To *disdain* or despise the poor, because of their *poverty,* is to reflect dishonor on the Creator.

144. *Dilu'vi-um,* a deluge, a flood.

1. Del'uge, *n.* a flood.
   Antedilu'vians, *n.* those who lived before the flood (7-1).

1. According to Usher's chronology, the *deluge* occurred 1656 A.M. or 2348 B.C.

LATIN DERIVATIVES.

145. *Discip'ul-us*, a learner.
1. Dis'cipline, *n.* training, physical or mental.
   Disci'ple, *n.* a follower; an adherent (92-6).

   1. *Parental discipline* was formerly so *rigid*, that a child was not allowed to sit, in presence of the *parent*, without permission.

146. *Di'v-us*, a god; God.
1. Divina'tion, *n.* foretelling.
2. Divine', *a.* having the nature of God.
3. Divine', *n.* a theologian.
   Divin'ity, *n.* the science of divine things (49-2).

   1. Fortune-tellers profess to practise *divination* with the *sediment* of coffee, the lines of the hand, wych-hazel, etc.

   2. The idea of the existence of a *divine* being, seems to be *innate* in the human mind.

   3. * Dr. Biles, a celebrated *divine* of Boston, was noted for his *humor*. In order to illuminate the darkness of their streets, the Selectmen of Boston had imported lamps from England, which, according to the *usual* practice, they proceeded to suspend from the lamp-posts by chains. There was, at this time, a religious sect called " New Lights." One of these, a *matron*, noted for her *illiberality*, had annoyed the doctor with her *loquacity* and *inquisitive* disposition. Meeting this lady one day, the following *colloquy* took place:— "Madam, have you heard the *important* news?" "News! What news?" "I do not wish to *grieve* you," said the doctor; "but a number of 'New Lights' arrived this morning, and the Selectmen have ordered them all to be put in irons!" "Doctor, are you certain of this?" "Madam," said the doctor, with *imperturbable gravity*, "I can testify to the truth of the statement, for I saw one of them hanging. But, remember, this is entirely *confidential*." "Oh! certainly," said madam; and with an *abrupt* "good-by," the lady hurried off to spread the intelligence.

147. *Do*, I give. *Da't-um*, to give. *Do'n-um*, a gift.
1. Ren'der, *v.* to furnish.
2. Donee', *n.* one who receives a gift.
3. Do'nor, *n.* giver.
   Condi'tion, *n.* state (11-3).
   Dona'tion, *n.* gift (36).
   Addi'tion, *n.* increase (1-6).
   Ed'itor, *n.* one who publishes (54-2).
   Uncondi'tional, *a.* without terms (11-8).
   Surren'der, *n.* giving up (11-8).
   Add, *v.* to join to (560).

---

* When scholars are required to combine a word contained in a long paragraph, they should make a clear, distinct statement similar to the model given. Dr. Biles, meeting a very *loquacious* lady, a witty *colloquy* took place Dr. Biles could preserve the most *imperturbable gravity*, while saying the funniest things.

1. When the French Government was unwilling to *render* any aid, Lafayette offered his services to the American cause.

2. Congress, grateful for the generous conduct of Lafayette, determined to make him the *donee* of a large tract of land.

3. Boston and Philadelphia are greatly indebted to Franklin, who was the *donor* of £2000, the *nucleus* of the Philadelphia Library, and of the Massachusetts Institute of Technology.

148. *Do'c-eo,* I teach.   *Doc't-um,* to teach.

1. DOCIL'ITY, *n.* teachableness.
2. DOC'TRINE, *n.* that which is taught.
3. DOC'ILE, *a.* teachable; willing to learn.

DOC'TOR, *n.* one who has received a diploma; a teacher (49-2).

DOC'UMENT, *n.* a paper containing evidence (11-5).

1. The most *inveterate* enemy of Charles I. longed to *condole* with him in the *grief* occasioned by the death of his little daughter, whose *docility* and *ingenuousness* had won the love of all who knew her.

2. Many Pagans admit the *doctrine*, that a part of man is *immortal*, even though they believe in the *annihilation* of the body.

3. A *docile* disposition in *infancy* and youth is the best indication of a learned old age.

149. *Do'le-o,* I grieve; I am in pain.

DOLE'FUL, *a.* sorrowful (68-3). | CONDOLE' (see page 29).

150. *Dom'in-us,* a master; a lord.

1. DOMIN'ION, *n.* sovereign power.

DOMINA'TION, *n.* tyranny (65-9).

DOMINEER', *v.* to rule with insolence (22-3).

PREDOM'INATE, *v.* to prevail over (27-1).

1. When the Colonies determined to throw off the *dominion* of Great Britain, the dominant power in Boston held Tory principles.

151. *Dom-o,* I subdue, I tame.   *Dom'it-um,* to subdue, to tame.

1. UNDAUNT'ED, *a.* not intimidated.

INDOM'ITABLE, *a.* not to be subdued (71-2).

UNDAUNT'EDLY, *adv.* intrepidly (46).

DAUNT'LESS, *a.* fearless; intrepid (618-1).

1. De Soto, *undaunted* by the dangers that surrounded him, pressed forward to the Mississippi, which he discovered in 1541.

152. Do'm-us, a house, a home.

1. Domes'ticate, v. to tame. 2. Dom'icile, n. mansion.

1. A man found a *serpent* in a *dormant* or *torpid* state, and took it home, intending to *domesticate* it; but he had reason to *repent* of his folly, when the *reptile* stung him.

2. Having *indubitable* proof, that the King was *implacable*, Wolsey resigned his *splendid domicile,* and, *disconsolate* and dejected, sought the hospitality of Leicester Abbey, where he died.

153. Dor'm-io, I sleep.   Dormi't-um, to sleep.

Dor'mant, a. insensible (152-1).

Dor'mitory, n. a sleeping-room (72).

154. Dor's-um, the back.

1. Endorse', v. to write one's name on the back of a paper.

1. To *transfer* a *promissory* note, it is necessary to *endorse* it.

155. Du'bi-um, doubt.   Dubita't-um, to doubt.

Du'bious, a. uncertain; doubtful (75-3).

Indu'bitable, a. not to be doubted (152-2).

156. Du'c-o, I lead.   Duc't-um, to lead.

1. Duc'tile, a. capable of being drawn into a wire; flexible.
2. Con'duit, n. a water-pipe.
3. Conduce', v. to tend.
4. Adduce', v. to bring forward.
4. Deduce', v. infer.
5. Duc'at, n. a silver coin worth about a dollar; and a gold of twice the value.

Con'duct, n. behavior; deportment (11-1).

Duke, n. one of the highest order of nobility (111-2).

Ed'ucate, v. to bring up (92-5).

Introduc'tory, a. preliminary (54-1).

Induce' (see page 30).
Produce' (see page 30).
Reduce' (see page 30).

1. The *ductile* quality of gold, enables the artificer to *attenuate* it in a most remarkable degree.

2. A *conduit,* intended to supply Jerusalem with water, was made *impervious* by a cement, known only to the ancients.

3. Public schools ought to *conduce* to morality, as well as to general intelligence.

4. We are accustomed to *adduce* the tax upon tea, as the cause of

the Revolution, but there were many other acts of *oppression*, from which we can *deduce* the righteousness of the war.

5. In the "Merchant of Venice," Antonio agrees, that if every *ducat* is not paid, he will forfeit a pound of flesh.

157. Du'-o, two. Duel'l-um, a fight between two.

1. Du'plicates, *n.* (plico,) copies; things which exactly resemble other things.
2. Duodec'imo, *n.* (decem,) a book in which the sheet is folded into 12 leaves.

Du'el, *n.* a combat between two (51).
Duplic'ity, *n.* (plico,) deception (71-2).
Doub'ly, *adv.* (plico,) in twice the degree (7-4).

1. *Duplicates* of letters had to be written by *manual* labor until a machine was invented to perform the *operation*.

2. Caxton published books of all sizes, from the cumbersome *folio* to the *duodecimo*, so convenient to peruse.

158. Du'r-us, hard.

1. Du'rable, *a.* lasting.
2. Dura'tion, *n.* continuance.
3. Ob'duracy, *n.* hardness of heart.

Ob'durate, *a.* stubborn; hardened in feelings (70-2).
Endure', *v.* to undergo; to sustain (92-5).

1. So *durable* are some kinds of wood, that there are stone bridges in a state of *dilapidation*, while the wooden piles on which they rest are in a good state of *preservation*.

2. Who can *comprehend* the *duration* of Eternity? Or even the *infinite* distance that exists between us and the nearest *constellation*.

3. The *flagrancy* of the crime, and the *obduracy* exhibited by Ravaillac, the murderer of "Good King Henry," made the people rejoice in his terrible punishment.

159. Eb'ri-us, drunken.

1. Ine'briate, *n.* a drunkard.
Ebri'ety, *n.* drunkenness (51).

Sobri'ety, *n.* freedom from intoxication; habitual temperance (75-7).

1. A home for the *inebriate*, in which he will be free from *temptation*, is one of the *noble* charities of the age.

160. Æd-es, a house, a building.

1. Ed'ify, *v.* to build up in knowledge.

Ed'ifice, *n.* (facio,) a building (65-1).

1. The study of history tends to *edify* and enlarge the mind.

161. *Ed-o,* I eat.

1. Ed'ible, *a.* eatable. | 2. Edac'ity, *n.* voracity.

1. "What articles are *edible?*" inquires the *naturalist.* "Rats and birds'-nests," says the Chinaman. "Frogs," says the Frenchman. "Rancid oil," says the Esquimaux. "Old cheese," says the Englishman. Yet all these are *disgusting* to persons not accustomed to them.

2. The *edacity* of pachyderms, such as the elephant, rhinoceros, hippopotamus, and tapir, is astonishing.

162. *Ego,* I.

1. E'gotism, *n.* talking much of one's self. | 2. Egotist'ical, *a.* self-conceited.

1. In the first person, the *plural we* is often used, for the singular *I,* by editors, etc., to avoid the appearance of *egotism.*

2. To avoid appearing *egotistical,* the plural *we* is often used for the singular *I,* by reviewers, etc.

163. *El'egans (elegan't-is),* elegant.

1. El'egance, *n.* the state or quality of being elegant.

1. *Elegance* implies a select style of beauty, usually produced by art or skill.

164. *Em-o,* I buy. *Emp't-um,* to buy.

1. Exemp'tion, *n.* freedom from that to which others are subject.
2. Per'emptory, *a.* decisive.
3. Redemp'tion, *n.* ransom.
4. Redeem', *v.* to ransom.
5. Redeem'able, *a.* capable of being redeemed.
Exempt', *v.* to release; to take from (15-2).

1. Only two (Enoch and Elijah) of the human race, have had *exemption* from *mortality.*

2. The command to General Scott, in 1846, to proceed to Mexico, was so *peremptory,* that delay was impossible.

3. Richard, the "Lion-hearted," was so esteemed, that the English melted the silver in the churches to obtain the sum necessary for his *redemption.*

4. The brigands demanded a large sum to *redeem* the captive.

5. The bonds of the United States, called "five-twenties," were *redeemable* in either five or twenty years.

165. *Æm'ulus,* a rival.

1. Emula'tion, *n.* rivalry; desire to equal or excel. | 2. Em'ulate, *v.* to strive to equal or excel.

1. The *pleasure* afforded by the possession of knowledge, ought to produce sufficient *emulation* among scholars.

2. Let the youth of America *emulate* the noble character of Washington, in *integrity*, *honesty*, and *self-sacrifice*.

166. Ens (en't-is), being. (See *Sum.*)

167. E'-o, I go. **I't-um,** to go.

1. AM'BIENT, *a.* floating on all sides.
2. EX'IT, *n.* departure.
3. INI'TIAL, *a.* placed at the beginning.
4. INI'TIATE, *v.* to introduce.
5. OBIT'UARY, *a.* relating to the decease of a person.
6. SEDI'TION, *n.* insurrection; rebellion.

CIR'CUIT, *n.* the division of a state visited by a judge to hold periodical courts (475).
CIRCU'ITOUS, *a.* indirect (72).
AMBI'TION, *n.* desire for advancement (42-3).
TRAN'SITORY, *a.* passing quickly away (125-8).
TRAN'SIENT, *a.* not lasting (48-1).

1. It is related of Constantine, that a flaming cross appeared to him in the heavens, and that, through the *ambient* air, there came a voice, saying, "By *this*, conquer."

2. The *exit* of some of the Royal Governors from the Colonies, was marked by acts calculated to *inflame* the minds of the people.

3. When a word begins with two consonants, the sounds of which will not coalesce, the *initial consonant* is silent; as, knife.

4. The ancient alchemists, before consenting to *initiate* a *novice* into the mysteries of their craft, required him to make a solemn *asseveration*, never to *divulge* its secrets.

5. The *obituary* notices of Lord Brougham (broo'-am, or broo'm), in 1839, were so *laudatory*, that some thought he *originated* the *false* report of his own death, to see what contemporary writers would say of him.

6. William Penn was known to *correspond* with James II., and, consequently, was accused of *sedition.*

168. E'ques (eq'uit-is), a horseman.

1. EQUES'TRIAN, *a.* pertaining to horsemanship.
2. EQ'UIPAGE, *n.* attendance, retinue.

1. *Equestrian* exercises are *promotive* of health and *vivacity*, and are *invaluable* for those who are *convalescent*.

2. According to Ancient History, the *equipage* of Queen Zenobia was magnificent.

169. Æ´qu-us, equal, just.

1. AD'EQUATE, a. equal to.
2. EQUA'TION, n. an expression of equality between quantities.
3. EQUILIB'RIUM, n. (libra,) equality of weight.
4. EQ'UITY, n. justice.
5. EQUIV'ALENT, n. (valeo,) that which is of equal value.
6. EQUIV'OCATE, v. (voco,) to use words in a deceptive manner.
7. INIQ'UITY, n. great wickedness.
8. E'QUALIZE, v. to make alike in amount or degree.
9. EQUIDIS'TANT, a. (sisto,) at the same distance.
10. E'QUAL, a. neither greater nor less.
    EQUATO'RIAL, a. relating to the equator (180-11).
    EQUINOC'TIAL, a. (nox,) pertaining to the equinox (320).

1. In 1779, Prevost threatened Charleston; although Lincoln feared that his force was not *adequate* to the *emergency*, he hastened to its relief, and in spite of the *disparity* of the forces, compelled the British to retreat.

2. An *equation* is not altered, if you *perform* the same operation on both sides.

3. The cultivation of the intellect tends to preserve the *equilibrium* of the mental and physical powers.

4. "The judicial power shall extend to all cases, in law and *equity*, arising under this Constitution."

5. William Penn considered it *dishonorable* to take anything from the Indians, without returning an *equivalent*.

6. Nathan Hale was able to *penetrate* into the very heart of the British camp, but, on his return, was *apprehended*, and carried before the Provost. When the usual *question*, "Are you a spy?" was put to Nathan Hale, he scorned to *equivocate*, and merely answered "Yes."

7. The *iniquity* of the massacre of Wyoming, in 1778, has made the name of Col. John Butler *infamous*.

8. Congress has made an effort to *equalize* the bounties paid to the soldiers.

9. The tropics are two small circles, *equidistant* from the equator, which mark the limit of the sun's *declination*.

10. Two lines which are *equal* and parallel express equality; thus, $6 + 4 = 10$.

170. Er´r-o, I wander. Erra´t-um, to wander.

1. ERRAT'IC, a. eccentric.
2. ERRO'NEOUS, a. incorrect.
3. ABERRA'TION, n. a wandering.
4. ERRA'TA, n. errors in writing or printing.
   ER'ROR, n. fault; blunder (675-1).

1. The *erratic* course of George III., greatly surprised the nation, until it was known that all the *premonitory* symptoms of *insanity* had appeared.

2. Until Columbus proved it to be *erroneous,* the opinion was prevalent, that the earth was a level *plain.*

3. *Aberration* of mind, was formerly attributed to *lunar* influences, and was, therefore, called *lunacy.*

4. The correction of *errata* in stereotype plates, *involves* a great deal of *labor.*

171. *Æs'tim-o,* I value.

1. Es'TIMATE, *v.* to compute.
2. Es'TIMABLE, *a.* worthy of esteem.
3. INES'TIMABLE, *a.* above all price.
ESTIMA'TION,*n.*opinion(76).

1. It is hardly possible to *estimate,* properly, the value of the territory acquired by the treaty of Guadaloupe Hidalgo.

2. The *estimable* character of Rose Standish, *consort* of Miles Standish, made her generally beloved in the Plymouth Colony.

3. The *inestimable* "right to a speedy and *public* trial, is a right belonging to the people, as individuals."

172. *Æter'n-us,* without beginning or end.

1. ETER'NITY, *n.* continuance without beginning or end.

1. The ancients represented *eternity* by a serpent with its tail in its mouth.

173. *Æ'-vum,* an age.

1. COE'VAL, *n.* existing at the same time.
2. PRIME'VAL, *a.* (primus,) primitive.
3. LONGEV'ITY, *n.* (longus,) long duration of life (7-1).

1. If, in a *stratum* of *granite,* we find the bones of a *quadruped,* or biped, it is fair to infer that those animals were *coeval* with the rocks.

2. Milton gives, in "Paradise Lost," a *vivid description* of the earth in its *primeval* state.

174. *Exam'en (exam'in-is),* a balance.

1. EXAM'INING, *part.* investigating closely (22-5).
2. EXAMINA'TION, *n.* investigation (125-3).

175. *Exem'pl-um,* a pattern.

1. EXEM'PLIFY, *v.* to illustrate by example.
2. SAM'PLE,*n.* specimen; a part presented for inspection.

LATIN DERIVATIVES.

EXAM'PLE, n. pattern (75-10).
EX'EMPLARY, a. worthy of imitation (38).
EXEMPLIFICA'TION, n. (facio,) illustration (125-8).
UNEXAM'PLED, a. without precedent (76-1).

1. The proficiency which Milton exhibited at college, served to *exemplify* the principle, that "ATTENTION IS THE SECRET OF SUCCESS."
2. When, in 1791, a *sample* of anthracite coal was exhibited, people treated with *derision* the idea, that it was *inflammable*.

176. *Exil'i-um*, banishment from one's country.
1. EX'ILE, n. banishment.

1. Charles II. was too *obtuse* to profit by his *experience* in *exile*, during the *Protectorate*.

177. *Ex'ter-us*, outer. ***Exte'rior*,** outer. ***Extre'm-us*,** the outermost. ***Ex'tra*,** on the outside.

1. EXTE'RIOR, n. the outer part; that which is external.
2. EXTER'NAL, a. outward.
3. EXTRA'NEOUS, a. not belonging to a thing.
4. EXTREM'ITY, n. the utmost point.
5. EXTRIN'SIC, a. unessential, outward.
STRANGE, a. peculiar (12-3).

1. The first *view* of the *exterior* of St. Peter's, usually disappoints the spectator.
2. The *Supreme* Being judges not by the *external* appearance, but by the heart.
3. As there was no surgeon to *probe* the wound of Smith, and remove any *extraneous* matter, he sought *medical* aid in England.
4. During the *famine* in Virginia, in 1610, the colonists were reduced to such *extremity*, that they *devoured* the skins of horses.
5. The *favorable* reception of Franklin, as ambassador to France, was attributable to no *extrinsic* aids or *adventitious* circumstances.

178. *Fab'ric-o*, I make or frame.
1. FAB'RIC, n. manufactured cloth.
2. FAB'RICATE, v. to manufacture.

1. We are indebted to a worm, for the beautiful *fabric* called silk, whose soft and *pliable texture* makes it so *suitable* for clothing.
2. The object of a tariff, is to induce the inhabitants of a country to *fabricate* everything they use.

10* H

179. Fa'ci-es, a face.

1. DEFACE', *v.* to disfigure.
2. EFFACE', *v.* expunge.
2. FACE, *n.* the countenance; the visage.

1. To *deface* a building, or its enclosure, by *scribbling*, or by drawing any figure, or by whittling, is a *vulgarism* of which no person, having the slightest *pretension* to gentility, would be guilty.

2. A young man having been guilty of some *immoral* act, Washington deemed it his duty to *remonstrate* with him; when the youth, greatly incensed, actually spit in his *face*. With the most perfect equanimity, Washington wiped it off, saying, " Young man, I wish you could *efface* the guilt from your soul, as easily as I can wipe this *insult* from my *face*."

180. Fa'ci-o, I do, I make. **Fac't-um,** to do, to make.

1. FAC'TION, *n.* a party opposed to the Government.
2. AFFECTA'TION, *n.* artificial appearance.
3. EFFICA'CIOUS, *a.* effectual.
4. OFFI'CIATE, *v.* to perform the duties of an office.
5. INFECT', *v.* taint with disease.
6. SUR'FEITED, *part.* satiated.
7. DIF'FICULTIES, *n.* embarrassments.
8. DEFEC'TIVE, *a.* deficient.
9. PON'TIFF, *n.* (pons,) the pope.
10. FASH'IONS, *n.* modes, styles.
11. FEAT'URES, *n.* lineaments.
AFFEC'TION, *n.* love (12-2).

FAC'ULTIES, *n.* powers (8-2).
DEFEAT', *v.* to overcome or to vanquish (57-5).
DEFEC'TION, *n.* the act of abandoning a cause (35-3).
EFFECT', *v.* produce (1-5).
FACIL'ITATE, *v.* to render easy (475-1).
FACIL'ITY, *n.* dexterity (26-2).
FAC'TORY, *n.* a place where things are manufactured (705-1).
OF'FICER, *n.* a person holding an office, or a commission from the President or from a governor (56-5).
SUFFI'CIENT, *n.* enough (11-4).

1. In 1645, a *faction,* headed by Clayborne, caused much *disturbance* in Maryland.

2. When Pocahontas was in England, her *simplicity*, and freedom from *affectation*, won the love of all.

3. When a person has swallowed poison, the most *efficacious* remedy at hand, is *usually* the white of an egg, to *neutralize* the poison; or mustard, in warm water, to produce *nausea*.

4. If the President and Vice-President are both *disqualified* to perform the duties of the office, the presiding officer of the *Senate* is to *officiate*.

LATIN DERIVATIVES.

5. Travellers are obliged to submit to *quarantine*, lest they should *infect* a city.

6. Alexander, the *conqueror* of the world, having **surfeited** himself, died, a *glutton* and a drunkard, 324 B. C.

7. Arnold's *pecuniary* **difficulties** led him to *peculate* the public funds, and to *defraud* the Government of *enormous* sums.

8. In relation to taxes, the Articles of Confederation were very **defective.**

9. When the Roman **Pontiff** refused to sanction the divorce, Henry called a Parliament, which *declared* the King's *supremacy*.

10. It is curious to walk in Pompeii (pom-pa′-yee), (destroyed by an *eruption* of Vesuvius), and see the **fashions** of a people who lived 1800 years ago.

11. Some of the tribes inhabiting the *equatorial* regions of Africa, have fine **features.**

181. *Fal′l-o,* I deceive.   *Fal′s-um,* to deceive.

1. FAL′LIBLE, *a.* liable to err.
2. FAL′SIFY, *v.* represent falsely.
3. FAIL′URE, *n.* want of success; omission.

FALLA′CIOUS, *a.* deceitful (69-2).
FAL′LACY, *n.* deceitfulness (56-5).
FALSE, *a.* untrue (167-5).

1. The *condemnation* of so many to the *penitentiary*, proves that some of the human race are **fallible.**

2. Whether Mr. Erskine really did **falsify** the instruction of his Government, in 1809, we know not; but the refusal of the British Government to *repeal* the injurious decrees, gave *umbrage* to the American people.

3. The numerous attempts to discover a North-West passage, have all resulted in **failure.**

182. *Fa′m-a,* fame.

1. FA′MOUS, *a.* renowned; much talked of.
1. DEFAME′, *v.* to injure one's reputation maliciously.

IN′FAMOUS, *a.* detestable (169-7).
IN′FAMY, *n.* public reproach (56-3).

1. After the surrender of Burgoyne, which rendered Gates so **famous,** persistent attempts were made to **defame** Washington.

183. *Fa′m-es,* hunger.

1. FAM′ISH, *v.* to die of hunger; to starve.

FAM′INE, *n.* scarcity of food (177-4).

1. After the battle of Flatbush, in 1776, General Woodhull was allowed to **famish** in a British prison.

184. *Famil'i-a*, a family.

FAMILIAR'ITY, *n.* intimate acquaintance (290-1).

FAMIL'IAR, *a.* acquainted (97).
FAM'ILY, *n.* household (125-7).

185. *Fa'n-um*, a temple.

1. PROFANE', *v.* to desecrate.
FANAT'IC, *a.* excessively enthusiastic (75-12).

FANAT'ICISM, *n.* wild and extravagant notions of religion (49-3).

1. A man's hand, tracing unknown characters on the wall, might well *terrify* Belshazzar, when he had dared to *profane* the vessels of the sanctuary, by using them in a *convivial* assembly.

186. *Fa'ri*, to speak.   *Fa't-um*, fate, destiny.

1. FA'TAL, *a.* mortal.
2. PREF'ACE, *n.* introduction.
AF'FABLE, *a.* courteous (50-1).
INFANT'ICIDE, *n.* (cædo,) the killing of an infant (57-4).

AFFABIL'ITY, *n.* kindness of manner in conversation (56-1).
IN'FANCY, *n.* childhood (148-3).
FATE, *n.* predetermined event (42-3).

1. At the taking of Quebec, by the English, in 1759, Wolfe and Montcalm received *fatal* wounds.
2. Bunyan, in the work, which alone was sufficient to *immortalize* his name, says in his *preface*, that in answer to the *query*, "Shall I print my book?"—

"Some said, 'John, print it.' Others said, 'Not so,'
Some said, 'It might do good.' Others said 'No.'"

187. *Fari'n-a*, meal.

1. FARI'NA, *n.* the flour of any grain, starch, etc.

1. FARINA'CEOUS, *a.* consisting of meal.

1. Large quantities of *farinaceous* food, such as oatmeal, cornstarch, *farina*, etc., were required for the army.

188. *Fav'e-o*, I favor.

FA'VORABLE, *a.* propitious (177-5).

189. *Feb'r-is*, a fever (from *Fer'veo*, I am hot).

1. FE'VERISH, *a.* affected by fever.

1. FEB'RILE, *a.* pertaining to fever.

1. In 1799, Washington, while superintending his *plantation*, took a cold, which produced a *feverish* condition of the whole system. Every effort was made to subdue the *febrile* symptoms, but without avail.

LATIN DERIVATIVES.

190. *Fœd'-us (fœd'er-is),* a league, or covenant.

1. CONFED'ERACY, *n.* a number of States united by a league.
2. CONFED'ERATE, *n.* one joined with others in a league.

1. Under the *Confederacy,* the Congress had no power to lay and collect taxes, duties, *imposts.*

2. Blannerhasset was unwilling to *confess* that he was a *confederate* of Aaron Burr.

191. *Fe'l-ix (felic'-is),* happy.

1. FELIC'ITOUS, *a.* happy.
2. FELIC'ITATE, *v.* to congratulate.
FELIC'ITY, *n.* happiness, prosperity; enjoyment of good (98-1).

1. The *felicitous* condition of the Wyoming Colony, so remote from the *commotion* of the war, made them disregard the danger of their *defenseless* position, until too late to remedy it.

2. The citizens of Geneva thought they had reason to *felicitate* themselves, that they were able to *extinguish* their debt by means of an enormous *legacy.*

192. *Fem'in-a,* a woman.

1. EFFEM'INATE, *a.* unmanly.
2. EFFEM'INACY, *n.* unmanly delicacy.
FEM'ININE, *a.* pertaining to the female sex; characteristic of woman (57-5).

1. Nothing but *confusion* and *turbulence* could result from the reign of a sovereign, so *effeminate* and *dilatory,* as Charles II.

2. Men of *sagacity* assert, that, when a people become very *prosperous,* they are in great danger of *effeminacy.*

193. *Fen'd-o,* I keep off, I strike. *Fen's-um,* to keep off, to strike.

1. DEFEN'DANT, *n.* one who makes a defence in a prosecution.
2. FEN'DER, *n.* a metallic frame to hinder coals of fire from rolling on the floor.
DEFENSE', *n.* protection (114-1).
DEFEN'SIVE, *a.* resisting attack (121-1).
OFFEN'SIVE, *a.* aggressive (35-5).
DEFENSE'LESS, *a.* without protection (191-1).
DEFEND' (see page 30).
OFFEND' (see page 30).

1. The suit for the *possession* of New Jersey, was decided in favor of the *defendant.*

2. A Spanish monarch being seated too near the *fender* for comfort, and the *exquisite* formality of court etiquette not allowing him to move himself, he was nearly roasted before an attendant came to his relief.

194. Fĕr-a, a wild beast. **Fĕrox (fero'cis),** ferocious.

FERO'CIOUS, *a.* savage (22-5). | FIERCE'NESS, *n.* fury (69-1).

195. Fĕr-o, I bear, I carry. **Lăt-um,** to bear, to carry.

1. CONFER', *v.* to consult one with another.
2. DEF'ERENCE, *n.* a yielding of judgment out of respect to another.
3. ELATE', *v.* to render proud by success.
4. OBLA'TION, *n.* a sacrifice.
5. PREF'ERENCE, *n.* predilection.
6. TRANS'LATE, *v.* to interpret into another language.
7. PESTIF'EROUS, *a.* (pestis, plague,) producing the plague.

CON'FERENCE, *n.* a meeting for consultation (143-2).
DIF'FERENT, *a.* distinct (8-2).
DIL'ATORY, *a.* procrastinating (192-1).
FER'TILE, *a.* producing plentifully (43-3).
PREF'ERABLE, *a.* more desirable (8-1).
REF'ERENCE, *n.* the act of referring (12-1).
SUF'FERING, *n.* distress (47-1).
TRANSFER' (see page 30).
DEFER' (see page 30).
OF'FER (see page 30).

    1. In 1811, the Indians asked Harrison that an *opportunity* to **confer** might be afforded, before deciding on his *proposition.* Harrison suspected that this was only a *pretext,* and the *sequel* showed his *surmise* to be correct.

    2. Both the Mosaic and Roman law, enjoin **deference** to the aged.

    3. The victory of Gates, in 1777, seemed to **elate** him beyond measure.

    4. It was *sacrilege* to proffer, as an **oblation,** an animal that was *infirm* or injured in any way.

    5. The **preference** which Queen Elizabeth felt for Raleigh, induced her to transfer the patent to him.

    6. It is necessary to *apply* ourselves closely to the *acquisition* of a *language,* in order to **translate** with facility.

    7. During the Great Plague, in 1665, Sir Isaac Newton went to the country, to escape the **pestiferous** air of London.

196. Fĕr'ul-a, a plant (giant-fennel).

1. FER'ULE, *v.* to punish by striking with a ferule.

    1. *Anciently,* the stalks of fennel, or the "ferula," were used to punish children; hence the expression "to *ferule* a child."

LATIN DERIVATIVES. 119

197. *Fer've-o*, I boil, I am hot. ***Fermen't-um*,** leaven, or yeast.

1. FER'VOR, *n.* zeal.
2. EFFERVES'CENCE, *n.* ebullition.
3. FERMENTA'TION, *n.* that change by which substances are decomposed, and their elements form new compounds.

1. Large numbers used to *congregate* around Peter the Hermit, A. D. 1096, attracted by the *fervor*, with which he would *portray* the advantages of rescuing the Holy *Sepulchre* from infidels.

2. Soda-water, in a state of *effervescence*, is agreeable to the taste; but when that has passed off, it becomes very *insipid*.

3. To commemorate the Passover, the Israelites were commanded to eat bread which had not gone through the process of *fermentation.*

198. *Fes's-um*, to own, to declare.

1. PROFESSED', *v.* claimed. | CONFESS', *v.* to own (190-2).

1. Tyler, elected by a party, which *professed* to be in favor of a United States Bank, *vetoed* two bills rechartering the Bank.

199. *Fes't-um*, a feast.

1. FESTIV'ITY, *n.* a festive celebration.
2. FEAST, *n.* a festival.
3. FES'TIVE, *a.* joyful.
4. FEAST'ING, *part.* eating sumptuously.
FES'TIVAL, *n.* an occasion of rejoicing (68-4).

1. Rahl was engaged in the *festivity* incident to Christmas, when surprised by Washington, at the battle of Trenton.

2. It is not difficult to *imagine* the feelings of Damocles (dam'-o-cles) when, amid the gayety and *music* of the *feast,* he saw a sword suspended over his head by a hair.

3. From time *immemorial*, the birthday has been a *festive* occasion.

4. Job's sons were *feasting*, when a whirlwind destroyed the house.

200. *Fi'd-o*, I trust. ***Fide'l-is*,** faithful.

1. DIF'FIDENCE, *n.* distrust of one's self.
2. AFFI'ANCED, *part.* betrothed.
FIDEL'ITY, *n.* faithfulness (63).
CON'FIDENCE, *n.* trust (63).
CONFIDEN'TIAL, *a.* private (146-3).
PER'FIDY, *n.* treachery (86-2).
CONFIDE' (see page 31).

1. Washington's *diffidence,* in accepting the important commission, only served to *elevate* him in the estimation of the Congress.

2. Prince Charles was *affianced* to the Infanta of Spain, before he married Henrietta of France.

201. Fi'g-o, I fix, I fasten. **Fix'-um,** to fix, to fasten.

1. CRUCIFIX'ION, *n.* (crux,) death upon a cross.
   TRANSFIX', *v.* to pierce through (40).
   FIXED, *a.* stationary; established (551).
   PRE'FIX (see page 31).
   SUF'FIX (see page 31).

1. *Crucifixion* was used only for a *malefactor* of the lowest grade

202. Figu'r-a, an image.

1. TRANSFIGURA'TION, *n.* the supernatural change in the appearance of our Saviour on the Mount; a change of form.
   FIG'URE, *n.* shape (643-2).

1. A little child, when asked how she knew that people lived after death, said, "because Moses and Elias were at the *transfiguration.*"

203. Fil'i-us, a son. **Fil'i-a,** a daughter.

1. AFFILIA'TION, *n.* adoption; association in the family.
   FIL'IAL, *a.* pertaining to a son or daughter (42-3).

1. The *affiliation* of a slave into the family of the Sultan is not an uncommon event.

204. Fin'g-o, I form, I fashion. **Fic't-um,** to form, to fashion.

1. FIC'TION, *n.* a feigned story.
2. FICTI'TIOUS, *a.* imaginary.
3. FEIGNED, *a.* pretended.
4. EF'FIGY, *n.* an image.

1. Defoe's "Robinson Crusoe" is a *fiction;* yet everything in it seems like a *reality.*

2. To witness distress, which we do not attempt to *alleviate,* renders the heart less *sensitive.* *Novels* depict only *fictitious* suffering, therefore the effect of such reading is to harden the heart.

3. A *feigned* attack on the lower town in 1759, enabled Wolfe to divert the attention of Montcalm.

4. "I do not *extenuate,*" said that *sage* observer, Benjamin Franklin, "such acts as burning the King in *effigy,* and treating his representative with *contumely;* but the Americans have had great *provocation;* and if they resort to arms, you will find them *invincible.*"

205. Fi'n-is, the end or limit.

1. AFFIN'ITY, *n.* attraction which exists between the particles of bodies.
2. DEFIN'ITIVE, *a.* conclusive.
3. DEF'INITE, *a.* precise.
4. INDEF'INITE, *a.* not precise.
5. FI'NITE, *a.* limited.

LATIN DERIVATIVES. 121

CONFINE'MENT, n. restraint (20-3).
FI'NALLY, adv. ultimately (22-2).

IN'FINITE, a. limitless (158-2).
FINE, n. payment of money imposed as punishment for an offence (125-1).

1. The *affinity* which the particles of one body have for those of another, enables chemists to perform many interesting experiments.
2. The *definitive* treaty between England and the United States was made in 1783.
3. Jay's treaty, in 1795, was *definite* on the subject of debts contracted *prior* to the war.
4. The intelligence from the army was very *indefinite*, but on the approach of the British, in 1777, Congress determined to remove to Lancaster.
5. Many things *transcend* man's *finite* powers. How *incomprehensible* is the *omnipresent* and *omniscient* God!

206. *Fir'm-us*, strong.

1. FIR'MAMENT, n. the heavens.
2. CONFIRMA'TION, n. proof.
3. AFFIRMA'TION, n. solemn asseveration.
3. AFFIRM', v. assert.

4. INFIRM'ARY, n. a hospital.
INFIRM', a. weak (195-4).
FIRM, a. stable; not easily moved (43-2).
CONFIRM' (see page 31).

1. Light was created on the first day, yet it was not till the fourth day that the great *luminary* was placed in the *firmament*.
2. The garrison at Fort Mimms heard of the intended attack; but, as the report needed *confirmation*, the commander resisted all *importunity* to send for more troops.
3. Before he (the President) shall enter on the duties of his office, he shall take the following *affirmation:* — "I do solemnly *affirm*, that I will faithfully execute the office of President of the United States."
4. In Girard College, there is an *apartment* used as an *infirmary*.

207. *Fis'c-us*, a money-bag; the public treasury.

1. CON'FISCATED, v. appropriated, as a penalty, to public use.
2. FIS'CAL, a. pertaining to the revenue.

CONFISCA'TION, n. transfer of forfeited goods to public use (106).
CONFIS'CABLE, a. liable to forfeiture (698).

1. During the Revolutionary War, the States *confiscated* the property of those who continued to *adhere* to the royal cause.
2. The *fiscal* arrangements of the Government caused great anxiety to the first Congress.

208. Fla'gr-o, I burn. Flagra't-um, to burn.

1. FLA'GRANT, *a.* enormous. FLA'GRANCY, *n.* enormity (158-3).

CONFLAGRA'TION, *n.* an extensive fire, or extending to many objects (76-2).

1. During the Revolution in France, the most *flagrant* crimes were committed, by those who had been accustomed to *inveigh* against the nobles for similar atrocities.

209. Flam'm-a, a flame.

INFLAME', *v.* to irritate; to excite (167-2).

INFLAM'MABLE, *a.* easily set on fire (175-2).

210. Flec't-o, I bend. Flex'-um, to bend.

1. FLEX'IBLE, *a.* pliable; easily bent.

REFLECT', *v.* to bend back (143-4).

1. By using India-rubber, we can have a *flexible* tube, convenient for many purposes.

211. Fli'g-o, I beat, I dash. Flic't-um, to beat, to dash.

1. CON'FLICT, *n.* contest.
2. PROF'LIGATE, *a.* dissolute.
2. AFFLIC'TION, *n.* suffering.

3. AFFLICT', *v.* to distress.
INFLICT', *v.* to impose (70-1).

1. After a long *conflict*, in South Carolina, all laws which were unjust to the Huguenots, were *abrogated* in 1697.

2. The administration of the *profligate* Lord Cornbury, 1702-1707, caused much *affliction* in New York and New Jersey.

3. In the leprosy, which continues to *afflict* the inhabitants of Eastern countries, the flesh assumes a *tumid* appearance, the limbs are *tremulous*, and the sufferer soon becomes a *vagabond*.

212. Flo, I blow. Fla't-um, to blow.

1. INFLATE', *v.* to fill with air.

1. To *inflate* the lungs, we must stand erect, expand the chest to its full size, and then make a long *inspiration*.

213. Flos (flo'r-is), a flower.

1. EFFLORES'CENCE, *n.* an appearance resembling flowers.
2. FLO'RIST, *n.* a cultivator of flowers.

3. FLOR'ID, *a.* having a lively red color.
4. FLORIF'EROUS, *a.* (fero,) bearing flowers.
5. FLOW'ERS, *n.* shrubs.

LATIN DERIVATIVES. 123

1. A beautiful *efflorescence,* which appears on the snow in Greenland, has given it the name of "Red Snow."

2. A *florist* thinks himself very *fortunate,* if he can add one new *specimen* to the floral beauties of his green-house, especially if it has a choice *perfume,* and beautiful *foliage.*

3. Magnus, a noted *depredator* from Norway, made an attempt to ravage England, in the *reign* of William Rufus, so called from his *florid complexion.*

4. Many plants, which are *fruit*-bearing in their native country, are *floriferous* when exotics; of this the *pomegranate* is an example.

5. Trees and *flowers* flourish in England, on account of the *humidity* of the air.

214. *Flu'-o,* I flow. *Flux'-um,* to flow.

1. FLU'ENCY, *n.* readiness of speech.
2. FLUCT'UATE, *v.* to wave.
3. CON'FLUENCE, *n.* junction.
3. FLUCTUA'TION, *n.* undulation.
4. AF'FLUENCE, *n.* wealth.
5. INFLUEN'TIAL, *a.* powerful.
6. IN'FLUX, *n.* a coming in.
6. SUPERFLU'ITY, *n.* a superabundance.
7. SUPER'FLUOUS, *a.* more than is wanted.
8. EFFLU'VIA, *n.* exhalations perceived by the smell.
IN'FLUENCE, *n.* power; ability to effect (65-15).

1. Whitfield possessed great *fluency* of speech, and his passionate *appeals* to his hearers, to *attend* to *religion,* were frequently followed by the conversion of hundreds.

2. A very light wind will cause the surface of the ocean to *fluctuate* sufficiently to produce sea-sickness.

3. At the *confluence* of two rapid streams, the *fluctuation* of the water is very great.

4. Robert Morris, in the midst of *affluence,* was willing to *entertain* the officers, and to provide *sustenance* for the privates.

5. Formerly, Spain was one of the most *influential* nations of Europe; but the *suicidal* policy adopted by her rulers, has greatly diminished her power.

6. On the discovery of gold in California, it was thought that the *influx* of that *commodity* would be so great that there would be a *superfluity.*

7. We find a foreign market for our *superfluous* cereals and *multifarious* manufactures.

8. Travellers seldom visit the catacombs of Paris and Rome in summer on account of the *effluvia.*

215. Fo'li-um, a leaf.

Fo'LIAGE, n. a collection of leaves (213-2).

Fo'LIO, n. a book in which paper is folded once (157-2).

216. For'm-a, form, shape, beauty.

1. CONFORM', v. to comply with.
2. DEFORM'ITY, n. state of being deformed.
3. INFORM'ER, n. informant.
4. INFORMA'TION, n. intelligence.
5. TRANSFORMA'TION, n. a change of condition.
6. TRANSFORM', v. to change.
7. REFORMA'TION, n. correction.
8. INFORMAL'ITY, n. absence of some legal form.

CONFORM'ITY, n. agreement (49-2).
FORM, n. shape (68-2).
DEFORM', v. (see page 31).
REFORM,' v. (see page 32).
PERFORM', v. (see page 32).

  1. The *Puritans,* unwilling to ***conform*** to the law prescribing ministerial *habiliments,* and many other things of which they could not *approve,* determined to emigrate to Holland.
  2. Lord Byron was *morbidly* sensitive on the subject of his ***deformity.***
  3. The ***informer,*** who apprised General Grey of the locality of Wayne's troops, must have felt great *remorse,* when he heard of the *cruel* massacre.
  4. A large reward was offered for ***information,*** which would lead to the recovery of the lost *regalia* of Scotland.
  5. Such is the ***transformation,*** which railroads have effected, that each *section* of our country seems in close *contiguity* with every other.
  6. Heathen mythology describes beings with power to ***transform*** a man into a *monster.*
  7. To *diminish* the amount of crime among the junior members of society, houses of ***reformation*** have been established.
  8. Some ***informality*** in the grant of New Hampshire to Mason, caused *continual* disputes.

217. Fors (for't-is), chance. **Fortu'na,** fortune.

FORTU'ITOUS, a. accidental (124-2).
MISFOR'TUNE, n. calamity (21-7).
UNFOR'TUNATE, a. unfavorable (56-4).
FOR'TUNATE, a. much favored; successful (213-2).

LATIN DERIVATIVES.

218. *For't-is,* brave, strong.

1. For'tify, *v.* to strengthen by forts, batteries, etc.
2. For'tress, *n.* a fort.
   Ef'fort, *n.* exertion (21-4).
   For'titude, *n.* courage (42-3).

Fortifica'tion, *n.* (facio,) military architecture for defence (76-3).
Force, *n.* power (66-3).
Com'fort, *n.* state of enjoyment (193-2).

1. In 1775, General Gage fearing a *rupture* between Great Britain and the Colonies, determined to *fortify* Boston.
2. The *fortress* of Ticonderoga surrendered in 1759 to Amherst, in 1775 to Ethan Allen, and in 1777 to Burgoyne.

219. *Fos's-um,* to dig.

1. Fos'sils, *n.* substances changed into stone.

1. Some *fossils* give *irrefragable* evidence that there has been a universal deluge.

220. *Fra'gr-o,* I smell sweetly.

1. Fra'grant, *a.* smelling sweetly.

1. At many of the railway stations in England, the air is *redolent* of flowers; *primroses,* mignonette, and other *fragrant* flowers, diffuse their sweet *odor* for a long distance.

221. *Fran'g-o,* I break. *Fract-um,* to break.

1. Fract'ure, *n.* a breaking.
2. Frag'ment, *n.* a broken part.
3. Fragil'ity, *n.* brittleness.
4. Refrac'tory, *a.* contumacious.
5. Refrac'tion, *n.* change in the direction of a ray of light.

Infringe'ment, *n.* violation (30-2).
Irref'ragable, *a.* not to be refuted (219).
Frag'ile, *a.* brittle (239-2).

1. In the battle of Vera Cruz, in 1836, a ball struck Santa Anna, and caused a *fracture* of his leg.
2. On the bursting of the Peace-maker, in 1844, a *fragment* of the gun struck Mr. Upshur, Secretary of State, killing him instantly.
3. An *experiment* has lately been made, by which it is hoped to manufacture glass without its *fragility.*
4. In 1664, Charles II. sent Commissioners to the *refractory* Colonies to compel them to obey.
5. A stick put into water, generally appears bent; this is owing to *refraction.*

222. Fra'ter, a brother.

1. FRATER'NAL, *a.* brotherly.
2. FRATER'NITY, *n.* brotherhood.
3. FRAT'RICIDE, *n.* (cædo,) the murder of a brother; one who murders a brother.

1. Penn's determination, to *treat* the Indians in an *honorable* manner, and to *compensate* them for everything needed by the settlers, served to *pacify* the Indians, and produce the most *fraternal* feelings.
2. The noble *fraternity*, founded by St. Bernard amid the *solitude* of the Alps, has for nine hundred years rendered most valuable services to thousands of travellers.
3. Had Cain subdued every feeling of jealousy and hatred, he would not have committed the crime of *fratricide.*

223. Fraus (frau'd-is), deceit.

DEFRAUD', *v.* to cheat (180-7).
FRAUD, *n.* cheating (42-1).
FRAUD'ULENT, *a.* treacherous (122-2).

224. Fre'quens (frequen't-is), frequent.

FRE'QUENT, *a.* occurring often (8-1).
FRE'QUENTLY, *adv.* often; not rarely (54-2).

225. Fri'g-us (frig'or-is), cold.

1. FRIGID'ITY, *n.* coldness; want of warmth.
2. FRIG'ID, *a.* cold; wanting warmth.

1. Arnold and Montgomery, disregarding the *frigidity* of a Canadian winter, attacked Quebec on the last night of 1775.
2. The *frigid* atmosphere, and the falling snow, increased the misery of the soldiers, in the *memorable* attack on Quebec, in 1775.

226. Frons (fron't-is), the forehead.

1. FRONT'ISPIECE, *n.* (specio,) a picture facing the title-page.
FRON'TIERS, *n.* borders (108-1).
CONFRONT' (see page 32).

1. The *frontispiece* is on the left-hand page, the vignette on the right.

227. Fru'-or, I enjoy. Fru'it-us, or Fruc't-us, enjoying.

1. FRUI'TION, *n.* pleasure derived from possession.
FRUIT, *n.* the part of plants containing the seed (213-4).

1. By patient continuance in well-doing, we may hope for the *fruition* of all our hopes, in another world.

LATIN DERIVATIVES.

228. *Fu'g-io,* I flee. *Fu'git-um,* to flee.

1. SUBTER'FUGE, *n.* evasion.
2. REF'UGE, *n.* shelter.
3. CENTRIF'UGAL, *a.* (centrum,) tending from the centre.

FU'GITIVE, *n.* one who flees (21-7).
REFUGEE', *n.* one who flees for protection (49-2).

1. By a mean *subterfuge,* Col. John Butler induced Zebulon Butler to come, with his force, into the woods of Wyoming.
2. Becket took *refuge* in the *sanctuary,* supposing the assassins would not dare to *desecrate* the sacred place; but even here he fell a *victim* to their *insatiable* desire for *vengeance.*
3. Two forces, the *centripetal* and *centrifugal,* keep the planets in their orbits.

229. *Ful'ge-o,* I shine.

1. FUL'GENCY, *n.* brightness.
1. REFUL'GENCE, *n.* fulgency.

EFFUL'GENCE, *n.* extreme brilliancy (64-4).

1. The opinion, that light is produced only by the *fulgency* of the sun, is not *tenable,* as light was created before the sun.

230. *Fu'm-us,* smoke. *Fu'mig-o,* I fumigate.

1. FUMIGA'TION, *n.* the application of vapor as a disinfectant.
2. PERFUM'ERY, *n.* perfumes in general.
PER'FUME, *n.* odor (213-2).

1. Many substances are good for *fumigation;* such as coffee, tobacco, sugar, tar, etc.
2. In the manufacture of *perfumery,* it is necessary to express the *essence* of flowers.

231. *Fun'd-o,* I pour, I melt. *Fu's-um,* to pour, to melt.

1. FU'SION, *n.* state of being dissolved by heat.
1. FU'SIBLE, *a.* capable of being melted.
2. EFFU'SION, *n.* pouring out.
3. CONFOUND'ED, *part.* dismayed.
4. FUSIBIL'ITY, *n.* the quality

of being convertible into a fluid by heat.
CONFU'SION, *n.* tumult (192-1).
PROFU'SION, *n.* abundance (89).
INFU'SION, *n.* the act of steeping in water (108-2).
DIFFUSE', *v.* pour out (220).
INFUSE,' *v.* (see page 32).

1. Substances, in a state of *fusion,* are called liquids. All metals are *fusible;* but intense heat is *requisite* to fuse iron.

2. The *humane* measures, which Penn adopted, to secure the pacification of the Indians, prevented the *effusion* of blood.

3. Braddock was *confounded* by the suddenness of the attack, in 1755.

4. *Fusibility* and insolubility are *predicable* of the 51 metals now known.

232. ***Fun'd-us,*** a foundation.

1. PROFOUND', *a.* intellectually deep.
2. FOUND, *v.* to establish.
   FOUNDA'TION, *n.* basis of an edifice (74-1).

FUNDAMENT'AL, *a.* lying at the foundation (121-2).
PROFUN'DITY, *n.* depth (52-1).
FOUND'ERED, *v.* sunk at sea (19-1).

1. Jefferson, who wrote the Declaration of Independence, was a *profound* reasoner on the most *abstruse* subjects.

2. Lord Clarendon had the most *extravagant* and *ludicrous* idea of the empire he expected to *found* in Carolina.

233. ***Fu'n-us (fu'ner-is),*** a burial, a funeral.

1. FU'NERAL, *n.* the ceremony of burying a dead human body.

1. Usually, the sovereign does not attend in person the *funeral* of a subject, but sends some one to represent him.

234. ***Fu'ri-a,*** a fury, or fiend.

1. FU'RIOUS, *a.* transported with passion.

1. Henry VIII. was *furious,* when he saw Ann of Cleves, his fourth wife; Cromwell, the King's *Vice-gerent*, had great difficulty to induce him to *solemnize* the marriage with the customary pomp and splendor.

235. ***Fu'til-is,*** leaky, trifling.
FU'TILE, *a.* unavailing (35-7).

236. ***Fu't-o,*** I disprove. ***Futa't-um,*** to disprove.
CONFUTA'TION, *n.* refutation (260-2).

237. ***Futu'r-us.*** See *Sum,* I am.

238. ***Fy,*** to make. See the suffix, ***Fy.***

239. ***Gel'-o,*** I freeze. ***Gela't-um,*** to freeze.

1. CONGEAL', *v.* to freeze. | 2. GELAT'INOUS, *a.* like jelly.

1. To *congeal* water, the *temperature* must be as low as 32 degrees Fahrenheit's thermometer.

2. To mend china, and other *fragile* articles, various *gelatinous* substances, such as the white of an egg, isinglass, etc., are used.

LATIN DERIVATIVES.

240. Ge'r-o, I bear, I carry. **Ges't-um,** to bear, to carry.

1. GEST'URE, *n.* a movement expressive of emotion.
2. JESTS, *n.* jokes.
   DIGES'TION, *n.* conversion of food into chyme; the act of digesting (1-5).

1. Lee's division was making a *retrograde* movement, at the battle of Monmouth, when Washington, with an *impatient gesture,* gave an imperative order for them to advance.
2. The King's Fool made *jests* to amuse the King and his courtiers.

241. Ge'n-us (gen'er-is), race, family. **Gen'itum,** to beget. **Gens (gen't-is),** a family, a nation.

1. GE'NIAL, *a.* causing production.
2. GEN'IUS, *n.* uncommon intellectual power.
3. GEN'UINE, *a.* real, natural.
4. PROGEN'ITOR, *n.* forefather.
5. INGEN'IOUS, *a.* inventive.
6. PRIMOGEN'ITURE, *n.* (primus,) the exclusive right of inheritance, which belongs to the eldest child.
   7. GENER'IC, *a.* pertaining to the genus.
   CONGEN'IAL, *a.* agreeable to the nature.
   GEN'ERATED, *part.* produced (60-1).
   GEN'TLE, *a.* refined in manners (576-7).
   INGENU'ITY, *n.* acuteness (57-5).
   INGEN'UOUSNESS, *n.* candor (148-1).

1. Notwithstanding the *genial* climate of Virginia, Lane could not *reconcile* the settlers to the thought of *remaining.*
2. The *genius* of Locke was well adapted to writing on such an *abstract* subject as the "Understanding."
3. *Genuine* sorrow was exhibited, by the people of Great Britain, when Washington died.
4. As the deluge was general, and destroyed all but one family, Noah is the great *progenitor* of the human race.
5. The patents issued every week exhibit the *ingenious* character of Americans, and *contribute* greatly to the wealth of the nation.
6. By the law of *primogeniture,* the Prince of Wales is heir-apparent
7. Bread is a *generic* term for all kinds of *nutriment.*

242. Gla'di-us, a sword.

1. GLADIATO'RIAL, *a.* relating to the Roman combats between gladiators.
   1. GLAD'IATOR, *n.* one who fought for the entertainment of the Romans.

1. The spectators of the *gladiatorial* shows would applaud the success of either the *gladiator* or the beast.

243. *Glo'b-us*, a globe.   ***Glob'ul-us*,** a little globe.
1. GLOB'ULAR, *a.* spherical. | GLOBE, *n.* a sphere (44-4).

1. To make shot perfectly *globular*, it is dropped from the top of a high tower into cold water.

244. *Glo'ri-a*, glory, honor.
GLO'RIOUS, *a.* magnificent (64-4). | GLORIFICA'TION, *n.* (facio,) the act of giving glory to (477-5).

245. *Glu't-io*, I swallow.
GLUT'TON, *n.* a gormandizer (180-6).

246. *Gra'di-or*, I go step by step.   ***Gres's-us*,** going step by step.

1. GRADA'TION, *n.* advance step by step.	CON'GRESS, *n.* the legislative department (121-2).
2. GRAD'UATE, *v.* receive a degree.	DEGREE', *n.* rank (18-4).
3. DEGRADES', *v.* debases.	GRAD'UAL, *a.* advancing by steps (116-2).
4. DEGRADA'TION, *n.* debasement.	PROG'RESS, *n.* advancement (77-1).
5. AGGRES'SIONS, *n.* encroachments.	RET'ROGRADE, *a.* backward (240-1).
6. TRANSGRES'SES, *v.* violates.	TRANSGRES'SION, *n.* violation (75-11).
7. DIGRES'SIONS, *n.* wanderings from the main subject.	IN'GRESS, *n.* entrance (65-1).

1. John Singleton Copley, a poor boy of Boston, is a striking instance of what can be effected by *assiduous attention* to business. He went to *reside* in England, was taken into the Government service, and rose by regular *gradation,* until he became Lord Chancellor of England.

2. Harvard College and Yale College, where so many of our erudite men *graduate,* were founded in 1637 and 1700.

3. To use bad language so *degrades* the character, that Washington forbade the practice in the army.

4. Commodore Decatur found the American prisoners in a state of great *degradation.* He compelled the Dey to release them, and to relinquish the *tribute,* which had been long exacted.

5. The *aggressions* of the British, on the rights of the colonists, strengthened their *determination* to *revolt.*

LATIN DERIVATIVES. 131

6. Disobedience to parents not only *transgresses* the law of God, but is *subversive* of all government.

7. In giving an account of any transaction, avoid useless *digressions*.

247. *Gra'men (gram'in-is),* grass.

1. GRAMINIV'OROUS, *a.* (voro,) eating grass.

1. Many of the *graminivorous* and *herbivorous* animals, such as the ox, camel, deer, sheep, and goat, are *ruminants*.

248. *Gran'd-is,* great, grand.

1. GRANDEE', *n.* a man of high rank.
2. AG'GRANDIZE, *v.* to increase.
3. GRAND'EUR, *n.* magnificence.
4. GRANDIL'OQUENCE, *n.* (loquor,) bombast.

1. Lord Clarendon, a *grandee* of England, received from Charles II. a large tract of land, which he called Carolina.

2. In 1683, Seth Sothel, a *proprietor* of North Carolina, arrived as *Deputy-Governor*. His only object seemed to be to *aggrandize* his own wealth and power, that he might return to England, and live in *grandeur*.

3. James I., of England, thought himself a prodigy of authorship; but the *grandiloquence* of the style makes his books ridiculous.

249. *Gra'n-um,* a grain of corn.

1. GRANIV'OROUS, *a.* (voro,) eating grain.
2. GRAN'ARY, *n.* a storehouse for grain.

GRAIN, *n.* cereals (75-6).
GRAN'ITE, *n.* a rock consisting of several minerals (quartz, feldspar, and mica) (178-1).

1. Man, being both *carnivorous* and *granivorous*, has teeth called incisors for cutting, and molars for grinding.

2. A *liberal* man will endeavor to *ameliorate* the condition of the poor, by dispensing corn from his well-filled *granary*.

250. *Gra't-us,* grateful, pleasing. *Gra't-ia,* favor.

1. CONGRAT'ULATE, *v.* to address with sympathetic pleasure.
2. GRAT'ITUDE, *n.* thankfulness.
3. INGRAT'ITUDE, *n.* unthankfulness.
4. GRATU'ITOUS, *a.* without remuneration.
5. GRA'CIOUS, *a.* benignant: bestowing mercy.
5. GRA'TIS, *adv.* for nothing.
6. IN'GRATE, *n.* an ungrateful person.

7. INGRA'TIATE, v. to commend to the favor of another.
GRAT'IFIED, part. indulged (31-1).
GRATE'FUL, a. thankful; acceptable (147-2).
AGREE', v. consent; yield assent to (264).

1. After two years of oppressive rule by Seth Sothel, the Carolinas were able to *congratulate* each other on the wise administration of John Archdale.
2. In 1824, the people showed their *gratitude* to the hero of Brandywine, by gifts more substantial than mere *honorary* titles.
3. Santa Anna charged the Mexicans with *ingratitude,* and bade them *remember* the service he rendered at Vera Cruz.
4. The cession of Florida, and of the adjoining islands to the United States, was not *gratuitous* on the part of Spain.
5. Penn's *gracious* manner, and friendly aid always given *gratis,* did much to humanize the Indians.
6. *Retributive* punishment is certain to visit the *ingrate,* who treats his parents with *disrespect.*
7. Harvey, when sent to England for impeachment, contrived to *ingratiate* himself with the king, and to *insinuate* so many doubts, as to the loyalty of the Virginians, that the king invested him with *plenary* power to punish the *complainants.*

251. *Gra'v-is,* heavy, grievous. *Grav'it-as,* weight.

1. GRIEV'OUS, a. mournful.
1. AGGRAVA'TION, n. increase (of evil).
AG'GRAVATE, v. increase an evil (68-3).
GRAVITA'TION, n. tendency of matter towards other matter (65-7).
GRAV'ITY, n. seriousness (146-3).
GRIEF, n. sorrow (148-1).
GRIEVE, v. to distress (146-3).

1. It was *grievous* to witness the *aggravation* of the sufferings of the soldiers at Valley Forge, by the intense cold.

252. *Grex (greg-is),* a flock.

1. EGRE'GIOUS, a. remarkably bad.
2. SEG'REGATE, v. to set apart in a flock.
CON'GREGATE, v. to assemble (197-1).
CONGREGA'TION, n. an assembly (65-1).

1. Clinton committed the *egregious* blunder of stopping to burn the towns on the Hudson, and Burgoyne was compelled to surrender a force, amounting in the aggregate to 10,000 men.
2. The prairie dogs *segregate* themselves in communities called "prairie-dog villages."

LATIN DERIVATIVES.

253. *Guber'n-o,* I rule, I govern. *Guberna'tor,* a governor, a steerer.

1. GUBERNATO'RIAL, *a.* pertaining to the governor.
1. GOV'ERN, *v.* to rule.

GOV'ERNMENT, *n.* the established form of law (16-2).

1. While Andross occupied the *gubernatorial* chair of New York, he made several attempts to *govern* Connecticut. His impotent efforts brought upon him *ridicule* and contempt.

254. *Gus't-us,* a taste, a relish.

1. DISGUST'ED, *v.* excited the aversion of.

DISGUST'ING, *a.* nauseous; offensive to the taste (161).

1. In 1692, Wadsworth *disgusted* Governor Fletcher, by refusing to *discuss* the question of jurisdiction.

255. *Hab'e-o,* I have. *Hab'it-um,* to have. *Hab'il-is,* able. *Deb'il-is,* weak, feeble.

1. HABIT'UAL, *a.* customary.
2. DEBIL'ITATED, *a.* enfeebled.
3. HAB'IT, *n.* custom.
4. PROHIB'IT, *v.* to forbid.
5. INHAB'IT, *v.* dwell in.
5. DEBIL'ITY, *n.* feebleness.
5. INHAB'ITANTS, *n.* residents.
   A'BLE, *a.* capable (11-3).

HABITA'TION, *n.* a place of abode (27-3).
HABIL'IMENTS, *n.* garments (216-1).
HABIT'UATING, *part.* accustoming (8-2).
UNA'BLE, *a.* not capable (22-3).

1. The present *tense* often expresses what is *habitual, universal,* or permanent; as, "The sun gives light."
2. Hunger and exposure had greatly *debilitated* the soldiers at Valley Forge.
3. It is easy to form a bad *habit;* it is hard to cure one.
4. An Embargo Law is a law to *prohibit* vessels leaving port.
5. Those who *inhabit* tropical climates, generally exhibit more *debility* in old age, than the *inhabitants* of colder regions.

256. *Hæ're-o,* I stick. *Hæ's-um,* to stick. *Hæs'it-o,* I hesitate.

1. INCOHER'ENT, *a.* inconsistent.
2. INHER'ENT, *a.* innate.
   ADHERE', *v.* to own allegiance (207-1).

HES'ITATE, *v.* scruple (100-1).
ADHER'ENCE, *n.* adhesion (56-2).
COHERE', *v.* (see page 32).

12

1. The ***incoherent*** *ravings* of the prisoners, confined in the Sugar-House, who were in a state of *inanition*, from want of food, etc., excited no compassion among the Tories.

2. The ***inherent*** right of all men to life, liberty, and protection, is fully recognized in the Constitution of the United States.

257. *Ha'l-o*, I breathe.   ***Hala't-um*,** to breathe.

1. EXHALES', *v.* breathes out. EXHALA'TIONS, *n.* vapors (68-3).

   INHALE', *v.* to breathe in; to inspire (129).

   1. A *robust* person ***exhales*** and inhales many times in a minute.

258. *Haus't-um*, to draw.

EXHAUST'ED, *a.* drawn out until nothing is left (65-4).

INEXHAUST'IBLE, *a.* unfailing (24-2).

259. *Her'b-a*, an herb; grass.

HERBIV'OROUS, *a.* (voro,) eating herbs (247).

260. *He'r-es (here'd-is)*, an heir. ***Hered'it-as*,** an inheritance.

1. HERED'ITARY, *a.* descended by inheritance.
1. INHER'ITANCE, *n.* patrimony.

   2. HEIR, *n.* one who inherits.
   DISINHER'IT, *v.* to cut off from succession (100-1).

   1. The friends of John Locke ridiculed the idea of an ***hereditary*** order of nobility among a people sparsely scattered through the wilderness, whose only ***inheritance*** would be a log-cabin.

   2. The Pretender, son of James II., would hear nothing in *confutation* of his theory, that he was ***heir*** to the throne of England.

261. *Ho'm-o (hom'in-is)*, a man.

HU'MAN, *a.* belonging to mankind (27-3).
HUMANE', *a.* benevolent (231-2).

HUMAN'ITY, *n.* the nature of man (47-1).
INHU'MAN, *a.* barbarous (103-2).

262. *Ho'nor*, respect, honor. ***Hones't-us*,** honorable.

DISHON'ORABLE, *a.* degrading (169-5).
HON'ORABLE, *a.* not base (222-1).

HON'ORARY, *a.* conferring honor (250-2).
HON'ESTY, *n.* uprightness (165-2).

LATIN DERIVATIVES.

263. *Hor're-o,* to be dreadful, to shudder.
Hor'rible, *a.* dreadful (56-3). | Hor'ror, *n.* dread (68-3).

264. *Hor't-or,* I exhort. *Horta't-us,* exhorting.
1. Exhort'ed, *v.* entreated.

1. Washington *exhorted* the Wyoming settlers to remove, but they would not *agree* to leave their homes.

265. *Hor't-us,* a garden.
1. Hor'ticulture, *n.* (colo,) the culture of gardens. | 2. Horticul'tural, *a.* (colo,) relating to horticulture.

1. To promote *horticulture,* the Patent-Office is allowed to *distribute* seeds.
2. The collection of ferns in *Horticultural* Hall is very fine.

266. *Hos'p-es (hos'pit-is),* a host or guest.
1. Hos'pitable, *a.* kind to visitors; entertaining strangers with kindness. | Host, *n.* one who receives guests (382).
Hotel', *n.* an inn (382).

1. Roger Williams *expostulated* with the Council; but finding he did not *prevail,* he sought refuge among the *hospitable* Narragansetts.

267. *Hos't-is,* an enemy.
Host, *n.* a multitude (42-2). | Hostil'ity, *n.* enmity (74-2).
Hos'tile, *a.* adverse (17-1). | Hostil'ities, *n.* hostile proceedings (17-2).

268. *Hu'm-us,* the ground. *Hu'mil-is,* humble.
Hu'me-o, to be wet or moist.
1. Humilia'tion, *n.* mortification. | Humid'ity, *n.* dampness (213-5).
2. Exhume', *v.* disinter. | Hum'ble, *v.* to free from pride (329-3).
3. Humil'iate, *v.* to humble. |
Hu'mid, *a.* damp (68-3). | Hu'mor, *n.* pleasantry (146-3).

1. The loss of Quebec, in 1759, was a great *humiliation* to France.
2. In 1661, Charles II. gave orders to *exhume* the body of Oliver Cromwell, and, as it was not entirely decomposed, it was easy to *prove* its *identity.*
3. To *humiliate* his son, the King Frederick William treated him in the most barbarous manner; "he was kicked, cudgelled, pulled by the hair, etc."

269. *I'dem,* the same.

IDEN'TICAL, *a.* the same (134-2).
IDEN'TITY, *n.* sameness (268-2).
IDEN'TIFY, *v.* to prove sameness (65-14).

270. *Ig'n-is,* fire.

1. IGNITE', *v.* to set on fire.

　1. In 1777, Col. Meigs was able to *ignite* the British vessels at Sag Harbor; and to explode the magazine.

271. *Ima'g-o (imag'in-is),* an image. *Imagina'-t-us,* fancying.

1. IMAGINA'TION, *n.* fancy.
　IM'AGE, *n.* statue (110).
　IMAG'INE, *v.* to conceive by the fancy (199-2).
　IMAG'INARY, *a.* fancied; visionary (64-6).
　IM'AGERY, *n.* figurative representation (64-1).

　1. *Imagination* can scarcely *depict* a more *desolate* situation, than the Colony of Virginia, *isolated* as it was, and surrounded by Indians, who desired its *extirpation.*

272. *Imbecill'l-is,* weak, feeble.

IM'BECILE, *a.* feeble (290-3).

273. *Im'it-or,* I imitate.

1. IMITA'TORS, *n.* those who pattern after.
2. IMITA'TION, *n.* the act of copying.

　1. Milton has had many *imitators,* since he wrote "Paradise Lost."
　2. Such an excellent *imitation* of the diamond has been made, that experts are sometimes deceived.

274. *Im'per-o,* I command. *Impera't-um,* to command.

EM'PIRE, *n.* the dominion of an emperor (75-3).
EM'PEROR, *n.* a monarch over an empire (98-1).
IMPE'RIAL, *a.* pertaining to an emperor (98-1).
IMPE'RIOUS, *a.* overbearing (65-3).

275. *Ina'n-is,* empty.

INANI'TION, *n.* exhaustion (256-1).

276. *Indi'gen-a,* a native, the native of a place.

INDI'GENOUS, *a.* native (56-7).

277. *Indus'tri-a*, industry.

1. IN'DUSTRY, *n.* habitual diligence.

1. By *industry* and economy France has been able to pay the war *indemnity*.

278. *In'fer-us* and *Infer'n-us*, below.

1. INFER'NAL, *a.* pertaining to the lower regions. | INFE'RIOR, *a.* lower in place (85-3).

1. "Stygian," in Heathen Mythology, refers to the Styx, a river of the *infernal* regions.

279. *In'sul-a*, an island.

1. IN'SULATE, *v.* to isolate.
2. IN'SULAR, *a.* belonging to an island.
PENIN'SULAS, *n.* (pene,) portions of land almost surrounded by water (444-1).
IS'OLATED, *a.* placed by itself (271).

1. Clinton hoped, by forming a junction with Burgoyne, to *insulate* New England from the Middle States.

2. The *insular* position of England led to the passage of the *Navigation* Acts, intended to increase her commerce.

280. *In'teg-er*, whole, entire.

1. DISIN'TEGRATE, *v.* to reduce to fragments.
2. IN'TEGRAL, *a.* whole, entire.
INTEG'RITY, *n.* purity of mind; honesty (165-2).

1. The power of moisture to *disintegrate* solid rock is shown by the sand on the sea-shore.

2. The action of the Berlin Congress was *tantamount* to deciding that Turkey should not be an *integral* part of Europe.

281. *Intrin'sec-us*, on the inside. ***In'tim-us*,** most intimate. ***Inter'n-us*,** inward. ***In't-us*,** within.

1. INTRIN'SIC, *a.* inherent.
INTE'RIOR, *a.* inner; internal (132-1).
IN'TIMATE, *a.* familiar; close in friendship (83-1).
INTIMA'TION, *n.* hint (103-2).

1. The pleasure experienced on receiving a gift, does not depend on its *intrinsic* value, but on the feeling which prompted it.

282. *I'ra*, anger. ***Ir'rit-o*,** I make angry.
IRAS'CIBLE, *a.* easily made angry (12-2).
IR'RITATED, *v.* provoked (12-2).
IR'RITABLE, *a.* irascible (508-2).

283. I'ter (itin'er-is), a journey. **I'ter-o,** I repeat.

It'erate, v. to repeat (110).
Reit'erate, v. to repeat again and again (65-5).

Itin'erant, a. journeying (92-3).
Itin'erate, v. travel (558-5).

284. Ja'ce-o, I lie.

1. Circumja'cent, a. lying around.

Adja'cent, a. lying near to (74-2).

1. Florida, and the *circumjacent* islands, were ceded to the United States in 1821.

285. Ja'c-io, I throw. **Jac't-um,** to throw.

1. Conject'ure, n. surmise.
2. Eject', v. to expel.
3. Dejec'tion, n. depression of spirits.
   Ab'ject, a. mean (125-6).

Ad'jective, n. a word added to a noun to describe it (8-1).
Sub'ject, n. that which is brought under thought (37-3).

1. Washington was right in his *conjecture*, that Howe intended to attack New York, in 1776.
2. Dunmore, the last Royal Governor of Virginia, was regarded with such *aversion*, that the colonists determined to *tolerate* him no longer, but to *eject* him by force.
3. The act of the *traitor*, Arnold, caused great *dejection* in the American army, and a few *timorous* citizens joined the Loyalists.

286. Jo'c-us, a joke.

1. Joc'ular, a. jocose.
2. Jocular'ity, n. gayety.

3. Joc'und, a. merry.
   Joke, n. jest (291).

1. "Colonel Washington is very *illiterate*, and cannot *subscribe* his name to a document," said Tarleton, who had been wounded by him at Cowpens. "Ah! Colonel," *retorted* Mrs. Jones, in a *jocular* manner, "you bear *evidence* that he can make his mark."
2. The *jocularity* of Charles II., and his *sociable* disposition, made him a general favorite.
3. Never were the *jocund* strains of the Highland pipe more welcome, than when they announced the relief of Lucknow, 1857.

287. Ju'dic-o, I judge. **Judica't-um,** to judge.

1. Judi'cious, a. wise.
2. Judi'cial, a. pertaining to courts of justice.

3. Ju'dicatory, n. a tribunal.
4. Misjudge', v. to form an erroneous opinion.

LATIN DERIVATIVES.

JUDI'CIARY, n. the system of courts of justice (475-1).

PREJUDI'CIAL, a. injurious (65-6).

1. By *judicious* management, Scott, who was sent to *supersede* Atkinson, induced Black Hawk to sign a treaty.
2. John Jay, who was at the head of the *Judicial* Department, under Washington, was an excellent *linguist*.
3. The giving of false *testimony* before a *judicatory*, is a crime which tends to subvert the very foundations of society.
4. Often we *misjudge* a case, for lack of careful examination.

288. *Jun'go,* I join. *Junc't-um,* to join. *Ju'g-um,* a yoke.

1. AD'JUNCT, n. a thing joined.
2. CONJUNCT'URE, n. combination.
   CON'JUGAL, a. relating to marriage (140-5).

SUB'JUGATE, v. conquer (11-3).
SUBJUGA'TION, n. the act of bringing under the power or absolute control of another (76-3).

1. The relative, with any *adjunct,* should be placed near its antecedent, to *prevent* ambiguity.
2. The invention of the *mariner's compass*, the discovery of America, and the invention of printing, formed a *conjuncture* of circumstances, very favorable to the *dissemination* of knowledge.

289. *Ju'r-o,* I swear. *Jura't-um,* to swear.

1. CON'JURE, v. to practise magical arts.

PER'JURY, n. false swearing (75-3).

1. Although the magicians of Chaldea professed to *conjure,* they could not read the handwriting on the wall.

290. *Jus (ju'r-is),* right, justice, law. *Jus't-us,* just.

1. JURISPRU'DENCE, n. (video,) science of law.
2. JURISDIC'TION, n. (dico,) extent of power.

3. INJUS'TICE, n. want of justice.
   INJU'RIOUS, a. hurtful (75-9).
   IN'JURES, v. damages (8-2).
   ADJUST', v. to set right (75-1).

1. Rufus Choate was noted for his *familiarity* with difficult questions in *jurisprudence.*
2. In 1688, New Jersey was *included* in the *jurisdiction* of Andross, although his *claim* to it had been *contested.*
3. The Indians never forgot the *injustice* of Major Waldron; having captured the *imbecile* old man, they proceeded to *excruciate* their prisoner, before inflicting a mortal wound.

291. Ju'ven-is, young; a young man; youth.

1. REJUVENES'CENCE, *n.* a renewing of youth.
JU'VENILE, *a.* youthful; pertaining to youth (97-1).

　1. It seems like a *joke*, rather than an historical fact, that Ponce de Leon hoped for *rejuvenescence.*

292. La'bor, work, labor.

ELAB'ORATE, *a.* wrought with labor (24-1).
LA'BORED, *v.* toiled (38-2).
LA'BOR, *n.* work (170-4).

293. Lap'sus, falling, sliding.

1. COLLAPSE', *v.* to fall inward or together.
2. ELAPSED', *v.* passed away.
3. RELAPSE', *v.* to fall back again.
LAPSE, *v.* to glide (679-2).

　1. Engineers are trying to discover what it is which causes a boiler to *collapse.*

　2. But fourteen years *elapsed,* after the settlement of Ohio, before it became a State.

　3. Washington adopted the most *lenient* measures with Aaron Burr, expostulated with him in *private,* and when he promised to improve, put him on *probation.* But Burr's *negligence* caused him to *relapse* into his old habits; and as he showed no signs of *penitence,* Washington, after much *deliberation,* dismissed him from his staff.

294. Lach'rym-a, a tear.

1. LACH'RYMAL, *a.* secreting tears.

　1. Pepper, when taken in large quantities, affects the *lachrymal* glands.

295. Lamen't-or, I bewail.

1. LAMENT', *n.* an expression of sorrow.
LAM'ENTABLE, *a.* deplorable (125-9).

　1. David's *lament* for his son Absalom is *unsurpassed* in classic literature.

296. La'p-is (lap'id-is), a stone.

DILAPIDA'TION, *n.* demolition (158-1).

297. La't-us, broad.

LAT'ITUDE, *n.* distance from the equator either north or south (107).
DILATE', *v.* to enlarge upon (195-3).
DILA'TION, *n.* expansion (485).

LATIN DERIVATIVES.

298. *La't-us (lat'er-is),* a side.

1. EQUILAT'ERAL, *a.* (æquus,) having equal sides.
2. COLLAT'ERAL, *a.* indirect; on the side of.

1. From a simple proposition in Geometry, we have the *corollary,* that it is impossible for a right-angled triangle to be *equilateral.*

2. The Treaty of Ghent settled some *collateral* questions, but made no *mention* of the main point at issue, viz.. the impressment of American seamen.

299. *Laus (lau'd-is),* praise. *Lauda't-um,* to praise.

1. LAUD'ABLE, *a.* praiseworthy. LAUD, *v.* praise (483-2).
   LAUD'ATORY, *a.* expressive of praise (167-5).

1. The settlement of Georgia, in 1733, resulted from the *laudable* desire of some *benevolent* gentlemen to provide an asylum for the oppressed of all nations.

300. *Lax'-us,* loose, open.

1. RELAXA'TION, *n.* diversion. | LAX, *a.* loose (308).

1. In Germany, families go to the beer gardens for *relaxation.*

301. *Le'g-o,* I send as an ambassador; I bequeath. *Lega't-um,* to send as ambassador; to bequeath.

1. ALLEGA'TIONS, *n.* declarations.
2. DEL'EGATE, *n.* a commissioner.
   LEG'ACY, *n.* a gift by will of personal property (191-2).
   LEGA'TION, *n.* a deputation (114-3).

1. King Charles considered the *allegations* against Harvey insig*nificant* and easily disproved.
2. Rhode Island did not send a *delegate* to the Convention in 1787.

302. *Le'g-o,* I gather, I select, I read. *Lec't-um,* to gather, to select, to read.

1. LEG'IBLE, *a.* that can be read.
2. LEG'END, *n.* narrative of fabulous character.
3. DI'ALECTS, *n.* peculiar modes of speech.
3. INTEL'LIGIBLE, *a.* that can be understood.
   INTEL'LIGENCE, *n.* information (19-1).
   ELEC'TION, *n.* the act of choosing (75-10).
   DIL'IGENT, *a.* industrious (97-1).
   EL'IGIBLE, *a.* fit to be chosen (12-1).

LECT'URE, n. a discourse conveying instruction (66-1).
NEG'LIGENCE, n. inattention (293-3).
NEGLECT'ED, v. omitted (113).
SELECT'ED, part. chosen (19-1).
COLLECT', v. to gather together (96-1).

1. A very ancient and *legible* copy of the Holy Scriptures has recently been found in Russia.
2. According to an Indian *legend,* "Alabama" means "Here I lay my bones."
3. In a great many *dialects,* there is a word meaning "amen," and so similar to it, that it is *intelligible* to a foreigner.

303. *Le'n-is,* mild, gentle. *Le'ni-o,* I soothe, I make gentle.

1. LEN'ITY, n. gentleness of treatment.
LE'NIENT, a. mild; gentle; soothing (293-3).

1. Charles II., on the restoration of monarchy, strove to *intimidate* his enemies by severity, rather than *appease* them by *lenity.*

304. *Le'-o,* or *Li'n-o,* to besmear; to blot.

1. INDEL'IBLE, a. not to be erased.
DELETE'RIOUS, a. injurious (11-10).

1. The execution of the Archbishop of Paris has left an *indelible* stain on the perpetrators of the deed.

305. *Le'v-is,* light. *Le'v-o,* I raise.

1. LEV'ITY, n. lightness.
2. IRREL'EVANT, a. not applicable.
EL'EVATE, v. to raise (200-1).
ALLE'VIATE, v. to lighten (204-2).
RELIEF', n. assistance; succor (370).

1. A person need not be a *devotee,* to avoid *levity* on serious subjects.
2. The reply of George III., to an *interrogation,* was frequently so *irrelevant,* as to excite grave doubts of his *sanity.*

306. *Lex (le'g-is),* a law. *Legit'im-us,* legal.

LE'GAL, a. pertaining to law (11-5).
ILLE'GAL, a. unlawful (75-10).
LEG'ISLATE, v. (fero,) to enact laws (121-2).
LEG'ISLATURE, n. (fero,) the law-making power; the supreme power of a state (14-2).
PRIV'ILEGES, n. (privus,) special advantages (85-2).

307. Li'ber, free.

1. LIB'ERALIZE, v. to remove narrow views.
2. DELIV'ERY, n. release.
   ILLIBERAL'ITY, n. narrowness of mind (146-3).

LIB'ERAL, a. generous (249).
LIB'ERATE, v. to set free (15-2).
LIB'ERTY, n. freedom (12-4).
LIBERA'TION, n. freedom from restraint (85-1).

1. A good education tends to *liberalize* the mind and free it from *superstition*.
2. The *delivery* of a person from prison is frequently effected by a writ of *Habeas Corpus*.

308. Li'b-er (lib'ri), a book.

1. LI'BEL, n. a defamatory writing.

LI'BRARY, n. a collection of books (147-3).

1. It is no *libel* to describe the English kings as exceedingly *lax* in morals.

309. Li'bra, a pound, a balance.

DELIBERA'TION, n. consideration (293-3).

310. Li'g-o, I bind. Liga't-um, to bind.

1. ALLE'GIANCE, n. acknowledged obligation to obey.
2. LIG'AMENT, n. a strong compact substance uniting two bones.

LI'ABLE, a. subject (598).
RELI'GION, n. duty to God and man (214-1).
OBLIGED', part. compelled (66-4).

1. The American Colonies did not *deny* that they owed *allegiance* to Great Britain.
2. In a ball and socket joint, (such as the shoulder,) the ball is kept in place by a *ligament*.

311. Li'men (lim'in-is), a threshold.

PRELIM'INARY, a. introductory (18-4).

312. Li'mes (lim'it-is), a limit, a boundary.

1. LIMITA'TION, n. restriction.

1. The *permanent limitation* to the power of *amendment* is as follows: "No State, without its consent, shall be deprived of its equal *suffrage* in the Senate."

313. Lĭ'ne-a, a line. **Lĭ'n-um,** flax.

1. Delin'eate, *v.* to draw.
2. Lin'eament, *n.* feature.
3. Lin'ear, *a.* relating to lines.
4. Rectilin'ear, *a.* (rectus,) having straight lines.
Lines, *n.* boundaries (60-2).

Lin'en, *n.* cloth made of flax (75-6).
Lin'seed, *n.* the seed of flax (75-6).
Lin'eage, *n.* family line (75-4).
Lin'eal, *a.* in a line (75-4).

1. One of the juvenile efforts of Benjamin West, was an attempt to *delineate* the *portrait* of his little niece.
2. Every *lineament* was so correct, that his mother was able to *recognize* it *immediately*.
3. Duodecimals are used both in *linear* and *square* measure.
4. Any figure bounded by straight *lines* is *rectilinear;* bounded by four lines is *quadrilateral*.

314. Lĭn'gu-a, the tongue; a language.

Lan'guage, *n.* the speech of a nation (195-6).
Lin'guist, *n.* one skilled in languages (287-2).

315. Lĭn'qu-o, I leave. **Lĭc't-um,** to leave.

Delin'quency, *n.* fault (113).
Rel'ic, *n.* something left (24-1).
Relin'quish, *v.* to abandon (17-3).

316. Lĭ'que-o, to melt, to be liquid.

Liq'uors, *n.* distilled liquids (51).

317. Lĭs (lĭt'-ĭs), strife.

1. Litiga'tion, *n.* (ago,) a suit at law; a judicial contest.
2. Litig'ious, *a.* (ago,) fond of litigation.

1. The people of New Hampshire regarded the demand for rent as an imposition, and resorted to *litigation,* to decide the point.
2. Whitney, the inventor of the cotton-gin, though not *litigious,* was constantly involved in lawsuits.

318. Lĭt'er-a, a letter.

1. Lit'eral, *a.* exact to the letter.
2. Oblit'erate, *v.* to rub out.

Illit'erate, *a.* ignorant (286-1).
Lit'erary, *a.* relating to learning (11-2).

LATIN DERIVATIVES.

1. To produce a *literal* copy of a long article requires close attention
2. Americans will never be able to *obliterate* from their remembrance the *despicable* attempt of Arnold to *betray* his country.

319. Lo'c-us, a place. Lo'co, I place.

1. LOCOMO'TION, *n.* (moveo,) power of changing place.
2. LO'CAL, *a.* relating to place.
LOCAL'ITY, *n.* place (56-3).

1. An oyster has not *locomotion,* yet it is classed among animals.
2. A knowledge of *local* geography is *valuable* in any *vocation.*

320. Lon'g-us, long.

1. ELON'GATE, *v.* to lengthen.
LON'GITUDE, *n.* distance, east or west, from any established meridian, as Greenwich (141-2).
PROLONG' (see page 33).

1. From the 21st of December, the days continue to *elongate* in the Northern Hemisphere, and diminish in the Southern, until the sun reaches the *equinoctial* line, when the days and nights are equal.

321. Lo'qu-or, I speak. Locu't-us, speaking.

1. ELOCU'TION, *n.* the art of oratorical delivery.
2. CIRCUMLOCU'TION, *n.* roundabout expression.
3. OB'LOQUY, *n.* censure; calumny.
4. SOLIL'OQUY, *n.* (solus,) a speech in solitude.

COLLO'QUIAL, *a.* relating to conversation (52-1).
COL'LOQUY, *n.* conversation (146-3).
EL'OQUENT, *a.* expressive of strong emotion (18-4).
LOQUA'CITY, *n.* talkativeness (146-3).

1. To excel in *elocution,* great attention should be paid to the correct *enunciation* of every *vowel.*
2. Perry used no *circumlocution* in announcing his great *victory* on Lake Erie, September, 1813.
3. Much *obloquy* was cast on William Penn, for his friendship for James II.
4. Cato's *soliloquy,* commencing, "It must be so, Plato, thou reasonest well," may have kept many from *suicide.*

**322. Lu'ce-o, I shine. Lu'men (lu'min-is), light.
Lus'tr-o, I make clear or bright.**

1. ELU'CIDATE, *v.* to explain.
2. ILLUMINA'TION, *n.* lighting up.
3. LU'MINOUS, *a.* emitting light.

ILLUSTRA'TION, *n.* exemplification (334-2).
LU'MINARY, *n.* the sun; any orb that gives light (206-1)

13   K

1. Newton was the first to clearly *elucidate* the principle of the attraction of gravitation.
2. There was a general *illumination,* on the repeal of the Stamp Act, in 1766.
3. The moon is not a *luminous* body, but is able to *irradiate* the earth by reflecting the *rays* of the sun.

323. *Lu'cr-um,* gain. *Lucra't-us,* gaining.

1. Lu'crative, *a.* profitable.

1. The great *diversity* in the productions of the United States, makes the foreign commerce very *lucrative.*

324. *Luc't-or,* I struggle.

1. Reluc'tant, *a.* unwilling.

1. Elizabeth was very *reluctant* to *sign* the death-warrant of Essex, but as she could find no *excuse* for his conduct, she was compelled to yield.

325. *Lu'd-o,* I play, I deceive. *Lu's-um,* to play, to deceive.

Allu'sions, *n.* references (97-1).	Lu'dicrous, *a.* exciting to laughter (232-2).
Elude', *v.* to evade (104-2).	Delude', *v.* to cheat (665).

326. *Lu'n-a,* the moon.

1. Lu'natic, *n.* an insane person.	Lu'nacy, *n.* madness; properly the kind which is broken by intervals of reason (170-3).
Lu'nar, *a.* pertaining to the moon (170-3).	

1. George III. was for many years a *lunatic;* in 1811, Prince George was appointed *Regent.*

327. *Lu'-o,* I wash away. *Lu't-um,* to wash away.

1. Ablu'tion, *n.* a washing. | 2. Dilute', *v.* to weaken.

1. The frequent *ablution* of the whole body is enjoined by the Mosaic Law.
2. It is a crime, in some countries, to *dilute* milk or *adulterate* articles of merchandise.

328. *Magis'ter (magis'tr-i),* a master.

1. Mag'istracy, *n.* the office of a magistrate. | 2. Magiste'rial, *a.* having the air of authority.

LATIN DERIVATIVES. 147

8. MAG'ISTRATE, *n.* one having civil authority.

MAS'TER, *n.* one having others under authority (128).

1. Prescott, the Governor of Rhode Island, appointed none to the *magistracy*, but those who would carry out his *malicious* designs.
2. Berkley, the aristocratic governor of Virginia, said with a *magisterial* air, "Thank God there are no free schools nor printing-presses in Virginia."
3. Bunyan was frequently brought before a *magistrate*, when his friends would *intercede* for him.

329. *Mag'n-us*, great. *Ma'jor*, greater. *Max'im-us*, greatest.

1. MAGNAN'IMOUS, *a.* (animus,) of noble mind.
2. MAG'NIFY, *v.* to enlarge.
3. MA'JESTY, *n.* title of a sovereign.

3. MAG'NA-CHAR'TA, *n.* (charta,) the great charter.
MAJOR'ITY, *n.* the part greater than the sum of all the other parts (97-3).

1. Had Washington been less *magnanimous*, he would have taken measures to punish Conway for his unprovoked attacks.
2. We use a microscope to *magnify*; a telescope to see distant objects.
3. His *Majesty*, King John, had many things to *humble* him, but the signing of *Magna*-Charta, 1215, reduced him to despair.

330. *Ma'l-us*, evil, bad. *Malig'n-us*, ill-disposed; malevolent.

MALADMINISTRA'TION, *n.* (ministri,) bad use of power (123-1).
MAL'CONTENT, *n.* (teneo,) a dissatisfied member of society (445).
MALIGN', *v.* to slander (672-2).

MALEFAC'TOR, *n.* (facio,) a criminal (201).
MAL'ICE, *n.* malevolence (140).
MALI'CIOUS, *a.* malevolent (328-1).
MALIG'NITY, *n.* extreme enmity (64-5).

331. *Man'd-o*, I command. *Manda't-um*, to command.

COMMAND', *n.* injunction (75-14).
COUNTERMAND', *v.* to revoke (124-2).
MAN'DATE, *n.* order (75-13).

REPRIMAND', *n.* reproof; censure (2).
COMMEND'ABLE, *a.* worthy of praise (491).
REMAND' (see page 38).

332. Ma'ne-o, I stay. **Man's-um,** to stay.
Per'manent, *a.* lasting (312). | Remain'ing, *part.* staying (241).

333. Ma'n-o, I flow. **Mana't-um,** to flow.
Em'anates, *v.* proceeds from (16-2).

334. Ma'n-us, the hand.
1. Amanuen'sis, *n.* one who writes for another.
2. Man'acles, *n.* fetters.
   Man'ual, *a.* performed by the hand (157).
   Maintain', *v.* (teneo,) to support (126-3).
   Manumis'sion, *n.* (mitto,) giving liberty to slaves (65-8).

Maneu'ver, *n.* (opera), a skilful movement (138-1).
Manufac'tory, *n.* (facio,) a place where goods are made (57-2).
Manufact'ure, *n.* (facio,) anything made by the hand or by art (35-6).
Man'uscript, *n.* (scribo), a writing (125-5).

1. Want of sight is considered an *insuperable* obstacle to literary pursuits, yet Milton by means of an *amanuensis* wrote "Paradise Lost," after he became blind.
2. Columbus, returning from the New World in *manacles*, is a striking *illustration* of the mutability of earthly things.

335. Ma'r-e, the sea.
1. Transmarine', *a.* across the sea.
2. Submarine', *a.* under the sea.

Mar'itime, *a.* bordering on the sea (132-1).
Mar'iner, *n.* one who follows the sea (288-2).

1. In 1763, England received a large accession to her *transmarine* possessions, by the acquisition of Canada.
2. The efforts of Cyrus W. Field, to lay a *submarine* telegraph, to *unite* England and America, have been successful.

336. Mars (mar't-is), the god of war.
Court-Mar'tial, *n.* a military court (2).

337. Mas'cul-us, the male.
Mas'culine, *a.* relating to the male sex (449-1).

LATIN DERIVATIVES. 149

338. *Ma'ter (mat'r-is)*, a mother.

1. MAT'RICIDE, *n.* (cædo,) the murder of a mother.
   MA'TRON, *n.* an elderly married lady (146-3).
   MATER'NAL, *a.* relating to a mother (696).
   MAT'RIMONY, *n.* marriage (545-2).

   1. *Matricide* is not the least crime of which the Emperor Nero is accused.

339. *Mate'ri-a*, matter.

1. MAT'TER, *n.* anything perceived by the senses.
   MATE'RIAL, *n.* matter; substance (78).

   1. It is easy to confute the old theory that heat and light are *matter*.

340. *Matu'r-us*, ripe.

1. MATURED', *p.* well digested.
   IMMATURE', *a.* unripe (119).
   MATU'RITY, *n.* ripeness (119).
   PRE'MATURE, *a.* too hasty (86-1)

   1. In 1838, the *insurgents* in Canada, having *matured* their plans, an *insurrection* took place.

341. *Med'e-or*, I cure.   *Med'ic-us*, a physician.

1. MEDIC'INAL, *a.* having the power of healing.
   MED'ICAL, *a.* relating to the art of healing (177-3).
   MED'ICINE, *n.* any substance used in curing disease (65-15).
   REME'DIAL, *a.* intended for a remedy (92-4).
   REM'EDY, *n.* cure (180-3).

   1. The Indians are well acquainted with the *medicinal* properties of the plantain.

342. *Med'it-or*, I muse.

1. PREMED'ITATED, *v.* planned previously.

   1. As the Indians of Virginia *premeditated* the attack, in 1644, they were well prepared for the contest.

343. *Med'i-us*, middle.   *Medi'ocr-is*, middling.

1. ME'DIUM, *n.* means.
   IMME'DIATELY, *adv.* instantly (313-2).
   MEDIA'TION, *n.* interposition (28-2).
   ME'DIATE, *v.* to interpose between parties, for the purpose of effecting a reconciliation (75-1).
   IMME'DIATE, *a.* present (504-2).

   1. A system of *signals* is usually adopted, as a *medium* of communication between the distant parts of an army.

13*

344. Mel'ior, better.

AME'LIORATE, *v.* to make better (249-2).

345. Me'mor, mindful.   **Mem'in-i,** I remember.

1. REMINIS'CENCE, *n.* recollection.
1. MEM'ORY, *n.* the faculty by which we remember.
2. MEMO'RIAL, *n.* a monument.
   COMMEM'ORATE, *v.* to preserve in memory by some public act (22-6).

IMMEMO'RIAL, *a.* beyond memory (199-3).
MEM'ORABLE, *a.* worthy to be remembered (225-2).
REMEM'BER, *v.* bear in mind (250-3).
MEN'TION, *n.* a calling to mind (298-2).

1. The following pleasing ***reminiscence*** of Washington is worth committing to ***memory.*** As Washington was about to leave a house, where he had made a call, a *modest* little girl opened the door, and courteously held it for him to pass out. "My dear," said Washington, "I wish you a better service." "Yes, sir," said the little girl, "*to let you in.*"

2. A library is a far more suitable ***memorial*** of Benjamin Franklin, than any useless *monument,* which *posterity* could erect.

346. Men'd-a, a blemish, a mistake.

AMEND'MENT, *n.* alteration for the better (312).

347. Mens (men't-is), the mind.

MEN'TAL, *a.* relating to the mind (105-2).

348. Mensu'ra, a measure.   **Me'ti-or,** I measure.

1. DIMEN'SION, *n.* extent.
   MEAS'URES, *n.* plans; the dimensions (43-2).

MEAS'UREMENT, *n.* the act of measuring (15-1).
IMMENSE', *a.* of vast extent (38).

1. To find the area of a *rectangular* figure, *multiply* one ***dimension*** by the other.

349. Me'-o, I go.   **Mœan'der,** a river in Phrygia.

1. MEAN'DERING, *a.* winding, or flowing round.
2. PER'MEATE, *v.* to pass through the interstices of.

1. Mythology gives the name Mæander to a river in Asia, remarkable for its ***meandering*** or *serpentine* course.

2. The *noxious* substances used in some wall paper, are often found to ***permeate*** the air and render it unwholesome.

LATIN DERIVATIVES. 151

350. *Mer'c-or*, I buy, I trade. *Mer'cans*, buying, trading.

1. MER'CENARY, *a.* serving for pay.
2. MER'CANTILE, *a.* pertaining to a merchant.

COM'MERCE, *n.* trade (130).
MER'CHANDISE, *n.* things bought and sold (75-6).
MER'CHANT, *n.* a trader (11-5).

1. Burgoyne's army was composed of a heterogeneous mass of ***mercenary*** troops, gathered by *conscription*.

2. The *assumption*, that the British Government had the right to seize deserters, was *destructive* of the ***mercantile*** *interests* of the United States.

351. *Mer'g-o*, I dip. *Mer's-um*, to dip.

EMER'GENCY, *n.* pressing necessity (169-1).
IMMER'SION, *n.* a dipping (125-2).

EMERGE', *v.* to rise out (see page 33).
IMMERSE', *v.* to dip; to sink (see page 33).

352. *Mig'r-o*, I remove. *Migra't-um*, to remove.

1. MI'GRATORY, *a.* roving.
EM'IGRATE, *v.* to remove from a place (62-1).
IMMIGRA'TION, *n.* the coming of foreigners into a country (92-5).

IM'MIGRANT, *n.* one who comes into a country to reside (132-1).
MIGRA'TION, *n.* departure to a distant place of residence (66-1).

1. In 1713, a ***migratory*** band of Tuscaroras arrived in New York, and joined the Five Nations.

353. *Mi'l-es (mil'it-is)*, a soldier.

MIL'ITARY, *a.* pertaining to soldiery (93-2).

MILI'TIA, *n.* the enrolled soldiers (96-1).

354. *Mil'le*, a thousand.

MILL'ION, *n.* ten hundred thousand (511).

355. *Mi'n-eo*, I jut out.

PROM'INENT, *a.* eminent; conspicuous (66-1).

EM'INENT, *a.* distinguished (65-11).

356. Minis'ter (minis'tr-i), a servant.

ADMINISTRA'TION, *n.* management of affairs (75-9). | ADMIN'ISTER, *v.* give; dispense (109-3).

357. Mi'n-or, less. **Min'u-o,** I lessen. **Minut'-um,** to lessen.

1. DIMINU'TION, *n.* decrease.
2. MINOR'ITY, *n.* the smaller number.
3. DIMIN'UTIVE, *a.* little.
   DIMIN'ISH, *v.* to lessen (216-7).

 1. Want and disease had caused such a *diminution* in the army, that Lincoln was compelled to surrender Charleston, in 1780.
 2. The *minority* in Congress may be authorized to compel the attendance of *absent* members.
 3. In making the soundings for the Atlantic Cable, the *plummet* brought up *diminutive* shells.

358. Mi'r-us, strange, wonderful. **Mira't-us,** wondering. **Mirac'ul-um,** a miracle.

1. MIRAC'ULOUS, *a.* exceeding the laws of nature; performed supernaturally.
   AD'MIRABLY, *adv.* wonderfully (27-3).
   ADMIRA'TION, *n.* wonder (37-3).

 1. According to an ancient *tradition,* the *veritable tabernacle,* described in the Pentateuch, is still in existence, having been preserved by *miraculous* power.

359. Mis'c-eo, I mix. **Mix't-um,** to mix.

1. MIS'CELLANY, *n.* a collection of various things.
2. MISCELLA'NEOUS, *a.* mixed.
3. PROMIS'CUOUS, *a.* consisting of individuals united in a mass without order.

 1. A good Cyclopedia contains an interesting *miscellany,* embracing Mechanics, Geometry, Geology, etc.
 2. The Patent-Office contains a *miscellaneous* collection of every kind of *apparatus.*
 3. A *promiscuous* multitude, composed of all classes, gain admission to the President on New-Year's day.

360. Mi'ser, wretched.

1. MI'SER, *n.* an extremely covetous person.
2. COMMIS'ERATE, *v.* to pity.
   MIS'ERABLE, *a.* unhappy (75-8).
   MIS'ERY, *n.* suffering (225).

 1. At the present day, a man is in more danger of being a spendthrift than a *miser.*

LATIN DERIVATIVES.

2. The intense sufferings of the prisoners, in the "Prison Ship," were *unmitigated* during the war. If any Royalist dared to **commiserate** these sufferings, and to provide a palliative, he soon received an *admonition*, which caused him to desist.

361. *Mit'ig-o*, I make mild, I assuage.
UNMIT'IGATED, *a.* unassuaged (360-2).

362. *Mit't-o*, I send. ***Mis's-um*,** to send.

1. INTERMIT'TENT, *a.* ceasing at intervals.
ADMIS'SION, *n.* admittance (359-3).
COM'MISSARY, *n.* the officer who provides food for the army (13-1).
COMMIT', *v.* to perpetrate (31-3).
COM'PROMISE, *n.* adjustment by concession (75-1).
COMMIT'TEE, *n.* persons appointed to perform some business (42-1).
EM'ISSARY, *n.* one sent as a secret agent (86-2).

MIS'SIONARY, *n.* one sent to propagate religion (31).
PERMIS'SION, *n.* leave granted (82-1).
PROM'ISING, *part.* engaging to give (21-4).
PROM'ISSORY, *a.* containing a promise (154).
SUBMIS'SION, *n.* a yielding to power or superior authority (14-4).
SURMISE', *n.* suspicion (195-1).
EMIT' (see page 33).
SUBMIT' (see page 33).
TRANSMIT' (see page 33).
PERMIT' (see page 33).

1. In some of the oil wells, the flow is uninterrupted, while in others it is *intermittent*.

363. *Mo'd-us*, a measure. ***Modes't-us*,** modest.

1. MOD'ERATE, *a.* observing proper bounds.
2. MOD'ESTY, *n.* humility.
3. MOD'IFY, *v.* to change the character of a thing.
4. COMMO'DIOUS, *a.* convenient.
4. INCOMMODE', *v.* to inconvenience.

ACCOM'MODATE, *v.* to supply with conveniences (65-1).
COMMOD'ITY, *n.* that which affords convenience — goods, wares, merchandise (214-6).
MOD'EL, *n.* a copy to be imitated (94-2).
MOD'EST, *a.* diffident (345).

1. Never eat to *satiety;* but be *moderate* in all things, if you would preserve health.
2. Washington had proved himself a *competent* General, yet when

appointed to the position of Commander-in-chief, he said, with great *modesty,* "I do not think myself equal to the command."

3. As Great Britain refused to repeal or *modify* the "Orders in Council," war was declared in 1812.

4. Nothing was found to *incommode* the settlers in Massachusetts so much as the lack of *commodious* habitations.

364. *Mo'li-or,* I rear or build. *Molit-us,* rearing or building.

1. DEMOLI'TION, *n.* destruction. | DEMOL'ISH, *v.* to destroy (78).

1. The *demolition* of Faneuil Hall, or an attempt to modernize it, would seem a sacrilege.

365. *Mol'l-is,* soft.

1. EMOL'LIENT, *n.* that which assuages. | MOL'LIFY, *v.* to assuage; to soften (140-4).

1. While the attendants of King —— were applying some *unctuous* substance, as an *emollient,* it took fire, and *enveloped* him in flames He soon expired, in great *torment.*

366. *Mo'n-eo,* I put in mind; I warn. *Mon'it-um,* to put in mind; to warn.

1. MON'ITOR, *n.* one who puts in mind. | PREMON'ITORY, *a.* giving warning beforehand (170-1).
1. SUM'MON, *v.* to call. | MON'UMENT, *n.* memorial (345).
ADMON'ISH, *v.* to remind of a fault (76-2). | ADMONI'TION, *n.* warning (360-2).

1. In the Lancasterian method of education, a *monitor* is employed to *summon* the classes to their exercises.

367. *Mons (mon't-is),* a mountain.

1. PAR'AMOUNT, *a.* superior. | MOUNT'AIN, *n.* a high hill (15-1).
AMOUNT', *n.* the sum total of several quantities (86-2). | SURMOUNT', *v.* to rise above (189-2).

1. Moral science (or ethics) teaches, that the duty we owe to God is *paramount* to any duty imposed by man.

368. *Mon'str-o,* I show. *Monstra't-um,* to show.

DEM'ONSTRATE, *v.* make evident (140-8). | REMON'STRATE, *v.* to expostulate (179-2).
MON'STER, *n.* anything horrible from ugliness (216-6). | MON'STROUS, *a.* horrible (434-3).

LATIN DERIVATIVES.

369. *Mor'b-us*, a disease.
MOR'BIDLY, *adv.* in a diseased manner (216-2).

370. *Mor'd-eo*, I bite. *Mor's-um*, to bite.
1. MOR'SEL, *n.* a small portion.
REMORSE', *n.* sense of guilt (216-3).

1. The missionaries in China could give but a *morsel* to each sufferer, yet it was some *relief* in the terrible famine of 1878.

371. *Mors (mor't-is)*, death. *Moribun'd-us*, dying.
1. MOR'IBUND, *a.* dying.
2. MORT'GAGE, *n.* the state of being pledged.
3. MOR'TALLY, *adv.* fatally.
4. MOR'TIFY, *v.* to humble.
   IMMOR'TAL, *a.* exempt from death (148-2).
MOR'TAL, *a.* deadly (118-2).
MORTAL'ITY, *n.* death (164-1).
IMMOR'TALIZE, *v.* to make immortal (186-2).
MORTIFICA'TION, *n.* (facio,) vexation (71-2).

1. Edward III., when in a *moribund* condition, had no friend to solace him.
2. Capitalists loan money on *mortgage* if the security is good.
3. To *mortally* wound a person, with malice *prepense*, is a capital crime, in most civilized countries.
4. Wayne determined to *vindicate* his honor, and to *mortify* the British, for his defeat at Paoli.

372. *Mos (mo'r-is)*, custom; practice.
DEMOR'ALIZE, *v.* to render corrupt in morals (139-2).
MOR'AL, *a.*, pertaining to right and wrong (8-2).
MORAL'ITY, *n.* correctness of life (156-3).
IMMOR'AL, *a.* not virtuous (179-2).

373. *Mo've-o*, I move. *Mo't-um*, to move. *Mob'ilis*, easily moved; excitable.
COMMO'TION, *n.* tumult (191).
EMO'TION, *n.* disturbance of mind (68-3).
MO'TIVE, *n.* inducement (11).
MOVE'MENT, *n.* motion (68-3).
REMOTE', *a.* distant (74-1).
MOB,' *n.* a riotous multitude (77-1).
PROMO'TION, *n.* advancement (86-2).
PROMO'TIVE, *a.* tending to advance (168-1).
PROMOTE' (see page 33).

374. *Mul't-us,* many.

1. MUL'TIFORM, *a.* (forma,) having many forms.
   MUL'TITUDE, *n.* a great number (359-3).
   MUL'TIPLY, *v.* (plico,) to take one quantity as many times as there are units in another quantity (348).
   MULTIFA'RIOUS, *a.* (fari,) diversified (214-7).

1. To those who *scrutinize* closely, Nature, in every department, exhibits *multiform* beauties.

375. *Mun'd-us,* the earth, the world.

1. MUN'DANE, *a.* earthly
   1. We hold every *mundane* treasure by a very *precarious tenure.*

376. *Mu'ni-o,* I fortify. *Munit'-um,* to fortify.

AMMUNI'TION, *n.* materials used in war (35-6).
MUNI'TIONS, *n.* materials used in war (75-5).

377. *Mu'n-us (mu'ner-is),* an office, a gift; duty.

1. MUNIF'ICENCE, *n.* (facio,) liberality.
2. MUNIC'IPAL, *a.* (capio), pertaining to a city.
3. COMMU'NICATIVE, *a.* ready to impart knowledge.
4. IMMU'NITIES, *n.* peculiar privileges.
5. REMU'NERATE, *v.* to repay.
   *COM'MON, *a.* usual (23).
   COMMU'NICATE, *v.* to impart (86-2).
   COMMU'NITY, *n.* society (11-5).
   REMUNERA'TION, *n.* recompense (62-1).

1. The *munificence* of Mr. Peabody confers *innumerable* blessings on the *poor* of London, and keeps many from *pauperism.*
2. One of the most important duties devolving upon *municipal* authorities, is to provide an abundant supply of water.
3. The first adventurers to the New World found the Indians friendly and *communicative.*
4. The citizens of each State shall be entitled to all the privileges and *immunities* of citizens in the several States.
5. The United States made arrangements to *remunerate* Spain for the *cession* of Florida, in 1821.

378. *Mu'r-us,* a wall.

1. IMMURED', *part.* imprisoned.
2. MU'RAL, *a.* pertaining to a wall.

1. "Why was Casper Hauser *immured* from infancy to manhood?"

"Why was he not allowed to mingle with his fellow-men?" are questions on which many have *speculated.*

2. A *mural* tablet on a building in Philadelphia, declares it to be the place in which George Washington and John Adams were inaugurated.

379. *Mu's-a,* a muse; a song.

1. Mu'ses, *n.* goddesses, in ancient mythology, who presided over the liberal arts.

Mu'sic, *n.* melody (199-2).
Musi'cian, *n.* one skilled in music (92-3).

1. Castalia was a fountain sacred to the Nine *Muses,* Calli'ope, Cli'o, Er'ato, Euter'pe, Melpom'ene, Polyhym'nia, Terpsich'ore, Thali'a, Ura'nia.

380. *Mu't-o,* I change. *Muta't-um,* to change.

1. Immu'table, *a.* unchangeable.
Commu'ted, *part.* changed (10-2).

Mutabil'ity, *n.* quality of being subject to change (334-2).
Transmute', *v.* to change from one nature to another (473).

1. The Medes and Persians boasted that their laws were *immutable,* yet not a *vestige* of them remains at the present day.

381. *Mu'tu-us,* mutual.

1. Mu'tual, *a.* reciprocal.

1. The *connection* of the New and the Old World by the Telegraph, has proved a *mutual* advantage.

382. *Nar'r-o,* to tell, to relate.

1. Narra'tion, *n.* story.

1. In the old-fashioned *hotel,* the *host* assembled his guests around the fire, to hear some wonderful *narration.*

383. *Nas'c-or,* I am born. *Na't-us,* born.

1. Nativ'ity, *n.* birth.
Innate', *a.* inborn (146-2).
Nat'ural, *a.* native (12-1).
Na'ture, *n.* essential quality (4).

Nat'uralist, *n.* one versed in natural history (161).
Supernat'ural, *a.* beyond nature (57-5).
Interna'tional *a.* pertaining to nations (22-6).

1. The place of Homer's *nativity* is a doubtful point:

"Seven cities contend for Homer dead,
Through which the living Homer begged his bread."

384. Na′s-us, the nose.
1. NA′SAL, *a.* relating to the nose.
   1. Europeans say they can tell an American by his **nasal** tones.

385. Nau′t-a, a sailor.
1. NAU′TICAL, *a.* pertaining to navigation. | NAU′SEA, *n.* sea-sickness (180-3).
   1. Before the invention of the mariner's compass, **nautical** skill was limited to *navigable* rivers, and the shores of the ocean.

386. Na′v-is, a ship. (See words under **Ago.**)
NAVE, *n.* the aisle of a church, from the choir to the principal entrance (120-4).

387. Nec′t-o, I tie or bind.   **Nex′-um,** to tie or bind.
1. ANNEXA′TION, *n.* the act of connecting. | CONNEC′TION, *n.* joining (381) CONNECT′ (see page 33).
   1. The **annexation** of Texas was a very unpopular measure with a large party in the North.

388. Nefa′ri-us, wicked.
NEFA′RIOUS, *a.* extremely wicked (389-2).

389. Ne′g-o, I deny.   **Nega′t-um,** to deny.
1. NEGA′TION, *n.* denial. | NEG′ATIVE, *a.* implying denial (124-2).
2. REN′EGADE, *n.* an apostate. |
   DENI′AL, *n.* refusal (120-2). | DENY′, *v.* declare untrue (310).
   1. Two negatives in the same sentence are improper, if intended to express the same **negation.**
   2. Richard III. employed any **renegade** to carry out his *nefarious* plans.

390. Neu′ter (neu′tr-um), neither.
NEU′TRAL, *a.* not engaged on either side (75-5). | NEU′TRALIZE, *v.* to destroy peculiar properties (699-2).

391. Ni′hil, nothing.
ANNIHILA′TION, *n.* the being reduced to nothing (148-2).

392. No′ce-o, I hurt; I harm.   **Nox′i-us,** hurtful.
1. IN′NOCENT, *a.* free from guilt. | 2. NUI′SANCE, *n.* that which incommodes.

LATIN DERIVATIVES.

3. Obnox'ious, *a.* offensive. | Nox'ious, *a.* hurtful (349-2).
In'nocence, *n.* purity (30-3). |

1. In Germany, during the 16th century, more than 100,000 *innocent* persons suffered death for witchcraft.

2. Scholars should be ashamed of conduct which makes a school-house a *nuisance.*

3. George III. found it impossible to make *obnoxious* laws operative in the American Colonies.

393. *Nor'm-a,* a rule or pattern.

1. Nor'mal, *a.* according to established principles. | Enor'mity, *n.* excessive greatness (42-1).
2. Abnor'mal, *a.* not natural. | Enor'mous, *a.* huge (180-7).

1. A good *Normal* School is essential to the existence of good Common Schools.

2. A physician must study the body in a healthy or normal state, to know when it is *abnormal.*

394. *Nos'c-o,* I know. *Not'-um,* to know. *Nob'il-is,* of high birth. *No'men (nom'in-is),* a name.

1. Noto'rious, *a.* remarkable. | No'tify, *v.* to make known (34).
2. Reconnoi'tring, *part.* surveying. | Rec'ognize, *v.* to remember as previously known (313-2).
3. Nom'inal, *a.* in name only. | No'tice, *v.* to regard (143-3).
Denomina'tion, *n.* religious sect (75-12). | Nomina'tion, *n.* the act of naming (94-1).
Enno'ble, *v.* to raise to the nobility (143-3). | No'ble, *a.* exalted (159-1).
Ig'nominy, *n.* dishonor (39). | Misno'mer, *n.* an incorrect name (467-2).
Nom'inate, *v.* to name for appointment (94-1). | Nobil'ity, *n.* the peerage (260).

1. Captain Kidd, a *notorious* pirate, was at one time the terror of sailors.

2. General Marion, a noted *partisan* of South Carolina, was invaluable for *reconnoitring.*

3. The treaty of Aix-la-Chapelle (aks-la-sha-pell') was but a *temporary* suspension of hostilities; the peace proved to be only *nominal,* especially where there was not a full *complement* of regular troops.

395. No'v-us, new.

1. Innova'tion, *n.* introduction of something new.
2. Ren'ovate, *v.* to make new.
   Nov'ice, *n.* one new in a business (167-4).

Nov'els, *n.* fictitious tales (204-2).
Nov'el, *a.* unusual (457).
Nov'elty, *n.* a new or strange thing (7-4).

1. Walter Scott, when *insolvent*, wrote a series of historical novels, which were a great ***innovation*** on the literature of that period.
2. One of the "Labors of Hercules" was to ***renovate*** and cleanse from all that was *odious* and *repugnant*, the Augean stables.

396. Nox (noc't-is), night.

1. Noctur'nal, *a.* nightly.
2. E'quinox, *n.* (æquus,) the time when the sun enters the equinoctial point.

Equinoc'tial, *a.* (æquus,) pertaining to the equinoxes; *n.* the celestial equator (320).

1. Nothing is so certain to *eradicate* the belief in *spectres* and ***nocturnal*** visitants as education.
2. At the ***equinox***, the night is everywhere twelve hours long.

397. Nu'b-o, I marry. ***Nup't-um,*** to marry.
Nup'tials, *n.* marriage ceremonies (465-3).

398. Nu'd-us, naked.

1. Denude', *v.* make bare. | Nu'dity, *n.* nakedness (22-3).

1. When the cold blasts from the north ***denude*** the trees, we should have sympathy with those who are poor and suffering.

399. Nul'l-us, no one.

1. Nul'lify, *v.* to render of no force.
2. Nul'lity, *n.* that which is void in law.

1. The "Non-Intercourse Act," was designed to ***nullify*** the Act, which imposed a duty on tea, glass, paper, painters' colors, etc.
2. The Charter of Massachusetts was declared a ***nullity***, in 1684, by Charles II.

400. Nu'mer-us, a number.

1. Supernu'meraries, *n.* persons beyond the usual number.
2. Enu'merate, *v.* to number; to compute.

Innu'merable, *a.* too many to be counted (377-1).
Numer'ical, *a.* pertaining to numbers (75-12).
Num'bers, *n.* multitudes (62-1).

1. Where large numbers of laborers are employed, it is common to have several *supernumeraries.*
2. It is impossible to *enumerate* the benefits resulting from the Centennial celebration.

401. *Nun'ci-o,* I announce. *Nuncia't-um,* to announce.

1. RENOUNCE', *v.* to disown.
2. NUN'CIO, *n.* ambassador.
ENUNCIA'TION, *n.* utterance (321-1).

ANNOUN'CING, *part.* proclaiming (47-2).
ANNOUNCE' (see page 39).
PRONOUNCED', *v.* uttered (140).

1. Such was the *odium* attached to the name of Quaker, that Admiral Penn determined to *renounce* his son for professing their principles.
2. Wolsey and the Pope's *nuncio* were appointed to try the question of the divorce of Henry VIII.

402. *Nu'tri-o,* to nourish.

1. NUTRI'TIOUS, *a.* nourishing.
1. NOUR'ISHING, *a.* nutritious; promoting growth.

2. NURSE', *n.* one who tends or nourishes.
NU'TRIMENT, *n.* that which nourishes (241-7).

1. The most *nutritious* or *nourishing* food comes from cereals, wheat, rye, etc.
2. Every *nurse* should have a knowledge of the *regimen* suitable for the sick.

403. *Nux (nu'c-is),* a nut.

NU'CLEUS, *n.* the central portion about which matter is gathered (147-3).

404. *Obliv'io,* forgetfulness.

1. OBLIV'ION, *n.* the state of being forgotten.

1. Stone pillars and monuments were instituted to prevent important acts from passing into *oblivion.*

405. *Oc'ul-us,* the eye.

1. INOC'ULATE, *v.* to insert infectious matter.

2. OC'ULAR, *a.* perceived by the eye.

1. In the spring of 1777, Washington determined to *inoculate* his army with the small-pox.
2. The sailors were on the point of mutiny, when they had *ocular* demonstration that they were approaching land.

406. O'di, I hate.

O'DIOUS, a. causing hatred; offensive (395-2).

O'DIUM, n. dislike; offensiveness (401-1).

407. O'dor, a scent, perfume.

O'DOR, n. scent; any smell (220).

408. O'l-eo, I emit odor; I grow. Ol'it-um, to emit odor, to grow.

1. OLFAC'TORY, a. (facio,) pertaining to the sense of smelling.
2. OB'SOLETE, a. grown out of use.
3. ADULT', n. one who has reached mature age.

ABOLI'TION, n. utter destruction (7-2).
RED'OLENT, a. diffusing a sweet scent (followed by *of*) (220).
ABOL'ISH, v. utterly destroy (661).

1. The *olfactory* nerves are very sensitive in birds of prey.
2. Shakespeare wrote three hundred years ago, and many of his words are now *obsolete*.
3. The bones of an *adult* are much more brittle than those of a child.

409. Om'n-is, every; all.

OMNIP'OTENT, a. (potens,) having all power (75-14).
OMNIPRES'ENT, a. (sum,) everywhere present (205-5).

OMNI'SCIENT, a. (scio,) having infinite knowledge (205-5).
OMNIV'OROUS, a. (voro,) eating everything (706).

410. O'n-us (on'er-is), a burden.

1. ON'EROUS, a. burdensome; oppressive.

EXON'ERATE, v. to exculpate (669-3).

1. Pitt, with all his *onerous* duties, found time to *investigate* the cause of the reverses in America, and to plan a successful campaign.

411. O'pus (o'per-is), work. Opera't-us, working.

1. INOP'ERATIVE, a. not producing effects.
2. OP'ERATE, v. to produce effects.

CO-OP'ERATE, v. to act together (413).
OPERA'TION, n. action; the act of operating (157).

1. The extraordinary powers granted to the President, by the Alien and *Sedition* Acts, rendered them *inoperative*.
2. With the *ordinary* covering, the telegraphic wire is not likely to *operate* under water.

LATIN DERIVATIVES.

412. *Opi'n-or*, I think; I imagine.

OPIN'ION, *n.* judgment (478-1).

413. *Op't-o*, I wish. ***Opta't-um*,** to wish.

1. OP'TION, *n.* choice. | ADOPT''(see page 34).

1. Unless James II. could have induced Louis XIV. of France to *co-operate* with him in a civil war, he had no *option*, but was compelled to abdicate.

414. *Or'b-is*, a circle; a circular body. ***Or'bit-a*,** the track of a rolling body.

1. EXOR'BITANT, *a.* extravagant. | 2. OR'BIT, *n.* path of a planet.
| 3. ORB, *n.* a sphere.

1. For such a *tract* of land as the Louisiana Territory, $15,000,000 was not an *exorbitant* price.

2. Astronomy teaches us, that the *orbit* of the earth is *oval*, and that the earth is nearer the sun in winter than in summer.

3. The Sun is an immense *orb*, whose volume is 1,400,000 times as great as that of the earth.

415. *Or'd-o (or'din-is)*, order.

1. OR'DINANCE, *n.* law.
2. INSUBORDINA'TION, *n.* disobedience to lawful authority.
3. INOR'DINATE, *a.* excessive.
OR'DER,*n.*command (124-2).
OR'DINARY, *a.* in the usual manner (411-2).

1. It was natural to suppose, that an *ordinance* imposing a *restriction* on business, would *eventually* lead to rebellion.

2. Braddock thought it showed *insubordination*, to express any doubt as to the expediency of his plans.

3. *Ostentation* and *inordinate* love of dress, have induced many persons to steal.

416. *O'ri-or*, I rise; I spring from. ***Ori'g-o (orig'-in-is)*,** beginning.

1. ORIGINAL'ITY, *n.* the quality of being original.
1. EXOR'DIUM, *n.* a formal introduction.
2. ORIG'INALLY, *a.* at first.
3. ORIG'INATE, *v.* to bring into existence.
ORIEN'TAL,*a.* eastern (64-1).
ORIG'INATED, *v.* brought into existence (167-5).

1. If an orator has eloquence and *originality*, whether his discourse has an *exordium* and a *peroration* or not, it is heard with interest.

2. If the Indians of North America *originally* came across the "big water," it is an argument for the *unity* of the human race.

3. A very trifling circumstance led Rowland Hill to *originate* the system of penny postage.

417. Or'n-o, I embellish. **Orna't-um,** to embellish.

1. ORNATE', *a.* highly ornamented.
2. SUBORN', *v.* to cause to take a false oath.

OR'NAMENT, *n.* embellishment (89).
ADORNED', *part.* ornamented (477-3).

1. Many of the cathedrals in England are exceedingly *ornate;* the most elevated portions *reveal* the handiwork of the *sculptor*.

2. It was easy for Henry VIII. to *suborn* bad men to bring charges against his wife.

418. O'r-o, I pray; I ask. **Ora't-um,** to pray; to ask.

1. OR'ATORY, *n.* eloquence.
2. OR'ISONS, *n.* prayers or supplications.
ADORA'TION, *n.* worship (64-3).
INEX'ORABLE, *a.* not to be moved by entreaty (39).

ORA'TION, *n.* a formal speech (64-3).
OR'ATOR, *n.* a public speaker (18-2).
PERORA'TION, *n.* the final summing up of a speech (416-1).
ADORE' (see page 34).

1. The orations of Cicero are still *extant*, and are regarded as models to be studied by all who would excel in *oratory*.

2. Amid the snows of Valley Forge, Washington offered his *devout orisons* for the *sanction* of a just God upon his undertaking.

419. Os (os's-is), a bone.

1. OSSIFICA'TION, *n.* (facio,) turning to bone.

1. Heart-disease is sometimes occasioned by the *ossification* of one of the valves.

420. O'ti-um, ease.

NEGO'TIATE, *v.* to establish by agreement (35-1).
NEGO'TIATING, *p.* procuring by mutual agreement (464-3).

421. O'v-um, an egg.

O'VAL, *a.* egg-shaped (414-2).

422. Pac't-us, stipulated; agreed.

1. COMPACT', *a.* firmly united. | 2. COM'PACT, *n.* bargain.

1. Jackson defended New Orleans by ramparts of cotton, which were so *compact* as to be *impenetrable* to cannon-balls.

2. Many attempts have been made to *disparage* the character of Osceola for *veracity*; but he always declared that the *compact* to remove was made without his knowledge.

423. *Pa'g-us,* a village.

1. Pa'ganism, *n.* heathenism.

1. Even in *paganism* man has a desire to *expiate* his sin.

424. *Pal'li-um,* a cloak.

Pall, *n.* a covering for the dead (68-3). | Pal'liate, *v.* extenuate; cover with excuse (57-1).

425. *Pan'd-o,* I lay open. *Pan's-um,* to lay open.

1. Expan'sion, *n.* the act of expanding; enlarging.
Expan'sive, *a.* expanding (490). | Expand', *v.* enlarge; to open (43-1).
Expanse', *n.* wide extent (75-13).

1. Montgolfier, the first aëronaut, made many attempts to effect the *expansion* of the first balloon.

426. *Pa'n-is,* bread.

Accom'pany, *v.* go with (112). | Com'pany, *n.* association (112).

427. *Par (pa'r-is),* equal; like.

1. Peer'age, *n.* the rank of a peer.
Peer, *n.* a nobleman (127). | Dispar'age, *v.* to vilify (422-2).
Dispar'ity, *n.* inequality (169).
Compare' (see page 34).

1. The *peerage* of England includes five degrees: Baron, *Viscount,* Earl, Marquis, and Duke.

428. *Pa'r-eo,* I am present. *Par'it-um,* to be present.

1. Appari'tion, *n.* ghost.
2. Transpar'ent, *a.* admitting the passage of light. | Appear'ance, *n.* a coming into sight (35-3).
Appear' (see page 39).

1. An *apparition* is not often *visible* in a well-lighted house inhabited by educated people.

2. Our comfort is greatly increased by the use of a substance which is *transparent,* and yet impervious to the air.

429. Pa'r-io, I bring forth. **Par't-um,** to bring forth.

PAR'ENT, *n.* a father or mother (145).
PARENT'AL, *a.* relating to parents (145).
PAR'RICIDE, *n.* (cædo,) the killing of a parent (57-4).
PAR'ENTAGE, *n.* birth; extraction (544-3).

430. Pa'r-o, I prepare. **Para't-um,** to prepare.

1. REPARA'TION, *n.* restitution.
1. PREPARED', *v.* made ready.
2. APPAR'EL, *n.* clothing.
   APPARA'TUS, *n.* implements
for a particular business (359-2).
SEPARA'TION, *n.* disconnection (11-9).
SEV'ERAL, *a.* divers (82-1).

1. As France refused to make *reparation* for the depredation of our commerce, the United States *prepared* for war.
2. Some of the *apparel* and household *utensils* of Stephen Girard are deposited in Girard College, Philadelphia.

431. Pars (part-is), a part. **Por't-io,** a share.

1. PARTI'TION, *n.* division.
   APART'MENT, *n.* a room (206).
   IMPAR'TIAL, *a.* not favoring either side (57).
   PAR'TICLE, *n.* a little portion (21-5).
PAR'TISAN, *n.* an adherent of a party (394-2).
PROPOR'TION, *n.* equal or just share (66-2).
POR'TION, *n.* part (27-1).
PART', *n.* portion (27-1).
IMPART', *v.* to bestow (98-1).

1. To induce the men on board of a privateer to *exert* themselves, there is usually a *partition* of the prize.

432. Pas'c-o, I feed. **Pas't-um,** to feed.

1. PAS'TORAL, *a.* rural.
2. PAST'URE, *n.* grazing.
2. PAS'TOR, *n.* a minister having the care of a congregation.

1. David, "the sweet singer of Israel," Burns, and many others whom we love to *extol*, spent their youth in *pastoral* occupations.
2. As early as 1638, the narrow limits of the Plymouth Colony seemed to *circumscribe* the settlers to such a degree, that *Pastor* Davenport and others determined to settle on the fertile *pasture* lands of Connecticut.

433. Pas's-us, a pace, a step.

COM'PASS, *n.* an instrument having a magnetized needle turning to the north (288-2).
UNSURPASSED', *a.* unexcelled (295).
PASSED, *v.* crossed (528).

434. *Pa'ter (pat'r-is),* a father. *Pat'ria,* one's native country.

1. PAT'RIMONY, *n.* inheritance.
2. PA'TRONAGE, *n.* special support.
3. PATRI'CIAN, *n.* one of the nobility of Rome; one who was not a plebeian.

PA'TRIOT, *n.* a lover of his country (105-2).
COMPA'TRIOT, *n.* one of the same country (50-1).
EXPA'TRIATE, *v.* to banish from one's country (57-3).

1. The *patrimony* of General Van Rensselaer comprised a territory in New York, forty-eight miles long and twenty-one broad.
2. The *patronage* of Benjamin Franklin was extended to any poor young man whose *aspiration* for something higher led him to apply for aid.
3. At one time, a *patrician* of Rome held the *monstrous* doctrine, that a *plebeian* had no rights that any one was bound to respect.

435. *Pa'ti-or,* I suffer. *Pas's-us,* suffering.

1. DISPAS'SIONATE, *a.* calm.
1. COMPAT'IBLE, *a.* consistent with.
COMPAS'SION, *n.* pity (47-1).

IMPA'TIENT, *a.* uneasy (240-1).
PA'TIENT, *n.* an invalid (65-15).
PA'TIENCE, *n.* endurance (38-2).

1. A *dispassionate* and *sedate* temper is perfectly *compatible* with great energy and activity.

436. *Pax (pa'c-is),* peace.

APPEASE', *v.* to pacify (303).
PACIF'IC, *a.* (facio,) peacemaking (66-5).

PAC'IFY, *v.* to quiet (222-1).
PEACE, *n.* quiet; a state of tranquillity (22-5).

437. *Pau'per,* poor.

PAU'PERISM, *n.* indigence (377-1).
POOR, *a.* needy (246-1).

POV'ERTY, *n.* state of being poor (143-4).
POOR, *n.* the indigent (377-1).

438. *Pec't-us (pec'tor-is),* the breast.

1. PAR'APET, *n.* breast-work.
2. EXPECTORA'TION, *n.* the act of discharging from the lungs.

1. In 1776, Sergeant Jasper jumped over the *parapet,* amid a *volley* of shot, and replaced the flag on Fort Moultrie.
2. Lobelia, or Indian tobacco, has often been used to produce *expectoration.*

439. *Pecu'li-um,* money. *Pecu'ni-a,* money.

PEC'ULATE, *v.* to steal public property (180-7). | PECU'NIARY, *a.* relating to money (180-7).

440. *Pel'l-o,* I call. *Pella't-um,* to call.

APPEALS', *n.* entreaties (214-1). | REPEAL', *v.* to rescind (181-2).

441. *Pel'l-o,* I drive. *Pul's-um,* to drive.

1. COMPUL'SORY, *a.* forcible.
EXPUL'SION, *n.* driving out (75-11).
IMPUL'SIVE, *a.* acting from impulse (118-2).
COMPELLED', *v.* constrained; forced (589).

REPUL'SIVE, *a.* forbidding; repelling (64-6).
REPUL'SIVENESS, *n.* the quality of being forbidding (9).
REPEL' (see page 34).
EXPEL' (see page 34).
IMPEL' (see page 34).

1. In all criminal prosecutions, the accused shall "have ***compulsory*** process for obtaining witnesses;" this is effected by means of a ***subpœna***, a writ commanding one to appear in court, which cannot be disregarded.

442. *Pen'd-eo,* I hang. *Pen'sum,* to hang.

1. PEN'DULUM, *n.* a vibrating body.
2. PROPEN'SITY, *n.* inclination.
3. APPEN'DIX, *n.* something added at the end.
INDEPEND'ENCE, *n.* state of not being subject to (14-4).

PERPENDIC'ULAR, *a.* at right angles to a given line (522-6).
PREPENSE', *a.* premeditated (371-3).
SUSPEND', *v.* to hang (146-3).
SUSPEN'SION, *n.* interruption (75-9).

1. The length of a yard-stick is determined by the ***pendulum*** of a clock.
2. Cattle have such a ***propensity*** for *salt,* that they will go a great distance to obtain it.
3. In some books, difficult or important points are placed in a ***compendious*** form, in an ***appendix***.

443. *Pen'd-o,* I weigh, I pay out. *Pen's-um,* to weigh, to pay out.

1. PEN'SION, *n.* stated allowance for past services.
COMPEN'DIOUS, *a.* comprehensive (442-3).

COMPEN'SATE, *v.* to give an equivalent for (222).
REC'OMPENSE, *n.* reward, compensation (86-2).

LATIN DERIVATIVES.

1. Every Government ought to *appreciate* the services of those wounded in its defense, and grant a *pension* or *annuity* which will enable them to live in *tranquillity* and *comfort*.

444. Pe'ne, almost.

1. PENIN'SULAS, n. (insula,) bodies of land nearly surrounded by water. but one; almost the last syllable.
2. PE'NULT, PENUL'TIMATE, n. (ultimus,) the last syllable
2. ANTEPENULT', ANTEPENUL'TIMATE, n. (ultimus,) the last syllable but two.

1. It is a fact that nearly all *peninsulas* point southward.
2. The ancient city of Alexandri'a has the accent on the *penult*, the modern on the *antepenult*, Alexan'dria.

445. Pen'etr-o, I pierce.

1. PENETRA'TION, n. acuteness. PEN'ETRATE, v. to pierce (169-6).
IMPEN'ETRABLE, a. not pierceable; incapable of being penetrated (422-1).

1. Had Charles I. possessed any *penetration*, it would have led him to *expedite* the departure of such a troublesome *malcontent* as Cromwell.

446. Pœnit't-eo, I repent. Pœ'na, punishment.

PE'NAL, a. enacting punishment (57-4).
PEN'ALTY, n. suffering in consequence of an act (82-1).
PEN'ITENCE, n. repentance (293-3).
REPENT', v. to feel sorrow for what one has done (152-1).
PENITEN'TIARY, n. a prison (181-1).
SUBPŒ'NA, n. a command to appear in court (441).

447. Per'i-or, I try. Perit'-us, trying.

EXPE'RIENCE, n. finding out by trial (176).
EXPERT', a. practised, skilful (138-3).
EXPER'IMENT, n. trial for the purpose of finding out (221).
EXPERT'NESS, n. skilfulness (576-5).

448. Persev'er-o, to persist (ā per and severus). See Severus.

449. Perso'n-a, a person.

1. PERSON'IFY, v. to ascribe life to inanimate objects.
2. PER'SONATED, v. represented the character of.

PER'SON, *n.* human being (12-1). PER'SONALLY, *adv.* in person (120-1).

1. In most European languages, nouns are of the *masculine* or feminine gender; but in the English, things without life are all neuter, and this enables us to *personify* them.

2. Alfred the Great *personated* a harper, and thus obtained access to the Danish camp.

450. *Pes (pe'd-is),* a foot.

1. PEDES'TRIAN, *n.* a foot traveller.
QUAD'RUPED, *n.* (quadra,) a four-footed animal (173-1).
EX'PEDITE, *v.* to hasten (445).
EXPEDI'TION, *n.* an important enterprise at a distance (35-2).
IMPED'IMENT, *n.* hindrance (96).
EXPE'DIENT, *n.* contrivance (38)

1. A peddler, especially if he is a *pedestrian,* has a fine opportunity to view a country.

451. *Pe't-o,* I seek. *Peti't-um,* to seek.

1. AP'PETITE, *n.* desire for food.
2. REPETI'TION, *n.* the doing or saying again.
3. COMPETI'TION, *n.* rivalry.
4. IMPET'UOUS, *a.* headstrong.
COMP'ETENT, *a.* capable (363-2).
CENTRIP'ETAL, *a.* (centrum,) tending to the centre (228-3).
IM'PETUS, *n.* force imparted (77-2).
REPEAT', *v.* to say or do again (456-2).
PET'ULANT. See PETULANS.

1. The climate of Greenland gives the Esquimeaux an *appetite* which enables him to eat train-oil and walrus flesh with *voracity.*

2. Constant *repetition* and close attention form the best " Art of Memorizing."

3. The Navigation Acts destroyed all *competition* in business by compelling the colonists to buy and sell in England.

4. The *impetuous* and *vindictive* character of General Lee brought him into many serious difficulties.

452. *Pet'ulans (petulan't-is),* saucy.
PET'ULANT, *a.* peevish (64-6).

453. *Pi'l-lo,* I pillage, I rob.

1. PIL'LAGE, *n.* robbing; the act of plundering.
PIL'FER, *v.* (facio,) to steal by petty theft (482).

1. Many of the Arabs perform no labor, but live entirely by *pillage.*

LATIN DERIVATIVES. 171

454. Pin'g-o, I paint. **Pic't-um,** to paint.

1. PICTURESQUE', a. forming a pleasing picture.
2. PAINT'ING, *part.* portraying in colors.

PICTS, n. a tribe of Germans who settled in Scotland (125-6).
DEPICT', v. picture (271).

1. The scenery of New Hampshire is so *picturesque* that the State is called the "Switzerland of America."
2. Michael Angelo (mī'-ka-el an'-gĕ-lo) was only twenty months in *painting* the Sistine (sis-teen) Chapel.

455. Pi'-o, I appease by sacrifice. **Pia't-um,** to appease by sacrifice.

1. EX'PIATORY, a. having power to atone.

EX'PIATE, v. to atone for (423).

1. The desire to offer *expiatory* sacrifices seems deeply *implanted* in the human heart.

456. Pi'-us, pious; religious.

1. IM'PIOUSLY, adv. profanely. | 2. PI'ETY, n. religion.

1. The Romans, knowing the antipathy of the Israelites to swine, *impiously* sacrificed them on the altar *consecrated* to the worship of God.
2. The *piety* of the prophet Daniel led him to *repeat* his *prayer* three times a day, though forbidden by Darius (da-rī'-us).

457. Pla'c-eo, I please. **Pla'cit-um,** to please.

1. COMPLA'CENCE, n. satisfaction.
PLA'CID, a. tranquil (64-5).

PLEAS'URE, n. satisfaction; enjoyment (165-1).
IMPLA'CABLE. See PLACO.

1. William Penn could not but feel *complacence* at the success of his *novel* peace policy.

458. Pla'c-o, I appease.
IMPLA'CABLE, a. not to be appeased (152-2).

459. Plan'g-o, I complain. **Planc't-um,** to complain.
COMPLAIN'ANTS, n. those who complain (250-7).

460. Plan't-a, a plant; the sole of the foot. **Plan't-o,** I plant. **Planta't-um,** to plant.

1. SUPPLANT', v. to displace; to undermine.

PLANT, n. a vegetable; a young tree or bush (22-4).

PLANTA'TION, *n.* a farm (189). | IMPLANT'ED, *v.* infixed; set in
TRANSPLANT'ING, *n.* removing | (455).
and planting in another place | TRANSPLANT' (see page 34).
(56-7). | IMPLANT' (see page 34).

1. Conway sent a letter to Washington, *explanatory* of his conduct in reference to the attempt to *supplant* Washington.

461. *Pla'n-us,* plain; smooth; evident.

1. PLANE, *n.* a level surface; an imaginary surface. | EXPLAN'ATORY, *a.* containing explanation (460).
PLAIN, *n.* a level surface; level land (170-2). | EXPLAIN', *v.* make intelligible (56-7).

1. Cut an orange into two equal parts, and each of the flat surfaces thus formed will be the *plane* of a great circle.

462. *Plau'd-o,* I clap; I applaud. ***Plau's-um,*** to applaud.

1. PLAUS'IBLE, *a.* right in appearance. | EXPLO'SIVE, *a.* liable to cause explosion (78-1).
EXPLO'SION, *n.* violent bursting (127). | EXPLODE', *v.* to burst with a loud report (270).

1. Duché, who opened the first Continental Congress with a solemn *invocation,* soon after addressed a letter to Washington, using the most *plausible* arguments to induce him to desert the American cause, and avow his loyalty to George III.

463. *Plebs (pleb'-is),* the common people.
PLEBE'IAN, *n.* one of the common people (434-3).

464. *Ple'-o,* I fill. ***Plet'-um,*** to fill. ***Ple'n-us,*** full.

1. EX'PLETIVE, *n.* something added to fill up. | ACCOM'PLISHED, *v.* performed (66-6).
2. IM'PLEMENTS, *n.* tools. | COM'PLEMENT, *n.* full number
3. COM'PLIMENT, *v.* to praise. | (394-3).
3. PLENIPOTEN'TIARY, *a.* (posse,) having full power; full. | REPLETE', *a.* filled again; completely filled (97-1).
4. PLEN'TIFUL, *a.* abundant. | SUPPLY'ING, *part.* providing
5. COMPLETE', *a.* perfect. | (18-1).
5. SUP'PLEMENT, *n.* an addition to supply defects. | PLE'NARY, *a.* full; sufficient (250-7).

1. The adverb "there" is frequently used simply to introduce a sentence, and is then considered a mere *expletive.*
2. There has been great improvement in all kinds of agricultural *implements.*
3. In 1795, the President was able to *compliment* Mr. Jay, our Minister *Plenipotentiary* to England, for his success in negotiating the treaty.
4. Artesian wells, which provide a *plentiful* supply of water, have been sunk in the deserts of Africa.
5. So many inventions are patented every year, that no Dictionary of Arts and Sciences is *complete* without a *supplement.*

465. *Pli'c-o,* I fold. *Plica't-um,* to fold. *Plec't-o,* I twine or weave. *Plex'-um,* to twine or weave.

1. COM'PLICATE, v. to render complex.
1. ACCOM'PLICE, n. a person joined in a plot.
2. EXPLIC'IT, a. clear.
3. DU'PLICATE, a. (duo,) twofold.
APPLICA'TION, n. the act of applying (124-2).
APPLY', v. to fix closely (195-6).

COMPLEX'ION, n. color of the skin (213-3).
DISPLAYED', v. exhibited (37-3).
IM'PLICATE, v. to involve (127).
PLI'ABLE, a. easily bent (178-1).
SIMPLIC'ITY, n. artlessness (180-2).
SIM'PLY, adv. merely (464-1).

1. When Aaron Burr was tried for treason, everything seemed to *complicate* the matter, but especially the difficulty of proving that he had an *accomplice.*
2. The laws of most of the States give *explicit* directions, in case a man dies *intestate.*
3. When Napoleon heard of the *nuptials* of Prince Jerome and Miss Patterson, of Baltimore, he sent to his brother a *duplicate* copy of the decree, prohibiting his sister-in-law from entering France.

466. *Plo'r-o,* I cry; I bewail. *Plora't-um,* to cry; to bewail.

1. IMPLORE', v. to entreat.
DEPLO'RABLE, a. lamentable (76-2).

DEPLORE', v. regret (66-6).
EXPLORE', v. to examine; to search through (562).

1. When the Northern foe invaded England, the wretched inhabitants sent a letter to *implore* the Romans to aid them in expelling their *assailant.*

467. *Plum'b-um,* lead.

1. PLUMBA'GO, *n.* a mineral consisting of carbon and, it may be, a little iron; black-lead.

PLUM'MET, *n.* a leaden weight at the end of a line used to sound the depth of water (357-3).

1. The term black-lead, for the *plumbago* of which pencils, etc., are made, is an unfortunate *misnomer*.

468. *Plus (plu'r-is),* more.

1. PLURAL'ITY, *n.* the greater number.
2. SUR'PLUS, *n.* what is over.

PLU'RAL, *a.* consisting of more than one; designating two or more (162).

1. In the Presidential election of 1800, neither Jefferson nor Burr had a *plurality* of votes.
2. In 1837, the *surplus* of revenue was distributed among the States.

469. *Po'li-o,* I polish.   *Polit'-um,* to polish.

1. POL'ISHED, *a.* smooth and glossy.
2. POLITE'NESS, *n.* elegance of manners.

1. Before glass was manufactured, *polished* plates of metal were used for mirrors.
2. Benjamin Franklin, at the French Court, was noted for his *politeness* and *suavity* of manners.

470. *Po'l-us,* the pole.

PO'LAR, *a.* relating to the pole (141-2).

471. *Po'm-um,* an apple; fruit.

1. POMOLOG'ICAL, *a.* (logos, Gr.,) relating to fruit.

POME'GRANATE, *n.* (granum,) a fruit (213-4).

1. *Pomological* societies have done much to improve the fruit-trees of the country.

472. *Pon'd-us (pon'der-is),* a weight.

1. PON'DERABLE, *a.* capable of being weighed.

PON'DEROUS, *a.* heavy (108-1).
PON'DER, *v.* consider (65-7).

1. What *sort* of bodies are *ponderable,* if all bodies have weight?

473. *Po'n-o,* I put or place.   *Pos'it-um,* to put or place.

1. POSTPONE', *v.* to put off; to defer to a future time.
2. DECOMPOSE', *v.* to resolve into the constituent parts.

LATIN DERIVATIVES.

Compos'ure, *n.* tranquillity (92-1).
Deposi'tion, *n.* removal from office (133-1).
Depos'it, *v.* to store (78).
Exposi'tion, *n.* a public exhibit (22-6).
Im'post, *n.* tax on imports (190-1).
Interpose', *v.* interfere (72).
Oppo'nent, *n.* an antagonist (21-5).

Propos'als, *n.* terms proposed (75-2).
Pos'itively, *adv.* peremptorily (75-5).
Proposi'tion, *n.* proposal (195-1).
Pos'itive, *a.* denoting quality without comparison (8-1).
Post'ure, *n.* attitude (126-3).
Depose' (see page 35).
Oppose', *v.* (see page 35).
Transpose', *v.* (see page 35).

1. Penn intended to visit Pennsylvania in 1692; but William III. having determined to *deprive* him of his charter, he was compelled to *postpone* his visit until 1699.

2. The ancient alchemists, while searching for a liquid that would *transmute* everything into gold, learned to *decompose* many substances.

474. *Pons (pon't-is)*, a bridge.

1. Pontif'icate, *n.* (facio,) the reign of a Pope.
2. Pontoon', *n.* a float used in forming a bridge.

1. The *pontificate* of Pius IX. began in 1846 and ended in 1878.
2. Both Darius (da-ri'-us) and Xerx'es crossed the Hellespont on *pontoon* bridges.

475. *Pop'ul-us*, the people. *Pub'lic-us*, public. *Publica't-io*, a publishing.

1. Popula'tion, *n.* the whole number of people.
1. Pop'ulous, *a.* full of people.
2. Public'ity, *n.* general notoriety.
2. Pub'lish, *v.* send out to the public.
    Peo'ple, *n.* a nation (11-3).

Pop'ulace, *n.* the common people (50-2).
Pop'ular, *a.* suitable to people in general (54-2).
Pub'lic, *a.* open to the knowledge of all (171-3).
Publica'tion, *n.* publishing; the act of offering a book to the public by sale (43-4).

1. To *facilitate* the administration of justice, the *judiciary* provides a judge for the *district*, if the *population* is *dense*; but in less *populous* portions of the country, one for each *circuit*.

2. To secure *publicity* to the Acts of Congress, the Constitution provides, that "Each House shall keep a journal of its proceedings, and, from time to time, *publish* the same."

476. Por'c-us, a hog.

1. Por'cupine, *n.* (spina, a thorn,) a rodent quadruped with quills on its body.
   1. The *porcupine* is a native of Africa and Asia, and also of Italy.

477. Por't-o, I carry. **Porta't-um,** to carry.

1. Port'able, *a.* easily carried.
2. Inopportune', *a.* unseasonable.
2. Port'ly, *a.* corpulent.
2. Portman'teau, *n.* (manus,) valise.
2. Portfo'lio, *n.* (folium,) a case for carrying loose sheets.
3. Port'als, *n.* entrances.
4. Porch, *n.* a portico.
5. Pur'port, *n.* design.
Export', *v.* to send out of the country (75-6).

Import'ant. *a.* momentous (146-3).
Import', *v.* to bring into a country (75-6).
Por'tico, *n.* an ornamental entrance (44-2).
Importu'nity, *n.* urgent solicitation (206-2).
Opportu'nity, *n.* fit time (195-1).
Report', *v.* narrate (5-1).
Report', *n.* rumor; an account received (114-1).
Transport' (see page 35).

1. Soldiers are generally compelled to cook their *victuals* in such utensils as are *portable.*
2. Doubtless, Gen. Prescott felt the *intrusion* of Col. Barton on his privacy to be very *inopportune;* while Barton felt no *compunction* of conscience in carrying off the *portly* old General, without giving him time to pack his *portmanteau,* or secure the *portfolio* containing his military plans.
3. One of the *portals* of the Temple at Jerusalem was beautifully *adorned.*
4. The Stoics derive their name from the stoa, or *porch,* in which Zeno taught.
5. The *purport* of every address made by Napoleon to his army was the *glorification* of France.

478. Pos'se, to be able. **Po'tens (poten't-is),** able, powerful.

1. Po'tent, *a.* powerful.
1. Pu'issant, *a.* powerful.

Po'tentate, *n.* a monarch (75-14).

LATIN DERIVATIVES.

POWER, *n.* might; influence; ability to act (98-1).
POS'SIBLE, *a.* that can be done (35-8).

1. Many circumstances seem to *corroborate* the *opinion*, that the Emperor of Russia will be one of the most *potent* (or *puissant*) monarchs of Europe.

479. *Pos'ter-us,* after.

1. PREPOS'TEROUS, *a.* absurd; utterly foolish.
POSTER'ITY, *n.* succeeding generations (345-2).

1. "How *preposterous,*" said some one to Columbus, "to suppose that we are on the surface of a ball that is turning round?"

480. *Pos'tul-o,* I demand. *Postula't-um,* to demand.

EXPOST'ULATED, *v.* reasoned earnestly with a view to dissuade (266).

481. *Po'tens (poten't-is).* See *Posse.*

482. *Pra'v-us,* crooked, wicked.

1. DEPRAV'ITY, *n.* wickedness.

1. The tendency that children have to *pilfer* and to *prevaricate*, proves the *depravity* of the human heart.

483. *Pre'ci-um* for *Pre'ti-um,* a price; esteem.

1. PRIZE, *v.* to esteem highly.
2. PRAISE, *v.* extol.
   APPRE'CIATE, *v.* to value; to estimate justly (443).
   PRICE, *n.* cost (414-1).
DEPRE'CIATED, *a.* lessened in value (43-2).
DEPRE'CIATE, *v.* to lessen in value (522-7).
PRE'CIOUS, *a.* valuable (24-1).

1. We cannot *prize* too highly the blessings of a just government.
2. The "Te Dē'um" is so called from the words with which the psalm commences, "We *praise* thee," or "We *laud* thee, O God."

484. *Pre'c-or,* I entreat. *Preca't-us,* entreating.

DEP'RECATE, *v.* regret deeply (35-8).
PRAYED, *v.* entreated; besought (125-6).
PRAYER, *n.* supplication (456-2).
PRECA'RIOUS, *a.* uncertain; unsettled (375).

485. *Præ'd-a,* prey ; plunder.

1. Prey, *n.* plunder.
Dep'redator, *n.* a robber; a plunderer (213-3).

Pred'atory, *a.* plundering; robbing (125-6).

1. The dilation and *contraction* of the eye enables a cat to seek her *prey* both night and day.

486. *Prehen'd-o,* I seize. *Prehen's-um,* to seize.

Apprehend', *v.* to arrest; to take hold of (509-3).
Apprehend'ed, *p.* arrested; seized (169-6).
Comprehend', *v.* take into the mind (158-2).
Comprehen'sion, *n.* perception (11-8).
En'terprise, *n.* undertaking (123-2).

Incomprehen'sible, *a.* not to be understood (205-5).
Impris'onment, *n.* incarceration (113).
Impreg'nable, *a.* not to be taken (76-3).
Prize, *n.* something captured (431).
Pris'oners, *n.* captives (85-1).
Surprise', *n.* wonder (11-7).

487. *Pre'm-o,* I press. *Pres's-um,* to press.

1. Compres'sible, *a.* yielding to pressure.
1. Pres'sure, *n.* force exerted against an obstacle.
2. Impres'sion, *n.* a mark made by pressure.

Oppres'sion, *n.* unjust severity (156-4).
Print, *v.* publish (186-2).
Expres'sion, *n.* the act of representing (112-1).
Compress', *v.* (see page 35).

1. Cotton is so *compressible* that, under a high *pressure,* its bulk can be greatly reduced.
2. Robinson Crusoe was startled when he saw the *impression* of a man's foot on the sand.

488. *Pri'm-us,* first. *Pri'or,* former.

1. Prior'ity, *n.* precedence.
Prim'rose, *n.* (rosa,) an early flowering plant (220).
Prime'val, *a.* (ævum,) primitive; original (173).

Prince, *n.* (capio,) son of a king (465-3).
Pri'or, *a.* antecedent (205-3).
Prin'cipal, *a.* (capio,) chief; highest in importance (7-1).

1. The Chinese claim *priority* in civilization over all other nations

LATIN DERIVATIVES.

489. *Pri'v-us*, one's own; not public.

1. PRIV'ILY, *adv.* secretly.
   DEPRIVE', *v.* to take from (473-1).

   PRI'VATE, *a.* secret (293-3).
   PRIVATEER', *n.* a private ship of war (431).

1. Many Puritans in England, perceiving that the *virulence* of their enemies increased, endeavored to leave *privily.*

490. *Pro'b-o*, I approve, I try. ***Proba't-um*,** to prove, to try.

1. PROB'ABLE, *a.* likely.
2. PROOF, *n.* confirmation.
   PROBA'TION, *n.* trial (293-3).
   PROB'ITY, *n.* integrity (696).
   APPROBA'TION, *n.* satisfaction (76-2).
   APPROVE', *v.* be pleased with (216-1).

   PROBE, *v.* to examine by thrusting in an instrument (177-3).
   PROVE, *v.* to test; to ascertain as truth (268-2).
   PROB'ABLY, *adv.* in a probable manner (74-1).
   REPROVE', *v.* to rebuke (75-13).

1. Is it *probable*, that Africa and South America were once united, and that the *disruption* was effected by some sudden *convulsion* of nature?
2. The lifting of the kettle-lid by the steam is *proof* of the *expansive* force of heat.

491. *Promp't-us*, prompt, ready.

1. PROMPT'ITUDE, *n.* cheerful alacrity.
   PROMPT'LY, *adv.* readily; quickly (92-4).

1. The Geneva Award of $15,500,000 was paid by Great Britain with *commendable* ***promptitude.***

492. *Pro'p-e*, near. ***Prox'im-us*,** nearest, next.

1. APPROX'IMATE, *v.* come near.
   APPROACH', *n.* advance (598-1).

   PROXIM'ITY, *n.* immediate nearness; the state of being next (60-2).

1. We cannot obtain exactly the square root of .1, but we can *approximate* to it by means of a *decimal.*

493. *Pro'pri-us*, one's own; fit; peculiar.

APPRO'PRIATE, *a.* suitable; proper (44-2).
PROP'ERTY, *n.* that which belongs to a person or thing (106).
PROPRI'ETY, *n.* justness (11-5).

PROP'ER, *a.* suitable; appropriate; right (66-6).
PROPRI'ETOR, *n.* a person who received a grant of land in letters-patent from the king (248-2).

494. Pros'per (ŭ pro and spero). See Spero.

495. Pu'er, a boy.
1. PU'ERILE, *a.* childish; boyish.

1. James I. spent much of his time in *diversions* of the most **puerile** character.

496. Pug'n-a, a battle. Pu'gil, a boxer.
1. PUGNA'CIOUS, *a.* disposed to fight.
2. PU'GILIST, *n.* one who fights with the fists.

REPUG'NANCE, *n.* aversion (62-3).
REPUG'NANT, *a.* adverse (395-2).

1. A **pugnacious,** quarrelsome disposition, will be very likely to bring a person into trouble.
2. A person must undergo a severe training, before he can be an expert **pugilist.**

497. Pul'mo (pulmo'n-is), the lungs.
1. PUL'MONARY, *a.* relating to the lungs.

1. In speaking of pleurisy, or any other **pulmonary** affection, it is incorrect to add the words "of the lungs." To speak of "lumbago in the back" is a similar error.

498. Pul'v-is (pul'ver-is), dust.
1. PUL'VERIZE, *v.* to reduce to fine powder by beating, grinding, etc.
2. PULVERIZA'TION, *n.* the reducing to powder.
3. POW'DER, *n.* dust.

1. Many spices are so *pungent*, that it is necessary to **pulverize** them before using.
2. The **pulverization** of many substances can be effected by grinding or beating.
3. Charcoal must be reduced to an impalpable **powder** before it is fit for a *dentifrice*.

499. Pun'g-o, I sting. Punc't-um, to sting, to point.
1. PUNCT'URE, *v.* pierce with a pointed instrument.
2. PUNCTUAL'ITY, *n.* exactness in regard to time.

LATIN DERIVATIVES. 181

3. PUNCT'UATE, *v.* to mark with points. | COMPUNC'TION, *n.* sting (477-2).
PUN'GENT, *a.* biting (498-1).

1. To perform *vaccination*, *puncture* the skin and insert a particle of *pure vaccine* matter.

2. The want of *punctuality* in business transactions has ruined many enterprising men.

3. To *punctuate* an article correctly is oftentimes a very difficult task.

500. *Pu'ni-o,* I punish. ***Puni't-um,*** to punish.

1. PU'NITIVE, *a.* inflicting punishment. | IMPU'NITY, *n.* freedom from punishment (31-3).

1. Every law has a *punitive* clause, definitely stating the punishment for its *violation*; imprisonment or fine is the punishment for refusing to obey a *subpœna*.

501. *Pur'g-o,* I make clean. ***Purga't-um,*** to make clean.

1. EX'PURGATED, *part.* purged.

1. The law allows objectionable books to be suppressed or *expurgated*.

502. *Pu'r-us,* pure.

PURE, *a.* free from impurity (499-1). | PU'RITAN, *n.* one of a religious sect (216-1).

503. *Pusil'l-us,* weak; small.

1. PUSILLANIM'ITY, *n.* (animus,) littleness of mind.

1. Even the friends of the Duke of Monmouth despised the *pusillanimity* which he exhibited after his defeat.

504. *Pu't-o,* I think; I cut or prune. ***Puta't-um,*** to think; to cut or prune.

1. IMPUTE', *v.* ascribe.
2. DEPUTA'TION, *n.* persons commissioned.
3. AMPUTA'TION, *n.* cutting off.
ACCOUNTS', *n.* reckonings (42-1).

DISPUT'ED, *a.* undecided (108-2).
DEP'UTY·GOV'ERNOR, *n.* one who acts in place of the Governor (248-2).
REPUTA'TION, *n.* character (114-2).

1. Historians *impute* many atrocities to Brant, but it does not appear that he was *responsible* for the Wyoming massacre.

2. In 1781, the soldiers at Morristown, having suffered greatly from want of their *regular* pay, mutinied; but on their way to Philadelphia they were met by a ***deputation*** from Congress, who relieved their *immediate* wants.

3. Santa Anna was so severely wounded in the leg that ***amputation*** was necessary.

505. ***Qua'l-is,*** such as; of what kind.

1. QUALIFICA'TIONS, *n.* (facio,) those things which fit a person for a place.
2. QUAL'ITY, *n.* character; degree of excellence.
3. QUAL'IFY, *v.* to render capable.
4. DISQUAL'IFY, *v.* render unfit.
 DISQUAL'IFIED, *p.* rendered unfit (180-4).

1. When the Constitution was framed, there were many diverse opinions as to the ***qualifications*** necessary for the Presidency.
2. The Tyrians manufactured a purple cloth, of very superior ***quality***, designed for the *vesture* of kings.
3. Lincoln spent months in the study of Geometry, in order to ***qualify*** himself to demonstrate any proposition in law.
4. Several things ***disqualify*** a person for the Presidency of the United States · such as holding another office, etc.

506. ***Quar't-us,*** the fourth. ***Quad'r-a,*** a square.

1. SQUAD'RON, *n.* a detachment of ships of war.
 QUAR'ANTINE, *n.* restraint of intercourse to which a ship is subjected on suspicion of infection (180-5).
 QUAR'TAN, *a.* returning every fourth day (512-4).
 QUADRILAT'ERAL, *a.* (latus,) having four sides (313-4).
 QUAD'RUMANE, *n.* (manus,) an animal having four feet that correspond to the hands of a man (52-2).
 SQUARE, *a.* applied to area or surface (313-3).

1. In 1778, France sent a ***squadron*** to aid the American cause; and the British evacuated Philadelphia.

507. ***Qua't-io*** (in compounds, ***cutio***), I shake.
 Quas's-um (in compounds, ***cussum***), to shake.

1. CONCUS'SION, *n.* violent agitation.
 DISCUSS,' *v.* to argue (254).
 DISCUS'SION, *n.* debate (21-2).

1. The mere ***concussion*** of the air, produced by cannonading, has often proved very *detrimental* to health.

LATIN DERIVATIVES.

508. *Que′r-or,* I complain.

1. QUAR′REL, *v.* to contend angrily.
1. QUAR′RELSOME, *a.* easily provoked to contest.
2. QUER′ULOUS, *a.* habitually complaining.
   QUAR′RELLING, *n.* angry contention (75-8).

1. It is easy to *quarrel,* if you are of a *quarrelsome* disposition.
2. Philip's neglect, joined to his *taciturn* disposition, rendered Queen Mary still more *querulous* and irritable.

509. *Quæ′r-o* (in compounds, *quiro*), I seek; I ask. *Quæsi′t-um* (in compounds, *quisitum*), to seek; to ask.

1. QUEST, *n.* search.
2. PER′QUISITE, *n.* fee.
3. REQUISI′TION, *n.* demand.
4. REQUEST′, *n.* demand.
   ACQUIRE′, *v.* to obtain (140-1).
   ACQUISI′TION, *n.* the act of obtaining (195-6).
   CON′QUEST, *n.* subjugation (75-8).

EX′QUISITE, *a.* excessively nice (193-2).
INQUIS′ITIVE, *a.* prying (146-3).
QUE′RY, *n.* question (186-2).
QUES′TION, *n.* query (169-6).
REQ′UISITE, *a.* necessary (231-1).
CON′QUEROR, *n.* one who subdues (180-6).

1. The sanguine *temperament* of Ponce de Leon, led him to go in *quest* of a fountain whose waters would restore youth and beauty to his wrinkled *visage.*
2. In some offices, no *perquisite* is allowed, the remuneration being a fixed *salary.*
3. When a *requisition* is made for a person charged with crime, it is the duty of the Governor to resort to no *evasion* to withhold him, but to *apprehend* him at once.
4. As soon as the *pusillanimous* king was opposed with firmness and *courage,* he acceded to every *request,* even to the signing of Magna-Charta.

510. *Qui′es (quie′t-is),* rest.

1. ACQUIESCE′, *v.* to comply.
2. QUIES′CENCE, *n.* state of repose.
3. RE′QUIEM, *n.* a hymn for the dead.
4. QUI′ET, *n.* rest; repose.
5. QUI′ETUDE, *n.* tranquillity; freedom from agitation.
   COY, *a.* reserved; shy (120-5).

1. When the "Three Lower Counties" resolved to separate from Pennsylvania, Penn determined to *acquiesce* in their decision.
2. Although Charles V. resigned his *regal* power, he did not find that *quiescence* which he expected.
3. The *requiem* for departed *royalty* has *rarely* come from sadder hearts than that sung for Mer'cedes, the young Queen of Spain.
4. Late researches make it *certain* that Charles V., in the *quiet* of the monastery, was busy with State affairs.
5. In a Shaker village we are impressed with the *quietude* that prevails.

511. *Quin'que,* five. *Quin'ta,* a fifth.

1. QUINTILL'ION, *n.* a million twice multiplied by a million.
2. QUINTES'SENCE, *n.* (esse,) pure or concentrated essence.

1. It requires seven figures to express a *million*, and nineteen to express one *quintillion*.
2. He who practises the Golden Rule will exhibit the *quintessence* of politeness.

512. *Quot,* how many; as many as.

1. QUO'TA, *n.* just share.
2. QUO'RUM, *n.* a number sufficient to transact business.
3. AL'IQUOT, *a.* (alius,) an aliquot part of a number is one that will divide it without a remainder.
4. QUOTID'IAN, *a.* (dies,) daily.

1. When war breaks out, every State is required to furnish its *quota* of troops.
2. In the Congress of the United States, "a majority of each House shall constitute a *quorum* to do business."
3. Each American coin, except the three-cent piece, is an *aliquot* part of the dollar and the eagle.
4. An ague which returns every day is called *quotidian;* every third day, or every other day, tertian; every fourth day, *quartan.*

513. *Ra'bi-es,* madness.

1. RAB'ID, *a.* mad.
2. RAVE, *v.* to talk wildly.
RA'VINGS, *n.* wild, delirious talk (256-1).

1. So many dogs become *rabid,* that in large cities it is *safer* to muzzle them.
2. It is painful to visit an insane asylum, and hear the unfortunate inmates *rave* on so many strange subjects.

LATIN DERIVATIVES.

514. *Ra'di-us,* a rod, a spoke.

1. Ra'dius, *n.* one-half of a diameter.
Irra'diate, *v.* to illuminate (322-3).
Ra'diance, *n.* effulgence; brilliancy (64-4).
Rays, *n.* lines of light (322-3).

1. The *radius* of the earth is a little less than four thousand miles.

515. *Ra'dix (radi'c-is),* a root.

1. Rad'ical, *a.* fundamental.
Erad'icate, *v.* to root out (396-1).
Rad'ically, *adv.* fundamentally; originally; primitively (8-2).

1. There are *radical* differences in the meanings of words, perceived by those only who know the derivation.

516. *Ra'd-o,* I shave; I scrape. ***Ra's-um,*** to shave; to scrape.

1. Razed, *v.* demolished.
2. Era'sure, *n.* obliteration; a scratching out.
3. Abra'sion, *n.* the act of rubbing off.
4. Erase', *v.* efface.

1. After the taking of Jerusalem, the city was first given over to *rapine,* and then *razed* to its foundations.
2. The *erasure* of lead-pencil marks is easily effected by means of India-rubber.
3. The process of cutting glass, stone, etc., by the sand-blast was suggested by the *abrasion* of windows on the coast of New Jersey.
4. India-rubber, or caoutchouc (kōō'chōōk), will *erase* lead-pencil marks.

517. *Ran'ce-o,* I am stale or rancid.

1. Ran'corous, *a.* malignant.

1. The Pequods secretly cherished the most *rancorous* feelings towards the Connecticut settlers.

518. *Ra'pi-o,* I snatch. ***Rapt'-um,*** to snatch.

1. Surrepti'tious, *a.* done by stealth.
Rapa'cious, *a.* greedy (36).
Rap'idly, *adv.* swiftly (35-8).
Rap'ine, *n.* plunder (516-1).
Rapt'ure, *n.* ecstasy (64-4).

1. Soldiers, in an enemy's country, sometimes resort to *surreptitious* means to obtain better food.

519. Ra'r-us, scarce; rare; not thick.

1. RAR'EFY, v. to make less dense.
   RARE'LY, adv. seldom; not often (510-3).

   1. Heat has a tendency to *rarefy* bodies; cold, to contract them.

520. Rat'-us, thinking; judging.

1. RAT'IFY, v. sanction.
2. RA'TION, n. fixed allowance.
2. IRRA'TIONAL, a. not according to reason.

   REA'SON, n. efficient cause (522-5).
   RA'TIONAL, a. agreeable to reason (76-2).

   1. Three-fourths of the States, either by their Legislatures or by conventions, must *ratify* an amendment.
   2. After the scanty *ration* which often falls to the soldier, it is not *irrational* to suppose that he is willing to *satiate* himself with food obtained from the enemy by *surreptitious* means.

521. Re'cens (recen't-is), new; recent.

RE'CENT, a. late (584-4). | RE'CENTLY, adv. lately (302-1).

522. Reg-o, I rule. **Rect-um,** to rule. **Rect-us,** right. **Reg'num,** a reign. **Reg'ul-a,** a rule.

1. REG'ULATE, v. to adjust methodically.
2. INCOR'RIGIBLE, a. irreclaimable.
3. CORREC'TION, n. making right.
4. INTERREG'NUM, n. the interval in which a throne is vacant between two reigns.
5. REC'TIFY, v. to correct.
6. RECT'ANGLE, n. (angulus,) a right-angled parallelogram.
7. ERECT', v. to build.
   CORRECT'LY, adv. properly (65-2).
   INCORRECT', a. wrong; erroneous (7-1).

   REC'TITUDE, n. uprightness (62-3).
   RE'GAL, a. kingly (510-2).
   RE'GENT, n. one who governs in place of the sovereign (326).
   REG'ULAR, a. according to established laws (504-2).
   REIGN, n. the time during which a sovereign exercises authority (213-3).
   REGA'LIA, n. ensigns of royalty (216-4).
   REG'IMEN, n. systematic course of living (402-2).
   ROY'ALTY, n. kingship (510-3).
   RULE, n. regulation (65-13).

   1. The Constitution *vests* in Congress "The power to coin money *regulate* the value thereof," etc.

2. Several States provide institutions in which ***incorrigible*** boys are subjected to a *rigorous* discipline.

3. The ***correction*** of a bad habit is so difficult that it is safest not to form any.

4. Louis XVI. was beheaded in 1793, and Napoleon became First Consul in 1800. During the ***interregnum,*** various changes were made in the Government.

5. There is no good *reason* for calling America after Amerigo, but it is too late to ***rectify*** the mistake.

6. In a ***rectangle*** the base is *perpendicular* to the height.

7. In some cities it is illegal to *erect* a frame *tenement*, as the danger of fire tends to *depreciate* all the surrounding property.

523. *Rep't-um,* to creep.

1. REP′TILE, *n.* an animal that crawls on its belly.

   1. The anaconda is the largest ***reptile*** found in America.

524. *Res,* a thing.

1. RE′ALLY, *adv.* actually.
REAL′ITY, *n.* actual existence (204-1).
RE′ALIZE, *v.* to consider as real (125-3).
RE′AL, *a.* actual (37-2).

   1. The Jewish nation never ***really*** submitted to the Roman yoke.

525. *Ri′de-o,* I laugh. ***Ri′s-um,*** to laugh.

DERIDE′, *v.* laugh at in a contemptuous manner (140-8).
DERI′SION, *n.* ridicule (175-2).
RID′ICULE, *n.* derision (253).
RIDIC′ULOUS, *a.* worthy of ridicule (22-3).
RIS′IBLE, *a.* pertaining to laughter (22-3).

526. *Ri′g-eo,* I am stiff (as with cold).

RI′GID, *a.* strict (145). | RIG′OROUS, *a.* severe (522-2).

527. *Ri′g-o,* I water. ***Riga′t-um,*** to water.

1. IR′RIGATE, *v.* to water.

   1. In many countries, it is necessary for the farmer to have a *reservoir* of water, from which to ***irrigate*** his land.

528. *Ri′v-us,* a stream. ***Ri′p-a,*** a bank, a shore.

1. RI′VAL, *n.* a competitor; an antagonist.
2. RIV′ULET, *n.* a little stream of water; a rill.
3. UNRI′VALLED, *a.* having no rival.
4. RIV′ER, *n.* a large stream of water.

DERIVA'TION, n. origin, act of tracing origin or descent (20).

ARRIVE', v. come to (see page 35).
DERIVE' (see page 35).

1. In 1632, Gustavus Adolphus, having found means to *subsidize* a large force in France, met his formidable *rival* at Lutzen.
2. The Rubicon was a *rivulet* separating Italy from Gaul. Cæsar having planned an *invasion* of Italy, paused when he arrived at this river; then, hurrying across, he exclaimed, "The Rubicon is *passed*."
3. England was for many years *unrivalled* in the production of tin.
4. Trace the *river* Danube to its *source*, in Baden, and you will find it a tiny rill.

529. *Ro'b-ur (rob'or-is)*, an oak; strength.

1. CORROB'ORATIVE, a. tending to confirm; having the power of giving strength.

ROBUST', a. vigorous (257).
CORROB'ORATE, v. to confirm (478).

1. Tradition specifies the exact mountain on which the ark rested; but travellers find nothing *corroborative* of the statement.

530. *Ro'g-o*, I ask. *Roga't-um*, to ask.

1. AR'ROGATE, v. to assume to one's self.
1. PREROG'ATIVE, n. an exclusive privilege.
2. INTERROG'ATIVE, a. containing a question.
3. PROROGUE', v. to continue the English Parliament from one session to another.

4. AB'ROGATE, v. to repeal.
DEROG'ATORY, a. tending to lessen in value (140-5).
AB'ROGATED, v. repealed (211-1).
INTERROGA'TION, n. a question (305-2).
AR'ROGANT, a. haughty (121-3).

1. The Stuarts imagined they had a "divine right" to *arrogate* every power, and to claim every *prerogative*.
2. The *interrogative* form of the verb is limited to the Indicative and Potential moods.
3. In England, only the Queen has power to *prorogue* Parliament, though she need not do it in person.
4. In despotic governments, the sovereign has power to *abrogate* a law.

531. *Ro's-a*, a rose.

1. RO'SEATE, a. rosy.

1. A *roseate* hue in the sky in the evening is a *presage* of fair weather on the morrow.

532. Ro't-a, a wheel.

1. Ro'tary, *a.* turning.
2. Rotun'da, *n.* any building that is round both on the outside and inside.

Rota'tion, *n.* rotary motion (14-3).
Rotund'ity, *n.* sphericity; roundness (140-8).

1. By the *rotary* motion of the earth, a person living on the equator, moves more than one thousand miles in an hour.
2. The paintings which *encircle* the *rotunda* of the Capitol at Washington are generally historical subjects.

533. Ru'd-is, rude, ignorant.

1. Ru'diments, *n.* the beginnings of any branch of knowledge.
2. Rude, *a.* uncivil.
Er'udite, *a.* well instructed; learned (140-10).

1. The most skilful teachers should be employed to instruct children in the *rudiments*.
2. Never be *rude* to the aged, but be attentive to their counsel.

534. Ru'men (ru'min-is), the throat.

Ru'minants, *n.* animals that chew the cud (247).

535. Ru'mor, a common report.

1. Ru'mor, *n.* a common report.

1. In 1778, the *rumor*, that a *simultaneous* attack by land and sea was to be made on Newport, alarmed the royalists.

536. Rup't-um, to break.

Abrupt', *a.* having a sudden termination (146-3).
Bank'rupt, *n.* one who cannot pay his debts (131-1).
Corrupt', *a.* decomposed (68-3).
Disrup'tion, *n.* the act of breaking asunder (490).
Erup'tion, *n.* a bursting out 180-10).
Rupt'ure, *n.* open hostility, breach of peace (218-1).

537. Rus (ru'r-is), the country.

1. Rus'ticate, *v.* to reside in the country.
Rus'tic, *a.* unpolished (85).
Ru'ral, *a.* belonging to the country (120-5).

1. It is pleasant in the summer-time to *rusticate* in the mountains, or at the sea-shore.

538. Sac'char-um, sugar.

Sac'charine, *a.* having the qualities of sugar (1-6).

539. Sa'cer (sac'r-i), holy, sacred.

1. Con'secrate, *v.* to devote to sacred purposes.
   Des'ecrate, *v.* to abuse a sacred thing (228-2).
   Sacerdo'tal, *a.* (dos, do'-tis, a dowry,) priestly (576).
   Con'secrated, *p.* devoted to sacred purposes (456-1).
   Sac'rifice, *n.* (facio,) consecration (165-2).
   Sac'rilege, *n.* (lego,) violation of what is sacred (195-4).

1. In 1101, the Normans were able to *consecrate* a "Round Church," modelled after the Church of the Holy Sepulchre, in Jerusalem.

540. Sa'gax (saga'c-is), knowing; foreseeing.

Sage, *a.* wise (204-4).
Saga'cious, *a.* discerning (140-6).
Pre'sage, *n.* sign (531).
Sagac'ity, *n.* discernment (192-2).

541. Sal, salt.

1. Saline', *a.* consisting of salt.
2. Sali'na, *n.* a salt marsh.
   Sal'ary, *n.* a fixed annual compensation for services (509-2).
   Salt, *n.* a substance used for seasoning (442-2).

1. To *satisfy* a natural craving for salt, there is, in many countries, a *superabundance* of *saline* substances.
2. Cattle will go a long distance to find a *salina*.

542. Sa'l-io, I leap; I spring. Sal't-um, to leap; to spring.

1. Des'ultory, *a.* immethodical.
2. Sal'ly, *v.* to rush out suddenly.
2. Assail', *v.* to attack.
3. Exult', *v.* triumph.
   Assail'ant, *n.* one who makes an attack (466).
   Assault', *n.* sudden attack (550).
   Sa'lient, *a.* forcing itself on the attention; prominent; conspicuous (135-2).
   In'sult, *n.* an affront (179-2).
   Result', *n.* effect; consequence (23).

1. *Desultory* reading is not only of little practical *utility*, but is generally a great *detriment* to the mind.

LATIN DERIVATIVES.

2. Gansevoort, besieged in Fort Schuyler, determined to **sally** from the fort and **assail** the enemy.

3. Wellington would never **exult** over a great victory. "Except a great defeat," said he, "there is nothing worse than a great victory."

543. *Sa'l-us (salu't-is),* health; safety. *Salu'br-is,* healthful.

1. SALUTA'TION, *n.* greeting.
2. SALU'TATORY, *n.* introductory oration at a commencement.
3. SALVA'TION, *n.* preservation.

SA'FER, *a.* more secure (513-1).
SALU'BRITY, *n.* tendency to promote health (125-7).
SAL'UTARY, *a.* advantageous; wholesome (76-2).

1. Great diversity exists in the *conventional* forms of **salutation**. The ancient Greeks avoided all *verbiage*, and simply said "Rejoice."

2. *Terseness* of style should characterize both the **salutatory** and the *valedictory*; the subject is so *trite* that there is always danger of *verbosity*.

3. In Sheridan's famous ride, the horse seemed to know that the **salvation** of the army depended on him.

544. *Sanc't-us,* holy; sacred.

1. SANC'TITY, *n.* sacredness.
2. SANC'TIFY, *v.* to make holy.
3. SAINT, *n.* a person sanctified.
SANC'TION, *n.* approval (418-2).

SANCTIMO'NIOUS, *a.* having an appearance of holiness (112-4).
SANCT'UARY, *n.* a sacred place; a consecrated spot; a place of worship (228-2).

1. The Mohammedans have such regard for the **sanctity** of the mosque, that they deem it *irreverent* to enter with the shoes on.

2. Many things in this *temporal* existence, which are *inscrutable* to man, may be intended to **sanctify** and prepare him for a happier condition.

3. Neither the humble *parentage* of Thomas à Becket, nor his enormous wealth, prevented the people from regarding him as a **saint**.

545. *San'gu-is (san'guin-is),* blood.

1. CONSANGUIN'ITY, *n.* relationship by blood.
2. COUS'IN, *n.* the child of an uncle or aunt.

SAN'GUINARY, *a.* bloody (42-3).
SAN'GUINE, *a.* confident (92-2).

1. As court etiquette does not allow a sovereign in Europe to *espouse* a subject, there is no alternative but to choose a person already connected by **consanguinity.**

2. On the question of *matrimony*, neither Queen Mary nor Queen Victoria gave the nation any opportunity to *speculate*. Mary married her ***cousin,*** William of Orange; Victoria, her cousin, Albert.

546. *Sa'n-us,* sound; healthy.

INSANE', *a.* deranged in mind; mad (20-3).
INSAN'ITY, *n.* derangement of mind (170-1).
SAN'ITARY, *a.* pertaining to health (558-2).
SAN'ITY, *n.* the condition or quality of being sane (305-2)

547. *Sa'pi-o,* I savor; I know.

1. SA'VORY, *a.* agreeable to the taste.
INSIP'ID, *a.* tasteless (197-2).
SA'PIENT, *a.* wise (115-1).

1. To an Esquimaux, the most *sumptuous* repast is not so ***savory*** as bread *saturated* with train-oil.

548. *Sa'po (sapo'nis),* soap.

1. SOAP, *n.* a substance used for cleansing (The result of the combination of acid obtained from fatty bodies, and an alkali.)
2. SAPONA'CEOUS, *a.* soapy.

1. The great *consumption* of ***soap*** and paper, makes it very desirable to find a substitute for each of these indispensable articles.

2. In Europe, there is a plant called soap-wort, because it has ***saponaceous*** qualities.

549. *Sa'tis,* enough. *Sa'tur,* full, sated.

INSA'TIABLE, *a.* not to be satisfied (228-2).
SA'TIATE, *v.* to feed to the full (520-2).
SATI'ETY, *n.* repletion (363-1).
SAT'ISFY, *v.* to gratify wants to the full extent (541-1).
SAT'URATED, *p.* soaked (547-1).

550. *Sca'l-a,* a ladder.

1. SCALE, *v.* to climb.

1. Although Montcalm was a *veteran*, yet Wolfe deceived him by a feigned *assault* on the Lower Town, while his *ulterior* design was to ***scale*** the Heights of Abraham, and attack the Upper Town.

LATIN DERIVATIVES.

551. Scan'd-o, I climb. **Scan's-um,** to climb.

1. SCAN, *v.* to examine carefully.
2. CONDESCEND', *v.* to stoop.
ASCENT', *n.* climbing (66-6).

DESCEND'ANTS, *n.* offspring (75-4).
TRANSCEND', *v.* rise beyond (205-5).
DESCEND' (see page 36).

1. *Science* enables us to *scan* the depths of *space* and measure the distances of the *fixed* stars.
2. "To **condescend** to argue with these rebels, or to *extenuate* their conduct," said Lord Grenville, "is to favor the rebellion."

552. Sci'-o, I know. **Scien'ti-a,** knowledge.

CON'SCIENCE, *n.* the knowledge of our own actions as right or wrong (92-5).
CONSCIEN'TIOUS, *a.* obedient to the dictates of conscience (114-1).

SCI'ENCE, *n.* truth ascertained (551-1).
SCIENTIF'IC, *a.* (facio,) well versed in science (18-3).
UNCON'SCIOUS, *a.* not conscious (112-4).

553. Scri'b-o, I write. **Script'-um,** to write.

CONSCRIP'TION, *n.* a compulsory enrolment for military service (350-1).
CIRCUMSCRIBE', *v.* to limit (432-2).
DESCRIP'TION, *n.* delineation (173-2).

SCRIB'BLING, *n.* writing carelessly (179-1).
SCRIPT'URES, *n.* the Bible (22-5).
DESCRIBE' (see page 36).
PRESCRIBE' (see page 36).
SUBSCRIBE' (see page 36).

554. Scru't-or, I examine. **Scruti'n-ium,** scrutiny.

INSCRU'TABLE, *a.* unsearchable (544-2).
SCRU'TINIZE, *v.* examine closely (374).

555. Scul'p-o (sculp't-um), to carve on stone.

SCULP'TOR, *n.* a carver (417-1).

556. Sec'o, I cut. **Sect'-um,** to cut.

1. IN'SECT, *n.* a small animal.
1. INSECTIV'OROUS, *a.* (voro,) eating insects.

2. BISECT', *v.* (bini,) to divide into two equal parts (Geom.); to cut into two parts.

3. **Intersec'tion**, *n.* the act or state of intersecting.

Sec'tion, *n.* division (216-5).
Intersect', *v.* (see page 36).

1. To watch a bird and see if it eats an *insect*, helps us to decide whether or not the bird is *insectivorous.* Do you think that a bird would eat a *centipede?*

2. You should learn to *bisect* straight lines without the aid of compasses.

3. It was an old custom in England, to bury a suicide at the *intersection* of two roads.

557. Sec'ul-um, an age.

1. **Sec'ular**, *a.* pertaining to the present world.

1. Solomon enjoins a proper *supervision* over *secular* affairs, and a wise *providence* in preparing for the future.

558. Se'd-eo, I sit. **Ses's-um,** to sit. **Seda't-us,** calm; peaceful.

1. **Subsid'iary**, *a.* aiding.
1. **Insid'ious**, *a.* treacherous.
2. **Sed'ulous**, *a.* assiduous.
3. **Siege**, *n.* the placing of an army before a place to take it.
4. **Res'idue**, *n.* remainder.
5. **Assize'**, *n.* a court of justice.
   Assid'uous, *a.* sedulous; unremitting (246-1).
   Assess'or, *n.* one who assesses (57-2).
   Besieg'ers, *n.* those who lay siege (60-2).
   Possessed', *v.* owned (10).
   Posses'sion, *n.* holding (193)

Pres'ident, *n.* one who presides (44-2).
Pres'idency, *n.* office of chief magistrate (12-1).
Reside', *v.* to dwell (246-1).
Sedate', *a.* calm (435-2).
Sed'entary, *a.* requiring much sitting (126-3).
Sed'iment, *n.* dregs (146-1).
Vice-Pres'ident, *n.* (vicis,) one in place of the President (21-3).
Ses'sion, *n.* a sitting (14-2).
Sub'sidize, *v.* to obtain by payment of a subsidy (528-1).
Supersede', *v.* to take the place of another (287-1).

1. St. Leger's expedition was *subsidiary* to Burgoyne's campaign; but, ignorant of the *insidious* character of the Indians, he found himself deserted by them in the time of his greatest need.

2. To secure sound minds in sound bodies, *sedulous* care should be taken of the *sanitary* condition of every *seminary.*

3. The most noted *siege* on record is probably the siege of Troy, which commenced 1194 and ended 1184 B. C.

LATIN DERIVATIVES. 195

4. Many of the American colonists in Palestine refused to *stay*; the *residue* sank into poverty.

5. Judges of *assize itinerate* through the counties of England and hold jury trials twice a year.

559. Se'm-en (sem'in-is), seed.

DISSEMINA'TION, *n.* general diffusion (288-2).

SEM'INARY, *n.* school, academy, college, etc. (558-2).

560. Se'nex (se'nis), old, aged.

1. SE'NIOR, *a.* older; prior in age or rank.

SEN'ATE, *n.* one of the Houses of Congress (180-4).

1. Where two members of a family have the same name, it is common to *add* the word *senior* to the elder of the two.

561. Sen'ti-o, I feel; I think. Sen's-um, to feel; to think.

1. ASSENT', *v.* to consent.
2. RESENT', *v.* consider as an affront.
3. SEN'TIMENTS, *n.* thoughts.
4. SCENT, *v.* perfume.
5. SENSE, *n.* sensation.
6. SENTEN'TIOUS, *a.* short and energetic.

SEN'TENCE, *n.* doom pronounced (10-2).
DISSENT', *v.* to differ in opinion (100-1).
PRESEN'TIMENT, *n.* foreboding (62-3).
SEN'SITIVE, *a.* easily affected (204-2).

1. Spain refuses to *assent* to the abolition of slavery in Cuba.
2. The Chinese Embassy *resent* the indignities inflicted on their countrymen, while *prosecuting* their lawful undertakings.
3. Many wise *sentiments* are contained in some of the Proverbs.
4. It is said that a *single* grain of musk will *scent* a room for years.
5. The *sense* of smell enables animals to track their prey for a great distance.
6. A *proverb* is sometimes a *sermon* in a *sententious* form.

562. Sepul'chr-um, a grave.

1. SEP'ULCHRE, *n.* a place of burial.

1. Those who have been able to *explore* the Great Pyramid are not convinced that it was intended for the *sepulchre* of kings.

563. Sep'tem, seven.

1. SEPTEM'BER, *n.* the ninth month.

1. In the old Roman year, *September* was the seventh month.

564. Se′qu-or, I follow. **Secu′t-us,** following.

1. CONSEC′UTIVE, *a.* following in regular order.
2. SUE, *v.* to prosecute.
   ENSUE′, *v.* follow (65-9).
   EXECU′TION, *n.* putting to death (92-7).
   CON′SEQUENCE, *n.* result; effect (75-9).
   OBSE′QUIOUS, *a.* complying in a servile manner (75-13).
   OB′SEQUIES, *n.* funeral solemnities (83-1).

PROS′ECUTE, *v.* to continue (75-2).
PURSUED′, *p.* followed (11-7).
PURSUIT′, *n.* the endeavor to attain (12-4).
SE′QUEL, *n.* that which follows (195-1).
SUB′SEQUENT, *a.* occurring at a later period (118-2).
SUIT′ABLE,*a.*appropriate(178).
PROS′ECUTING, *part.* carrying on (561-2).

1. In all text-books, the paragraphs should be numbered in *consecutive* order.
2. The Constitution does not permit an individual to *sue* a State.

565. Se′r-o, I knit together. **Ser′t-um,** to knit together. **Ser′ni-o (sermo′n-is),** a discourse.

DESERT′ERS, *n.* those who desert (19-2).
EXERT′, *v.* to put into action (431).
SE′RIES, *n.* a succession of things (75-9).

ASSERT′ING, *part.* affirming positively (37-4).
ASSERTS′, *v.* affirms positively (16-2).
SER′MON, *n.* a serious discourse (561-6).

566. Ser′p-o, I creep.

SER′PENTINE, *a.* winding (349). | SER′PENT, *n.* snake (152-1).

567. Ser′v-io, I serve. **Servi′t-um,** to serve.

DESERVED′, *a.* merited (6).
SERV′ANT, *n.* one who serves (68-2).

SERV′ITUDE, *n.* bondage (70-2).
SUBSERV′IENT, *a.* serving to promote some end (15-2).

568. Ser′v-o, I keep; I preserve. **Serva′t-um,** to keep; to preserve.

OBSERV′ING, *n.* watching (27-2).
PRESERVA′TION, *n.* being kept from decay (158-1).

RESERVOIR′, *n.* a cavity for holding a fluid (527).
OBSERVA′TION, *n.* notice (104-2).

LATIN DERIVATIVES.

569. *Seve′r-us,* severe.

ASSEV′ERATION, *n.* solemn assertion (167-4).
SEVERE′LY, *adv.* sharply (21-3).
SEVE′RER, *a.* harsher (70-1).
PERSEVE′RANCE, *n.* constancy in pursuit (38-2).

570. *Sex,* six. *Sexagin′ta,* sixty.

1. SEXAGENA′RIAN, *n.* a person sixty years old.

1. John Adams was a *sexagenarian,* when he became President of the United States.

571. *Sig′n-um,* a sign, a seal.

1. EN′SIGN, *n.* a standard; a flag or banner.
2. DES′IGNATE, *v.* to point out.
INSIGNIF′ICANT, *a.* unimportant (301-1).
SIG′NALS, *n.* those things which give notice (343).
SIGN, *v.* to affix the signature (324).
DESIGN,′ *n.* intention (37-1).

1. In battle, each of the tribes of Israel carried an *ensign,* to *designate* its place in the field.

572. *Sim′il-is,* like. *Si′mul,* at the same time.

1. ASSIM′ILATE, *v.* become like.
2. DISSEM′BLE, *v.* to hide under a false appearance.
DISSIMULA′TION, *n.* hypocrisy (57-3).
SIMILAR′ITY, *n.* resemblance; likeness (49-1).
SIM′ILAR, *a.* like (83-2).
SIMULTA′NEOUS, *a.* at the same time (535).
SIMIL′ITUDE, *n.* resemblance; likeness (68-2).
RESEM′BLANCE, *n.* similarity; likeness (643-2).

1. Insensibly, we *assimilate* in character to the persons with whom we *associate.*

2. There is something beautiful in the character of one who resolves never to *dissemble,* nor to act from a *sinister* motive, but always to speak the words of *verity* and soberness.

573. *Sin′gul-us,* one; single.
SIN′GLE, *a.* one alone (561-4).

574. *Sinis′ter,* on the left hand; bad.
SIN′ISTER, *a.* dishonest; on the left hand (572-2).

575. Si'n-us, a fold, a bosom.

INSIN'UATE, v. to introduce by artful means (250-7). | INSINUA'TION, n. a hint; an intimation (140-5).

576. Sis't-o or **St-o,** I stand; I set up. **Sta't-um,** to stand, to set up.

1. IN'TERSTICES, n. narrow spaces between things.
2. STA'TIONARY, a. fixed.
2. CON'STITUTE, v. compose.
3. SUBSIST'ENCE, n. support; provisions.
3. RESTITU'TION, n. giving back.
3. STABIL'ITY, n. steadiness; firmness.
4. DIS'TANCE, n. remoteness of place.
5. REST'IVE, a. obstinate in refusing to move forward.
6. SOL'STICE, n. (sol,) the point in the ecliptic in which the sun is farthest from the equator.
7. STAID, a. sober; grave.
ASSIST', v. help (1-4).
CIR'CUMSTANCE, n. event (124-2).
CON'STANT, a. continual; without cessation (14-1).

CON'STANTLY, adv. continually (43-1).
CONSTITU'TION, n. established system of laws (12-1).
DES'TITUTE, a. needy; without resources (105-1).
ESTAB'LISH, v. to settle firmly (121-2).
EXTANT', a. now in being; continuing to exist (418-1).
EXIST'ED, v. continued to be (17-1).
IN'STITUTE, n. association; society (11-2).
OB'STACLE, n. that which stands in the way (105-1).
RESIST'ANCE, n. opposition; the act of resisting (66-4).
RESIST', v. to withstand (22-3).
STATE, n. condition (1-4).
STAY, v. to remain (558-4).
SUPERSTI'TION, n. belief in omens and prognostics; false religion (307-1).

1. The settlers of America built their houses of logs, filling the *interstices* with clay.

2. Stars are *stationary* bodies; the planets which *constitute* our *solar* system *revolve* around the sun.

3. The Arabs depend on plunder for *subsistence;* and though the Pacha often promises *restitution* of the stolen goods, yet, such is the lack of *stability* in the government, that the promise is seldom kept.

4. Priests whose homes were at a *distance* remained in the *vicinity* of the temple, while performing the *special* duties of the *sacerdotal* office.

5. When Bucephalus was so *restive*, that no attendant could manage him, Alexander, with great *expertness*, mounted him without difficulty.

6. At the time of the summer *solstice*, the sun is *vertical* to the Tropic of Cancer, which is the northern boundary of the *Torrid* Zone.

7. Elizabeth Fry, with her *gentle, staid* demeanor, and sweet expression, was a welcome visitor in the London prisons.

577. So'ci-us, a companion.

Asso'ciate, *v.* keep company (572-2).
Associa'tion, *n.* society (112-2).
So'ciable, *a.* companionable (286-2).
So'cial, *a.* pertaining to society (139-2).
Soci'ety, *n.* the community (101-1).
Asso'ciated, *p.* connected (7-2).

578. Sol (so'l-is), the sun.

So'lar, *a.* pertaining to the sun (576-2).

579. Solem'n-is, solemn, serious.

Sol'emn, *a.* serious; fitted to awaken reflection (167-4).
Sol'emnize, *v.* to perform with proper ceremonies (234).

580. So'l-eo, to use, to be accustomed.

In'solence, *n.* impertinence (41).

581. Sol'id-us, solid.

Consol'idate, *v.* to form into a compact mass (666).
Sol'id, *a.* not fluid; having particles that cohere (27-1).
Solid'ify, *v.* to make solid (135-1).
Sol'diery, *n.* the body of military men (11-3).

582. So'l-or, I comfort; I soothe. **Sola't-us,** comforting; soothing.

1. Inconsol'able, *a.* not to be comforted.
   Consoled', *v.* cheered and solaced (687-2).
Discon'solate, *a.* sorrowful (152-2).
Sol'ace, *v.* to alleviate in distress (371-1).

1. If there were no *resurrection*, and the *spiritual* nature could be reduced to *nonentity*, we might well be ***inconsolable*** at the death of friends.

583. So'l-us, alone ; only.

DES'OLATE, *a.* cheerless (271).
SOL'ITARY, *a.* living alone (20).
SOL'ITUDE, *n.* remoteness from society (222-2).

584. Sol'v-o, I loose.   **Solu't-um,** to loose.

1. SOL'UBLE, *a.* capable of being dissolved.
1. SOLU'TION, *n.* the state of being diffused through a fluid.
2. SOL'VENCY, *n.* ability to pay.
3. DIS'SOLUTE, *a.* loose in morals.
3. ABSOLU'TION, *n.* remission.
4. ABSOLVE', *v.* to acquit.
   AB'SOLUTE, *a.* unconditional (131-1).
   INSOL'VENT, *a.* not able to pay (395-1).
   RESOLU'TION, *n.* determination (56-2).

1. Many substances, not *soluble* in water, can be held in *solution* by alcohol.
2. In the "Great Money Pressure" of 1837, many merchants, whose *solvency* there had never been reason to *suspect*, became bankrupt.
3. When Charles II. took a *retrospect* of his *dissolute* life, he was terrified at the thought of the *retribution* that awaited him; and, borne down by the *prostration* of disease, he besought *absolution* for all his sins.
4. The effect of the *recent* bankrupt laws was to *absolve* the debtor from legal obligation to pay.

585. Som'n-us, sleep.

1. SOMNAM'BULIST, *n.* (ambulo,) one who walks in his sleep.

   1. A *somnambulist* will sometimes *traverse* a dangerous path, and not *evince* the slightest fear.

586. So'n-us, a sound.

1. SONO'ROUS, *a.* clear ; high-sounding.
   SOUND, *n.* a noise (110).
   CON'SONANT, *n.* a letter which can be sounded only in connection with a vowel (167-3).

1. According to an old superstition, when the great bell of St. Paul's London, pours forth its *sonorous* tones, all the beer in the neighborhood turns sour.

587. Sor'did-us, mean ; covetous.

SOR'DID, *a.* mean ; covetous (6).

LATIN DERIVATIVES.

588. *Sors (sor't-is),* a sort, lot, share.

Con'sort, *n.* a partner, especially a wife or husband (171). | Sort, *n.* kind or species; a class or order (472-1).

589. *Spar's-um,* to strew; to scatter.

1. Interspers'ing, *part.* scattering between. | 2. Asper'sion, *n.* calumny. Disperse', *v.* scatter (700).

1. In the *tuition* of little children, care should be taken to *diversify* the exercises, by *interspersing* recreations and lighter studies with those which are more wearisome.

2. St. Clair, in order to prove the severe *strictures* passed upon him to be an *aspersion* of his character, was wont to *expatiate* on the various *contingent* circumstances, which *compelled* him to surrender Ticonderoga; but his *specious* arguments had little weight after his defeat in 1791.

590. *Spa'ti-um,* space.

Expa'tiate, *v.* to enlarge in discourse (589-2). | Space, *n.* extent; a portion of extension (551-1).

591. *Spe'ci-o,* I look; I see. ***Spec't-um,*** to look; to see.

1. Conspic'uous, *a.* prominent.
2. Specif'ic, *a.* specified.
2. Perspicu'ity, *n.* freedom from obscurity.
  Des'picable, *a.* worthy of contempt (318-2).
  Disrespect', *n.* dishonor (250-6).
  Ret'rospect, *n.* looking back on the past (584-3).
  Spe'cial, *a.* particular (576-4).
  Spe'cie, *n.* coin (75-9).
  Spe'cies, *n.* a kind (64-2).

Spec'imen, *n.* a sample (213-2).
Spe'cious, *a.* plausible (589-2).
Spec'tres, *n.* apparitions (396-1).
Spec'ulate, *v.* to theorize (545-2).
Suspect', *v.* to mistrust (584-2).
Pros'pect, *n.* view (62-1).
Specta'tor, *n.* one who views (37-3).
Espe'cially, *adv.* particularly (7-3).

1. In the District of Columbia, and in those parts of Maryland and Virginia which lie *contiguous*, the most ***conspicuous*** and *attractive* object is the Capitol.

2. The ***specific*** duty of the President, to "give to Congress information of the state of the Union," was formerly performed in person; but as most men *write* with more ***perspicuity*** than they speak, this information is now, by *tacit* consent, given in writing.

592. Spe'r-o, I hope.

DES'PERATE, a. hopeless (21-4).

DESPERA'DO, n. a desperate fellow (20-3).

DESPERA'TION, n. hopelessness (618-1).

DESPAIR', n. loss of hope (75-15).

PROSPER'ITY, n. successful progress (76-1).

PROS'PEROUS, a. successful (192-2).

593. Spi'r-o, I breathe. Spira't-um, to breathe.

1. ASPI'RANT, n. one who aims at something elevated.
2. INSPIR'IT, v. to animate.
   ASPIRA'TION, n. desire for something higher (434-2).
   CONSPIR'ACY, n. a plot (127).
   INSPIRE', v. to infuse into the mind (56-1).

INSPIRA'TION, n. a drawing in of the breath (212).

SPIR'ITUAL, a. immaterial (582).

SPIR'ITS, n. supernatural apparitions (64-3).

SPIR'ITUOUS, a. containing spirit (51).

CONSPIRE' (see page 36).

TRANSPIRE' (see page 36).

1. The Duke of Monmouth was an *aspirant* to the throne of England, and so *tenacious* of his rights that all efforts to *dissuade* him from invading England, 1685, were useless.

2. During Queen Mary's long *detention* in prison, her attendants tried to lessen the *intensity* of her grief, and *inspirit* her with fresh hopes.

594. Splen'd-eo, I shine.

SPLEN'DID, a. magnificent; celebrated (152-2).

SPLEN'DOR, n. brilliancy (76-1).

RESPLEN'DENT, a. very bright; shining with brilliant lustre (111-1).

595. Spo'li-um, spoil.

SPOLIA'TION, n. plunder taken from a neutral (130).

596. Spon'd-eo, I promise. Spon's-um, to promise.

CORRESPOND', v. to communicate by letters (167-6).

ESPOUSE', v. to marry (545-1).

DESPOND'ENCY, n. dejection (73).

RESPON'SIBLE, a. liable for consequences (504-1).

RESPOND' (see page 37).

597. Stel'la, a star.

CONSTELLA'TION, n. a cluster of fixed stars (158-2).

LATIN DERIVATIVES. 203

598. *Ster'n-o,* I spread; I strew. *Stra't-um,* to spread; to strew.

1. CONSTERNA'TION, *n.* surprise mingled with terror.
STRA'TUM, *n.* a layer (173-1).
PROSTRA'TION, *n.* depression (584-3).
PROS'TRATE, *a.* lying flat (64).

1. During "the dark ages," the *approach* of a comet spread *consternation* among the ignorant masses, as it was thought to *portend* war, or some other calamity to which men are *liable.*

599. *Stil'l-a,* a drop.
DISTIL'LERY, *n.* the place where distilling is carried on (75-7).

600. *Stin'gu-o,* I mark. *Stinc't-um,* to mark.

1. EXTINCT', *a.* extinguished.
DISTIN'GUISH, *v.* to recognize by characteristic qualities (90-1).
EXTIN'GUISH, *v.* to put an end to (191-2).
DISTINCT', *a.* clear (38-1).
DISTINCT'LY, *adv.* clearly (38-2).

1. In the West, there are numerous mounds, which *entomb* the remains of an *extinct* race.

601. *Stip'ul-a,* a bargain.
STIPULA'TION, *n.* agreement (134-1).

602. *Stirps,* a root, or stock.
EXTIRPA'TION, *n.* total destruction (271).
EX'TIRPATE, *v.* to root out (93-3).

603. *Sto,* I stand; I set up. See *Sisto.*

604. *Stren'u-us,* brave, vigorous.
STREN'UOUS, *a.* vigorous (39).

605. *Strin'g-o,* I bind. *Stric't-um,* to bind.

1. ASTRIN'GENT, *a.* contracting, binding.
2. STRAIN, *v.* to draw with force.
3. STRAIT, *n.* a narrow passage of water.
DIS'TRICT, *n.* circuit of authority (475-1).
RESTRAIN', *v.* to repress (22-3).
RESTRIC'TION, *n.* limitation; restraint (415-1).
STRICT'URES, *n.* critical censures (589).
STRICT'EST, *a.* most rigorous (121-4).

1. Some articles, as green persimmons, are so *astringent,* that, when taken into the mouth, they distort the features.
2. The power of the waves to *strain* a ship is easily perceived, when you are at sea in a tempest.
3. The *Strait* of Gibraltar is not more than fifteen miles wide.

606. *Stru'-o,* I build, I construct. *Struc't-um,* to build, to construct.

1. Construc'tion, *n.* formation.
1. In'strument, *n.* tool.
2. Instruct', *v.* to teach.
 Con'strue, *v.* to interpret (608-1).
 Destruc'tive, *a.* ruinous (350-2).

Superstruct'ure, *n.* an edifice (78).
Destroy', *v.* to demolish (127).
Instruc'tion, *n.* information imparted (26-1).
Destruc'tion, *n.* ruin (56-5).
Obstruct' (see page 37).

1. In the *construction* of Solomon's Temple, no *instrument* of iron was "heard in the house, while it was in building."
2. No matter what the *abstruseness* of the subject, it is pleasant to *instruct* those who desire to learn.

607. *Stu'd-eo,* I study, I strive.

Stu'dent, *n.* one engaged in study (97-1).

Stud'y, *n.* application of the mind (11-10).

608. *Sua'd-eo,* I advise. *Sua's-um,* to advise.

1. Dissua'sive, *a.* advising against.
2. Persuade', *v.* to induce.

Dissuade', *v.* to divert from any measure by persuasion (593-1).

1. To the *dissuasive* advice of his friends, Wolsey replied, "the King's words are not *equivocal;* it is impossible to *construe* them favorably; I shall resign the great seal."
2. All efforts to *persuade* Charles Edward, *alias* "The Pretender,' to relinquish his design of invading Scotland, in 1745, were of no avail

609. *Sua'v-is,* sweet, pleasant.

1. Assuage', *v.* to mitigate; to palliate.

Suav'ity, *n.* softness; pleasantness; gentleness (469-2).

1. In the late *contest* between Russia and Turkey, little was done to *assuage* the horrors of war.

LATIN DERIVATIVES.

610. *Suffra'gi-um,* a vote.
SUF'FRAGE, *n.* vote (312).

611. *Su'i,* of one's self.
SUICI'DAL, *a.* (cædo,) destructive to one's self (214-5).

612. *Sum,* I am. *Es'e-e,* to be. *Ens (en't-is),* being. *Futu'r-us,* about to be.

FUTU'RITY, *n.* the future.
AB'SENT, *a.* not present (357-2).
ES'SENCE, *n.* the peculiar quality (230-2).
IN'TERESTS, *n.* advantages (350-2).

NONEN'TITY, *n.* nothing; nonexistence (582).
PRES'ENCE, *n.* state of being present (1-2).
REPRESENT', *v.* portray (7-5).
ESSEN'TIAL, *a.* necessary; indispensable (62-3).

1. Astrologers professed to look into *futurity,* and prophesy good or evil, from the position of the stars.

613. *Su'm-o,* I take. *Sump't-um,* to take.

ASSUMP'TION, *n.* supposition (350-2).
CONSUMP'TION, *n.* use (548-1).
ASSUME', *v.* to take (121-3).

PRESUMP'TION, *n.* arrogance (121-3).
SUMPT'UOUS, *a.* expensive (547).
CONSUME' (see page 37).

614. *Su'per,* high. *Supe'rior,* higher. *Suprem-us,* highest.

1. SUPER'LATIVE, *a.* (latum,) highest in degree.
INSU'PERABLE, *a.* not to be overcome (334-1).
SUPERCIL'IOUS, *a.* (cilium, the eyelid,) haughty (22-3).
SUPERB', *a.* grand (651-1).

SUPE'RIOR, *a.* higher in excellence (66-3).
SUPREM'ACY, *n.* supreme power (180-9).
SUPREME', *a.* highest in power (177-2).
SOV'EREIGN, *n.* king or queen (75-4).

1. As the adjective "perfect" has a *superlative* meaning, the expression, "more perfect," seems to be *redundant.*

615. *Sur'g-o,* I rise. *Surrec't-um,* to rise.

INSUR'GENT, *n.* a rebel; one who rises in opposition to
civil or political authority (701-2).

INSURREC'TION, n. a rising in rebellion; opposition to the execution of law (340).

RESURREC'TION, n. rising again from the dead (582).
SOURCE, n, origin (528-4).

616. *Taber'na,* a shed; an inn.

1. TAV'ERN, n. an inn; a public house for entertainment.

TAB'ERNACLE, n. a temporary habitation (358-1).

1. A favorite sign for a *tavern*, was "The Silent Woman," represented by a woman with her head cut off.

617. *Ta'c-eo,* I am silent. ***Tac'it-um,*** to be silent.

TAC'IT, a. implied, but not expressed (591-2).

TAC'ITURN, a. not free to converse (508-2).

618. *Tan'g-o,* I touch. ***Tact-um,*** to touch.

1. INTACT', a. uninjured.
2. INTAN'GIBLE, a. not capable of being touched.
CONTA'GION, n. communication of disease by touch (129).
CON'TACT, n. a touching (129).

CONTIGU'ITY, n. contact (216-5).
CONTIG'UOUS, a. touching (591-1).
CONTIN'GENT, a. accidental (589-2).
ENTIRE'LY, adv. wholly (21-3).
TACT, n. peculiar aptness (124-1).

1. The *dauntless* Poles fought with *desperation* to preserve their littl territory *intact;* but, assailed at every *vulnerable* part by such an *adversary*, they first became *tributary*, and finally were compelled to accept the *ultimatum* of Russia, viz., the total extinguishment of their kingdom.

2. We believe in many things which are *intangible* and *invisible;* for instance, light, heat, and electricity.

619. *Tan't-us,* so great; as great.

TAN'TAMOUNT, a. (mons,) equivalent (280-2).

620. *Tæ'di-um,* weariness.

TE'DIOUS, a. wearisome from its length (18-2).

621. *Te'g-o,* I cover. ***Tec't-um,*** to cover.

1. DETECT', v. to discover.
PROTEC'TION, n. preservation (13-2).

PROTECT'ORATE, n. government by a Protector; government of Eng., 1653-1658 (176).

1. A remarkable *trait* in Indian character is the power to *detect* the trail of a person *several* days after he has passed.

LATIN DERIVATIVES.

622. *Tem'per-o,* I moderate. ***Tempera't-um,*** to moderate.

TEM'PERAMENT, *n.* natural organization (509-1).
TEM'PERANCE, *n.* moderation (121-4).

TEM'PERATURE, *n.* degree of heat or cold; condition with respect to heat and cold (239-1).

623. *Tem'p-us (tem'por-is),* time.

1. TEM'PORIZE, *v.* to yield to the current of opinion.
EXTEMPORA'NEOUS, *a.* produced at the time (125-5).
TEM'PORAL, *a.* not everlasting (544-2).

TENSE, *n.* that attribute of a verb by which it expresses the distinction of time (255-1).
TEM'PORARY, *a.* lasting only a time (394-3).

1. "The more you are willing to *temporize,* the more *contumacious* will these rebels become," said the opponents of Lord North's Conciliatory Bill.

624. *Ten'd-o,* I stretch. ***Ten's-um*** or ***Ten't-um,*** to stretch.

ATTEN'TION, *n.* application (246-1).
EXTEN'SIVE, *a.* wide-spread (66-1).
INTEN'SITY, *n.* vehemence (593-2).
INTEN'TION, *n.* design; purpose; aim (78-1).
OSTENTA'TION, *n.* ambitious display (415-3).
OSTEN'SIBLE, *a.* seeming (78-1).
PRETEN'SION, *n.* claim laid (179).
PORTEND', *v.* to foretoken (598).

EXTENT', *n.* compass (125-3).
SUPERINTEN'DING, *part.* overseeing (189).
TEN'DENCY, *n.* inclination (18-2).
ATTEND'ANTS, *n.* servants (56-1).
CONTEND'ED, *v.* argued (43-6).
INTEN'SIVE, *a.* serving to give force (8-1).
ATTEND', *v.* to listen to (214).
PORTENT'OUS, *a.* serving to foretoken; ominous (92-2).

625. *Ten'-eo,* I hold. ***Ten't-um,*** to hold.

1. AB'STINENCE, *n.* the refraining from indulgence of appetite.

2. CONTINU'ITY, *n.* unbroken connection.
3. RETEN'TIVE, *a.* retaining.

CONTIN'UAL, *a.* uninterrupted (216-8).
DETEN'TION, *n.* confinement (593-2).
ENTERTAIN', *v.* to receive with hospitality (214-4).
IMPER'TINENT, *a.* intrusive (56-5).
PERTINA'CIOUS, *a.* inflexible (56-2).
PERTINAC'ITY, *n.* inflexibility (75-1).
SUS'TENANCE, *n.* support (214-4).
TEN'ABLE, *a.* capable of being maintained (229).
TENA'CIOUS, *a.* holding fast (593-1).
TEN'EMENT, *n.* habitation (522-7).
TEN'URE, *n.* a holding (375).
DETAIN', *v.* to retain (65-6).
OBTAIN', *v.* to acquire (37-4).
CONTAIN', *v.* comprise (64-1).
CONTINEN'TAL, *a.* relating to a continent (54-1).
CONTIN'UED, *v.* persisted (28-2).

1. Much *animadversion* has been cast on Cranmer; but it should be remembered, that, weakened by imprisonment and long **abstinence**, he was unable to *controvert* the statements of those opposed to him.
2. Some truths are perceived by *intuition*; but others are only arrived at by an argument, which requires *continuity* of thought.
3. Attention and application to study are worth far more than a **retentive** memory.

626. *Ten't-o,* I try. *Tenta't-um,* to try.

ATTEMPT', *n.* endeavor; an effort to gain a point (11-6).
TEMPTA'TION, *n.* inducement (159).

627. *Ten'u-is,* thin, slender.

ATTEN'UATE, *v.* to make thin (156-1).
EXTEN'UATE, *v.* to palliate (551-2).

628. *Ter'g-o,* I make clean. *Ter's-um,* to make clean.

TERSE, *a.* elegant and concise (18-4).
TERSE'NESS, *n.* elegance and conciseness (543-2).

629. *Ter'min-us,* a bound or limit.

1. CONTER'MINOUS, *a.* having a common boundary.
   DETERMINA'TION, *n.* resolution (246-5).
   EXTER'MINATE, *v.* to destroy utterly (103-2).
   INTER'MINABLE, *a.* endless (68-3).
   TER'MINATE, *v.* to come to an end (85-1).
   DETER'MINED, *v.* resolved; concluded (638).

1. As Canada and the United States are *conterminous,* it is of *vital* importance that friendly relations should be maintained.

630. *Te'r-o,* I rub. *Tri't-um,* to rub.

1. CONTRI'TION, *n.* repentance; sorrow for sin.
   DET'RIMENT, *n.* injury (542-1).
   DETRIMENT'AL, *a.* injurious (507).
   TRITE, *a.* well-worn; having lost its novelty (543-2).

1. To tear the dress and put ashes on the head was, in ancient times, a common mode of expressing *contrition* and sorrow.

631. *Ter'r-a,* the earth.

1. MEDITERRA'NEAN, *n.* (medius,) the sea between Europe and Africa.
1. TERRES'TRIAL, *a.* pertaining to the earth.
   SUBTERRA'NEAN, *a.* under the surface of the earth (68-3).
   TER'RITORY, *n.* a district (17-3).

1. The ancients gave the name of *Mediterranean,* because they supposed it to be in the middle of this *terrestrial* habitation.

632. *Ter'r-eo,* I fill with fear. *Ter'rit-um,* to fill with fear.

1. TERRIF'IC, *a.* frightful.
   DETER', *v.* to stop by fear (641).
   TER'RIBLE, *a.* fearful (20-3).
   TER'RIFY, *v.* to fill with fear (641).

1. The *terrific* explosion caused by the bursting of a *torpedo* will destroy a large ship, though it is an iron-clad.

633. *Tes't-is,* a witness.

1. TES'TAMENT, *n.* a will.
1. ATTEST', *v.* to certify.
1. TESTA'TOR, *n.* one who makes a will.
   CONTEST'ED, *p.* disputed (290-2).
   INTES'TATE, *a.* without a will (465-2).
   PROTEST', *v.* to make a formal declaration against (98-2).
   PROT'ESTANTS, *n.* those who join in a protest (85-2).
   TES'TIMONY, *n.* that which is affirmed by a witness (287-3).
   CON'TEST, *n.* conflict (609).

1. It would *invalidate* a will or *testament,* if there were no witnesses to *attest* the fact that the *testator* was of sound mind.

634. *Text'-um,* to weave.

1. Con'text, *n.* connected passages.
1. Text, *n.* a passage of Scripture.

Pre'text, *n.* a pretence (195-1).
Text'ure, *n.* the manner in which a fabric is woven (178-1).

1. A gross *perversion* of truth may be made by taking a *text* without the *context.*

635. *Tim'-eo,* I fear.

Intim'idate, *v.* to terrify (303).
Tim'orous, *a.* full of fear (285).
Tim'id, *a.* full of fear; wanting courage (120-5).

636. *Tin'g-o,* I dye. *Tinct'-um,* to dye.

Tint, *n.* slight coloring (117-1).

637. *Tit'ul-us,* title.

1. Ti'tle, *n.* appellation of dignity.

1. In France, an Archbishop has the *title* of Monseigneur, usually abbreviated to Mgr.

638. *Tol'er-o,* I bear. *Toll'-o,* I lift up.

1. Tolera'tion, *n.* the act of tolerating.

Tol'erate, *v.* to endure (285-2).
Extol', *v.* to praise highly (432).

1. Some of the Colonies *determined* to grant *toleration* to every religious faith.

639. *Tor'p-eo,* I am numb or torpid.

Torpe'do, *n.* a machine for blowing up ships (632).
Tor'pid, *a.* inactive; having lost motion (152-1).

640. *Tor'r-eo,* I parch; I burn.

Tor'rents, *n.* strong currents (65-4).
Tor'rid, *a.* parched with heat (576-6).

641. *Tort'-um,* to twist. *Tormen't-um,* extreme pain.

1. Tort'uous, *a.* crooked.
Extort', *v.* to wrest from (120-2).
Extor'tion, *n.* oppressive exaction (66-1).

Retort'ed, *v.* threw back an objection (286-1).
Tor'ment, *n.* suffering (365).
Tort'ure, *n.* extreme pain; suffering (120-2).

LATIN DERIVATIVES. 211

1. The *tortuous* course of some African rivers, and the *ferocious* beasts (which lurk on the *umbrageous* banks), were formerly sufficient to *terrify* explorers, and *deter* them from even making an attempt.

642. *To't-us*, whole; all.

1. Total'ity, n. the whole. | To'tal, a. entire (133-1).

1. During the period of *totality*, in the eclipse of 1878, there was a fine opportunity to observe the *corona* of the sun.

643. *Tra'd-o*, I deliver. *Trad'it-um*, to deliver.

1. Trea'son, n. disloyalty.
2. Betray', v. to disclose.
    Tradi'tion, n. that which is transmitted from age to age by oral communication (358).

Trai'tor, n. one who levies war against his country, or who adheres to its enemies, giving them aid, etc. (285-3).

1. "*Treason* against the United States consists only in levying war against them, adhering to their enemies, etc."
2. Hamlet determined not to *betray* his suspicions, but to keep *vigil* himself, and see if a *figure* bearing any *resemblance* to his father would appear.

644. *Tra'h-o*, I draw. *Tract'-um*, to draw.

1. Protract', v. to prolong.
2. Distract', v. to draw away.
    Ab'stract, a. existing in the mind only (241-2).
    Attract'ive, a. engaging (591-1).
    Detrac'tion, n. slander (56-2).
    Extract', v. to draw out (134-2).
    Portray', v. depict (197-1).
    Tract'able, a. easily managed (138-2).

Treat, v. to use (222-1).
Trea'ty, n. a league; a covenant (17-1).
Contrac'tion, n. the act of lessening (485).
Contract', v. to lessen (60-2).
Por'trait, n. likeness (313-1).
Tract, n. district (414-1).
Trait, n. distinguishing characteristic (621).
Treat'ment, n. usage (133-1).
Attract' (see page 37).

1. There was no desire in the Berlin Congress to *protract* the war.
2. A sentry must be *vigilant*, and allow nothing to *distract* his attention.

645. *Tranquill'-us*, tranquil, calm.

Tranquil'lity, n. quietness (443).

646. *Trĕm-o,* I shake.

TREMEN'DOUS, *a.* terrible; exciting terror (127).

TREM'ULOUS, *a.* quivering; shaking (211-3).

647. *Tres (trī'a),* three.

1. TRIV'IAL, *a.* (via,) unimportant.

   1. During the voyage to Virginia, the most *trivial* remark of John Smith's, was regarded as *intrusive* by his companions.

648. *Trĭb'u-o,* I give.   *Tribu't-um,* to give.

ATTRIB'UTABLE, *a.* ascribable (76-8).
ATTRIB'UTE, *v.* to ascribe; to impute (7-1).
CONTRIB'UTE, *v.* give in common with others (241-5).
DISTRIB'UTE, *v.* to dispense (265-1).

RETRIBU'TION, *n.* requital; punishment (584-3).
RETRIB'UTIVE, *a.* requiting (250-6).
TRIB'UTARY, *a.* contributive (618-1).
TRIB'UTE, *n.* a tax paid to secure peace (246-4).

649. *Tru'd-o,* I thrust.   *Tru's-um,* to thrust.

1. INTRUDE', *v.* thrust themselves in.
1. INTRUD'ER, *n.* one who enters without right.
2. PROTRUDE', *v.* to thrust out.
  INTRU'SIVE, *a.* entering without right (647).

INTRU'SION, *n.* entrance without right (477-2).
ABSTRUSE', *a.* difficult to be comprehended (232-1).
ABSTRUSE'NESS, *n.* quality of being abstruse (606-2).
OBTRUDE' (see page 37).

   1. Cuckoos *intrude* upon any nest, whose occupants dare not venture to repel the *intruder.*

   2. In a prairie-dog village, do not be surprised to see a rattlesnake *protrude* its head from one of the openings.

650. *Tu'e-or,* I view; I guard.   *Tu'it-us,* viewing; guarding.

INTUI'TION, *n.* immediate perception of truth (625-2).

TUI'TION, *n.* instruction; the act of teaching (589-1).

651. *Tu'me-o,* I swell.   *Tum'b-a,* a tomb.

1. TOMB, *n.* sepulchre.
2. ENTOMB'MENT, *n.* interment.

ENTOMB', *v.* inter; deposit in a tomb (600).

CONTUMA'CIOUS, *a.* obstinate (623).
CON'TUMACY, *n.* contempt of authority (71-2).
CON'TUMELY, *n.* insolence (204).
TU'MID, *a.* swollen; distended; inflated (211-3).
TU'MULT, *n.* a commotion (661).

1. The Taj, at Agra, in India, is probably the most *superb tomb* in the world; it cost £3,174,802.
2. The buildings designed for the *entombment* of the native princes of India are marvels of beauty.

652. *Tun'd-o,* I beat; I bruise. ***Tu's-um,*** to beat; to bruise.

CONTU'SION, *n.* a bruise (124-4). | OBTUSE', *a.* dull (176).

653. *Tur'b-a,* a crowd; a bustle.

DISTURB'ANCE, *n.* confusion (180-1).
IMPERTUR'BABLE, *a.* not to be agitated (146-3).
PERTURBA'TION, *n.* agitation of mind (64-5).
TUR'BULENCE, *n.* insubordination (192-1).
TUR'PULENT, *a.* tumultuous (54-3).
TROUB'LESOME, *a.* causing disturbance (54-3).

654. *Tur'g-eo,* I swell.

1. TUR'GID, *a.* bombastic.

1. At a time when a *turgid* style was common, Bunyan wrote with great simplicity.

655. *Tur'r-is,* a tower.

1. TUR'RET, *n.* a little tower.

1. A *turret* placed at the corner of a building is called an angle-turret.

656. *Ul'tim-us,* the last. ***Ul'tra,*** beyond.

1. OUT'RAGE, *n.* gross injury.
UL'TIMATELY, *adv.* finally (92-2).
ULTE'RIOR, *a.* further (550).
ULTIMA'TUM, *n.* a final proposition (618-1).

1. The *umbrella* was unknown in England till the reign of Queen Anne, and then its *advent* in the hands of a man subjected him to *abuse* and *outrage.*

657. *Um'br-a,* a shade.

UM'BRAGE, *n.* offence (181-2).
UMBRA'GEOUS, *a.* affording a shade; shady (641).
UMBREL'LA, *n.* a shade carried in the hand for shelter from rain or sun (656).

658. Un'd-a, a wave.

1. ABOUNDS', v. exists in profusion.
2. INUN'DATE, v. to overflow.
2. UN'DULATE, v. to rise in waves.
REDUN'DANT, a. superfluous (614).

UN'DULATING, a. rising in waves (75-14).
ABUN'DANCE, n. profusion (107).
SUPERABUN'DANCE, n. excessive abundance (541-1).
ABUN'DANT, a. plentiful; fully sufficient (377-2).

1. The Californian *vulture abounds* only on the west side of the Rocky Mountains.
2. Though the Nile rises sufficiently to *inundate* the country, yet its waters are found to *undulate* so little as to be scarcely perceptible.

659. Un'gu-o, I anoint. **Unc't-um,** to anoint.

1. OINT'MENT, n. that which serves to anoint.

1. ANOINT', v. to pour oil upon.
UNCT'UOUS, a. oily (365).

1. To *anoint* the head with oil or with some precious *ointment* was, in oriental countries, a mark of special favor.

660. U'n-us, one.

U'NITY, n. oneness (416-2).
UNITE', v. to join (335-2).
U'NIVERSE, n. (verto,) the whole system of created things (18-3).

UNIVER'SAL, a. (verto,) comprising the whole (255-1).
UNIVERSAL'ITY, n. (verto,) unlimited application (65-7).

661. U't-or, I use. **U's-us,** using.

1. USURP', v. (rapio,) to seize without right.
DISUSE', n. cessation of use (35-4).
US'AGE, n. treatment (133-1).
U'SUAL, a. common (146-3).

U'SUALLY, adv. ordinarily (180).
UTEN'SILS, n. implements (430-2).
UTIL'ITY, n. profitableness (542-1).
ABUSE', n. ill treatment (656).

1. *Vague* rumors, that Cæsar intended to *usurp* the supreme authority, *abolish* long established customs, and proclaim himself Emperor, produced a great *tumult* in Rome.

662. Vac'c-a, a cow.

VACCINA'TION, n. insertion of vaccine matter (499).

VAC'CINE, a. relating to a cow (499-1).

LATIN DERIVATIVES. 215

663. Va'c-o, I am empty.

EVACUA'TION, *n.* the act of going out (21-6).
VACATE', *v.* to make empty (97-2).

VAC'UUM, *n.* an empty space; (some assert there is no such thing as a vacuum; "Nature abhors a vacuum.") (55-1).

664. Va'd-o, I go. **Va's-um,** to go.

1. EVA'SIVELY, *adv.* in a manner to avoid a direct reply or a charge.
EVA'SION, *n.* an artifice to elude (509-3).

INVA'SION, *n.* entrance with hostile intentions (528-2).
EVADE' (see page 38).
INVADE' (see page 38).
PERVADE' (see page 38).

1. To the question, "Are you a spy?" Nathan Hale did not answer *evasively,* but simply said "Yes."

665. Va'g-us, wandering.

1. VAGA'RIES, *n.* fancies.
EXTRAV'AGANCE, *n.* excess (66-1).
EXTRAV'AGANT, *a.* excessive (232-2).

VAG'ABOND, *n.* an outcast (211-3).
VA'GRANT, *a.* wandering (94-3).
VAGUE, *a.* indefinite (661).

1. Who can account for the strange *vagaries* which are apt to *delude* us in our sleep?

666. Va'l-eo, I am strong. **Va'le,** farewell.

1. INVAL'ID, *a.* of no legal force.
AVAIL'ABLE, *a.* capable of being used with advantage (54-2).
CONVALES'CENT, *a.* recovering health (168-1).
INVAL'IDATE, *v.* lessen the force of (633).
INVAL'UABLE, *a.* inestimable (168-1).

PREV'ALENT, *a.* current (170-2).
PREVAIL', *v.* succeed (266).
VALEDIC'TORY, *n.* (dico,) a farewell address (543-2).
VAL'IANT, *a.* brave (24-2).
VAL'ID, *a.* of legal force (11-5).
VAL'OR, *n.* bravery (92-3).
VAL'UABLE, *a.* having worth (319-2).
VAL'UE, *n.* worth (43-2).

1. In 1687, Andross determined to declare the Charter of Connecticut *invalid,* and *consolidate* the province with New York; by an adroit stratagem the Assembly managed to *circumvent* him.

667. Val'l-um, a rampart; a bulwark.

CIRCUMVALLA'TION, *n.* a line of defences surrounding the camp of a besieging army (60-2).

668. Var'ic-o, I straddle.

PREVAR'ICATE, *v.* to equivocate (482).

669. Ve'h-o, I carry. **Vec't-um,** to carry.

1. CONVEX'ITY, *n.* state of bulging out.
2. CON'VEX, *a.* swelling into a rounded form.
3. VEX, *v.* to irritate.
4. VE'HICLE, *n.* a carriage.
5. VEXA'TION, *n.* irritation.
INVEIGH', *v.* to rail against (208).
INVEC'TIVE, *n.* reproach (39).

1. To convey the idea of *convexity,* use the outside of an orange.

2. What proofs can you bring to *verify* the statement, that the surface of the earth is *convex?*

3. Few events in Washington's administration seemed to *vex* him so much as St. Clair's defeat by the Indians; none of the excuses served to *exonerate* St. Clair from the charge of mismanagement.

4. The jaunting-car of Ireland is a curious *vehicle,* which a *voluptuary* would not find quite so easy as a palace-car.

5. The numerous failures of Palissy the potter, caused much *vexation* to his wife and family.

670. Vel'l-o, I tear. **Vul's-um,** to tear.

CONVUL'SION, *n.* any violent and irregular motion (490).

671. Ve'l-o, I cover; I conceal. **Vo'lup,** agreeably.

1. DEVEL'OP, *v.* to disclose.
2. VEIL, *n.* a cover.
2. ENVEL'OP, *v.* to enclose.
REVEAL', *v.* disclose (417-1).
REVELA'TION, *n.* a disclosing of what was hidden (115-1).

1. When yellow fever is about to *develop* itself, physicians are aware that other diseases are likely to *supervene.*

2. When a Moslem woman goes in the street she thinks it necessary to *envelop* herself in a *veil.*

672. Ven'd-o, I sell.

1. VEND, *v.* sell.
1. VEND'ER, *n.* seller.
2. VE'NAL, *a.* corrupt.
VENDUE', *n.* an auction (43).

1. In London, the term costermonger is applied to a *vender* of small wares, or to those who *vend* articles on the streets.

2. A corrupt sovereign can usually find a *venal* press to *malign* the character of any one who opposes him.

673. *Ve'ni-o,* I come. *Ven't-um,* to come.

1. CONTRAVENE', *v.* to contradict.
AV'ENUE, *n.* any opening by which a place may be reached (688-1).
AD'VENT, *n.* a coming to; appearance (656).
ADVENTI'TIOUS, *a.* accidental (177-5).
CIRCUMVENT', *v.* to deceive by stratagem (666).
CONVEN'TION, *n.* assembly (94-1).
CONVEN'TIONAL, *a.* sanctioned by usage (543-1).
VEN'TURE, *n.* to dare (649).
COV'ENANTERS, *n.* those who have signed a covenant (120-2).
EVENT', *n.* circumstance (23).
EVENT'UALLY, *adv.* in the issue (415-1).
INVEN'TION, *n.* the making of that which did not exist before (35-4).
SUPERVENE', *v.* to come upon as something extraneous (671-1).
REV'ENUE, *n.* income (11-6).
PREVENT'IVE, *n.* that which hinders (52-3).
PREVENT', *v.* to hinder (288-1).
INTERVENE' (see page 38).
CONVENE' (see page 38).

1. The opponents of Galileo (gal-e-lee'-o) tried every method to *contravene* his theory, and to *convince* the people that the sun moved around the earth.

674. *Ven't-us,* the wind.

1. VEN'TILATE, *v.* to afford free circulation of air.
2. VENT, *n.* an opening for air or any fluid to escape.

1. The air of a school-room soon becomes impure; to *obviate* the defect, it is necessary to *ventilate* the room.
2. In every mine there should be a *vent* for the escape of foul air.

675. *Ver'b-um,* a word.

1. VERBA'TIM, *a.* word for word.
2. VERB, *n.* a word which affirms.
3. VERB'AL, *a.* oral; not written.
AD'VERB, *n.* a part of speech (8-1).
PROV'ERB, *n.* maxim; an old, common saying (561-6).
VER'BIAGE, *n.* superabundance of words (543-1).
VERBOS'ITY, *n.* the use of more words than are necessary (543-2).

1. Rules and definitions should be studied ***verbatim***, lest, by some *inadvertence*, an important *error* should occur.

2. In acquiring a language, it is necessary to *devote* much time to the study of the ***verb***.

3. Some ***verbal*** changes have taken place, since King James gave us the present *version* of the Bible, in 1611.

676. *Ve're-or,* I fear.

1. Rev'erend, *a.* worthy of reverence.
Revere', *v.* to regard with respect and fear (50-2).

Irrev'erent, *a.* wanting in respect (544-1).
Reveren'tial, *a.* expressing reverence (125-7).

1. The word reverend occurs but once in the Bible — "Holy and *reverend* is his name."

677. *Ver'g-o,* I bend, I incline.

1. Converge', *v.* tend towards each other.

Verge, *n.* the brink (85-4).
Diverge' (see page 38).

1. Lines which diverge in one direction must necessarily ***converge*** in the opposite direction; and the *converse*, of course, is true that converging lines must diverge.

678. *Ver'm-is,* a worm.

Ver'min, *n.* noxious little animals, insects, etc. (64-2).

679. *Ver't-o,* I turn.   *Ver's-um,* to turn.

1. Irrevers'ible, *a.* not capable of being revoked.
1. Adver'sity, *n.* calamity.
2. Con'troversy, *n.* disputation.
3. Versatil'ity, *n.* capability of turning to new subjects.
4. Inverse'ly, *a.* in an inverted manner.
Ad'versary, *n.* an enemy (618-1).
Advertise', *v.* to publish a notice (11-2).
Animadver'sion, *n.* (animus,) censure (625-1).

Aver'sion, *n.* dislike (285-2).
Ad'verse, *a.* calamitous (75-8).
Conversa'tion, *n.* intercourse (8-1).
Conver'sion, *n.* radical change of moral character (214-1).
Con'verse, *n.* a proposition in which the order is inverted (677).
Con'trovert, *v.* to oppose in argument (625-1).
Divorce', *n.* dissolution of the marriage contract (48-4).
Diver'sions, *n.* **amusements** (495).

LATIN DERIVATIVES.

Diver'sity, n. variety (323).
Diver'sify, v. to vary (589-1).
Inadver'tence, n. heedlessness (675-1).
Perver'sion, n. a wrong interpretation (634).
Reversed', v. changed to an opposite course (22-2).
Subver'sive, a. tending to overthrow (246-6).
Ver'tex, n. the point where the lines of an angle meet (20-1).
Versed, a. skilled (93-2).
Ver'tical, a. directly overhead (576-6).
Ver'sion, n. translation (675-3).
Convert' (see page 38).
Di'verse (see page 38).
Pervert' (see page 38).
Subvert' (see page 38).
Advert' (see page 38).
Avert' (see page 38).
Trav'erse (see page 38).

1. Haman, supposing the King's decree to be *irreversible*, rejoiced greatly at the *adversity* he was bringing upon the Jews. Esther, after *devout* supplication to God, *revealed* the plot to the King, and obtained a complete victory over the wicked Haman.

2. Henry VIII. delighted in *controversy;* but as he would maintain an opinion which was *obviously* incorrect, his opponent had no alternative but to *lapse* into silence.

3. The graphic descriptions in Milton's beautiful epic exhibit the wonderful *versatility* of his genius.

4. Light, heat, and gravitation are *inversely* as the square of the distance.

680. *Ve'r-us,* true. *Ve'rax (vera'cis),* veracious.

Verac'ity, n. truthfulness (422-2).
Ver'itable, a. genuine (358-1).
Ver'ify, v. to prove to be true (669-2).
Ver'ity, n. truth (572-2).

681. *Vestig'i-um,* a footstep.

Inves'tigate, v. to search into (410-2).
Ves'tige, n. a trace; a track or footstep (380-1).

682. *Ves't-is,* a garment.

Vest'ure, n. a robe; garments; dress (505-2).
Vests, v. puts in possession of (522-1).

683. *Ve'to,* I forbid.

Ve'toed, v. said; "I forbid" (198-1).

684. Vet'-us (vet'er-is), old; ancient.

INVET'ERATE, *a.* fixed by long continuance (148-1).

VET'ERAN, *n.* an old soldier (550).

685. Vi'-a, a way.

DEVIA'TION, *n.* turning aside (65-11).

IMPER'VIOUS, *a.* impenetrable (156-2).

OB'VIATE, *v.* to remove (674-1).

OB'VIOUS, *a.* evident (140-8).

OB'VIOUSLY, *adv.* evidently (679-2).

PRE'VIOUSLY, *adv.* in time preceding (94-3).

VOY'AGE, *n.* a journey, especially by water (44-1).

686. Vici'n-us, near in place.

VICIN'ITY, *n.* nearness (576-4).

687. Vic-is, change.

1. VIC'AR, *n.* one deputed to perform the functions of another.
2. VICIS'SITUDE, *n.* change; revolution.

VICE-GE'RENT, *n.* (gero,) an officer deputed to exercise the powers of a sovereign (234).

VICE-PRES'IDENT, *n.* (sedeo,) one in place of the President (21-3).

1. Goldsmith, in the "*Vicar* of Wakefield," has made the Primrose family famous.
2. In every *vicissitude* of fortune, Margaret, Queen of Henry VI., was *consoled* by the steady adherence of the House of Lancaster.

688. Vid'e-o, I see. **Vi's-um,** to see.

1. SURVEY', *v.* to look over.
1. VIS'TA, *n.* prospect through an avenue.
2. PROVI'SO, *n.* exception provided for.

EV'IDENCE, *n.* proof (286-1).

EV'IDENT, *a.* apparent (138-3).

INVIS'IBLE, *a.* not to be seen (618-2).

PROVIDE', *v.* to prepare; to supply (13-1).

PROV'IDENCE, *n.* forethought (557).

ADVICE', *n.* counsel; intelligence (56-5).

PROVI'DING, *part.* supplying (18-1).

PROVIS'ION, *n.* special enactment (62-2).

PRU'DENT, *a.* careful; wise (140-6).

SUPERVIS'ION, *n.* oversight (557).

LATIN DERIVATIVES. 221

Vis'age, *n.* the countenance (509).

View, *n.* appearance (177-1).

Vis'ible, *a.* capable of being seen (428-1).

Vis'ion, *n.* sight (42-2).

1. To *survey* the Chapel of Trinity College, England, through the *vista* formed by a noble *avenue* of trees, affords one of the finest sights in Cambridge.

2. The Constitution makes this *proviso* to the power of amendment: "That no State shall, without its consent, be deprived of its" *vote* in the Senate.

689. *Vĭ'gĭl,* awake; watchful.

Vig'ilant, *n.* attentive to discover and avoid danger (644-2).

Vig'il, *n.* watch; abstinence from sleep (643-2).

690. *Vĭ'gor,* strength; energy.

Invig'orate, *v.* to strengthen (115-2).

Vig'or, *n.* energy; strength of mind or body (75-2).

691. *Vĭn'c-o,* I conquer. *Vĭc't-um,* to conquer.

1. Convict', *v.* to pronounce guilty.
2. Van'quish, *v.* to conquer.
3. Vic'tor, *n.* conqueror.
   Convince', *v.* to persuade (673).
   Convinced', *p.* persuaded (11-3).
   Convic'tion, *n.* belief (54).

Evince', *v.* to exhibit (585).
Invin'cible, *a.* unconquerable (204-4).
Prov'ince, *n.* a country subject to a foreign power (22).
Vic'tory, *n.* success over an enemy (321-2).
Vic'tim, *n.* a sacrifice; a person or thing sacrificed (228-2).

1. Two witnesses to the same overt act are necessary, in the United States, to *convict* a person of treason.

2. From 334 to 324 B. C., Alexander the Great was able to *vanquish* all who opposed him.

3. The *victor* in ancient games was crowned with a wreath of laurel.

692. *Vĭn'd-ex (vĭn'dĭc-ĭs),* a defender; an avenger.

Revenge', *v.* to vindicate (21-5).

Ven'geance, *n.* recompense of evil (228-2).

Vin'dicate, *v.* to defend (371-4).

Vindic'tive, *a.* revengeful (451-4).

693. Vi'n-um, wine.

1. Vi′nous, *a.* having the qualities of wine.
2. Vin′tage, *n.* the gathering of the crop of grapes.

Grape-vine, *n.* a climbing-plant (56-8).
Vin′egar, *n.* (acer,) an acid liquor (3-1).

1. Many articles besides grapes have *vinous* qualities; large quantities of wine are made from berries.
2. The time of the *vintage* in France is a period of great hilarity.

694. Viola't-um, to injure.

1. Vi′olent, *a.* forcible; vehement.

Viola′tion, *n.* transgression (500).

1. Care should be taken that gymnastic exercises are not too *violent*.

695. Vir, a man.

1. Vira′go, *n.* a bold woman.

1. Xantippe, the wife of Socrates, was a *virago*, noted for her *vulgarity* and *voluble* tongue.

696. Vir't-us, valor; moral goodness.

1. Vir′tue, *n.* moral excellence.

1. Cornelia, a Roman matron, noted for her *virtue* and *probity* snowed her *maternal* affection by exhibiting her sons as her "jewels."

697. Vi'r-us, poison.

Vir′ulence, *n.* malignancy (489-2).
Vir′ulent, *a.* malignant (699-2).

698. Vi't-o, I shun, I avoid.

1. Inev′itably, *adv.* unavoidably.

Inev′itable, *a.* unavoidable (35-8).

1. Knowing what must *inevitably* follow the occupation of New York by the British, the patriots hastened to remove all *confiscable* property.

699. Vit'r-um, glass.

1. Vit′rify, *v.* to convert into glass.
2. Vit′riol, *n.* sulphuric acid; a soluble sulphate of a metal.

1. In Scotland, there are old stone enclosures which look like coarse glass, but what has caused the stone to *vitrify* is not known.

2. When *virulent* poisons, such as *vitriol,* arsenic, etc., have been taken in small quantities, a physician may be able to *neutralize* their effects.

700. *Viv'-o,* I live. *Vict-um,* to live.

1. Viv'ify, *v.* endue with life.
2. Survive', *v.* to continue to live.
   Conviv'ial, *a.* festive (185).
   Viv'id, *a.* lively (173-2).

Vic'tuals, *n.* food (477-1).
Vi'tal, *a.* highly important (629-1).
Vivac'ity, *n.* liveliness (168-1).
Revive' (see page 39).

1. How quickly, after a long winter, does the returning sun *disperse* the clouds and gloom, and *vivify* the face of nature.

2. Few persons from a southern latitude are likely to *survive* the rigors of an Arctic winter.

701. *Vo'c-o,* I call. *Vocat'-um,* to call.

1. Vocif'erates, *v.* (fero,) utters with a loud voice.
2. Invoke', *v.* to ask solemnly.
   Ad'vocate, *n.* a pleader (64-5).
   Avoca'tion, *n.* employment (140-7).
   Convoca'tion, *n.* an assembly (22-2).
   Equiv'ocal, *a.* (æquus,) ambiguous (608-1).
   Invoca'tion, *n.* prayer (462).
   Irrev'ocable, *a.* not capable of being repealed (64-5).

Provoke', *v.* to irritate (121-1).
Provoca'tion, *n.* cause of resentment (204-4).
Vocab'ulary, *n.* a dictionary; a list of words (139-3).
Vo'cal, *a.* relating to the voice (94-2).
Voca'tion, *n.* business (319-2).
Voice, *n.* sound uttered by the mouth (42-2).
Vocif'erous, *a.* (fero,) noisy (43-1).
Vow'el, *n.* a letter (321-1).
Revoke', *v.* to repeal (140-7).
Convoke' (see page 39).

1. Before making a proclamation in court, a crier *vociferates,* three times, "O yes;" meaning "*oyez,*" attend.

2. Rev. Mr. Duché, appointed by the First Congress to *invoke* the blessing of God upon the American cause, was so afraid of being considered an *insurgent* that he fled to Nova Scotia.

702. *Vo'l-o,* I fly. *Volat'-um,* to fly.

Vol'atile, *a.* fickle; easily evaporated (124-1).
Vol'ley, *n.* a flight of shot (438-1).

703. Vo'l-o, I will, I desire. **Volun't-as,** will; desire.

1. BENEV'OLENCE, *n.* (bene,) desire to do good.
2. MALEV'OLENCE, *n.* (malus,) ill-will.
1. VOL'UNTARY, *a.* without compulsion.
VOLUNTEERS', *n.* voluntary soldiers (30-1).

1. The ***benevolence*** of Regulus and his ***voluntary*** return to Carthage, have immortalized him in Roman history.
2. Such was the ***malevolence*** of Cato, towards Carthage, that every speech on the subject ended with "Carthage must be destroyed."

704. Volup't-as, pleasure.

VOLUP'TUOUS, *a.* devoted to luxury and pleasure (124-1).
VOLUP'TUARY, *n.* one who is devoted to pleasure (669-4).

705. Vol'v-o, I roll. **Volu't-um,** to roll.

1. EVOLVE', *v.* to roll out; produce; disclose.
2. VOL'UME, *n.* a book.
   INVOLVES', *v.* implies, implicates (170-4).
   REVOLT', *v.* to renounce allegiance (246-5).

REVOLU'TION, *n.* an entire change in government (11-6).
VOL'UBLE, *a.* fluent in speech (695).
REVOLVE', *v.* move round a centre (576-2).

1. It is interesting to go into a *factory* and watch the workmen, as they ***evolve*** the beautiful white paper from rags.
2. We call a book a ***volume***, although it is no longer a roll.

706. Vo'ro, I devour.

1. OMNIV'OROUS, *a.* (omnis,) eating everything.
   DEVOURED', *v.* ate up greedily (177-4).

VORAC'ITY, *n.* greediness of appetite (451-1).
CARNIV'OROUS, *a.* (caro,) eating flesh (249-1).

1. Man is ***omnivorous***; this is shown by the shape of the teeth.

707. Vo've-o, I vow. **Vot'-um,** to vow.

1. VO'TARY, *n.* one devoted to some particular object.
2. AVOWED', *v.* declared openly.
   DEVOUT', *a.* earnest and solemn (679-1).

DEVOTE', *v.* to give up wholly (675-2).
DEVOTEE', *n.* one who is dedicated (305-1).
VOTE, *n.* suffrage (688-2).

1. Queen Elizabeth, the *votary* of pleasure, was subject to attacks of the deepest melancholy.
2. In 1776, the Marquis de Lafayette *avowed* his determination to espouse the cause of the American Colonies.

708. *Vul'g-us,* the common people.

DIVULGE', *v.* to make known (167).

VUL'GAR, *a.* common (75-12).

VUL'GARISM, *n.* vulgarity (179-1).

VULGAR'ITY, *n.* grossness (695).

709. *Vul'n-us (vul'ner-is),* a wound.

1. INVUL'NERABLE, *a.* not capable of being wounded.

VUL'NERABLE, *a.* capable of being wounded (618-1).

1. The mother of Achilles, in order to render him *invulnerable,* dipped him in the river Styx.

710. *Vul'tur,* a vulture.

VUL'TURE, *n.* a ravenous and carnivorous bird (658-1).

REVIEW OF ROOTS.

25. — 1. Acidulate. 2. Centennial. 3. Pusillanimous. 4. Acetification. 5. Cogent. 6. Coalesce. 7. Preamble. 8. Anguish. 9. Ancient. 10. Acumen. 11. Adulation. 12. Cogitate. 13. Enemy. 14. Acerbity. 15. Inimical. 16. Pilgrims. 17. Agile. 18. Litigious. 19. Navigable. 20. Aperture. 21. Amplification. 22. Inalienable. 23. Centennial. 24. Unanimity. 25. Acrid.

50. — 1. Terraqueous. 2. Coerce. 3. Aviary. 4. Inertia. 5. Benefice. 6. Adapt. 7. Argentiferous. 8. Arbitrament. 9. Exercise. 10. Articles. 11. Arduous. 12. Obedience. 13. Auspices. 14. Author. 15. Arboriculture. 16. Armada. 17. Benign. 18. Belligerent. 19. Atrocities. 20. Audience. 21. Audacious. 22. Auriferous. 23. Aqueduct. 24. Arson. 25. Adulterate.

75. — 1. Charms. 2. Decisive. 3. Scald. 4. Boil. 5. Incensed. 6. Incident. 7. Biscuit. 8. Bounty. 9. Imbibed. 10. Abbreviate. 11. Calamitous. 12. Suicide. 13. Recipe (re'-ci-pē). 14. Cherished. 15. Precipice. 16. Ceaseless. 17. Armament. 18. Barbarous. 19. Auxiliary. 20. Exercise. 21. Aviary. 22. Authority. 23. Incentive. 24. Ancestor. 25. Peregrinations.

P

100.—1. Discriminating. 2. Centennial. 3. Celebration. 4. Incinerate. 5. Disconcert. 6. Cloister. 7. Concern. 8. Ascertain. 9. Succinct. 10. Chart. 11. Clinical. 12. Seclusion. 13. Clandestinely. 14. Clarion. 15. Civic. 16. Quadrangle. 17. Arduous. 18. Exaggeration. 19. Enmity. 20. Coerce. 21. Exigency. 22. Agrarian. 23. Altercation. 24. Inert. 25. Concise.

150.—1. Render. 2. Digit. 3. Dentifrice. 4. Contradictory. 5. Recourse. 6. Condemn. 7. Codicil. 8. Cultivate. 9. Dial. 10. Incredulity. 11. Corpulency. 12. Discouragement. 13. Corollary. 14. Procrastination. 15. Discrepancy. 16. Recriminate. 17. Proxy. 18. Crusade. 19. Decennial. 20. Dictates. 21. Indicate. 22. Predominate. 23. Divination. 24. Sinecure. 25. Cruel.

200.—1. Festival. 2. Sobriety. 3. Equilibrium. 4. Ambient. 5. Fallacious. 6. Pontiff. 7. Preface. 8. Confederacy. 9. Extraneous. 10. Conduit. 11. Domicile. 12. Dormitory. 13. Domineer. 14. Condole. 15. Indomitable. 16. Fatal. 17. Edacity. 18. Familiar. 19. Sample. 20. Strange. 21. Fanatic. 22. Fierce. 23. Affability. 24. Pestiferous. 25. Deign.

250.—1. Effigy. 2. Granite. 3. Glutton. 4. Degree. 5. Primogeniture. 6. Generated. 7. Perfumery. 8. Fratricide. 9. Flagrant. 10. Flexible. 11. Fluctuate. 12. Confute. 13. Fictitious. 14. Feigned. 15. Fixed. 16. Efflorescence. 17. Fruition. 18. Comfort. 19. Fossils. 20. Irrefragable. 21. Agree. 22. Gesture. 23. Effluvium. 24. Florid. 25. Funeral.

300.—1. Hosts. 2. Cite. 3. Rejuvenescence. 4. Fine. 5. Intrinsic. 6. Isolated. 7. Host. 8. Grief. 9. Hesitate. 10. Govern. 11. Horrible. 12. Inanition. 13. Adjacent. 14. Con'jure. 15. Injurious. 16. Joke. 17. Prolix. 18. Collateral. 19. Dilate. 20. Lachrymal. 21. Collapse. 22. Dejection. 23. Itinerant. 24. Imitation. 25. Egregious.

350.—1. Dialects. 2. Merchandise. 3. Reminiscence. 4. Maritime. 5. Circumlocution. 6. Lunatic. 7. Heir. 8. Emanate. 9. Soliloquy. 10. Allegiance. 11. Relief. 12. Mercenary. 13. Alleviate. 14. Delivery. 15. Relinquish. 16. Malicious. 17. Remain. 18. Medical. 19. Premeditated. 20. Permeate. 21. Relic. 22. Ludicrous. 23. Professed. 24. Efficacious. 25. Locomotion. 26. Deliberation.

400.—1. Litigious. 2. Immigration. 3. Eminent. 4. Nuptials. 5. Deny. 6. Maladministration. 7. Misery. 8. Moribund. 9. Paramount. 10. Summon. 11. Nudity. 12. Multifarious. 13. Reconnoitring. 14. Diminish. 15. Promiscuous. 16. Ammunition. 17. Nautical. 18. Equinoctial. 19. Nefarious. 20. Supernumeraries. 21. Meandering. 22. Matter. 23. Admonish. 24. Municipal. 25. Musician.

REVIEW OF ROOTS.

450.—1. Ocular. 2. Enunciation. 3. Adult. 4. Oriental. 5. Peer. 6. Circuit. 7. Enumerate. 8. Impediment. 9. Penitence. 10. Peculate. 11. Impatient. 12. Particle. 13. Expansion. 14. Reparation. 15. Ordinary. 16. Exonerate. 17. Redolent. 18. Omnipotent. 19. Ornata 20. Oval. 21. Peroration. 22. Exorbitant. 23. Obsolete. 24. Compensate. 25. Oblivion.

500.—1. Pulverization. 2. Punctuate. 3. Accomplice. 4. Complement. 5. Plebeian. 6. Complacence. 7. Deplorable. 8. Potentate. 9. Competition. 10. Preposterous. 11. Deprecate. 12. Prove. 13. Propriety. 14. Repugnant. 15. Petulant. 16. Pomological. 17. Pedestrian. 18. Impunity. 19. Pusillanimity. 20. Implacable. 21. Expiatory. 22. Explosion. 23. Pontoon. 24. Publish. 25. Comprehend.

550.—1. Acquiesce. 2. Multifarious. 3. Insatiable. 4. Sanguinary. 5. Sagacious. 6. Amputation. 7. Inquisitive. 8. Abrogate. 9. Risible. 10. Corroborate. 11. Eradicate. 12. Irradiate. 13. Rotation. 14. Coy. 15. Raving. 16. Abrasion. 17. Incorrigible. 18. Reason. 19. Surreptitious. 20. Irrigate. 21. Erudite. 22. Rusticate. 23. Presage. 24. Sacrilege. 25. Saccharine.

600.—1. Consternation. 2. Dissemination. 3. Obsequious. 4. Extant. 5. Assimilate. 6. Subservient. 7. Disconsolate. 8. Asseveration. 9. Subsidiary. 10. Dissertation. 11. Assiduous. 12. Inscrutable. 13. Secular. 14. Sexagenarian. 15. Sinister. 16. Sociable. 17. Solvency. 18. Sordid. 19. Expatiate. 20. Extinct. 21. Strain. 22. Desperado. 23. Sound. 24. Specie. 25. Solar.

650.—1. Extirpation. 2. Perspicuity. 3. Determination. 4. Tuition. 5. Extortion. 6. Sustenance. 7. Temporal. 8. Contiguous. 9. Suicidal. 10. Destructive. 11. Supercilious. 12. Insurrection. 13. Strenuous. 14. Assuage. 15. Dissuade. 16. Entirely. 17. Contingent. 18. Extensive. 19. Tantamount. 20. Detriment. 21. Intestate. 22. Intrusive. 23. Tomb. 24. Conterminous. 25. Pertinacity.

710.—1. Imperturbable. 2. Valedictory. 3. Redundant. 4. Umbrage. 5. Virulent. 6. Avocation. 7. Impervious. 8. Invigorate. 9. Equivocal. 10. Ventilate. 11. Envelop. 12. Contumaciousness. 13. Prevalent. 14. Universal. 15. Veritable. 16. Subversive. 17. Revere. 18. Abuse. 19. Vaccination. 20. Unctuous. 21. Invulnerable. 22. Vindictive. 23. Avow. 24. Survey. 25. Voyage.

KEY.

IT has not been deemed advisable to insert in the Key many simple words, whose analysis is perfectly obvious; thus, if *anciently* is given, *ancient* is not; *affable* is not inserted, because if *affability* contains *ble*, *affable*, from which it is derived, must also contain it; if *choleric* has not *er*, it is equally absent from *choler*; *ambition* is exactly the same as *ambitious*, except in the suffix. Every word is given about which the slightest doubt could exist, and the greatest care has been taken to decide the difficult questions which constantly arise.

Words derived from Greek roots are indicated by (Gr.).

A root commences with a capital; a prefix or suffix, with a small letter.

Roots *defined* in the Key, are not found in the body of the work.

A few words are analyzed, which are not inserted under their roots.

When the orthography of the derivative differs materially from its root, the explanation is given in parenthesis: *Ex.*, Affiance, *Fido*. (Fr. Fiancé.) It is not intended that such explanations should be learned; they are inserted to show the changes which words undergo.

An interrogation mark indicates a doubt.

Abbreviate, ab. *Brevis; ate.*
Abdicate, ab. *Dico; ate.*
Aberration, ab. *Erratum; ion.*
Abject, ab. *Jactum.*
Able. *Habeo; ble.*
Ablution, ab. *Lutum; ion.*
Abnormal, ab. *Norma; al.*
Abolish, ab. *Oleo; ish.*
Abolition, ab. *Olitum; ion.*
Abound, ab. *Unda.*
Abrasion, ab. *Rasum; ion.*
Abrogate, ab. *Rogo; ate.*
Abrupt, ab. *Ruptum.*
Absent, abs. *Entis.*
Absolutely, ab. *Solutum; ly.*
Absolution, ab. *Solutum; ion.*
Absolve, ab. *Solvo.*
Abstinence, abs. *Teneo; ence.*
Abstract, abs. *Tractum.*
Abstruseness, abs. *Trusum; ness.*
Abundance, ab. *Unda; ance.*
Abuse, ab. *Usus.*

Academic, (Gr.) *Akademia; ic.*
Accede, ac. *Cedo.*
Accelerate, ac. *Celer; ate.*
Acceptable, ac. *Captum; able.*
Accessory, ac. *Cessum; ory.*
Acclamation, ac. *Clamatum; ion.*
Acclivity, ac. *Clivus; ity.*
Accommodate, ac, com. *Modus; ate.*
Accompany, ac, com. *Panis.*
Accomplished, ac, com. *Pleo; ish.*
Accordance, ac *Cordis; ance.*
Account, ac, con. *Puto.*
Accumulate, ac. *Cumulus; ate*
Accurate, ac. *Cura; ate.*
Accusation, ac. *Causatum; ion.*
Accuse, ac. *Causa.*
Accrues, ac. *Cresco.*
Acephalous, (Gr.) a. *Kephale; ous.*
Acerbity. *Acerbus; ity.*
Acetic. *Acetum; ic.*
Acetification. *Acetum, Factum; ion.*
Acetose. *Acetum; ose.*

KEY. 229

Ache, (Gr.) *Achos.*
Achromatic, (Gr.) a. *Chroma; ic.*
Acidity. *Aceo; id, ity.*
Acidulate. *Acidulus; ate.*
Acknowledge, a.c. *Nosco.* (Some derive this from the Saxon.)
Acoustics, (Gr.) *Akouo; ics.*
Acquiesce, a.c. *Quies.*
Acquire, a.c. *Quæro.*
Acquisition, a.c. *Quæsitum; ion.*
Acrid. *Acris; id.*
Acrimony. *Acris; mony.*
Acropolis, (Gr.) *Akron, Polis.*
Acrospire, (Gr.) *Akron, Sperma.*
Acrostic, (Gr.) *Akron, Stichos.*
Active. *Actum; ive.*
Actual. *Actum; al.*
Acumen. *Acuo.*
Acute. *Acutum.*
Adamantine, (Gr.) a. *Damao; ant, ine.*
Adapt, ad. *Aptus.*
Add, ad. *Do.*
Addition, ad. *Datum; ion.*
Adduce, ad. *Duco.*
Adequate, ad. *Æquus; ate.*
Adherence, ad. *Hæreo; ence.*
Adjacent, ad. *Jaceo; ent.*
Adjective, ad. *Jactum; ive.*
Adjoining, ad. *Jungo; ing.*
Adjunct, ad. *Junctum.*
Adjust, ad. *Justus.*
Administer. ad. *Minister.*
Administration, ad. *Ministri; ate, ion.*
Admirably, ad. *Mirus; able, ly.*
Admiration, ad. *Miratus; ion.*
Admission, ad. *Missum; ion.*
Admit, ad. *Mitto.*
Admonish, ad. *Moneo; ish.*
Admonition, ad. *Monitum; ion.*
Adopt, ad. *Opto.*
Adoration, ad. *Oratum; ion.*
Adorn, ad. *Orno.*
Adulation. *Adulatum; ion.*
Adult, ad. *Olitum.*
Adulterate, ad. *Alter; ate.*
Advent, ad. *Ventum.*
Adventitious, ad. *Ventum; ous.*
Adverb, ad. *Verbum.*
Adversary, ad. *Versum; ary.*
Adversity, ad. *Versum; ity.*
Advert, ad. *Verto.*
Advertise, ad. *Vertum; ise.*
Advice, ad. *Visum.*
Advocate, ad. *Voco; ate.*
Aerial, (Gr.) *Aer; al.*
Aerography, (Gr.) *Aer, Grapho; y.*
Aerolite, (Gr.) *Aer, Lithos.*
Aeromancy, (Gr.) *Aer, Manteia; y.*
Aerometer, (Gr.) *Aer, Metron.*
Aeronaut, (Gr.) *Aer, Nauta.*
Affability, af. *Fari; ble, ity.*
Affectation, af. *Factum; ion.*
Affection, af. *Factum; ion.*
Affiance, af. *Fido.* (Fr. Fiancé.)
Affiliation, af. *Filius; ate, ion.*
Affinity, af. *Finis; ity.*
Affirm, af. *Firmus.*
Affirmation, af. *Firmus; ion.* (Affirmatio.)
Affliction, af. *Flictum; ion.*

Affluence, af. *Fluo; ence.*
Agent. *Ago; ent.*
Aggrandize, ag. *Grandis; ise.*
Aggravation, ag. *Gravis; ate, ion.*
Agile. *Agilis* (from *Ago*); *ile.*
Agility. *Agilis* (from *Ago*); *ile, ity.*
Agitation. *Agito; ate, ion.*
Agony, (Gr.) *Agon; y.*
Agrarianism. *Agri; an, ism.*
Agree, a. *Gratia.*
Agriculture. *Agri, Cultum; ure.*
Alchemist, (Gr.) al. *Chymos; ist.*
Alchemy, (Gr.) al. *Chymos; y.*
Alienation. *Alienus; ate, ion.*
Alien. *Alienus.*
Aliment. *Alitum; ment.*
Aliquot. *Alius, Quot.*
Allegation, al. *Legatum; ion.*
Allegiance, al. *Ligo; ance.*
Allegory, (Gr.) *Allos, Agora; y.*
Alleviate, al. *Levis; ate.*
Alliance, al. *Ligo; ance.*
Allude, al. *Ludo.*
Allusion, a). *Lusum; ion.*
Alphabetically, (Gr.) *Alpha, Beta; ical, ly.*
Altercation. *Alter; ion.* (L. Altercatio.)
Alternation. *Alternus; ate, ion.*
Altitude. *Alti; tude.*
Amalgamate, (Gr.) *Ama,* together. *Gameo; ate,* or *Malagma,* a poultice.
Amanuensis, a. *Manus.*
Ambidexter, ambo. *Dexter.*
Ambient. amb. *Itum; ent.*
Ambiguity, ambi. *Ago; ity.*
Ambition, amb. *Itum; ion.*
Ameliorate, a. *Melior; ate.*
Amendment, a. *Menda; ment.*
Amiable. *Amo; able.*
Amicable. *Amicus; able.*
Amity. *Amo; ity.*
Ammunition. am. *Munitum; ion.*
Amnesty, (Gr.) a. *Mneo; ty.*
Amorphous, (Gr.) a. *Morphe; ous.*
Amphibious, (Gr.) amphi. *Bios; ous.*
Amphiscii. (Gr.) amphi. *Skia.*
Amphitheatre, (Gr.) amphi. *Theatron.*
Amplification. *Amplus, Factum; ion.*
Amplify. *Amplus; fy.*
Amplitude. *Amplus; tude.*
Amply. *Amplus; ly.*
Amputation, am. *Puto; ate, ion.*
Amputate, am. *Puto; ate.*
Anabaptist, (Gr.) ana. *Bapto; ist.*
Anachronism, (Gr.) ana. *Chronos; ism.*
Anagram. (Gr.) ana. *Gramma.*
Analogy, (Gr.) ana. *Logos; y.*
Analysis, (Gr.) ana. *Lysis.*
Analytical, (Gr.) ana. *Lytikos; ical.*
Anarchy, (Gr.) ana. *Arche; y.*
Anathema, (Gr.) ana. *Thema.*
Anatomy, (Gr.) ana. *Tomos; y.*
Ancestor, ante. *Cessum; or.*
Anchorite, (Gr.) ana. *Choreo; ite.*
Anciently. *Antiquus; ent, ly.*
Androphagus, (Gr.) *Andros, Phago.*
Anecdote, (Gr.) an, ec. *Dotos.*
Anemography, (Gr.) *Anemos, Grapho; y.*
Anemometer, (Gr.) *Anemos, Metron.*
Anemone. (Gr.) *Anemos.*
Angel, (Gr.) *Angelle.*

20

Anger. *Ango.*
Angle. *Angulus.*
Anguish. *Ango.*
Angular. *Angulus; ar.*
Animadversion. *Animus; ad. Versum; ion.*
Animadvert. *Animus; ad. Verto.*
Animalcule. *Anima; al, cule.*
Animation. *Anima; ate, ion.*
Animosity. *Animus; ity.*
Annals. *Annus; al.*
Annexation, an. *Nexum; ion.*
Annihilation, an. *Nihil; ate, ion.*
Anniversary. *Annus, Versum; ary.*
Anno Domini. *Annus, Dominus.*
Anno Mundi. *Annus, Mundus.*
Announce, an. *Nuncio.*
Annual. *Annus; al.*
Annuity. *Annus; ity.*
Annular. *Annulus; ar.*
Anoint, an. *Unctum.*
Anomalous, (Gr.) an. *Omalos; ous.*
Anomaly, (Gr.) an. *Omalos; y.*
Anonymous, (Gr.) an. *Onyma; ous.*
Antagonist, (Gr.) ant. *Agon; ist.*
Antarctic, (Gr.) ant. *Arktos; ic.*
Antecedent, ante. *Cedo; ent.*
Antediluvian, ante. *Diluvium; an.*
Antepenultimate, ante. *Pene, Ultimus; ate.*
Anther, (Gr.) *Anthos.*
Anthology, (Gr.) *Anthos, Logos; y.*
Anthropology, (Gr.) *Anthropos, Logos; y.*
Anthropophagi, (Gr.) *Anthropos, Phago.*
Antichrist, (Gr.) anti. *Christos.*
Anticipation, anti. *Capio; ate, ion.*
Antidote, (Gr.) anti. *Dotos.*
Antinomy, (Gr.) anti. *Nomos; y.*
Antinomian, (Gr.) anti. *Nomos; ian.*
Antipathy, (Gr.) anti. *Pathos; y.*
Antiphlogistic, (Gr.) anti. *Phlegma; ic.*
Antipodes, (Gr.) anti. *Podos.*
Antiquary. *Antiquus; ary.*
Antiquate. *Antiquus; ate.*
Antique. *Antiquus.*
Antiscii, (Gr.) anti. *Skia.*
Antithesis, (Gr.) anti. *Thesis.*
Anxiety. *Anxi; ety.*
Apathy, (Gr.) a. *Pathos; y.*
Aperture. *Apertum; ure.*
Apetalous, (Gr.) a. *Petalon; ous.*
Aphelion, (Gr.) ap. *Helios.*
Aphæresis, (Gr.) ap. *Hairesis.*
Aphorism, (Gr.) ap. *Horos; ism.*
Apocalypse, (Gr.) apo. *Kalypto.*
Apocope, (Gr.) apo. *Kope.*
Apocrypha, (Gr.) apo. *Krypto.*
Apocryphal, (Gr.) apo. *Krypto; al.*
Apogee, (Gr.) apo. *Ge.*
Apologue, (Gr.), apo. *Logos.*
Apology, (Gr.) apo. *Logos; y.*
Apostasy, (Gr.) apo. *Stasis; y.*
Apostle, (Gr.) apo. *Stello.*
Apostolic, (Gr.) apo. *Stello; ic.*
Apostrophe, (Gr.) apo. *Strophe.*
Apothecary, (Gr.) apo. *Theke; ary.*
Apothegm, or Apophthegm, (Gr.) apo. *Phthegma.*
Apotheosis, (Gr.) apo. *Theos.*

Apothesis, (Gr.) apo. *Thesis.*
Apparatus, ap. *Paratum.*
Apparel, ap. *Paro.*
Apparent, ap. *Pareo; ent.*
Apparition, ap. *Paritum; ion.*
Appeal, ap. *Pello.*
Appearance, ap. *Pareo; ance.*
Appease, ap. *Pacis.*
Appendix, ap. *Pendeo.*
Appetite, ap. *Petitum.*
Applaud, ap. *Plaudo.*
Application, ap. *Plicatum; ion.*
Apply, ap. *Plico.*
Appreciate, ap. *Precium; ate.*
Apprehend, ap. *Prehendo.*
Apprise, ap. *Prehensum.* (Fr. Prise.)
Approach, ap. *Proximus.* (Fr. Approcher.)
Approbation, ap. *Probatum; ion.*
Appropriate, ap. *Proprius; ate.*
Approve, ap. *Probo.*
Approximate, ap. *Proximus; ate.*
Aptitude. *Aptus; tude.*
Aquarium. *Aqua*
Aquatic. *Aqua; ic.*
Aqueduct. *Aqua, Ductum.*
Aqueous. *Aqua; ous.*
Arable. *Aro; uble.*
Arbitrament. *Arbitri; ment.*
Arbitrary. *Arbitri; ary.*
Arbitration. *Arbitri; ate, ion.*
Arbitrator. *Arbitri; ate, or.*
Arboriculture. *Arbor, Cultum; ure.*
Archæology, (Gr.) *Arche, Logos; y*
Archaism, (Gr.) *Arche; ism.*
Archangel, (Gr.) *Arche, Angello.*
Archbishop, (Gr.) *Arche; epi. Skopeo.*
Archetype, (Gr.) *Arche, Typos.*
Architecture, (Gr.) *Arche, Tekton; ure.*
Archives, (Gr.) *Arche.*
Arctic, (Gr.) *Arktos; ic.*
Ardent. *Ardeo; ent.*
Ardor. *Ardeo; or.*
Arduous. *Arduus; ous.*
Argentiferous. *Argentum, Fero; ous.*
Argue. *Arguo.*
Argument. *Arguo; ment.*
Argumentative. *Arguo; ment, ive.*
Aristocracy, (Gr.) *Aristos, Kratos; y.*
Aristocrat, (Gr.) *Aristos, Kratos.*
Arithmancy, (Gr.) *Arithmos, Manteia; y*
Arithmetic, (Gr.) *Arithmos; ic.*
Arm. *Arma.*
Armada. *Arma.*
Armament. *Arma; ment.*
Armistice. *Arma, Sto; ice.*
Armor. *Arma; or.*
Armorer. *Arma; or, er.*
Armory. *Arma; ory.*
Army. *Arma; y.*
Aroma, (Gr.) *Aroma.*
Aromatics, (Gr.) *Aromata; ics.*
Arrest, ar, re. *Sto.*
Arrive, ar. *Rivus.*
Arrogant, ar. *Rogo; ant.*
Arrogate, ar. *Rogo; ate.*
Arsenic, (Gr.) *Arsen,* strong, *Nike.*
Arson. *Arsum.*
Art. *Artis.*
Article. *Articulus.*
Articulation. *Articulus; ate, ion.*

KEY. 231

Artificer. *Artis, Facio; er.*
Artificial. *Artis, Facio; al.*
Artisan. *Artis; an.*
Artless. *Artis; less.*
Ascertain, a.s. *Certus.*
Asperity. *Asper; ity.*
Aspersion, a for ad. *Sparsum; ion.*
Aspirant, a. *Spiro; ant.*
Aspiration, a. *Spiro; ate, ion.*
Assailant, a.s. *Salio; ant.*
Assault, a.s. *Saltum.*
Assenting, a.s. *Sentio; ing.*
Assertor, a.s. *Sertum; or.*
Assessor, a.s. *Sessum; or.*
Asseveration, a.s. *Severus; ate, ion.*
Assiduous, a.s. *Sedeo; ous.*
Assimilate. a.s. *Similis; ate.*
Associate, a.s. *Socius; ate.*
Association, a.s. *Socius; ate, ion.*
Assuage, a.s. *Suavis.*
Assumption, a.s. *Sumptum; ion.*
Asterisk, (Gr.) *Astron; isk.*
Asteroid, (Gr.) *Astron, Eidos.*
Asteroidal, (Gr.) *Astron, Eidos; al.*
Astral, (Gr.) *Astron; al.*
Astringent, a. *Stringo; ent.*
Astrologer, (Gr.) *Astron, Logos; er.*
Astronomy, (Gr.) *Astron, Nomos; y.*
Asymptote, (Gr.) a, sym. *Ptoma.*
Atheism, (Gr.) a. *Theos; ism.*
Athletic, (Gr.) *Athlos; ic.*
Atmospheric, (Gr.) *Atmos, Sphaira; ic.*
Atom, (Gr.) a. *Tomos.*
Atonic, (Gr.) a. *Tonos.*
Atrocity. *Atrocis; ity.*
Attain, at. *Tango.* (Fr. Atteindre.)
Attempt, at. *Tento.*
Attendant, at. *Tendo; ant.*
Attention, at. *Tentum; ion.*
Attentive, at. *Tentum; ive.*
Attenuate, at. *Tenuis; ate.*
Attest, at. *Testis.*
Attractive, at. *Tractum; ive.*
Attribute, at. *Tributum.*
Attune, (Gr.) at. *Tonos.*
Auctioneer. *Auctum; ion, eer.*
Audacious. *Audeo; acious.*
Audible. *Audio; ble.*
Audience. *Audio; ence.*
Audit. *Auditum.*
Auditory. *Auditum; ory.*
Augment. *Augeo; ment.*
Augur. *Augur.*
Augury. *Augur; y.*
Auriferous. *Aurum, Fero; ous.*
Auspices. *Avis, Specio.*
Auspicious. *Avis, Specio; ous.*
Authentic, (Gr.) *Authenteo; ic.*
Authenticity, (Gr.) *Authenteo; ic, ity.*
Author. *Augeo; or.*
Authority. *Augeo; or, ity.*
Autobiography, (Gr.) *Autos, Bios, Grapho; y.*
Autograph, (Gr.) *Autos, Grapho.*
Automatical, (Gr.) *Autos, Matos; ical.*
Automaton, (Gr.) *Autos, Matos.*
Autonomous, (Gr.) *Autos, Nomos; ous.*
Autonomy, (Gr.) *Autos, Nomos; y.*
Autopsy, (Gr.) *Autos, Opsis; y.*
Auxiliary. *Auxilium; ary.*

Available, a. *Valeo; able.*
Avenue, a. *Venio.*
Aversion, a. *Versum; ion.*
Avert, a for ab. *Verto.*
Aviary. *Avis; ary.*
Avocation, a. *Vocatum; ion.*
Avowal, a. *Voveo; al.*
Avow, a. *Voveo.*
Axiom, (Gr.) *Axioma.*

Balmy, (Gr.) *Balsamon; y.*
Balsam, (Gr.) *Balsamon.*
Bankrupt. *Abacus,* a bench. *Ruptum.*
Baptist, (Gr.) *Bapto; ist.*
Baptize, (Gr.) *Bapto; ize.*
Barbarous. *Barbarus; ous.*
Barometer, (Gr.) *Baros, Metron.*
Baroscope, (Gr.) *Baros, Skopeo.*
Barytone, (Gr.) *Baros, Tonos.*
Base, (Gr.) *Basis.*
Basilica, (Gr.) *Basileus.*
Basilicon, (Gr.) *Basileus.*
Basilisk, (Gr.) *Basileus; isk.*
Beatific. *Beatus, Facio.*
Beatitude. *Beatus; tude.*
Belligerent. *Bellum, Gero; ent.*
Benediction. *Bene, Dictum; ion.*
Benefaction. *Bene, Factum; ion.*
Benefice. *Bene, Facio.*
Beneficence. *Bene, Facio; ence.*
Beneficial. *Bene, Facio; al.*
Benefit. *Bene, Facio.*
Benevolence. *Bene, Volo; ence.*
Benignity. *Benignus; ity.*
Bible, (Gr.) *Biblos.*
Bibliographer, (Gr.) *Biblos, Grapho; er.*
Bibliomania, (Gr.) *Biblos, Mania.*
Bibliopolist, (Gr.) *Biblos, Poleo; ist.*
Bibliothecal, (Gr.) *Biblos, Theke; al.*
Biennial. *Bis, Annus; al.*
Bigamist, (Gr.) L. *Bis. Gameo; ist.*
Bigamy, (Gr.) L. *Bis. Gameo; y.*
Biography, (Gr.) *Bios, Grapho; y.*
Biped. *Bis, Pedis.*
Bipetalous, (Gr.) L. *Bis. Petalon; ous.*
Biscuit. *Bis.* (Fr. Cuit, baked.)
Bisect. *Bis, Sectum.*
Bishop, (Gr.) epi. *Skopeo.*
Blasphemy, (Gr.) *Blapto, Phano; y.*
Boil. *Bulla.*
Botanical, (Gr.) *Botane; ical.*
Botanology, (Gr.) *Botane, Logos; y.*
Botany, (Gr.) *Botane; y.*
Bounty. *Bonus; ty.*
Brevity. *Brevis; ity.*
Brief. *Brevis.*
Bronchial (Gr.) *Bronchos; al.*
Bronchocele, (Gr.) *Bronchos, Kele.*
Bronchotomy, (Gr.) *Bronchos, Tomos; y.*
Bucolic, (Gr.) *Boukolos; ic.*

Cachexy, (Gr.) *Kakos, Hexis,* state of mind or body; *y.*
Cacophony, (Gr.) *Kakos, Phone; y.*
Cadence. *Cado; ence.*
Calamitous. *Calamitas; ous.*
Calamity. *Calamitas; ity.*
Calculate. *Calculus; ate.*
Caligraphy, (Gr.) *Kalos, Grapho; y.*
Caloric. *Calor; ic.*

Calumny. *Calumnia; y.*
Candidate. *Candeo; id, ate.*
Candor. *Candeo; or.*
Canine. *Canis; ine.*
Canon, (Gr.) *Kanon.*
Canonical, (Gr.) *Kanon; ical.*
Canonize, (Gr.) *Kanon; ize.*
Canticle. *Canto; cle.*
Capacious. *Capio; acious.*
Capacity. *Capio; ity;* (state of being capacious.)
Capacitate. *Capio; ity, ate.*
Capital. *Capitis; al.*
Capitol. *Caput.* (Capitol, a building in ancient Rome where the Senate met.)
Capitation. *Capitis; ate, ion.*
Capitulate. *Capitulum; ate.*
Captain. *Caput.* (Old Fr. Capitain.)
Captious. *Captum; ous.*
Captivate. *Captum; ive, ate.*
Carcass. *Caro.* L. Capsa, chest.
Career. *Curro.* (Fr. Carrière.)
Caress. *Carus.*
Carnival. *Carnis, Vale.*
Carnivorous. *Carnis, Voro; ous.*
Castigate. *Castigo; ate.*
Castigation. *Castigo; ate, ion.*
Casualty. *Casum; al, ty.*
Catalepsy, (Gr.) kata. *Lepsis; y.*
Catalogue, (Gr.) kata. *Logos.*
Cataplasm, (Gr.) kata. *Plasso.*
Catarrh, (Gr.) kata. *Rheo.*
Catastrophe, (Gr.) kata. *Strophe.*
Catechise, (Gr.) kata. *Echeo; ise.*
Catechism, (Gr.) kata. *Echeo; ism.*
Catechumen, (Gr.) kata. *Echeo.*
Category, (Gr.) kata. *Agora; y.*
Cathedral, (Gr.) kata. *Hedra.*
Catholic, (Gr.) kata. *Holos; ic.*
Catholicism, (Gr.) kata. *Holos; ic, ism.*
Catoptrics, (Gr.) kata. *Optomai; ics.*
Cause. *Causa.*
Caustic, (Gr.) *Kaustikos.*
Cauterize, (Gr.) *Kaustikos; ize.*
Caution. *Cautum; ion.*
Cavern. *Caverna.*
Cavil. *Cavilla.*
Ceaseless. *Cessum; less.*
Celebration. *Celebris; ate, ion.*
Celebrity. *Celebris; ity.*
Celerity. *Celer; ity.*
Celestial. *Coelestis; al.*
Cellar. *Cella.*
Cenobite, (Gr.) *Koinos,* common. *Bios;* ite.
Cenotaph, (Gr.) *Kenos,* empty. *Taphos.*
Censor. *Censeo; or.*
Censorious. *Censeo; or, ous.*
Censurable. *Censeo; ure, able.*
Census. *Censeo.*
Century. *Centum; ry.*
Centenarian. *Centum, Annus; ian.*
Centennial. *Centum. Annus; al.*
Center, (Gr.) *Kentron.*
Centigrade. *Centum, Gradior.*
Centipede. *Centum. Pedis.*
Centrifugal. *Centrum,* the centre, or Gr. *Kentron. Fugio; al.*
Centripetal. *Centrum,* the centre, or Gr. *Kentron. Peto; al.*

Centurion. *Centum.*
Cephalalgy, (Gr.) *Kephale, Algos; y.*
Ceremonial. *Ceremonia; al.*
Ceremonious. *Ceremonia; ous.*
Ceremony. *Ceremonia; y.*
Certain. *Certus.*
Certificate. *Certus, Facio; ate.*
Certify. *Certus; fy.*
Cessation. *Cessatum; ion.*
Cession. *Cessum; ion.*
Chant. *Canto.*
Chaotic, (Gr.) *Chaos; ic.*
Characterize, (Gr.) *Charakter; ize.*
Charity, (Gr.) *Charis; ity.*
Charm. *Canto.*
Charnel. *Carnis.*
Chart. *Charta.*
Charter. *Charta.*
Chemical, (Gr.) *Chymos; ical.*
Chemistry, (Gr.) *Chymos; ist, ry.*
Cherish. *Carus; ish.* (Fr. Cher, dear.)
Chimerical. (Gr.) *Chimaira; ical.*
Chirography, (Gr.) *Cheir, Grapho; y.*
Chirology, (Gr.) *Cheir, Logos; y.*
Chiromancy, (Gr.) *Cheir, Manteia; y.*
Chirurgeon, (Gr.) *Cheir, Ergon.*
Cholera, (Gr.) *Chole.*
Choleric, (Gr.) *Chole; ic.*
Chord, (Gr.) *Chorde.*
Chrism, (Gr.) *Christos.*
Christ, (Gr.) *Christos.*
Christendom, (Gr.) *Christos; dom.*
Christmas, (Gr.) *Christos, Massa,* a feast. (?)
Chromatic, (Gr.) *Chroma; ic.*
Chronic, (Gr.) *Chronos; ic.*
Chronology, (Gr.) *Chronos, Logos; y.*
Chronometer, (Gr.) *Chronos, Metron.*
Chrysalis, (Gr.) *Chrysos.*
Chrysanthemum, (Gr.) *Chrysos, Anthos.*
Chrysolite, (Gr.) *Chrysos, Lithos.*
Chrysology, (Gr.) *Chrysos, Logos; y.*
Chyle, (Gr.) *Chylos.*
Chylification, (Gr.) *Chylos, Factum; ion.*
Cinerary. *Cineris; ary.*
Circuitous. *circum, Itum; ous.*
Circulate. *Circulus; ate.*
Circumgyration,(Gr.) circum. *Gyros; ate, ion.*
Circumjacent, circum. *Jaceo, ent.*
Circumlocution, circum. *Locutus; ion.*
Circumnavigation, circum. *Navis, Ago, ate, ion.*
Circumscribe, circum. *Scribo.*
Circumstance, circum. *Sto; ance.*
Circumvallation, circum. *Vallum; ate, ion.*
Circumvent, circum. *Ventum.*
Citation. *Citatum; ion.*
Cite. *Cito.*
Citizen. *Civis.*
Civic. *Civis; ic.*
Civilian. *Civis; ile, ian.*
Civilization. *Civis; ile, ize, ion.*
Claimant. *Clamo; ant.*
Clamorous. *Clamo; or, ous.*
Clandestinely. *Clandestinus; ly.*
Clarify. *Clarus; fy.*
Clarion. *Clarus.*
Classical. *Classis; ical.*
Classification. *Classis, Factum; ion.*
Classify. *Classis; fy.*

Clause. *Clausum.*
Clemency. *Clemens; ency.*
Clepsydra, (Gr.) *Klepto, Hydor.*
Clinical. *Clino; ical.*
Cloister. *Clausum; er.*
Coagulation, co. *Ago; ate, ion.*
Coalesce, co. *Alo.* (Alesco, I grow up.)
Coalition, co. *Alitum; ion.*
Code. *Codex.*
Codicil. *Codicis.*
Coercion, co. *Arceo* or *Erceo; ion.*
Coeval, co. *Ævum; al.*
Cogent, co. *Ago; ent.*
Cogitate, co. *Agito; ate.*
Coincide, co, in. *Cado.*
Coincidence, co, in. *Cado; ence.*
Collapse, col. *Lapsus.*
Collateral, col. *Lateris; al.*
Colleague, col. *Lego.*
Collect, col. *Lectum.*
Colloquy, col. *Loquor; y.*
Colony. *Colonus; y.*
Colonist. *Colonus; ist.*
Color. *Color.*
Combine, com. *Bini.*
Comedy, (Gr.) *Komos, Ode; y.*
Comfort, com. *Fortis.*
Comic, (Gr.) *Komos; ic.*
Comity. *Comis; ity.*
Command, com. *Mando.*
Commemorate, com. *Memor; ate.*
Commendable, com. *Mando; able.*
Commerce, com. *Mercor.*
Commiserate, com. *Miser; ate.*
Commissary, com. *Missum; ary.*
Committee, com. *Mitto; ee.*
Commodious, com. *Modus; ous.*
Commodity, com. *Modus; ity.*
Common, com. *Munus.*
Commotion, com. *Motum; ion.*
Communicative, com. *Munus; ate, ive.*
Community, com. *Munus; ity.*
Commute, com. *Muto.*
Compact, com. *Pactus.*
Company, com. *Panis; y.*
Compare, com. *Par.*
Compassionate, com. *Passus; ion, ate.*
Compatible, com. *Patior; ible.*
Compatriot, com. *Patria.*
Compel, com. *Pello.*
Compendious, com. *Pendo; ous.*
Compensate, com. *Pensum; ate.*
Competent, com. *Peto; ent.*
Competition, com. *Petitum; ion.*
Compile, com. *Pilo.*
Complacence, com. *Placeo; ence.*
Complainant, com. *Plango; ant.*
Complement, com. *Pleo; ment.*
Completely, com. *Pletum; ly.*
Complexion, com. *Plexum; ion.*
Complicate, com. *Plico; ate.*
Compliment. com. *Pleo; ment.*
Composure, com. *Positum; ure.*
Compotator, com. *Potatum; or.*
Comprehend, com. *Prehendo.*
Comprehension, com. *Prehensum; ion.*
Compressible, com. *Pressum; ible.*
Comprise, com. *Prehendo.* (Fr. Prise.)
Compromise, com, pro. *Missum.*
Compulsory, com. *Pulsum; ory.*

Compunction, com. *Punctum; ion.*
Concealment, con. *Celo; ment.*
Concede, con. *Cedo.*
Conceive, con. *Capio.*
Concentrate, (Gr.) con. *Kentron; ate.*
Concentric, (Gr.) con. *Kentron; ic.*
Conception, con. *Captum; ion.*
Concern, con. *Cerno.*
Concert, con. *Certo.*
Conciliation. *Concilium; ate, ion.*
Conciliatory. *Concilium; ate, ory.*
Concise, con. *Cæsum.*
Conclude, con. *Cludo.*
Couclusive, con. *Clusum; ive.*
Concoct, con. *Coctum.*
Concomitant, con. *Comitis; ant.*
Concordance, con. *Cordis; ance.*
Concourse. con. *Cursum.*
Concurrence. con. *Curro; ence.*
Concussion, con. *Cussum; ion.*
Condemn, con. *Damnum.*
Condensation, con. *Densus; ion.*
Condense, con. *Densus.*
Condescend, con. de. *Scando.*
Condign, con. *Dignus.*
Condition, con. *Do; ion.*
Condole, con. *Doleo.*
Conduce. con. *Duco.*
Conduct, con. *Ductum.*
Conduit con. *Ductum.*
Confederacy, con. *Fœderis; acy.*
Confederate. con. *Fœderis; ate.*
Conference, con. *Fero; ence.*
Confess, con. *Fessum.*
Confidence, con. *Fido; ence.*
Confidential, con. *Fido; ent, al.*
Confinement. con. *Finis; ment.*
Confirmation, con. *Firmus; ion.*
Confiscate, con. *Fiscus; ate.*
Confiscation, con. *Fiscus; ate, ion.*
Conflagration, con. *Flagratum; ion.*
Conflict, con. *Flictum.*
Confluence, con. *Fluo; ence.*
Conformity, con. *Forma; ity.*
Confound, con. *Fundo.*
Confront, con. *Frontis.*
Confusion, con. *Fusum; ion.*
Confutation, con. *Futatum; ion.*
Congeal, con. *Gelo.*
Congenial, con. *Genus; al.*
Congratulate, con. *Gratus; ate.*
Congregation, con. *Gregis; ate, ion.*
Congress, con. *Gressus.*
Conic, (Gr.) *Konos; ic.*
Conjecture, con. *Jactum; ure.*
Conjugal, con. *Jugum; al.*
Conjuncture, con. *Junctum; ion.*
Conjure, con. *Juro.*
Connection, con. *Necto; ion.*
Conoid, (Gr.) *Konos, Eidos.*
Conqueror, con. *Quæro; or.*
Conquest, con. *Quæsitum.*
Consanguinity, con. *Sanguinis; ity.*
Conscience. con. *Scio; ence.*
Conscientious, con. *Scientia; ous.*
Consciousness, con. *Scio; ous, ness.*
Conscription, con. *Scriptum; ion.*
Consecrate. con. *Sacer; ate.*
Consecutive, con. *Secutus; ive.*
Consequence, con. *Sequor; ence.*

Consideration, con. *Sedeo; ion.* (Some derive it from Sidus, a star.)
Console, con. *Solor.*
Consolidate, con. *Solidus; ate.*
Consonant, con. *Sonus; ant.*
Consort, con. *Sortis.*
Conspicuous, con. *Specio; ous.*
Conspiracy, con. *Spiro; acy.*
Constant, con. *Sto; ant.*
Constellation, con. *Stella; ion.*
Consternation, con. *Sterno; ion.*
Constitution, con. *Statum; ion.*
Construction, con. *Structum; ion.*
Construe, con. *Struo.*
Consult. *Consultum,* to consult.
Consumption, con. *Sumptum; ion.*
Contact, con. *Tactum.*
Contagion, con. *Tango; ion.*
Contain, con. *Teneo.*
Contemporary, con. *Temporis; ary.*
Contend, con. *Tendo.*
Conterminous, con. *Terminus; ous.*
Contest, con. *Testis.*
Context, con. *Textum.*
Contiguous, con. *Tango; ous.*
Continental, con. *Teneo; ent, al.*
Contingent, con. *Tango; ent.*
Continual, con. *Teneo; al.*
Continuity, con. *Teneo; ity.*
Contortion, con. *Tortum; ion.*
Contraction, con. *Tractum; ion.*
Contradiction, contra. *Dictum; ion.*
Contravene, contra. *Venio.*
Contribute, con. *Tributum.*
Contrition, con. *Tritum; ion.*
Controversy, contro. *Versum; y.*
Controvert, contro. *Verto.*
Contumacy, con. *Tumeo; acy.*
Contumely, con. *Tumeo; y.*
Contusion, con. *Tusum; ion.*
Convalescent, con. *Valeo; escent.*
Convene, con. *Venio.*
Convenient, con. *Venio; ent.*
Conventional, con. *Ventum; ion, al.*
Converge, con. *Vergo.*
Conversation, con. *Versum; ion.*
Conversion, con. *Versum; ion.*
Convert, con. *Verto.*
Convexity, con. *Vectum; ity.*
Convex, con. *Veho.*
Conviction, con. *Victum; ion.*
Convince, con. *Vinco.*
Convivial, con. *Vivo; al.*
Convocation, con. *Vocatum; ion.*
Convoke, con. *Voco.*
Convulsion, con. *Vulsum; ion.*
Co-operate, co. *Operis; ate.*
Cordage, (Gr.) *Chorde; age.*
Cordial. *Cordis; al.*
Cordiality. *Cordis; al, ity.*
Cornet. *Cornu; et.*
Cornucopia. *Cornu, Copia.*
Corollary. *Corona; ary.*
Corona. *Corona.*
Coronation. *Corona; ion.*
Coroner. *Corona; er.*
Coronet. *Corona; et.*
Corporal. *Corporis; al.*
Corporation. *Corporis; ate, ion.*
Corporeal. *Corporis; al.*

Corpulency. *Corpus; ency;* (state of being corpulent.)
Corpulent. *Corpus; ulent.*
Corpuscle. *Corpus; cle.*
Correction, cor. *Rectum; ion.*
Correspond, cor, re. *Spondeo.*
Corroborative, cor. *Roboris; ate, ive.*
Corrupt, cor. *Ruptum.*
Cosmetic, (Gr.) *Kosmos; ic.*
Cosmogony. (Gr.) *Kosmos, Genea; y.*
Cosmopolitan, (Gr.) *Kosmos, Politeia; an*
Cosmopolite, (Gr.) *Kosmos. Polis; ite.*
Council. *Concilium.*
Counsel. *Consulo,* I consult.
Count. *Comitis.*
Countenance, con. *Teneo; ance.*
Counteract, counter. *Actum.*
Courage. *Cor; age.*
Courier. *Curro; ier.*
Course. *Cursum.*
Court, (Gr.) *Chortos.*
Cousin, con. *Sanguinis.* (?)
Covenanter, co. *Venio; ant, er.*
Creator. *Creatum; or.*
Creature. *Creatum; ure.*
Credence. *Credo; ence.*
Credential. *Credo; al.* (Credenda, articles of faith.)
Credible. *Credo; ible.*
Credit. *Creditum.*
Credulous. *Credo; ous.*
Crescent. *Cresco; ent.*
Crime. *Crimen.*
Criminal. *Criminis; al.*
Crisis, (Gr.) *Krites.*
Criterion, (Gr.) *Krites; ion.*
Criticise, (Gr.) *Krites; ic, ise.*
Criticism, (Gr.) *Krites; ic, ism.*
Critique, (Gr.) *Krites.*
Crocodile, (Gr.) *Krokos, Deilos,* fearful (Webster, Krokodilos.)
Crocus, (Gr.) *Krokos.*
Cross. *Crucis.*
Crown. *Corona.*
Crucial. *Crucis; al.*
Crucible. *Crucis; ible.*
Crucifixion. *Crucis, Fixum; ion.*
Cruciform. *Crucis, Forma.*
Crude. *Crudis.*
Cruel. *Crudelis.*
Crusade. *Crucis.*
Crypt, (Gr.) *Krypto.*
Cryptogamous, (Gr.) *Krypto, Gameo; ous*
Cryptography, (Gr.) *Krypto, Grapho; y*
Crystalline, (Gr.) *Krystallos; ine.*
Crystallize, (Gr.) *Krystallos; ise.*
Culpable. *Culpa; able.*
Cultivate. *Cultum; ate.*
Cumulative. *Cumulus; ate, ive.*
Curable. *Cura; able.*
Curate. *Cura; ate.*
Curious. *Cura; ous.*
Currency. *Curro; ency.*
Current. *Curro; ent.*
Cursory. *Cursum; ory.*
Curve. *Curvus.*
Curvilinear. *Curvus,* Linea; ar.
Custody. *Custodis; y.*
Cutaneous. *Cutis; ous.*
Cycle, (Gr.) *Kyklos.*

KEY. 235

Cycloid, (Gr.) *Kyklos, Eidos.*
Cyclopedia, (Gr.) *Kyklos, Paideia.*
Cylinder, (Gr.) *Kylindros; er.*
Cylindric, (Gr.) *Kylindros; ic.*
Cynic, (Gr.) *Kyon; ic.*
Cynosure. *Kyon, Oura,* the tail.

Dactylology, (Gr.) *Daktylos, Logos; y.*
Damage. *Damnum; age.*
Dauntless. *Domo; less.*
Deacon, (Gr.), dia. *Koneo.*
Dean, (Gr.) *Deka.*
Debase, (Gr.) de. *Basis.*
Debilitate, de. *Habeo; ate.* (Debilis.)
Debility, de. *Habeo; ity.* (Debilis.)
Debit. *Debitum.*
Debtor. *Debitum; or.*
Decade, (Gr.) *Deka,* or L. *Decem.*
Decagon, (Gr.) *Deka, Gonia.*
Decalogue, (Gr.) *Deka, Logos.*
Decapolis, (Gr.) *Deka, Polis.*
Decay, de. *Cado.*
Decease, de. *Cessum.*
December. *Decem.*
Decemvirate. *Decem, Vir; ate.*
Decency. *Decens; y.*
Decennial. *Decem, Annus; al.*
Decide, de. *Cædo.*
Deciduous, de. *Cado; ous.*
Decimal. *Decem; al.*
Decimation. *Decem; ate, al.*
Decision, de. *Cæsum; ion.*
Decisive, de. *Cæsum; ive.*
Declamation, de. *Clamatum; ion.*
Declaration, de. *Clarus; ion.*
Declination, de. *Clinatum; ion.*
Decline, de. *Clino.*
Declivity, de. *Clivus; ity.*
Decoction, de. *Coctum; ion.*
Decompose, de, com. *Positum.*
Decorate. *Decor; ate.*
Decorum. *Decor.*
Decree, de. *Cretum.*
Decrepitude, de. *Crepitum; ude.*
Dedicate. de. *Dico; ate.*
Deduce, de. *Duco.*
Deface, de. *Facies.*
Defamatory, de. *Fama; ory.*
Defame, de. *Fama.*
Defeat, de. *Factum.*
Defection, de. *Factum; ion.*
Defective, de. *Factum; ive.*
Defendant, de. *Fendo; ant.*
Defenseless, de. *Fensum; less.*
Defensive, de. *Fensum; ive.*
Deference, de. *Fero; ence.*
Definite, de. *Finis.*
Definition, de. *Finis; ion.*
Definitive, de. *Finis; ive.*
Deform, de. *Forma.*
Deformity, de. *Forma; ity.*
Defraud, de. *Fraudis.*
Degradation, de. *Gradior; ion.*
Degrade, de. *Gradior.*
Deign. *Dignus.*
Deist. *Deus; ist.*
Deity. *Deus; ity.*
Dejection, de. *Jactum; ion.*
Delegate, de. *Lego; ate.*
Deleterious, de. *Leo; ous.*

Deliberation, de. *Libra; ate, ion.*
Delineate, de. *Linea; ate.*
Delinquency, de. *Linquo; ency.*
Delude, de. *Ludo.*
Deluge. *Diluvium.*
Delusion. de. *Lusum, ion.*
Demagogue, (Gr.) *Demos, Agogeus.*
Democracy, (Gr.) *Demos, Kratos; y.*
Demolish, de. *Molior; ish.*
Demolition, de. *Molitus; ion.*
Demoniac, (Gr.) *Daimon; ac.*
Demonocracy, (Gr.) *Daimon, Kratos; y.*
Demonolatry, (Gr.) *Daimon, Latreia; y.*
Demonology, (Gr.) *Daimon, Logos; y.*
Demonstrate, de. *Monstro; ate.*
Demoralize, de. *Moris; al, ize.*
Denial, de. *Nego; al.*
Denomination, de. *Nominis; ate, ion.*
Denote, de. *Nota.*
Denounce, de. *Nuncio.*
Dense. *Densus.*
Density. *Densus; ity.*
Dental. *Dentis; al.*
Dentifrice. *Dentis, Frico,* I rub.
Dentist. *Dentis; ist.*
Denude, de. *Nudus.*
Denunciation, de. *Nuncio; ate, ion*
Deny, de. *Nego.*
Depart, de. *Partis.*
Depict, de. *Pictum.*
Deplorable, de. *Ploro; able.*
Deposition, de. *Positum; ion.*
Depravity, de. *Pravus; ity.*
Depreciate, de. *Precium; ate.*
Depredation, de. *Præda; ate, ion.*
Depredator, de. *Præda; ate, or.*
Deprive, de. *Privus.*
Deputation, de. *Putatum; ion.*
Deputy, de. *Puto; y.*
Deride, de. *Rideo.*
Derision, de. *Risum; ion.*
Derivation, de. *Rivus; ion.*
Derive, de. *Rivus.*
Derogatory, de. *Rogo; ate, ory.*
Descant, dis. *Canto.*
Descendant, de. *Scando; ant.*
Describe, de. *Scribo.*
Description, de. *Scriptum; ion.*
Desecrate, de. *Sacer; ate.*
Desert, de. *Sertum.*
Design, de, *Signum.*
Designate, de. *Signum; ate.*
Desolate, de. *Solus; ate.*
Despair, de. *Spero.*
Desperado. *Spero.*
Desperation, de. *Spero; ate, ion.*
Despicable, de. *Specio; able.*
Despondency, de. *Spondeo; ency.*
Despot, (Gr.) *Despotes.*
Despotic, (Gr.) *Despotes; ic.*
Destitute, de. *Sisto* or *Statum.*
Destruction, de. *Structum; ion.*
Destructive, de. *Structum; ive.*
Desultory, de. *Saltum; ory.*
Detain, de. *Teneo.*
Detect, de. *Tectum.*
Detention, de. *Tentum; ion.*
Deter, de. *Terreo.*
Deterioration. *Deterior; ate, ion.*
Determination, de. *Terminus; ion.*

Determine, de. *Terminus.*
Detraction, de. *Tractum; ion.*
Detrimental, de. *Tritum; ment, al.*
Deuterogamy, (Gr.) *Deuteros, Gameo; y.*
Deuteronomy, (Gr.) *Deuteros, Nomos; y.*
Develop. de. *Volup.*
Deviation, de. *Via; ate, ion.*
Devise. *Divisus,* dividing.
Devolving. de. *Volvo; ing.*
Devotee, de. *Votum; ee.*
Devour. de. *Voro.*
Devout. de. *Votum.*
Dexterity. *Dexter; ity.*
Dexterous. *Dexter; ous.*
Diabolical, (Gr.) dia. *Boleo; ical.*
Diæresis, (Gr.) dia. *Hairesis.*
Diagonal, (Gr.) dia. *Gonia; al.*
Diagram, (Gr.) dia. *Gramma.*
Dial. *Dies; al.*
Dialects, (L. and Gr.) dia. *Lectum.*
Dialogue. (Gr.) dia. *Logos.*
Diameter, (Gr.) dia. *Metron.*
Diamond, (Gr.) a. *Damao.* (Corrupted from Adamant.)
Diaphanous, (Gr.) dia. *Phano; ous.*
Diarrhœa, (Gr.) dia. *Rheo.*
Diary. *Dies; ary.*
Dictate. *Dictum; ate.*
Dictator. *Dictum; ate, or.*
Dictatorial. *Dictum; ate, or, al.*
Diction. *Dictum; ion.*
Dictionary. *Dictum; ion, ary.*
Dictum. *Dictum.*
Didactic, (Gr.) *Didasko; ic.*
Diet. (Gr.) *Diaita.*
Dietetic, (Gr.) *Diaita; ic.*
Different, dif. *Fero; ent.*
Difficulty, dif. *Facio; ty.* (Facilis.)
Diffidence, dif. *Fido; ence.*
Diffuse, dif. *Fusum.*
Digit. *Digitus.*
Dignify. *Dignus; fy.*
Dignity. *Dignus; ity.*
Digression, di. *Gressus; ion.*
Dilapidation, di. *Lapidis; ate, ion.*
Dilate, di. *Latus.*
Dilation, di. *Latus; ion.*
Dilatory, di. *Latum; ory.*
Dilemma, (Gr.) di. *Lemma.*
Diligent, di. *Lego; ent.*
Dilute, di. *Lutum.*
Dimension, di. *Mensura; ion.*
Diminish, di. *Minuo; -ish.*
Diminutive, di. *Minutum; ive.*
Diocese, (Gr.) dia. *Oikos.*
Dioptrics, (Gr.) dia. *Optomai; ics.*
Diorama, (Gr.) dia. *Orama.*
Diphthong, (Gr.) di. *Phthegma.*
Diplomatist, (Gr.) *Diploma; ist.*
Direction, di. *Rectum; ion.*
Diruption, di. *Ruptum; ion.*
Disaster, (Gr.) dis. *Astron; er.*
Discernment, dis. *Cerno; ment.*
Disciple. *Discipulus.*
Discipline. *Discipulus; ine.*
Disclaim, dis. *Clamo.*
Discoloration, dis. *Color; ion.*
Disconcert, dis. con. *Certo.*
Disconnect, dis, con. *Necto.*
Disconsolate, dis, con. *Solor; ate.*

Discouragement, dis. *Cor; age, ment.*
Discourse, dis. *Cursum.*
Discreet, dis. *Cretum.*
Discrepancy, dis. *Crepo; ancy.*
Discretion, dis. *Cretum; ion.*
Discrimination, dis. *Cerno; ate, ion.*
Discursive, dis. *Cursum; ive.*
Discussion, dis. *Cussum; ion.*
Disdain, dis. *Dignus.*
Disgrace, dis. *Gratia.*
Disgust, dis. *Gustus.*
Dishonest, dis. *Honestus.*
Dishonor. dis. *Honor.*
Dishonorable, dis. *Honor; able.*
Disinherit, dis, in. *Hereditas.*
Disintegrate, dis. *Integer; ate.*
Dismount. dis. *Montis.*
Disorganize, (Gr.) dis. *Organon; ise.*
Disparagement, dis. *Par; age, ment.*
Disparity, dis. *Par; ity.*
Dispassionate, dis. *Passus; ion, ate.*
Dispensing, dis. *Pensum; ing.*
Disperse, dis. *Sparsum.*
Display, dis. *Plico.*
Disposition, dis. *Positum; ion.*
Disprove, dis. *Probo.*
Dispute, dis. *Puto.*
Disqualified, dis. *Qualis; fy, ed.*
Disrespect, dis, re. *Spectum.*
Disruption, dis. *Ruptum; ion.*
Dissatisfied, dis. *Satis; fy, ed.*
Dissemble, dis. *Similis; ble.*
Dissemination, dis. *Seminis; ate, ion.*
Dissent, dis. *Sentio.*
Dissertation, dis. *Sertum; ion.*
Dissimulation, dis. *Simul; ate, ion.*
Dissolute, dis. *Solutum.*
Dissuade, dis. *Suadeo.*
Dissuasive, dis. *Suasum; ive.*
Dissyllable, (Gr.) *Dis,* syl. *Labo.*
Distance, dis. *Sto; ance.*
Distant, dis. *Sto; ant.*
Distich, (Gr.) *Dis, Stichos.*
Distillery, dis. *Stilla; ery.*
Distinct, dis. *Stinctum.*
Distinguish, dis. *Stinguo; ish.*
Distort, dis. *Tortum.*
Distraction, dis. *Tractum; ion.*
Disturbance, dis. *Turba; ance.*
Disuse, dis. *Usus.*
Diurnal. *Dies,* al. (Diurnus, daily.)
Diverge, di. *Vergo.*
Diverse, di. *Versum.*
Diversify, di. *Versum; fy.*
Divide. *Divido,* I divide.
Divine. *Divus; ine.*
Divinity. *Divus; ine, ity.*
Divisor. *Divisum,* to divide; *or.*
Divorce, di. *Verto.*
Divulge, di. *Vulgus.*
Docility. *Doceo; ile, ity.*
Doctor. *Doctum; or.*
Doctrine. *Doctum; ine.*
Document. *Doceo; ment.*
Dogmatic, (Gr.) *Dogmatos; ic.*
Doleful. *Doleo; ful.*
Domesticate. *Domus; ic, ate.*
Domicile. *Domus.* (Domicilium, a house.)
Dominant. *Dominus; ant.*

KEY. 237

Domination. *Dominus; ate, ion.*
Domineer. *Dominus.*
Dominion. *Dominus; ion.*
Donation. *Donum; ate, ion.*
Donee. *Donum; ee.*
Donor. *Donum; or.*
Dormant. *Dormio; ant.*
Dormitory. *Dormitum; ory.*
Dose, (Gr.) *Dosis.*
Doubly. *Duo, Plico.*
Doubt. *Dubium, fr. Dubito, I doubt.*
Doxology, (Gr.) *Doxa, Logos; y.*
Dramatic, (Gr.) *Drama; ic.*
Dramatist, (Gr.) *Drama: ist.*
Dramatize, (Gr.) *Drama; ize.*
Dromedary, (Gr.) *Dromos.*
Dropsy, (Gr.) *Hydor, Ops: y.*
Dubious. *Dubium; ous.*
Ducat. *Ductum.*
Ductile. *Ductum; ile.*
Duel. *Duellum.*
Duke. *Ductum.*
Duodecagon, (Gr.) *Duo, Deka, Gonia.*
Duodecimal. *Duo, Decem; al.*
Duodecimo. *Duo, Decem.*
Duplicate. *Duo, Plico; ate.*
Duplicity. *Duo, Plico; ity.*
Durable. *Durus; able.*
Duration. *Durus; ion.*
During. *Durus; ing.*
Dynamics, (Gr.) *Dynamis; ics.*
Dynasty, (Gr.) *Dynamis; y.*
Dyspepsy, (Gr.) *Dys, Peptos; y.*
Dyspeptic, (Gr.) *Dys, Peptos; ic.*
Dysphony, (Gr.) *Dys, Phone; y.*

Ebriety. *Ebrius; ety.*
Ebullition, e. *Bullitum; ion.*
Eccentric, (Gr.) ec. *Kentron; ic.*
Eccentrical, ec. *Kentron; ical.*
Eccentricity, (Gr.) ec. *Kentron; ic, ity.*
Ecclesiastic, (Gr.) ec. *Klesis; ic.*
Echo, (Gr.) *Echeo.*
Eclipse, (Gr.) ec. *Leipo.*
Ecliptic, (Gr.) ec. *Leipo; ic.*
Eclogue, (Gr.) ec. *Logos.*
Economy, (Gr.) *Oikos, Nomos; y.*
Ecstasy, (Gr.) ec. *Stasis; y.*
Ecstatical, (Gr.) ec. *Stasis; ical.*
Ecumenical, (Gr.) *Oikos; ical.*
Edacity. *Edo; ity;* (state of being edacious.)
Edible. *Edo; ible.*
Edict, e. *Dictum.*
Edifice. *Ædes, Facio.*
Edify. *Ædes; fy.*
Editor, e. *Datum; or.*
Education, e. *Duco; ate, ion.*
Efface, ef. *Facies.*
Effect, ef. *Factum.*
Effeminacy, ef. *Femina; acy.*
Effervescence, ef. *Ferveo; escence.*
Efficacious, ef. *Facio; acious.*
Effigy, ef. *Fingo; y.*
Efflorescence, ef. *Floris; escence.*
Effluvium, ef. *Fluo.* (L. Effluvium; plural, Effluvia.)
Effort, ef. *Fortis.*
Effulgence, ef. *Fulgeo; ence.*
Effusion, ef. *Fusum; ion.*

Egotism. *Ego; ism.*
Egotistical. *Ego; ist, ical.*
Egregious, e. *Gregis; ous.*
Egress, e. *Gressus.*
Eject, e. *Jactum.*
Elaborate, e. *Labor; ate.*
Elapse, e. *Lapsus.*
Elasticity, (Gr.) *Elao; ic, ity.*
Elate, e. *Latum.*
Election, e. *Lectum; ion.*
Electricity, (Gr.) *Elektron; ic, ity.*
Electrometer, (Gr.) *Elektron, Metron.*
Elegance. *Elegans; ance.*
Elegiac, (Gr.) *Elegeia; ac.*
Elegy, (Gr.) *Elegeia; y.*
Elevate, e. *Levo; ate.*
Ellipses, (Gr.) el (ec). *Leipo.*
Elliptical, (Gr.) el (ec). *Leipo; ical.*
Elocution, e *Locutus; ion.*
Elongate, e. *Longus; ate.*
Eloquent, e. *Loquor; ent.*
Elucidate, e. *Luceo; id, ate.*
Elude, e. *Ludo.*
Elusion, e. *Lusum; ion.*
Emanates, e. *Mano; ate.*
Emancipate, e. *Manus, Capio; ate.*
Embalm, (Gr.) em. *Balsamon.*
Emblem, (Gr.) em. *Boleo.*
Emergency, e. *Mergo; ency.*
Emetic, (Gr.) *Emeo; ic.*
Emigrate, e. *Migro; ate.*
Eminence, e. *Mineo; ence.*
Eminent, e. *Mineo; ent.*
Emissary, e. *Missum; ary.*
Emit, e. *Mitto.*
Emotion, e. *Motum; ion.*
Emperor. *Impero; or.*
Emphasis, (Gr.) em. *Phano.*
Empire. *Impero.*
Empiric, (Gr.) em. *Peirates, fr. Peirao, I try, I attempt. ic.*
Empyrean, (Gr.) em. *Pyr; ean.*
Emulation. *Æmulus; ate, ion.*
Enable, en. *Habeo; ble.*
Enchant, en. *Canto.*
Encircle, en. *Circulus.*
Encomium, (Gr.) en. *Komos.*
Encumber, en. *Cumbo.*
Encumbrance, en. *Cumbo; ance.*
Encyclical, (Gr.) en. *Kyklos; ical.*
Encyclopædia, (Gr.) en. *Kyklos, Pas deia.*
Endecagon, (Gr.) *En, Deka, Gonia.*
Endemic, (Gr.) en. *Demos; ic.*
Endorse, en. *Dorsum.*
Endure, en. *Durus.*
Enemy. en. *Amicus.*
Energetic, (Gr.) en. *Ergon; ic.*
Energize, (Gr.) en. *Ergon; ize.*
Energy, (Gr.) en. *Ergon; y.*
Enervate, e. *Nervus; ate.*
Engraver, (Gr.) en. *Grapho; er.*
Enjoin, en. *Junctum.*
Enigma, (Gr.) *Ænigma.*
Enigmatical, (Gr.) *Ænigma; ical.*
Enmity, en. *Amicus; ty.*
Ennoble, en. *Nobilis.*
Enormous, e. *Norma; ous.*
Ensign, en. *Signum.*
Ensue, en. *Secutus.*

Enterprise, enter. *Prehensum.* (Fr. Prise, taken.)
Entertain, enter. *Teneo.*
Enthusiasm, (Gr.) en. *Theos; asm.*
Entombment, en. *Tumba; ment.*
Entomology, (Gr.) *Entomon, Logos; y.*
Enumeration, e. *Numerus; ate, ion.*
Enunciate, e. *Nuncio; ate.*
Envelop, en. *Volup.*
Ephemeral, (Gr.) epi. *Hemera; al.*
Ephemeris, (Gr.) epi. *Hemera.*
Epic, (Gr.) *Epos; ic.*
Epicure, (Gr.) *Epikouros.*
Epicurean, (Gr.) *Epikouros; ean.*
Epicycle, (Gr.) epi. *Kuklos.*
Epidemic, (Gr.) epi. *Demos; ic.*
Epiglottis, (Gr.) epi. *Glossa* or *Glotta.*
Epigram, (Gr.) epi. *Gramma.*
Epilepsy, (Gr.) epi. *Lepsis; y.*
Epiphany, (Gr.) epi. *Phano; y.*
Episcopacy, (Gr.) epi. *Skopeo; acy.*
Episode, (Gr.) epi. *Odos.*
Epispastic, (Gr.) epi. *Spao; ic.*
Epistle, (Gr.) epi. *Stello.*
Epitaph, (Gr.) epi. *Taphos.*
Epithet, (Gr.) epi. *Thesis.*
Epitome, (Gr.) epi. *Tomos.*
Epoch. *Epocha,* an epoch.
Equalize. *Æquus; al, ize.*
Equanimity. *Æquus, Animus; ity.*
Equator. *Æquus.*
Equatorial. *Æquus; al.*
Equestrian. *Eques; an.*
Equiangular. *Æquus, Angulus; ar.*
Equidistant. *Æquus; di, Sto, ant.*
Equilateral. *Æquus, Lateris; al.*
Equilibrium. *Æquus, Libra.*
Equinoctial. *Æquus, Noctis; al.*
Equinox. *Æquus, Nox.*
Equipage. *Eques.* (Sp. Equipage.)
Equity. *Æquus; ity.*
Equivalent. *Æquus, Valeo; ent.*
Equivocal. *Æquus, Voco; al.*
Equivocate. *Æquus, Voco; ate.*
Eradicate, e. *Radicis; ate.*
Erase, e. *Rasum.*
Erasure, e. *Rasum; ure.*
Erecting, e. *Rectum; ing.*
Eremite, (Gr.) *Eremos; ite.*
Errata. *Erratum.*
Erratic. *Erratum; ic.*
Erroneous. *Erro; ous.*
Error. *Erro; or.*
Erudite, e. *Rudis.*
Eruption, e. *Ruptum; ion.*
Esoteric, (Gr.) *Eso; ic.*
Especially, e. *Specio; al, ly.*
Espouse, e. *Sponsum.*
Essence. *Esse; ence.*
Essential. *Esse; ent, al.*
Establish, e. *Sto; able, ish.*
Esteem. *Æstimo.*
Estimable. *Æstimo; able.*
Estimation. *Æstimo; ate, ion.*
Eternity. *Æternus; ity.*
Ethereal, (Gr.) *Æther,* the sky; *al.*
Ethics, (Gr.) *Ethos; ics.*
Ethical, (Gr.) *Ethos; ical.*
Ethnical, (Gr.) *Ethnos; ical.*
Ethnography, (Gr.) *Ethnos, Grapho; y.*

Ethology, (Gr.) *Ethos, Logos; y.*
Etymology, (Gr.) *Etymon, Logos; y.*
Eucharist, (Gr.) *Eu, Charitos.*
Eulogium, (Gr.) *Eu, Logos.*
Eulogize, (Gr.) *Eu, Logos; ize.*
Euphemism, (Gr.) *Eu, Phano; ism.*
Euphony, (Gr.) *Eu, Phone; y.*
Euthanasia, (Gr.) *Eu, Thanatos.*
Euthanasy, (Gr.) *Eu, Thanatos; y.*
Evacuation, e. *Vaco; ate, ion.*
Evade, e. *Vasum.*
Evangelical, (Gr.) *Eu, Angello; ical.*
Evangelist, (Gr.) *Eu, Angello; ist.*
Evasion, e. *Vasum; ion.*
Evasively, e. *Vasum; ive, ly.*
Eventually, e. *Ventum; al, iy.*
Event, e. *Ventum.*
Evident, e. *Video; ent.*
Evince, e. *Vinco.*
Evolve, e. *Volvo.*
Exact, ex. *Act.*
Exaggeration, ex. *Agger; ate, ion.*
Exaltation, ex. *Altus; ion.*
Examination. *Examinis; ion.*
Example. *Exemplum.*
Exasperate, ex. *Asper; ate.*
Excavation, ex. *Cavus; ate, ion.*
Exceed, ex. *Cedo.*
Excellent, ex. *Celsus; ent.*
Except, ex. *Captum.*
Excessive, ex. *Cessum; ive.*
Excise, ex. *Cæsum.*
Excision, ex. *Cæsum; ion.*
Excitable, ex. *Cito; able.*
Exclaim, ex. *Clamo.*
Excrescence, ex. *Cresco; ence.*
Excruciate, ex. *Crucis; ate.*
Exculpate, ex. *Culpa; ate.*
Excursion, ex. *Cursum; ion.*
Execute, ex. *Secutus.*
Excuse, ex. *Causa.*
Exegesis, (Gr.) ex. *Egesis.*
Exegetical, (Gr.) ex. *Egesis; ical.*
Exemplar. *Exemplum; ar.*
Exemplary. *Exemplum; ary.*
Exemplify. *Exemplum; fy.*
Exemption, ex. *Emptum; ion.*
Exercise, ex. *Arceo; ise.*
Exert, ex. *Sertum.*
Exhale, ex. *Halo.*
Exhaust, ex. *Haustum.*
Exhibit, ex. *Habitum.*
Exhort, ex. *Hortor.*
Exhumed, ex. *Humus; ed.*
Exigency, ex. *Ago; ency.*
Exile. *Exilium.*
Existence, ex. *Sisto; ence.*
Exit, ex. *Itum.*
Exodus, (Gr.) ex. *Odos.*
Exonerate, ex. *Oneris; ate.*
Exorbitant, ex. *Orbita; ant.*
Exorcise, (Gr.) ex. *Orkos; ise.*
Exorcism, (Gr.) ex. *Orkos; ism.*
Exordium, ex. *Orior.* (Ordior, I begin.)
Exotic, (Gr.) *Exo; ic.*
Expansion, ex. *Pansum; ion.*
Expatiate, ex. *Spatium; ate.*
Expatriate, ex. *Patris; ate.*
Expect, ex. *Spectum.*
Expectoration, ex. *Pectoris; ate, ion.*

Expediency, ex. *Pedis; ency.*
Expedite, ex. *Pedis.*
Expensive, ex. *Pensum; ive.*
Experience, ex. *Perior; ence.*
Expert, ex. *Peritus.*
Expiatory, ex. *Pio; ate, ory.*
Expiration, ex. *Spiratum; ion.*
Expire, ex. *Spiro.*
Explanatory, ex. *Planus; ory.*
Expletive, ex. *Pletum; ive.*
Explicit, ex. *Plico.*
Explode, ex. *Plaudo.*
Exploration, ex. *Ploratum; ion.*
Explore, ex. *Ploro.*
Explosion, ex. *Plausum; ion.*
Exposition, ex. *Positum; ion.*
Expostulate, ex. *Postulo; ate.*
Expression, ex. *Pressum; ion.*
Expulsion, ex. *Pulsum; ion.*
Expurgate, ex. *Purgo; ate.*
Exquisite, ex. *Quæsitum.*
Extant, ex. *Sto; ant.*
Extemporaneous, ex. *Temporis; ous.*
Extent, ex. *Tentum.*
Extenuate, ex. *Tenuis; ate.*
Exterior. *Exterior.*
Exterminate, ex. *Terminus; ate.*
External. *Exterus; al.*
Extinguishment, ex. *Stinguo; ish, ment.*
Extirpate, ex. *Stirps; ate.*
Extol, ex. *Tollo.*
Extort, ex. *Tortum.*
Extract, ex. *Tractum.*
Extraneous. *Extra; ous.*
Extravagant, extra. *Vagus; ant.*
Extremity. *Extremus; ity.*
Extramural, Extra. *Murus; al.*
Extrinsic. *Exterus; ic.*
Exult, ex. *Saltum.*

Fabricate. *Fabrico; ate.*
Face. *Facies.*
Facilitate. *Facio; ile, ate.*
Factory. *Factum; ory.*
Faculty. *Facio; ile, ty.*
Faith. *Fido.*
Fallacious. *Fallo; acious.*
Fallacy. *Fallo; acy.*
Falsify. *Falsum; fy.*
Familiarity. *Familia; ar, ity.*
Family. *Familia; y.*
Famish. *Fames; ish.*
Famous. *Fama; ous.*
Fanaticism. *Fanum; ic, ism.*
Fancy, (Gr.) *Phano; y.*
Fantastic, (Gr.) *Phano; ic.*
Farinaceous. *Farina; aceous.*
Fashion. *Facio; ion.*
Fatal. *Fatum; al.*
Fault. *Fallo.*
Favorable. *Faveo; or, able.*
Feast. *Festum.*
Features. *Facio; ure.*
Febrile. *Febris; ile.*
Federal. *Fœderis; al.*
Felicitate. *Felicis; ate.*
Felicity. *Felicis; ity.*
Feminine. *Femina; ine.*
Fermentation. *Fermentum; ion.*

Ferocious. *Ferocis; ous.*
Fertile. *Fero; ile.*
Ferule. *Ferula.*
Fervor. *Ferveo; or.*
Festival. *Festum; ive, al.*
Festivity. *Festum; ive, ity.*
Feverish. *Febris; ish.*
Fictitious. *Fictum; ous.*
Fidelity. *Fidelis; ity.*
Fierce. *Ferocis.*
Figurative. *Figura; ive.*
Filial. *Filius; al.*
Finally. *Finis; al, ly.*
Fine. *Finis.*
Finite. *Finis.*
Firmament. *Firmus; ment.*
Fiscal. *Fiscus; al.*
Fix. *Fixum.*
Flagrancy. *Flagro; ancy.*
Flexible. *Flexum; ible.*
Florid. *Floris; id.*
Floriferous. *Floris, Fero; ous.*
Florin. *Floris.*
Flourish. *Floris; ish.*
Flowers. *Floris.*
Fluctuate. *Fluctum; ate.*
Fluency. *Fluo; ency.*
Foliage. *Folium; age.*
Folio. *Folium.*
Force. *Fortis.*
Forfeit. *Foris,* out of doors; *Factum.*
Formality. *Forma; al, ity.*
Fortification. *Fortis, Factum; ion.*
Fortitude. *Fortis; ude.*
Fortress. *Fortis.*
Fortuitous. *Fortis; ous.*
Fortunate. *Fortuna; ate.*
Fossil. *Fossum.*
Foundation. *Fundus; ion.*
Fraction. *Fractum; ion.*
Fragility. *Frango; ile, ity.*
Fragment. *Frango; ment.*
Fragrant. *Fragro; ant.*
Frantic, (Gr.) *Phren; ic.*
Fraternity. *Frater; ity.* (Fraternus.?)
Fratricide. *Frater. Cædo.*
Fraudulent. *Fraudis; ulent.*
Frenetic, (Gr.) *Phren; ic.*
Frenzy, (Gr.) *Phren; y.*
Frequent. *Frequentis.*
Frigid. *Frigus; id.*
Frontispiece. *Frontis, Specio.*
Fruit. *Fruitus.*
Fruition. *Fruitus; ion.*
Fugitive. *Fugitum; ive.*
Fulgency. *Fulgeo; ency.*
Fumigation. *Fumigo; ate, ion.*
Fundamental. *Fundus; ment, al.*
Funeral. *Funeris; al.*
Furious. *Furia; ous.*
Fusibility. *Fusum; ible, ity.*
Futile. *Futilis; ile.* (*Fundo?*)

Galaxy, (Gr.) *Galaktos; y.*
Gasometer, (Gr.) Gas, *Metron.*
Gastric, (Gr.) *Gaster; ic.*
Gastriloquy, (Gr.) *Gaster, Loquor; y*
Gelatinous. *Gelatum; ine, ous.*
Genealogy, (Gr.) *Genea, Logos; y.*
General. *Generis; al.*

Generate. *Generis; ate.*
Generic. *Generis; ic.*
Genesis, (Gr.) *Genea.*
Genial. *Genus; al.*
Genius. *Genus.*
Gentility. *Gentis; ile, ity.* (L. Gentilis, belonging to the same race.)
Gentle, Gentile. See Gentility.
Genuine. *Genus; ine.*
Geocentric. (Gr.) *Ge, Kentron; ic.*
Geography, (Gr.) *Ge, Grapho; y.*
Geology. (Gr.) *Ge, Logos; y.*
Geometry, (Gr.) *Ge, Metron; y.*
Geoponic, (Gr.) *Ge, Ponos; ic.*
Georgic, (Gr.) *Ge, Ergon; ic.*
Gesture. *Gestum; ure.*
Gladiatorial. *Gladius; or, al.*
Glands. *Glans,* an acorn.
Globe. *Globus.*
Globular. *Globulus; ar.*
Glorification. *Gloria, Factum; ion.*
Glossary, (Gr.) *Glossa; ary.*
Gloss, (Gr.) *Glossa.*
Glottis, (Gr.) *Glotta.*
Glutton. *Glutio.*
Glyptic, (Gr.) *Glypho; ic.*
Gnomon, (Gr.) *Gnomon.*
Gnostic, (Gr.) *Gnostos; ic.*
Government. *Guberno; ment.*
Gracious. *Gratia; ous.* (In Latin before two vowels *t* frequently changes to c.)
Gradation. *Gradior; ion.*
Grain. *Granum.*
Graminivorous. *Graminis, Voro; ous.*
Grammar, (Gr.) *Gramma.*
Granary. *Granum; ary.*
Grandeur. *Grandis.*
Grandiloquence. *Grandis, Loquor; ence.*
Granite. *Granum.* Gr. *Lithos.*
Granivorous. *Granum, Voro; ous.*
Graphic, (Gr.) *Grapho; ic.*
Grateful. *Gratus; ful.*
Gratis. *Gratia.*
Gratuitous. *Gratia; ity, ous.*
Gravitation. *Gravitas; ate, ion.*
Gravity. *Gravis; ity.*
Grecian, (Gr.) *Graikia; ian.*
Grief. *Gravis.*
Grievous. *Gravis; ous.*
Gubernatorial. *Gubernator; al.*
Gymnastic, (Gr.) *Gymnos; ic.*
Gymnosophist, (Gr.) *Gymnos, Sophia; ist.*
Gymnospermous, (Gr.) *Gymnos, Sperma; ous.*
Gyneocracy, (Gr.) *Gyne, Kratos; y.*
Gyration, (Gr.) *Gyros; ate, ion.*

Habeas Corpus. *Habeo, Corpus.*
Habiliments. *Habilis; ment.*
Habit. *Habitum.*
Habitation. *Habitum; ion.*
Habituate. *Habitum; ate.*
Harmonious, (Gr.) *Harmonia; ous.*
Harmony, (Gr.) *Harmonia; y.*
Hebdomadal, (Gr.) *Hebdomas; al.*
Hecatomb, (Gr.) *Hekaton, Bous,* an ox.
Heir. *Heres.*
Heliocentric, (Gr.) *Helios, Kentron; ic.*
Heliometer, (Gr.) *Helios, Metron.*
Helioscope, (Gr.) *Helios, Skopeo.*
Heliotrope, (Gr.) *Helios, Tropos.*
Hellenic, (Gr.) *Hellen; ic.*
Hemicycle, (Gr.) *hemi. Kyklos.*
Hemisphere, (Gr.) *hemi. Sphaira.*
Hemistich, (Gr.) *hemi. Stichos.*
Hemoptysis, (Gr.) *Haima, Ptyo,* I spit
Hemorrhage, (Gr.) *Haima. Rheo.*
Heptagonal, (Gr.) *Hepta, Gonia; al.*
Heptarchy, (Gr.) *Hepta, Arche; y.*
Herbivorous. *Herba, Voro; ous.*
Hereditary. *Hereditas; ary.*
Heresiarch, (Gr.) *Hairesis, Arche.*
Heresy, (Gr.) *Hairesis; y.*
Hermetic, (Gr.) *Hermes; ic.*
Hermit, (Gr.) *Eremos.*
Hermitage, (Gr.) *Eremos.*
Heroic, (Gr.) *Heros; ic.*
Heroine, (Gr.) *Heros; ine.*
Hesitate. *Hæsitum; ate.*
Heterarchy, (Gr.) *Heteros, Arche; y.*
Heteroscii, (Gr.) *Heteros, Skia.*
Heterodox, (Gr.) *Heteros, Doxa.*
Heterogeneous, (Gr.) *Heteros, Genea; ous.*
Hexagon, (Gr.) *Hex. Gonia.*
Hexahedron, (Gr.) *Hex, Hedra.*
Hexameter, (Gr.) *Hex, Metron.*
Hierarchy, (Gr.) *Hieros, Arche; y.*
Hieroglyphic, (Gr.) *Hieros, Glypho; ic.*
Hierophant, (Gr.) *Hieros, Phano.*
Hippodrome, (Gr.) *Hippos, Dromos.*
Hippopotamus, (Gr.) *Hippos, Potamos.*
Historian, (Gr.) *Historia; an.*
Historiography, (Gr.) *Historia, Grapho; y.*
Holocaust, (Gr.) *Holos, Kaustikos.*
Holograph, (Gr.) *Holos, Grapho.*
Homicide. *Homo, Cædo.*
Homily, (Gr.) *Homilos; y.*
Homogeneous, (Gr.) *Homos, Genea; ous.*
Homologous, (Gr.) *Homos, Logos; ous.*
Honesty. *Honestus; y.*
Honorable. *Honor; able.*
Honorary. *Honor; ary.*
Horal, (Gr.) *Hora; al.*
Horizon, (Gr.) *Horizo.*
Horography, (Gr.) *Hora, Grapho; y.*
Horologe, (Gr.) *Hora, Logos.*
Horrible. *Horreo; ible.*
Horror. *Horreo; or.*
Horticulture. *Hortus, Cultum; ure.*
Hospitable. *Hospitis; able.*
Hospital. *Hospitis.*
Hospitality. *Hospitis; ity.*
Host. *Hospitis.*
Hosts. *Hostis.*
Hostility. *Hostis; ile, ity.*
Hotel, Hostel. *Hospitis.*
Hour, (Gr.) *Hora.*
Human. *Homo; an.*
Humane. *Homo; ane.*
Humanize. *Homo; an, ize.*
Humble. *Humus; ble.*
Humidity. *Humus; id, ity.*
Humility. *Humilis; ity.*
Humor. *Humeo; or.*
Hydra, (Gr.) *Hydra.*
Hydrant, (Gr.) *Hydor; ant.*
Hydraulic, (Gr.) *Hydor, Aulos; ic.*

Hydrocele, (Gr.) *Hydor, Kele.*
Hydrocephalus, (Gr.) *Hydor, Kephale.*
Hydrogen, (Gr.) *Hydor, Genea.*
Hydrography, (Gr.) *Hydor, Grapho; y.*
Hydromel, (Gr.) *Hydor, Meli.*
Hydrometer, (Gr.) *Hydor, Metron.*
Hydrophobia, (Gr.) *Hydor, Phobos.*
Hydrostatic, (Gr.) *Hydor, Stasis; ic.*
Hygrometer, (Gr.) *Hygros, Metron.*
Hymeneal, (Gr.) *Hymen; al.*
Hymnology, (Gr.) *Hymnos,* a hymn; *Logos; y.*
Hyperbola, (Gr.) hyper. *Boleo.*
Hyperbole, (Gr.) hyper. *Boleo.*
Hypercritical, (Gr.) hyper. *Krites; ical.*
Hypochondriac, (Gr.) hypo. *Chondros; ac.*
Hypocrisy, (Gr.) hypo. *Krites; y.*
Hypocrite, (Gr.) hypo. *Krites; ite.*
Hypotenuse, (Gr.) hypo. *Tonos.*
Hypothecate, (Gr.) hypo. *Thesis; ate.*
Hypothesis, (Gr.) hypo. *Thesis.*

Ichthyology, (Gr.) *Ichthys, Logos; y.*
Ichthyophagy, (Gr.) *Ichthys, Phago; y.*
Iconoclast, (Gr.) *Eikon, Klastes,* a breaker.
Idealize, (Gr.) *Idea; al, ize.*
Identical. *Idem; ical.*
Idiom, (Gr.) *Idios.*
Idiosyncrasy, (Gr.) *Idios;* syn. *Krasis,* temperament. *y.*
Idiocy, (Gr.) *Idios; y.*
Idolatry, (Gr.) *Eidolon, Latreia; y.*
Ignite. *Ignis.*
Ignominious, ig. *Nomen (nominis); y, ous.*
Ignorant, ig. *Gnorus* for *Gnarus,* knowing.
Iliad, (Gr.) *Ilion.*
Illegal, il. *Legis; al.*
Illiberality, il. *Liber; al, ity.*
Illiterate, il. *Litera; ate.*
Illogical, (Gr.) il. *Logos; ical.*
Illumination, il. *Luminis; ate, ion.*
Illustration, il. *Lustro; ate, ion.*
Imagery. *Imago; ery.*
Imagination. *Imaginatus; ion.*
Imagine. *Imaginis.*
Imbecile. *Imbecillis.*
Imbibe, im. *Bibo.*
Imitate. *Imitor; ate.*
Immature, im. *Maturus.*
Immediate, im. *Medius; ate.*
Immemorial, im. *Memor; y, al.*
Immense, im. *Mensura.*
Immersion, im. *Mersum; ion.*
Immigrant, im. *Migro; ant.*
Immoral, im. *Moris; al.*
Immortal, im. *Mortis; al.*
Immunity, im. *Munus; ity.*
Immure, im. *Murus.*
Immutable, im. *Muto; able.*
Impart, im. *Partis.*
Impartial, im. *Partis; al.*
Impatient, im. *Patior; ent.*
Impediment, im. *Pedis; ment.*
Impel, im. *Pello.*
Impend, im. *Pendeo.*
Impenetrable, im. *Penetro; able.*

Imperial. *Impero; al.*
Imperious. *Impero; ous.*
Impertinent, im, per. *Teneo; ent.*
Imperturbable, im, per. *Turba; able.*
Impervious, im, per. *Via, ous.*
Impetuous, im. *Peto; ous.*
Impetus, im. *Peto.*
Impiously, im. *Pius; ous, ly.*
Implacable, im. *Placo; able.*
Implant, im. *Planta.*
Implement, im. *Pleo; ment.*
Implicate, im. *Plico; ate.*
Implore, im. *Ploro.*
Impolitic, (Gr.) im. *Politeia; ic.*
Importunity, im. *Porto; ity.*
Imposition, im. *Positum; ion.*
Impossible, im. *Posse; ible.*
Impotent, im. *Potentis.*
Impregnable, im. *Prehendo; able.*
Impression, im. *Pressum; ion.*
Improve, im. *Probo.*
Impugn, im. *Pugna.*
Impulsive, im. *Pulsum; ive.*
Impunity, im. *Punio; ity.*
Impute, im. *Puto.*
Inalienable, in. *Alienus; able.*
Inanition. *Inanis; ity, ion.*
Inarable, in. *Aro; able.*
Inarticulate, in. *Articulus; ate.*
Inaugurate, in. *Augur; ate.*
Inauspicious, in. *Avis, Specio; ous.*
Incantation, in. *Cantatum; ion.*
Incarcerate, in. *Carcer; ate.*
Incarnate, in. *Carnis; ate.*
Incautious, in. *Cautum; ous.*
Incendiary, in. *Candeo; ary.*
Incense, in. *Candeo.*
Incentive, in. *Candeo; ive.*
Incessant, in. *Cessum; ant.*
Incident, in. *Cado; ent.*
Incinerate, in. *Cineris; ate.*
Incipient, in. *Capio; ent.*
Incision, in. *Cæsum; ion.*
Incitement, in. *Cito; ment.*
Inclement, in. *Clementis.*
Inclination, in. *Clinatum; ion.*
Include, in. *Cludo.*
Incoherent, in, co. *Hæreo; ent.*
Incommode, in, com. *Modus.*
Incomprehensible, in, com. *Prehensum; ible.*
Inconsolable, in, con. *Solor; able.*
Incorrect, in, cor. *Rectum.*
Incorrigible, in, cor. *Rego; ible.*
Increase, in. *Cresco.*
Incredible, in. *Credo; ible.*
Incredulity, in. *Credo; ity.*
Incumbent, in. *Cumbo; ent.*
Incurable, in. *Cura; able.*
Incursion, in. *Cursum; ion.*
Incurvate, in. *Curvus; ate.*
Indecorum, in. *Decor.*
Indefinite, in, de. *Finis.*
Indelible, in, de. *Leo; ible.*
Indemnification, in. *Damnum, Factum; ion.*
Indemnify, in. *Damnum; fy.*
Indenture, in. *Dentis; ure.*
Independence, in, de. *Pendeo; ence.*
Index, in. *Dico.*

Indication, in. *Dico; ate, ion.*
Indict, in. *Dictum.*
Indifferent, in, dif. *Fero; ent.*
Indigenous. *Indigena; ous.*
Indigestion, in, di. *Gestum; ion.*
Indignity, in. *Dignus; ity.*
Indispensable, in, dis. *Pensum; able.*
Indisputable, in, dis. *Puto; able.*
Indite, in. *Dictum.*
Individual, in. *Dividuus,* divisible.
Indomitable, in. *Domitum; able.*
Indubitable, in. *Dubitatum; able.*
Industry. *Industria; y.*
Inebriate, in. *Ebrius; ate.*
Inert, in. *Artis.*
Inertia, in. *Artis.*
Inestimable, in. *Æstimo; able.*
Inevitably, in, e. *Vito; able, y.*
Inexhaustible, in, ex. *Haustum; ible.*
Inexorable, in, ex. *Oro; able.*
Infamous, in. *Fama; ous.*
Infancy, in. *Fari; ancy.*
Infanta, in. *Fari; ant.*
Infanticide, in. *Fari; ant. Cædo.*
Infatuate, in. *Fatuus,* foolish; *ate.*
Infect, in. *Factum.*
Inferior. *Inferus.*
Infernal. *Infernus; al.*
Infest. *Infesto,* I trouble.
Infidelity, in. *Fidelis; ity.*
Infinite, in. *Finis.*
Infirmary, in. *Firmus; ary.*
Inflame, in. *Flamma.*
Inflammation, in. *Flamma; ion.*
Inflexible, in. *Flexum; ible.*
Influence, in. *Fluo; ence.*
Influential, in. *Fluo; al.*
Influx, in. *Fluxum.*
Information, in. *Forma; ion.*
Infraction, in. *Fractum; ion.*
Infringement, in. *Frango; ment.*
Infusion, in. *Fusum; ion.*
Ingenious, in. *Genus; ous.*
Ingenuity, in. *Genus; ity.*
Ingenuousness, in. *Genus; ous, ness.*
Ingrate, in. *Gratus.*
Ingratitude, in. *Gratus; tude.*
Inhabitant, in. *Habitum; ant.*
Inhale, in. *Halo.*
Inherent, in. *Hæreo; ent.*
Inheritance, in. *Heredis; ance.*
Inhuman, in. *Homo; an.*
Inimical, in. *Amicus; al.*
Iniquity, in. *Æquus; ity.*
Initial, in. *Itum; al.*
Initiation, in. *Itum; ate, ion,*
Injurious, in. *Juris; ous.*
Injustice, in. *Justus; ice.*
Innate, in. *Natus.*
Innocent, in. *Noceo; ent.*
Innovation, in. *Novus; ate, ion.*
Innumerable, in. *Numerus; able.*
Inoculate, in. *Oculus; ate.*
Inoperative, in. *Operis; ate, ive.*
Inopportune, in. op. *Porto.*
Inordinate, in. *Ordinis; ate.*
Inquiries, in. *Quæro; y.*
Inquisitive, in. *Quæsitum; ive.*
Insanity, in. *Sanus; ity.*
Insatiable, in. *Satis; able.*

Inscrutable, in. *Scrutor; able.*
Insectivorous, in. *Sectum, Voro; ous.*
Insert, in. *Sertum.*
Insidious, in. *Sedeo; ous.*
Insignificant, in. *Signum, Facio; ant.*
Insinuation, in. *Sinus; ate, ion.*
Insipid, in. *Sapio; id.*
Insolubility, in. *Solutum; ble, ity.*
Insolvent, in. *Solvo; ent.*
Inspiration, in. *Spiratum; ion.*
Inspirit, in. *Spiratum.* (L. Spiritus.)
Instance, in. *Sto; ance.*
Instant, in. *Sto; ant.*
Institute, in. *Statum.*
Instruction, in. *Structum; ion.*
Instrument, in. *Struo; ment.*
Insubordination, in, sub. *Ordinis; ate, ion.*
Insular. *Insula; ar.*
Insulate. *Insula; ate.*
Insult, in. *Saltum.*
Insuperable, in. *Super; able.*
Insurgent, in. *Surgo; ent.*
Insurrection, in. *Surrectum; ion.*
Intact, in. *Tactum.*
Intangible, in. *Tango; ible.*
Integral. *Integer; al.*
Integrity. *Integer; ity.*
Intellect, intel. *Lectum.*
Intelligence, intel. *Lego; ence.*
Intend, in. *Tendo.*
Intensity, in. *Tensum; ity.*
Intention, in. *Tentum; ion.*
Inter, in. *Terra.*
Intercede, inter. *Cedo.*
Intercept, inter. *Captum.*
Intercession, inter. *Cessum; ion.*
Interdict, inter. *Dictum.*
Interest, inter. *Entis.*
Interior. *Intus.*
Interminable, in. *Terminus; able.*
Intermittent, inter. *Mitto; ent.*
Intermural, inter. *Murus; al,*
International, inter. *Natus; ion, al.*
Interpolation, (Gr.) inter. *Polis; ate, ion.*
Interpose, inter. *Positum.*
Interregnum, inter. *Regnum.*
Interrogative, inter. *Rogo; ate, ive.*
Interruption, inter. *Ruptum; ion.*
Interspersing, inter. *Sparsum.*
Interstices, inter. *Sto; ice.*
Intervene, inter. *Venio.*
Intestate, inter. *Testis; ate.*
Intimately. *Intimus; ate, ly.*
Intimidate, in. *Timeo; id, ate.*
Intoxicate, (Gr.) in. *Toxikon; ate.*
Intrinsic. *Intrinsecus; ic.*
Introductory, intro. *Ductum; ory.*
Intrude, in. *Trudo.*
Intrusive, in. *Trusum; ive.*
Intuition, in. *Tuitus; ion.*
Inundate, in. *Unda; ate.*
Invade, in. *Vado.*
Invalidate, in. *Valeo; id, ate.*
Invaluable, in. *Valeo; able.*
Invasion, in. *Vasum; ion.*
Invective, in. *Vectum; ive.*
Inveigh, in. *Veho.*
Invention, in. *Ventum; ion*

Inversely, in. *Versum ; ly.*
Invert, in. *Verto.*
Invest, in. *Vestis.*
Investigate, in. *Vestigium ; ate.*
Inveterate, in. *Veteris ; ate.*
Invigorate, in. *Vigor ; ate.*
Invincible, in. *Vinco ; ible.*
Invisible, in. *Visum ; ible.*
Invocation, in. *Vocatum ; ion.*
Invoke, in. *Voco.*
Involves, in. *Volvo.*
Invulnerable, in. *Vulneris ; able.*
Iota, the Greek letter i.
Iris, (Gr.) *Iris.*
Iriscope, (Gr.) *Iris, Skopeo.*
Irradiate, ir. *Radius ; ate.*
Irrational, ir. *Ratus ; ion, al.*
Irrefragable, ir, re. *Frango ; able.*
Irrelevant, ir, re. *Levo ; ant.*
Irremediable, ir, re. *Medeor ; able.*
Irresponsible, ir, re. *Sponsum ; ible.*
Irreverent, ir, re. *Vereor ; ent.*
Irreversible, ir, re. *Versum ; ible.*
Irrevocable, ir, re. *Voco ; able.*
Irrigate, ir. *Rigo ; ate.*
Irritate. *Irrito ; ate.*
Isle. *Insula.*
Isosceles, (Gr.) *Isos, Skelos.*
Isochronal, (Gr.) *Isos, Chronos ; al.*
Isochronous, (Gr.) *Isos, Chronos ; ous.*
Isolate. *Insula ; ate.*
Isothermal, (Gr.) *Isos, Thermos ; al.*
Iterate. *Itero ; ate.*
Itinerant. *Itineris ; ant.*

Jests. *Gestum.*
Jocose. *Jocus ; ose.*
Jocularity. *Jocus ; ar, ity.*
Joke. *Jocus.*
Jot, (Gr.) *Iota.*
Judicatory. *Judicatum ; ory.*
Judicial. *Judico ; al.*
Judiciary. *Judico ; ary.*
Judicious. *Judico ; ous.*
Junction. *Junctum ; ion.*
Junior. *Juvenis ; or.*
Jurisdiction. *Juris, Dictum ; ion.*
Jurisprudence. *Juris ; pru. Video ; ence.*
Justice. *Justus ; ice.*
Juvenile. *Juvenis ; ile.*

Kaleidoscope, (Gr.) *Kalos, Eidos, Skopeo.*
Kaleidophone, (Gr.) *Kalos, Eidos, Phone.*

Labor. *Labor.*
Laborious. *Labor ; ous.*
Lachrymal. *Lachryma ; al.*
Laity, (Gr.) *Laos ; ity.*
Lamentable. *Lamentor ; able.*
Language. *Lingua ; age.*
Lapse. *Lapsus.*
Latitude. *Latus ; tude.*
Latria, (Gr.) *Latreia.*
Laudable. *Laudis ; able.*
Laudatory. *Laudis ; ory.*
Laureate. *Laurus,* laurel ; *ate.*
Lax. *Laxus.*
Legal. *Legis ; al.*
Legation. *Lego ; ate, ion.*
Legend. *Lego.*

Legible. *Lego ; ible.*
Legislate. *Legis, Latum.*
Legislator. *Legis, Latum ; or.*
Legislature *Legis, Latum ; ure.*
Legitimate. *Legitimus ; ate.*
Lenient. *Lenis ; ent.*
Lenity. *Lenis ; ity.*
Lethargic, (Gr.) *Lethe, Argos,* idle, inactive ; *ic.*
Lethargy, (Gr.) *Lethe, Argos,* idle, inactive ; *y.*
Lethean, (Gr.) *Lethe ; an.*
Levity. *Levis ; ity.*
Lexicography, (Gr.) *Lexis, Grapho ; y.*
Liable. *Ligo ; able.*
Libel. *Liber.*
Liberal. *Liber ; al.*
Liberalize. *Liber ; al, ize.*
Liberation. *Liber ; ate, ion.*
Liberty. *Liber ; ty.*
Library. *Liber ; ary.*
Libration. *Libra ; ate, ion.*
Lictor. *Ligo ; or.*
Ligament. *Ligo ; ment.*
Ligneous. *Lignum,* wood ; *ous.*
Limitation. *Limitis ; ion.*
Lines. *Linea.*
Lineage. *Linea ; age.*
Lineal. *Linea ; al.*
Lineament. *Linea ; ment.*
Linear. *Linea ; ar.*
Linen. *Linum.*
Linguist. *Lingua ; ist.*
Linseed. *Linum,* Seed.
Liquor. *Liqueo ; or.*
Litany, (Gr.) *Litaneia ; y.*
Literal. *Litera ; al.*
Literary. *Litera ; ary.*
Literature. *Litera ; yre.*
Litharge, (Gr.) *Lithos, Argyros,* silver.
Lithographer, (Gr.) *Lithos, Grapho ; er*
Lithography, (Gr.) *Lithos, Grapho ; y.*
Lithotomy, (Gr.) *Lithos, Tomos ; y.*
Lithoxyl, (Gr.) *Lithos, Xylon.*
Litigation. *Litis, Ago ; ion.*
Litigious. *Litis, Ago ; ous.*
Liturgy, (Gr.) *Leitos, Ergon ; y.*
Locality. *Locus ; al, ity.*
Locomotion. *Locus, Motum ; ion.*
Logarithms, (Gr.) *Logos, Arithmos.*
Logician, (Gr.) *Logos ; ic, ian.*
Logomachy, (Gr.) *Logos, Machomai ; y*
Longevity. *Longus, Ævum ; ity.*
Longitude. *Longus ; tude.*
Loquacity. *Loquor ; ity,* (state of being loquacious.)
Lucid. *Luceo ; id.*
Lucrative. *Lucratus ; ive.*
Ludicrous. *Ludo ; ous.*
Luminary. *Luminis ; ary.*
Luminous. *Luminis ; ous.*
Lunacy. *Luna ; acy.*
Lunar. *Luna ; ar.*
Lunatic. *Luna ; ic.*
Luxury, (Gr.) *Luxuria ; y.*

Macrocosm, (Gr.) *Makros, Kosmos.*
Magician, (Gr.) *Magus ; ic, ian.*
Magisterial. *Magister ; al.*
Magistracy. *Magistri ; acy.*

244   THE MODEL ETYMOLOGY.

Magistrate. *Magistri; ate.*
Magna Charta. *Magnus, Charta.*
Magnanimous. *Magnus, Animus; ous.*
Magnify. *Magnus; fy.*
Magnitude. *Magnus; tude.*
Maintain. *Manus, Teneo.*
Majesty. *Magnus; y.*
Majority. *Major; ity.*
Maladministration. *Malus; ad. Ministri; ate, ion.*
Malcontent. *Malus; con; Tentum.*
Malediction. *Malus, Dictum; ion.*
Malefactor. *Malus, Factum; or.*
Malevolence. *Malus, Volo; ence.*
Malevolent. *Malus, Volo; ent.*
Malice. *Malus; ice.*
Malicious. *Malus; ice, ous.*
Malign. *Malignus.*
Malignity. *Malignus; ity.*
Manacle. *Manus; cle.*
Mandatory. *Mandatum; ory.*
Mandate. *Mandatum.*
Maneuver. *Manus, Operis.*
Mania, (Gr.) *Mania.*
Maniac, (Gr.) *Mania; ac.*
Manual. *Manus; al.*
Manufactory. *Manus, Factum; ory.*
Manufactures. *Manus, Factum; ure.*
Manumission. *Manus, Missum; ion.*
Manuscript. *Manus, Scriptum.*
Mariner. *Mare; ine, er.*
Maritime. *Mare.*
Martyrdom, (Gr.) *Martyr; dom.*
Martyrology, (Gr.) *Martyr, Logos; y.*
Masculine. *Masculus; ine.*
Master. *Magister.*
Material. *Materia; al.*
Maternal. *Mater; al.* (Maternus, motherly.)
Mathematics, (Gr.) *Mathematos; ics.*
Matricide. *Matris, Cædo.*
Matron. *Matris.*
Matter. *Materia.*
Mature. *Maturus.*
Maturity. *Maturus; ity.*
Maximum. *Maximus.*
Maxim. *Maximus.*
Meandering. *Meo.* (L. Meander.)
Measurement. *Mensura; ure, ment.*
Mechanics, (Gr.) *Mechanao; ics.*
Mechanician, (Gr.) *Mechanao; ic, ian.*
Mechanism, (Gr.) *Mechanao; ism.*
Mediate. *Medius; ate.*
Meditation. *Meditor; ate, ion.*
Medical. *Medeor; ical.*
Medicinal. *Medicus; ine, al.*
Medicine. *Medicus; ine.*
Mediterranean. *Medius, Terra.*
Medium. *Medius.*
Melancholy, (Gr.) *Melan, Kole; y.*
Melanite, (Gr.) *Melan;* Gr. *ite.*
Melioration. *Melior; ate, ion.*
Melodrama, (Gr.) *Melos, Drama.*
Melody, (Gr.) *Melos, Ode; y.*
Memorable. *Memor; able.*
Memorial. *Memor; y, al.*
Memorizing. *Memor; ize, ing.*
Memory. *Memor; y.*
Menology, (Gr.) *Men, Logos; y.*
Mental. *Mentis; al.*

Mention. *Memor; ion.*
Mercantile. *Mercans; ile.*
Mercenary. *Mercor; ary.*
Merchandise. *Mercans; ise.* (Fr. Marchand.)
Merchant. *Mercans; ant.*
Meridian. *Medius, Dies; an.*
Mesopotamia, (Gr.) *Mesos, Potamos.*
Metalliferous, (Gr.) *Metallon,* L. Fero; *ous*
Metalloid, (Gr.) *Metallon, Eidos.*
Metallurgy, (Gr.) *Metallon, Ergon; y.*
Metamorphic, (Gr.) meta. *Morphe; ic.*
Metaphor, (Gr.) meta. *Phero; or.*
Metaphysics, (Gr.) meta. *Physis; ics.*
Metempsychosis, (Gr.) meta. *Psyche.*
Meteor, (Gr.) *Meteora.*
Meteoric, (Gr.) *Meteora; ic.*
Meteorolite, (Gr.) *Meteora, Lithos.*
Meteorology, (Gr.) *Meteora, Logos; y.*
Meter, (Gr.) *Metron.*
Method, (Gr.) meta. *Odos.*
Methodical, (Gr.) meta. *Odos; ical.*
Metonymy, (Gr.) meta. *Onyma; y.*
Metropolis, (Gr.) *Metros, Polis.*
Metropolitan, (Gr.) *Metros, Politeia; an.*
Mezzotinto, (Gr.) *Mesos, Tinctum.*
Miasmatic, (Gr.) *Miasma; ic.*
Microcosm, (Gr.) *Mikros, Kosmos.*
Micrometer, (Gr.) *Mikros, Metron.*
Microphone, (Gr.) *Mikros, Phone.*
Microscope, (Gr.) *Mikros, Skopeo.*
Migration. *Migro; ate, ion.*
Migratory. *Migro; ate, ory.*
Militant. *Militis; ant.*
Military. *Militis; ary.*
Militia. *Militis.*
Millennium. *Mille, Annus.*
Mimic, (Gr.) *Mimos; ic.*
Mimicry, (Gr.) *Mimos; ic, ry.*
Mineralogy, (Gr.) Fr. Mineral, *Logos; y*
Minim. *Minimus,* smallest.
Minimum. *Minuo.* (L. Minimus.)
Ministerial. *Minister; al.*
Minority. *Minor; ity.*
Minute. *Minutum.*
Miracle. *Mirus; cle.*
Miraculous. *Miraculum; ous.*
Misanthrope, (Gr.) *Misos, Anthropos.*
Misanthropy, (Gr.) *Misos, Anthropos; y*
Miscellaneous. *Misceo; ous.* (L. Miscellaneus, mixed.)
Miscellany. *Misceo; y.*
Miserable. *Miser; able.*
Misery. *Miser; y.*
Misfortune, mis. *Fortuna.*
Misnomer, mis. *Nomos.*
Misogamy, (Gr.) *Misos, Gameo; y.*
Missionary. *Missum; ion, ary.*
Missive. *Missum; ive.*
Mitigate. *Mitigo; ate.*
Mnemonics, (Gr.) *Mneo; ics.*
Mob. *Mobths.*
Model. *Modus.*
Moderate. *Modus; ate.*
Modernize. *Modo,* just now; *ize.*
Modesty. *Modestus; y.*
Modification. *Modus, Factum; ion.*
Modify. *Modus; fy.*
Mollify. *Mollis; fy.*
Monad, (Gr.) *Monos.*

Monarch, (Gr.) *Monos, Arche.*
Monarchical, (Gr.) *Monos, Arche; ical.*
Monarchy, (Gr.) *Monos, Arche; y.*
Monastery, (Gr.) *Monos; ery.*
Monastic, (Gr.) *Monos; ic.*
Monitor. *Monitum; or.*
Monk, (Gr.) *Monos.*
Monoceros, (Gr.) *Monos, Keras.*
Monody, (Gr.) *Monos, Ode; y.*
Monogamy, (Gr.) *Monos, Gameo; y.*
Monogram, (Gr.) *Monos, Gramma.*
Monologue, (Gr.) *Monos, Logos.*
Monopetalous, (Gr.) *Monos, Petalon; ous.*
Monophyllous, (Gr.) *Monos, Phyllon; ous.*
Monopolize, (Gr.) *Monos, Poleo; ize.*
Monopoly, (Gr.) *Monos, Poleo; y.*
Monostich, (Gr.) *Monos, Stichos.*
Monotheism, (Gr.) *Monos, Theos; ism.*
Monotone, (Gr.) *Monos, Tonos.*
Monotony, (Gr.) *Monos, Tonos; y.*
Monster. *Monstro; er.*
Monstrous. *Monstro; ous.*
Monument. *Moneo; ment.*
Mood. *Modus.*
Morality. *Moris; al, ity.*
Moralize. *Moris; al, ize.*
Morbidly. *Morbus; id, ly.*
Moribund. *Moribundus.*
Morsel. *Morsum.*
Mortal. *Mortis; al.*
Mortality. *Mortis; al, ity.*
Mortgage. *Mortis, Gage*, a pledge.
Mortification. *Mortis, Factum; ion.*
Mortify. *Mortis; fy.*
Motion. *Motum; ion.*
Motor. *Motum; or.*
Motory. *Motum; ory.*
Mount. *Montis.*
Mountain. *Montis.*
Movable. *Moveo; able.*
Movement. *Moveo; ment.*
Multangular. *Multus, Angulus; ar.*
Multifarious. *Multus, Fari; ous.*
Multiform. *Multus, Forma.*
Multiply. *Multus, Plico.*
Multitude. *Multus; tude.*
Mundane. *Mundus; ane.*
Municipal. *Munus, Capio; al.*
Munificence. *Munus, Facio; ence.*
Munificent. *Munus, Facio; ent.*
Munition. *Munitum; ion.*
Mural. *Murus; al.*
Muriform. *Murus, Forma.*
Muses. *Musa.*
Musician. *Musica;* (or *Musa; ic,*) *ian.*
Mutability. *Muto; able, ity.*
Mutilate. *Mutilus,* maimed; *ate.*
Mutual. *Mutuus; al.*
Myopy, (Gr.) *Myo, Ops; y.*
Myriad, (Gr.) *Myriados.*
Mysterious, (Gr.) *Mystikos; ery, ous.*
Mystic, (Gr.) *Mystikos; ic.*
Mysticism, (Gr.) *Mystikos; ic, ism.*
Mythical, (Gr.) *Mythos; ical.*
Mythology, (Gr.) *Mythos, Logos; y.*

Narcissus, (Gr.) *Narke.*
Narcotic, (Gr.) *Narke; ic.*
Narration. *Narro; ate, ion.*
Nasal. *Nasus; al.*

Nativity. *Natus; ive, ity.*
Natural. *Natus; ure, al.*
Naumachy, (Gr.) *Naus, Machomai; y.*
Nauseous. *Nauta; ous.* (L. *Nausea*, sea sickness, fr. (Gr.) *Naus.*)
Nautical. *Nauta; ical.*
Naval. *Navis; al.*
Navigable. *Navis; Ago, able.*
Navigation. *Navis; Ago, ate, ion.*
Navy. *Navis; y.*
Necessitate. *Necesse,* needful; *ate.*
Necrology, (Gr.) *Nekros, Logos; y.*
Necromancy, (Gr.) *Nekros, Manteia; y.*
Nefarious. *Nefarius; ous.*
Negation. *Negatum; ion.*
Neglect, neg. *Lectum.*
Negligence, neg. *Lego; ence.*
Negotiate, neg. *Otium; ate.*
Neology, (Gr.) *Neos, Logos; y.*
Neophyte, (Gr.) *Neos, Phyton.*
Nervous. *Nervus,* a sinew; *ous.*
Neurology, (Gr.) *Neuron, Logos; y.*
Neurotic, (Gr.) *Neuron; ic.*
Neuter. *Neuter.*
Neutrality. *Neutrum; al, ity.*
Neutral. *Neutrum; al.*
Nihility. *Nihil; ity.*
Nitrogen, (Gr.) *Nitron,* natron, *Genea.*
Nobility. *Nobilis; ity.*
Noble. *Nobilis.*
Nocturnal. *Noctis; al.* (L. Nocturnus.)
Nomadic, (Gr.) *Nomados; ic.*
Nominal. *Nominis; al.*
Nominate. *Nominis; ate.*
Nomination. *Nominis; ate, ion.*
Nonagon. *Novem,* nine; (Gr.) *Gonia.*
Nonentity, non. *Entis; ity.*
Normal. *Norma; al.*
Nosology, (Gr.) *Nosos, Logos; y.*
Notify. *Notum; fy.*
Notorious. *Notum; ous.*
Nourish. *Nutrio; ish.*
Novels. *Novus.*
Novice. *Novus.*
Noxious. *Noxius; ous.*
Nucleus. *Nux.*
Nudity. *Nudus; ity.*
Nuisance. *Noceo; ance.*
Nullify. *Nullus; fy.*
Numbers. *Numerus.*
Numerical. *Numerus; ical.*
Numismatics, (Gr.) *Nomisma; ics.*
Nuptials. *Nuptum; al.*
Nurse. *Nutrio.*
Nutriment. *Nutrio; ment.*
Nymph, (Gr.) *Nympha.*

Obduracy, ob. *Durus; acy.*
Obdurate, ob. *Durus; ate.*
Obey, ob. *Audio.*
Obedience, ob. *Audio; ence.*
Obelisk, (Gr.) *Obeliskos.*
Obituary, ob. *Itum; ary.*
Object, ob. *Jactum.*
Oblation, ob. *Latum; ion.*
Obligation, ob. *Ligatum; ion.*
Oblige, ob. *Ligo.*
Obliterate, ob. *Litera; ate.*
Oblivion. *Oblivio; ion.*
Obloquy, ob. *Loquor; y.*

Obnoxious, ob. *Noxius; ous.*
Obsequies, ob. *Sequor; y.*
Obsequious, ob. *Sequor; y, ous.*
Observations, ob. *Servatum; ion.*
Observing, ob. *Servo; ing.*
Obstacle, ob. *Sto; cle.*
Obtain, ob. *Teneo.*
Obtrude, ob. *Trudo.*
Obtuse, ob. *Tusum.*
Obviate, ob. *Via; ate.*
Obviously, ob. *Via; ous, ly.*
Occasion. oc. *Casum; ion.*
Occupant. oc. *Capio; ant.*
Occupation, oc. *Captum; ion.*
Occupied, oc. *Capio.*
Occurrence, oc. *Curro; ence.*
Octagon, (Gr.) *Okto, Gonia.*
Octahedron, (Gr.) *Okto, Hedra.*
Octandria, (Gr.) *Okto, Andros.*
Octopetalous, (Gr.) *Okto, Petalon; ous.*
Octospermous, (Gr.) *Okto, Sperma; ous.*
Ocular. *Oculus; ar.*
Ode, (Gr.) *Ode.*
Odious. *Odi; ous.*
Odium. *Odi.*
Odontalgia, (Gr.) *Odontos, Algos.*
Odontalgic, (Gr.) *Odontos, Algos; ic.*
Odor. *Odor.*
Offensive, of. *Fensum; ive.*
Officiate, of. *Facio; ate.*
Ointment *Unctum; ment.*
Olfactory. *Oleo, Factum; ory.*
Oligarchical, (Gr.) *Oligos, Arche; ical.*
Oligarchy, (Gr.) *Oligos, Arche; y.*
Olympiad, (Gr.) *Olympos.*
Olympic, (Gr.) *Olympos; ic.*
Omnipotent. *Omnis, Potentis.*
Omnipresent. *Omnis; pre. Esse; ent.*
Omniscient. *Omnis, Scientia.*
Onerous. *Oneris; ous.*
Onomatopœia, (Gr.) *Onoma. Poieo.*
Operation. *Operis; ate, ion.*
Ophthalmia, (Gr.) *Ophthalmos.*
Opinion. *Opinor; ion.*
Opponent, op. *Pono; ent.*
Opportunity, op. *Porto; ity.* (L. Op- portunus.)
Oppress, op. *Pressum.*
Optician, (Gr.) *Optomai: ic, ian.*
Optics, (Gr.) *Optomai; ics.*
Option. *Opto; ion.*
Oracle. *Oraculum,* an oracle.
Oration. *Oratum; ion.*
Orator. *Oratum; or.*
Orb. *Orbis.*
Orbit. *Orbita.*
Orbital. *Orbita; al.*
Order. *Ordo.*
Ordinance. *Ordinis; ance.*
Organs, (Gr.) *Organon.*
Organization, (Gr.) *Organon; ize, ion.*
Oriental. *Orior; ent, al.*
Originality. *Originis; al, ity.*
Originate. *Originis; ate.*
Orison. *Oro.*
Ornament. *Ornatum; ment.*
Ornate. *Ornatum.*
Ornithology, (Gr.) *Ornithos, Logos; y.*
Ornithomancy, (Gr.) *Ornithos, Manteia; y.*
Orphanage, (Gr.) *Orphanos; age.*

Orthodromics, (Gr.) *Orthos, Dromos; ics*
Orthodox, (Gr.) *Orthos, Doxa.*
Orthoepy, (Gr.) *Orthos, Epos; y.*
Orthography, (Gr.) *Orthos, Grapho; y.*
Orthology, (Gr.) *Orthos, Logos; y.*
Orthometry, (Gr.) *Orthos, Metron; y.*
Ossification. *Ossis, Factum; ion.*
Ostensible. os. *Tensum; ible.*
Ostentation. os. *Tentum; ion.*
Osteology, (Gr.) *Osteon, Logos; y.*
Ostracism, (Gr.) *Ostrakon; ism.*
Ostracize, (Gr.) *Ostrakon; ize.*
Otacoustic, (Gr.) *Otos, Akouo; ic.*
Ouranography, (Gr.) *Ouranos, Grapho; y.*
Outrage. *Ultra.*
Oval. *Ovum; al.*
Ovate. *Ovum; ate.*
Oxide, (Gr.) *Oxys; ide.* (Fr. Acide.)
Oxygen, (Gr.) *Oxys, Genea.*
Oxymel, (Gr.) *Oxys, Meli.*

Pachyderm, (Gr.) *Pachys, Derma.*
Pacification. *Pacis, Factum; ion.*
Paganism. *Pagus; an, ism.*
Painting. *Pingo; ing.*
Paleograph, (Gr.) *Paleos, Grapho; y.*
Palindrome, (Gr.) *Palin, Dromos.*
Pall. *Pallium.*
Palliative. *Pallium; ate, ive.*
Palsy, (Gr.) para. *Lysis; y.*
Panacea, (Gr.) *Pan, Akeo,* I cure.
Pandect, (Gr.) *Pan, Dechomai.*
Pandemonium, (Gr.) *Pan, Daimon.*
Panegyric, (Gr.) *Pan, Agora.*
Panic, (Gr.) *Pan; ic.*
Panoply, (Gr.) *Pan, Oplon; y.*
Panorama, (Gr.) *Pan, Orama.*
Pantheism, (Gr.) *Pan, Theos; ism.*
Pantheon, (Gr.) *Pan, Theos.*
Pantomime, (Gr.) *Pantos, Mimos.*
Paper, (Gr.) *Papyros.*
Parable, (Gr.) para. *Boleo.*
Parabola, Gr.) para. *Boleo.*
Paraboloid, (Gr.) para. *Boleo, Eidos.*
Paradise, (Gr.) *Paradeisos.*
Paradox, (Gr.) para. *Doxa.*
Paragoge, (Gr.) para. *Agogeus.*
Parallax, (Gr.) para. *Allaxis.*
Parallel, (Gr.) para. *Allelon.*
Parallelogram, (Gr.) para. *Allelon, Gramma.*
Parallelopiped, (Gr.) para. *Allelon; epi Pedon,* a plain.
Paralysis, (Gr.) para. *Lysis.*
Paralyze, (Gr.) para. *Lysis; ize.*
Paramount, per, a for ad. *Montis.*
Parapet. *Paro, Pectus.*
Paraphernalia, (Gr.) para. *Pherne.*
Paraphrase, (Gr.) para. *Phrasis.*
Paraselene, (Gr.) para. *Selene.*
Parasite, (Gr.) para. *Sitos.*
Parasitical, (Gr.) para. *Sitos; ical.*
Parentage. *Pario; ent, age.*
Parenthesis, (Gr.) para, en. *Thesis.*
Parhelion, (Gr.) para. *Helios.*
Parish, (Gr.) para. *Oikos.*
Parochial, (Gr.) para. *Oikos; al.*
Parody, (Gr.) para. *Ode; y.*
Paronomasia, (Gr.) para. *Onoma.*
Parotid, (Gr.) para. *Otos.*

Paroxysm, (Gr.) para. *Oxys; sm.*
Parricide. *Pater, Cædo.*
Part. *Partis.*
Participate. *Partis, Capio; ate.*
Particle. *Partis; cle.*
Partisan. *Partis; an.*
Partition. *Partis; ion.*
Passionate. *Passus; ion, ate.*
Passive. *Passus; ive.*
Pastor. *Pastum,* to pasture; *or.*
Paternal. *Pater; al.* (L. Paternus.)
Paternoster, (Gr.) *Pater.* L. *Noster,* our.
Pathetic, (Gr.) *Pathos; ic.*
Pathology, (Gr.) *Pathos, Logos; y.*
Pathos, (Gr.) *Pathos.*
Patience. *Patior; ence.*
Patriarch, (Gr.) *Patros, Arche.*
Patrician. *Patris; ian.*
Patriot. *Patris.*
Patrimony. *Patris; mony.*
Patronage. *Patris; age.*
Patronymic, (Gr.) *Patros, Onyma; ic.*
Pauperism. *Pauper; ism.*
Peace. *Pacis.*
Peculate. *Peculium; ate.*
Peculiar. *Peculium; ar.*
Pecuniary. *Pecunia; ary.*
Pedagogue, (Gr.) *Paideia, Agogeus.*
Pedant, (Gr.) *Paideia; ant.*
Peddler. *Pedis; er.* (Pad, to go. ?)
Pedestrian. *Pedis; ian.*
Pedobaptist, (Gr.) *Paidos, Bapto; ist.*
Peer. *Par; eer.*
Peerage. *Par; eer, age.*
Peloponnesus, (Gr.) *Pelops,* the Mores, *Nesos.*
Penalty. *Pœna; al, ty.*
Pendulum. *Pendeo.*
Penetration. *Penetro; ate, ion.*
Peninsulas. *Pene, Insula.*
Penitence. *Pœniteo; ence.*
Penitentiary. *Pœniteo; ent, ary.*
Pension. *Pensum; ion.*
Pentachord, (Gr.) *Pente, Chorde.*
Pentagon, (Gr.) *Pente, Gonia.*
Pentameter, (Gr.) *Pente, Metron.*
Pentarchy, (Gr.) *Pente, Arche; y.*
Pentateuch, (Gr.) *Pente, Teuchos.*
Pentecost, (Gr.) *Pentekoste.*
Penultimate. *Pene, Ultimus; ate.*
People. *Populus.*
Perambulate, per. *Ambulo; ate.*
Perceiving, per. *Capio; ing.*
Perceptible, per. *Captum; ible.*
Peregrination, per. *Agri; ate, ion.*
Peremptory, per. *Emptum; ory.*
Perennial, per. *Annus; al.*
Perfectly, per. *Factum; ly.*
Perfidy, per. *Fido; y.*
Performance, per. *Forma; ance.*
Perfumery, per. *Fumus; ery.*
Pericardium, (Gr.) peri. *Kardia.*
Perihelion, (Gr) peri. *Helios.*
Perimeter, (Gr) peri. *Metron.*
Period, (Gr.) peri. *Odos.*
Periosteum, (Gr.) peri. *Osteon.*
Peripatetic, (Gr.) peri. *Pateo; ic.*
Periphery, (Gr.) peri. *Phero; y.*
Periphrase, (Gr.) peri. *Phrasis.*
Periscii, (Gr.) peri. *Skia.*

Perish, per. *Rum.*
Peristaltic, peri. *Stello; ic.*
Perjury, per. *Juro; y.*
Permanent, per. *Maneo; ent.*
Permeate, per. *Meo; ate.*
Permission, per. *Missum; ion.*
Peroration, per. *Oratum; ion.*
Perpendicular, per. *Pendeo; ar.*
Perplexity, per. *Plexum; ity.*
Perquisites, per. *Quæsitum.*
Persecution, per. *Secutus; ion.*
Perseverance, per. *Severus; ance.*
Persistent, per. *Sisto; ent.*
Personate. *Persona; ate.*
Perspicuity, per. *Specio; ity.*
Persuade per. *Suadeo.*
Pertinacious, per. *Teneo; acious.*
Pertinacity, per. *Teneo; ity.*
Pertinent, per. *Teneo; ent.*
Perturbation, per. *Turba; ion.*
Peruse, per. *Visum.*
Pervade, per. *Vado.*
Perversion, per. *Versum; ion.*
Pervert, per. *Verto.*
Pestiferous. *Pestis, Fero; ous.*
Petal, (Gr.) *Petalon.*
Petrifaction, (Gr.) *Petra,* L. *Factum ion.*
Petrify, (Gr.) *Petra; fy.*
Petulant. *Petulantis.*
Phantom, (Gr.) *Phano.*
Pharmaceutic, (Gr.) *Pharmakon; ic.*
Pharmacopœia, (Gr.) *Pharmakon, Poieo.*
Pharmacy, (Gr.) *Pharmakon; y.*
Phase, (Gr.) *Phano.*
Phenix, (Gr.) *Phoinix.*
Phenomenon, (Gr.) *Phano.*
Philanthropy, (Gr.) *Philos, Anthropos; y.*
Philology, (Gr.) *Philos, Logos; y.*
Philomath, (Gr.) *Philos, Mathema.*
Philomela, (Gr.) *Philos, Melos.*
Philosophy, (Gr.) *Philos, Sophia; y.*
Phlebotomy, (Gr.) *Phlebos, Tomos; y.*
Phlegm, (Gr.) *Phlegma.*
Phlegmatic, (Gr.) *Phlegma; ic.*
Phlogiston, (Gr.) *Phlegma.*
Phonics, (Gr.) *Phone; ics.*
Phosphate, (Gr.) *Phos.* (Gr.) *ate.*
Phosphorescent, (Gr.) *Phos, Phero; escent.*
Photography, (Gr.) *Photos, Grapho; y.*
Photometer, (Gr.) *Photos, Metron.*
Phraseology, (Gr.) *Phrasis, Logos; y.*
Phrenology, (Gr.) *Phren, Logos; y.*
Phyllophorous, (Gr.) *Phyllon, Phero; ous.*
Physical, (Gr.) *Physis; ic, al.*
Physician, (Gr.) *Physis; ic, ian.*
Physiognomy, (Gr.) *Physis, Gnomon; y.*
Physiology, (Gr.) *Physis, Logos; y.*
Phytology, (Gr.) *Phyton, Logos; y.*
Pict. *Pictum.*
Picturesque. *Pictum; ure, esque.*
Piety. *Pius; ety.*
Pilfer. *Pilo, Facio.*
Pilgrim, per. *Agri.*
Pillage. *Pilo, age.*
Piracy, (Gr.) *Peirates; acy.*
Placid. *Placeo; id.*

Plane. *Planus.*
Planet, (Gr.) *Plane.*
Planisphere, L. *Planus,* (Gr.) *Sphaira.*
Plant. *Planta.*
Planifolious. *Planus, Folium; ous.*
Plantation. *Plantatum; ion.*
Plastic, (Gr.) *Plasso; ic.*
Platonic, (Gr.) *Platon; ic.*
Plausible. *Plausum; ible.*
Pleasure. *Placeo; ure.*
Plebeian. *Plebs; ian.*
Plenary. *Plenus; ary.*
Plenipotentiary. *Plenus, Potentis; ary.*
Plentiful. *Plenus; ty, ful.*
Pleonasm. *Pleo; asm.*
Pleurisy, (Gr.) *Pleura; y.*
Pliant. *Plico; ant.*
Plumbago. *Plumbum.* (L. Plumbago.)
Plurality. *Pluris; al, ity.*
Pneumonia, (Gr.) *Pneumon.*
Poem, (Gr.) *Poieo.*
Poesy, (Gr.) *Poieo; y.*
Polarization. *Polus; ar, ize, ion.*
Polemic, (Gr.) *Polemos; ic.*
Police, (Gr.) *Polis.*
Policy, (Gr.) *Polis; y.*
Politeness. *Politum* (or Gr. *Politeia*); *ness.*
Political, (Gr.) *Politeia; ical.*
Polyadelphia, (Gr.) *Poly, Adelphos.*
Polyanthus, (Gr.) *Poly, Anthos.*
Polygamy, (Gr.) *Poly, Gameo; y.*
Polygenous, (Gr.) *Poly, Genea; ous.*
Polyglot (Gr.) *Poly, Glotta.*
Polygon, (Gr.) *Poly, Gonia.*
Polyhedron, (Gr.) *Poly, Hedra.*
Polypetalous, (Gr.) *Poly, Petalon; ous.*
Polypus, (Gr.) *Poly, Pous.*
Polyspermous, (Gr.) *Poly, Sperma; ous.*
Polysyllable, (Gr.) *Poly; syl. Labo.*
Polytheism, (Gr.) *Poly, Theos; ism.*
Pomegranate. *Pomum, Granum.*
Pomological. *Pomum,* Gr. *Logos; ical.*
Pomp, (Gr.) *Pompe.*
Pomposity, (Gr.) *Pompe; ous, ity.*
Ponderous. *Pondus; ous.*
Pontiff. *Pontis, Facio.*
Pontoon. *Pontis.*
Poor. *Pauper.*
Pope, (Gr.) *Papas.*
Populace. *Populus.*
Population. *Populus; ate, ion.*
Porch. *Porto.*
Porphyritic, (Gr.) *Porphyra; ic.*
Portal. *Porto; al.*
Portend, por. *Tendo.*
Portentous, por. *Tentum; ous.*
Portfolio. *Porto, Folium.*
Portico. *Porto.*
Portmanteau. *Porto, Manus.*
Portray, por. *Traho.*
Positively. *Positum; ive, ly.*
Possess, po, an inseparable preposition denoting power. *Sessum.*
Possibility. *Posse; ible, ity.*
Post-diluvian, post. *Diluvium; an.*
Posterity. *Posterus; ity.*
Postpone, post. *Pono.*
Posture. *Positum; ure.*
Potentate. *Potentis; ate.*

Potential. *Potentis; al.*
Potion. *Poto,* I drink; *ion.*
Powder. *Pulveris.*
Power. *Posse.*
Practicable, (Gr.) *Praktios; ice, able.*
Pragmatic, (Gr.) *Pragma; ic.*
Praise. *Precium.*
Prayer. *Precor; er.*
Preadmonish, pre, ad. *Moneo; ish.*
Preamble, pre. *Ambulo.*
Precarious. *Precor; ous.*
Precaution, pre. *Cautum; ion.*
Precedent, pre. *Cedo; ent.*
Preceptor, pre. *Captum; or.*
Precinct, pre. *Cinctum.*
Precious. *Precium; ous.*
Precipice, pre. *Caput.*
Precipitate, pre. *Capitis; ate.*
Precise, pre. *Cæsum.*
Precision, pre. *Cæsur*; *ion.*
Preclude, pre. *Cludo.*
Preconcert, pre, con. *Certo.*
Precursor, pre. *Cursum; or.*
Predatory. *Præda; ory.*
Predecessor, pre, de. *Cessum; or.*
Predicable, pre. *Dico; able.*
Predict, pre. *Dictum.*
Predominate, pre. *Dominus; ate.*
Preface, pre. *Fari.*
Preferable, pre. *Fero; able.*
Prejudice, pre. *Judico.*
Prejudicial, pre. *Judico; al.*
Preliminary, pre. *Liminis; ary.*
Premature, pre. *Maturus.*
Premeditate, pre. *Meditor; ate.*
Premonitory, pre. *Monitum; ory.*
Prepare, pre. *Puro.*
Prepense, pre. *Pensum.*
Preposterous, pre. *Posterus; ous.*
Prerogative, pre. *Rogatum; ive.*
Presage, pre. *Sagacis.*
Presbyterian, (Gr.) *Presbyteros; ian.*
Prescribe, pre. *Scribo.*
Presence, pre. *Esse; ence.*
Present, pre. *Esse; ent.*
Preservation, pre. *Servatum; ion.*
Presidency, pre. *Sedeo; ency.*
Pressure. *Pressum; ure.*
Presumption, pre. *Sumptum; ion.*
Pretension, pre. *Tensum; ion.*
Pretext, pre. *Textum.*
Prevail, pre. *Valeo.*
Prevaricate, pre. *Varico; ate.*
Preventive, pre. *Ventum; ive.*
Previously, pre. *Via; ous, ly.*
Prey. *Præda; y.*
Price. *Precium.*
Primacy. *Primus; acy.*
Primeval. *Primus, Ævum; al.*
Primogeniture. *Primus, Genitum;* ure
Primroses. *Primus, Rosa,* a rose.
Prince. *Primus, Capio.*
Principle. *Primus, Capio.*
Print. *Premo.*
Priority. *Prio; ty.*
Prismoid, (Gr.) *Prisma, Eidos.*
Prisoner. *Prehensum; er.*
Privacy. *Privus; acy.*
Privateer. *Privus; ate, eer.*
Privilege. *Privus, Legis.*

Prize. *Prehendo.* (Fr. Prise, taken.)
Prize. *Precium; ize.*
Probable. *Probo; able.*
Probation. *Probatum; ion.*
Probity. *Probo; ity.*
Problematical, (Gr.) pro. *Boleo; ical.*
Procedure. pro. *Cedo; ure.*
Proclamation, pro. *Clamatum; ion.*
Proclivity, pro. *Clivus; ity.*
Procrastinate, pro. *Cras; ate.*
Procurement, pro. *Cura; ment.*
Prodigal. *Prodigium; al.*
Prodigy. *Prodigium; y.*
Production, pro. *Ductum; ion.*
Profane, pro. *Fanum.*
Profess, pro. *Fessum.*
Proffer, pro, of. *Fero.*
Proficiency, pro. *Facio; ency.*
Profligate, pro. *Fligo; ate.*
Profound, pro. *Fundus.*
Profundity, pro. *Fundus; ity.*
Profusion, pro. *Fusum; ion.*
Progenitor, pro. *Genitum; or.*
Prognosticate. (Gr.) pro. *Gnostos; ate.*
Programme, (Gr.) pro. *Gramma.*
Progress, pro. *Gressus.*
Prohibit, pro. *Habeo.*
Prolepsis, (Gr.) pro. *Lepsis.*
Prologue, (Gr.) pro. *Logos.*
Prominent, pro. *Mineo; ent.*
Promiscuous, pro. *Misceo; ous.*
Promising, pro. *Missum; ing.*
Promotion, pro. *Motum; ion.*
Promptitude. *Promptus; tude.*
Pronounce, pro. *Nuncio.*
Proof. *Probo.*
Propensity, pro. *Pensum; ity.*
Proper. *Proprius.*
Property. *Proprius; ty.*
Prophesy, (Gr.) pro. *Phano; y.*
Prophet, (Gr.) pro. *Phano.*
Proportion, pro. *Portio; ion.*
Proposition, pro. *Positum; ion.*
Proprietor. *Proprius; or.*
Prorogue, pro. *Rogo.*
Prosecute, pro. *Secutus.*
Proselyte, (Gr.) *Proselytos.*
Prosody, (Gr.) *Pros, to, Ode; y.*
Prosopopoeia, (Gr.) *Prosopon, Poieo.*
Prospect, pro. *Spectum.*
Prosperity, pro. *Spero; ity.*
Prosthesis, (Gr.) pros, to. *Thesis.*
Prostration, pro. *Stratum; ion.*
Protectorate, pro. *Tectum; or, ate.*
Protestant, pro. *Testis; ant.*
Prothonotary, (Gr.) *Protos,* L. *Nota; ary.*
Protocol, (Gr.) *Protos, Kolla,* glue.
Protomartyr, (Gr.) *Protos, Martyr.*
Protoplast, (Gr.) *Protos, Plasso.*
Prototype, (Gr.) *Protos, Typos.*
Protract. *Pro, Tractum.*
Protrude. *Pro, Trudo.*
Prove. *Probo.*
Proverb, pro. *Verbum.*
Provide, pro. *Video.*
Providence, pro. *Video; ence.*
Province. pro. *Vinco.*
Provision, pro. *Visum; ion.*
Proviso, pro. *Visum.*
Provocation, pro. *Vocatum; ion.*

Provoke, pro. *Voco.*
Proximity. *Proximus; ity.*
Proxy, pro. *Cura; y.* (L. Procuracy.)
Prudent, pru. *Video; ent.*
Psalmody, (Gr.) *Psalma, Ode; y.*
Psaltery, (Gr.) *Psalma; ery.*
Pseudo-apostle, (Gr.) *Pseudos; apo. Stello.*
Pseudonym, (Gr.) *Pseudo, Onyma.*
Psychology, (Gr.) *Psyche, Logos; y.*
Publicity. *Publicus; ity.*
Publish. *Publicus; ish.*
Puerility. *Puer; ile, ity.*
Pugilist. *Pugil; ist.*
Pugnacious. *Pugna; acious.*
Puissant. *Posse; ant.*
Pulmonary. *Pulmonis; ary.*
Pulverization. *Pulveris; ize, ion.*
Punctuation. *Punctum; ate, ion.*
Puncture. *Punctum; ure.*
Pungent. *Pungo; ent.*
Punishment. *Punio; ish, ment.*
Punitive. *Punitum; ive.*
Pure. *Purus.*
Puritan. *Purus; an.*
Purport, pur. *Porto.*
Purpose, pur. *Positum.*
Pursue, pur. *Secutus.*
Pursuit, pur. *Secutus.*
Pusillanimity. *Pusillus, Animus; ity.*
Pygmean, (Gr.) *Pygme; an.*
Pyre, (Gr.) *Pyr.*
Pyrites, (Gr.) *Pyr;* Gr. *ite.*
Pyrolatry, (Gr.) *Pyr, Latreia; y.*
Pyroligneous, (Gr.) *Pyr, Lignum; ous.*
Pyrometer, (Gr.) *Pyr, Metron.*
Pyrotechnic, (Gr.) *Pyr, Techne.*

Quadrangle. *Quadra, Angulus.*
Quadrilateral. *Quadra, Lateris; al.*
Quadrumane. *Quadra, Manus.*
Quadruped. *Quadra, Pedis.*
Qualify. *Qualis; fy.*
Quarantine. *Quadra; ine.* (Fr. Quarante, forty.)
Quantity. *Quantus; ity.*
Quarrel. *Queror.*
Quart. *Quadra.*
Quartan. *Quadra.*
Querulous. *Queror; ous.*
Query. *Quaero; y.*
Question. *Quaesitum; ion.*
Quiescence. *Quies; escence.*
Quietude. *Quietis; ude.*
Quinquedentate. *Quinque, Dentis; ate.*
Quintessence. *Quinta, Esse; ence.*
Quintillion. *Quinta, Mille; ion.*
Quorum. *Quot.*
Quotidian. *Quot, Dies; an.*

Rabid. *Rabies; id.*
Radiance. *Radius; ance.*
Radically. *Radicis; al, ly.*
Rancorous. *Ranceo; or, ous.*
Rapacity. *Rapio; ity.*
Rapacious. *Rapio; acious.*
Rapidly. *Rapio; id, ly.*
Rapine. *Rapio; ine.*
Rarefy. *Rarus; fy.*
Ratification. *Ratus, Factum; ion.*

THE MODEL ETYMOLOGY.

Rational. *Ratus; ion, al.*
Ravage. *Rapio.*
Ravish. *Rapio; ish.*
Rays. *Radius.*
Raze. *Rasum.*
Reality. *Res; al, ity.*
Reason. *Ratus.*
Rebellion, re. *Bellum; ion.*
Recantation, re. *Cantatum; ion.*
Recapitulate, re. *Capitulum; ate.*
Receipt, re. *Captum.*
Receive, re. *Capio.*
Recently. *Recentis; ly.*
Receptacle, re. *Captum; cle.*
Recharter, re. *Charta.*
Recipe, re. *Capio.*
Recipient, re. *Capio; ent.*
Recitation, re. *Citatum; ion.*
Reclaim, re. *Clamo.*
Recline, re. *Clino.*
Recognize, re, co. *Nosco; ize.*
Recommend, re, com. *Mando.*
Recompense, re, com. *Pensum.*
Reconcile, re. *Concilium.*
Reconnoiter, re, con. *Notum.*
Record, re. *Cordis.*
Recourse, re. *Cursum.*
Recriminate. re. *Criminis; ate.*
Rectangular. *Rectus, Angulus; ar.*
Rectilineal. *Rectus, Linea; al.*
Rectitude. *Rectus; tude.*
Recumbent, re. *Cumbo; ent.*
Redeem. red. *Emo.*
Redolent, red. *Oleo; ent.*
Redundant, red. *Unda; ate.*
Reference, re. *Fero; ence.*
Reflect. re. *Flecto.*
Reformation, re. *Forma; ion.*
Refraction, re. *Fractum; ion.*
Refrigerate, re. *Frigoris; ate.*
Refugee. re. *Fugio; ee.*
Refulgence. re. *Fulgeo; ence.*
Regal. *Rego; al.*
Regalia. *Rego; al.*
Regent. *Rego; ent.*
Regimen. *Rego.*
Regulate. *Regula; ate.*
Reiterate, re. *Itero; ate.*
Relaxation, re. *Laxus; ion.*
Relevant, re. *Levo; ant.*
Relic. re. *Lictum.*
Relief, re. *Levo.*
Relieve, re. *Levo.*
Religion, re. *Ligo; ion.*
Relinquish, re. *Linquo; ish.*
Reluctant, re. *Luctor; ant.*
Remain. re. *Maneo.*
Remedial, re. *Medeor; al.*
Remember, re. *Memor.*
Reminiscence, re. *Memini; escence.*
Remonstrance, re. *Monstro; ance.*
Remorse, re. *Morsum.*
Remote, re. *Motum.*
Removal, re. *Moveo; al.*
Render, ren. *Do.*
Renegade, re. *Nego.*
Rendition, re. *Datum; ion.*
Renounce, re. *Nuncio.*
Renovate, re. *Novus; ate.*
Reparation, re. *Paratum; ion.*

Repeal. re. *Pello.*
Repeat, re. *Petitum.*
Repent. re. *Pœniteo.*
Repetition, re. *Petitum; ion.*
Replete, re. *Pletum.*
Reply, re. *Plico.*
Report, re. *Porto.*
Repose, re. *Positum.*
Reprehensible, re. *Prehensum; ible.*
Represent, re, pre. *Esse; ent.*
Representative, re, pre. *Esse; ent, ive.*
Reprove, re. *Probo.*
Reptile. *Reptum; ile.*
Repugnance, re. *Pugna; ance.*
Repulsive, re. *Pulsum; ive.*
Reputation, re. *Putatum; ion.*
Request, re. *Quæsitum.*
Requiem, re. *Quies.*
Require, re. *Quæro.*
Requisite, re. *Quæsitum.*
Resemblance, re. *Similis; ance.* (Fr Sembler, to appear.)
Resent, re. *Sentio.*
Reservoir, re. *Servo.*
Reside, re. *Sedeo.*
Residue, re. *Sedeo.*
Resign, re. *Signum.*
Resin, (Gr.) *Rheo.*
Resistance, re. *Sisto; ance.*
Resolution, re. *Solutum; ion.*
Resolve, re. *Solvo.*
Resonant. re. *Sonus; ant.*
Respectable. re. *Spectum; able.*
Resplendent, re. *Splendeo; ent.*
Responsible, re. *Sponsum; ible.*
Restitution, re. *Sisto,* or *Statum; ion.*
Restive, re. *Sto; ive.*
Restrain, re. *Stringo.*
Restriction, re. *Strictum; ion.*
Result, re. *Saltum.*
Resurrection, re. *Surrectum; ion.*
Resuscitate, re. sus. *Cito; ate.*
Retentive, re. *Tentum; ive.*
Retort. re. *Tortum.*
Retribution, re. *Tributum; ion.*
Retrograde. retro. *Gradior.*
Retrospect, retro. *Spectum.*
Reveal, re. *Velo.*
Revelation, re. *Velo; ion.*
Revenge, re. *Vindex.*
Revenue, re. *Venio.* (Fr. Venue, come.)
Revere, re. *Vereor.*
Reverend. re. *Vereor.*
Reverential, re. *Vereor; ent, al.*
Reverse, re. *Versum.*
Revert, re. *Verto.*
Reviewer, re. *Video; er.*
Revive. re. *Vivo.*
Revoke, re. *Voco.*
Revolt. re. *Volutum.*
Revolution, re. *Volutum; ion.*
Revolve. re. *Volvo.*
Rhapsodical, (Gr.) *Rhapto, Ode; ical.*
Rhapsody, (Gr.) *Rhapto, Ode; y.*
Rhetoric, (Gr.) *Rhetor; ic.*
Rheum, (Gr.) *Rheuma.*
Rheumatism, (Gr.) *Rheuma; ism.*
Rhinoceros, (Gr.) *Rhin,* the nose, *Keras*
Rhomb, (Gr.) *Rhombos.*
Rhomboid, (Gr.) *Rhombos, Eidos.*

Rhyme, (Gr.) *Rhythmos*.
Rhythm, (Gr.) *Rhythmos*.
Ridiculous. *Rideo; ous*. (L. Ridiculus.)
Rigid. *Rigeo; id*.
Rigorous. *Rigeo; or, ous*.
Riparian. *Ripa*, a bank; *ar, ian*.
Risible. *Risum; ible*.
Rival. *Rivus*.
River. *Rivus*.
Rivulet. *Rivus; let*.
Robust. *Robur*.
Roman. *Roma, Rome; an*.
Roseate. *Rosa; ate*.
Rotary. *Rota; ary*.
Rotunda. *Rota*. (L. Rotundus, round.)
Rotundity. *Rota; ity*.
Royalty. *Rego; al, ty*. (Fr. Roi, king.)
Rudeness. *Rudis; ness*.
Rudiments. *Rudis; ment*.
Rule. *Regula*.
Ruminant. *Ruminis; ant*.
Rumor. *Rumor*.
Rural. *Ruris; al*.
Rustic. *Rus; ic*. (L. Rusticus.)
Rusticate. *Rus; ic, ate*.

Saccharine. *Saccharum; ine*.
Sacerdotal. *Sacer, Dotis; al*.
Sacrament. *Sacri, ment*.
Sacred. *Sacri*.
Sacrifice. *Sacri, Facio*.
Sacrilege. *Sacri, Lego*.
Safer. *Salus; er*.
Sagacious. *Sagax; acious*.
Sagacity. *Sagacis; ity*.
Sage. *Sagax*. (L. Sapio?)
Saint. *Sanctus*.
Salary. *Sal; ary*. (L. Salarium, money for salt.)
Salient. *Salio; ent*.
Saline. *Sal; ine*.
Sally. *Salio; y*.
Salt. *Sal*.
Saltpetre. *Sal*. Gr. *Petra*.
Salubrity. *Salubris; ity*.
Salutary. *Salutis; ary*.
Salutatory. *Salutis; ory*.
Salvation. *Salus; ion*. (L. Salvus.)
Sample. *Exemplum*.
Sanative. *Sanus; ive*.
Sanctify. *Sanctus; fy*.
Sanctimonious. *Sanctus; mony, ous*.
Sanctuary. *Sanctus; ary*.
Sanguinary. *Sanguis; ine, ary*.
Sanguine. *Sanguis; ine*.
Sanity. *Sanus; ity*.
Saponaceous. *Saponis; aceous*.
Sarcasm, (Gr.) *Sarkos; asm*.
Sarcastic, (Gr.) *Sarkos; ic*.
Sarcophagus, (Gr.) *Sarkos, Phago*.
Sarcophagy, (Gr.) *Sarkos, Phago; y*.
Satiate. *Satis; ate*.
Satiety. *Satis; ety*.
Satisfactory. *Satis, Factum; ory*.
Saturate. *Satur; ate*.
Savor. *Sapio; or*.
Savory. *Sapio; ory*.
Scald, ex. *Caleo; id*.
Scale. *Scala*.
Scalene, (Gr.) *Skalenos*.

Scan. *Scando*.
Scarify, (Gr.) *Skariphos; fy*.
Scenery, (Gr.) *Skene; ery*.
Scenography, (Gr.) *Skene, Grapho; y*.
Scent. *Sentio*.
Scepter, (Gr.) *Skeptron*.
Scheme, (Gr.) *Schema*.
Schismatic, (Gr.) *Schisma; ic*.
Scholar, (Gr.) *Schole; ar*.
Scholasticism, (Gr.) *Schole; ic, ism*.
Scholium, (Gr.) *Schole*.
School, (Gr.) *Schole*.
Sciatica. *Sriatica*.
Science. *Scio; ence*.
Scientific. *Scientia, Facio*.
Scope, (Gr.) *Skopeo*.
Scoptic, (Gr.) *Skopto; ic*.
Scribbling. *Scribo; ing*.
Scripture. *Scriptum; ure*.
Sculptor. *Sculptum; or*.
Secession, se. *Cessum; ion*.
Seclude, se. *Cludo*.
Seclusion, se. *Clusum; ion*.
Secret, se. *Cretum*.
Secretary, se. *Cretum; ary*.
Secrete, se. *Cretum*.
Section. *Sectum; ion*.
Secular. *Seculum; ar*.
Security, se. *Cura; ity*.
Sedate. *Sedatus*.
Sedentary. *Sedeo; ary*.
Sedition, se. *Itum; ion*.
Sedulous. *Sedeo; ous*.
Segregate, se. *Gregis; ate*.
Select, se. *Lectum*.
Selenite, (Gr.) *Selene*; Gr. *ite*.
Selenography, (Gr.) *Selene, Grapho; y*.
Semi-diameter, (Gr.) semi, dia. *Metron*.
Seminary. *Seminis; ary*.
Semitone, (Gr.) semi. *Tonos*.
Senate. *Senex*. (L. Senatus.)
Senior. *Senex; or*. (L. Senior.)
Sensible. *Sensum; ible*.
Sentence. *Sentio; ence*.
Sententious. *Sentio; ence, ous*.
Sentimental. *Sentio; ment, al*.
Separable, se. *Paro; able*.
Separation, se. *Paro; ate, ion*.
September. *Septem*.
Septennial. *Septem, Annus; al*.
Sepulchre. *Sepulchrum*.
Sequel. *Sequor*.
Sermon. *Sermonis*.
Serpentine. *Serpo; ent, ine*.
Servant. *Servio; ant*.
Servitude. *Servio; tude*.
Session. *Sessum; ion*.
Several, se. *Paro; al*.
Severer. *Severus; er*.
Severity. *Severus; ity*.
Sexagenarian. *Sexaginta; ian*.
Sideroscope, (Gr.) *Sideros, Skopeo*.
Siege. *Sedeo*.
Sign. *Signum*.
Signal. *Signum; al*.
Similarity. *Similis; ar, ity*.
Similitude. *Similis; tude*.
Simplicity. sine. *Plico; ity*.
Simultaneous. *Simul; ous*.
Sinecure, sine. *Cura*.

Tragi-comedy, (Gr.) *Tragodia, Komos, Ode; y.*
Tragi-comic, (Gr.) *Tragodia, Komos; ic.*
Traitor. *Traditum; or.*
Tranquil. *Tranquillus.*
Transact, trans. *Actum.*
Transcend, tran. *Scando.*
Transcribe, tran. *Scribo.*
Transfer, trans. *Fero.*
Transfiguration, trans. *Figura; ion.* (L. Transfiguratio.)
Transfix, trans. *Fixum.*
Transformation, trans. *Forma; ion.*
Transgression, trans. *Gressus; ion.*
Transit, trans. *Itum.*
Transitory, trans. *Itum; ory.*
Translate, trans. *Latum.*
Translucent, trans. *Luceo; ent.*
Transmarine, trans. *Mare; ine.*
Transmigration, trans. *Migro; ate, ion.*
Transmit, trans. *Mitto.*
Transmute, trans. *Muto.*
Transparent, trans. *Pareo; ent.*
Transplant, trans. *Planto.*
Transport, trans. *Porto.*
Transposing, trans. *Positum; ing.*
Trapezium, (Gr.) *Trapezion.*
Trapezoid, (Gr.) *Trapezion, Eidos.*
Traverse, tra. *Versum.*
Treason. *Trado.*
Treaty. *Tractum; y.*
Tremendous. *Tremo; ous.* (L. Tremendus.)
Tremulous. *Tremo; ous.*
Triadelphous, (Gr.) *Tria, Adelphos; ous.*
Triandrian, (Gr.) *Tria, Andros; ian.*
Triangle. *Tria, Angulus.*
Tributary. *Tributum; ary.*
Tribute. *Tributum.*
Trigon, (Gr.) *Tria, Gonia.*
Trigonometry, (Gr.) *Tria, Gonia, Metron; y.*
Trimeter, (Gr.) *Tria, Metron.*
Triphthong, (Gr.) *Tria, Phthegma.*
Tripod, (Gr.) *Tria, Podos.*
Trite. *Tritum.*
Triton, (Gr.) *Tria, Tomos.*
Trivial. *Tria, Via; al.*
Trochee, (Gr.) *Trochaios.*
Trope, (Gr.) *Tropos.*
Trophy. (Gr.) *Tropos; y.*
Tropical, (Gr.) *Tropos; ical.*
Trouble. *Turba; ble.*
Truck, (Gr.) *Trochaios.*
Tubular. *Tubus,* a tube; *ar.*
Tuition. *Tuitus; ion.*
Tumid. *Tumeo; id.*
Tumult. *Tumeo.*
Tune, (Gr.) *Tonos.*
Turbulence. *Turba; ence.*
Turret. *Turris; et.*
Typhoid, (Gr.) *Typhos, Eidos.*
Typhus, (Gr.) *Typhos.*
Typical, (Gr.) *Typos; ical.*
Typify. *Typos; fy.*
Typography, (Gr.) *Typos, Grapho; y.*
Tyrannical, (Gr.) *Tyrannos; ical.*
Tyrannicide, (Gr.) *Tyrannos.* L. Cædo.
Tyrannize, (Gr.) *Tyrannos; ize.*
Tyrant, (Gr.) *Tyrannos.*

Ulterior. *Ultimus.*
Ultimately. *Ultimus; ate, ly.*
Ultimatum. *Ultimus.* (L. Ultimatum.)
Umbrage. *Umbra; age.*
Umbrageous. *Umbra; age, ous.*
Umbrella. *Umbra.*
Unanimous. *Unus, Animus; ous.*
Unctuous. *Unctum; ous.*
Undauntedly, un. *Domo; ed, ly.*
Undecagon, (Gr.) L. Unus. *Deka, Gonia.*
Undulate. *Unda; ate.* (L. Undula, a little wave.)
Uniformity. *Unus, Forma; ity.*
Unite. *Unus.*
Unity. *Unus; ity.*
Universal. *Unus, Versum; al.*
Universe. *Unus, Versum.*
Unprepared, un, pre. *Paro; ed.*
Unrivalled, un. *Rivus; al, ed.*
Unsurpassed, un, sur, for super. *Passus; ed.*
Unsymmetrical,(Gr.)un,sym. *Metron;ical.*
Uranography, (Gr.) *Ouranos, Grapho; y.*
Uranology, (Gr.) *Ouranos, Logos; y.*
Usage. *Usus; age.*
Usually. *Usus; al, ly.*
Usurp. *Usus, Rapio.*
Utensils. *Utor.*
Utility. *Utor; fle, ity.*

Vacate. *Vaco; ate.*
Vacation. *Vaco; ate, ion.*
Vacuum. *Vaco.*
Vagabond. *Vagus.* (L. Vagabundus.)
Vagaries. *Vagus; ury.*
Vagrant. *Vagus; ant.*
Vague. *Vagus.*
Valedictory. *Vale, Dictum; ory.*
Valiant. *Valeo; ant.*
Valid. *Valeo; id.*
Valor. *Valeo; or.*
Valuable. *Valeo; able.*
Value. *Valeo.*
Vanquish. *Vinco; ish.*
Varioloid, (Gr.) *Variola, Eidos.*
Vehement. *Vehemens,* violent.
Vehicle. *Veho; cle.*
Veil. *Velo.*
Venal. *Vendo; al.* (L. Venus, sale.)
Vender. *Vendo; er.*
Vendue. *Vendo.* (Fr. Vendue, sold.)
Vengeance. *Vindex; ance.* (Fr. Venger, to revenge.)
Ventilate. *Ventus; ate.*
Venture. *Ventum; ure.*
Veracity. *Veracis; ity.*
Verbal. *Verbum; al.*
Verbatim. *Verbum.*
Verbose. *Verbum; ose.*
Verdict. *Verus; dictum.*
Verge. *Vergo.*
Verify. *Verus; fy.*
Veritable. *Verus; ity, able.*
Verity. *Verus; ity.*
Vermin. *Vermis.*
Versatility. *Versum; fle, ity.*
Version. *Versum; ion.*
Vertex. *Verto.* (L. Vertex.)
Vertical. *Verto; ical.*
Vests. *Vestis.*

Vestige. *Vestigium.*
Vesture. *Vestis; ure.*
Veteran. *Veteris; an.*
Vetoed. *Veto; ed.*
Vex. *Veho.* (L. Vexo, I harass.)
Vice-(president). *Vicis.*
Vicinity. *Vicinus; ity.*
Victim. *Victum.* (L. Victima, a sacrifice.)
Victor. *Victum; or.*
Victory. *Victum; ory.*
Victuals. *Victum.*
View. *Video.*
Vigorous. *Vigor; ous.*
Vindicate. *Vindicis; ate.*
Vine. *Vinum.*
Vinegar. *Vinum, Acer.* (Fr. Aigre, sour.)
Vintage. *Vinum; age.*
Violation. *Violatum; ion.*
Violent. *Violo,* I injure; *ent.*
Virago. *Vir.* (L. Virago.)
Virtue. *Virtus.*
Virulent. *Virus; ulent.*
Visage. *Visum; age.*
Viscount. *Vicis, Comitis.*
Visible. *Visum; ible.*
Vision. *Visum; ion.*
Visionary. *Visum; ion, ary.*
Visitant. *Visum; ant.*
Vista. *Visum.*
Vital. *Vivo; al.* (L. Vita, life.)
Vitrify. *Vitrum; fy.*
Vitriol. *Vitrum.*
Vivacity. *Vivo; ity.*
Vivid. *Vivo; id.*
Vocabulary. *Voco; ary.*
Vocal. *Voco; al.*
Vocation. *Vocatum; ion.*

Vociferates. *Voco, Fero; ate.*
Vociferous. *Voco, Fero; ous.*
Voice. *Voco.*
Volatile. *Volatum; ile.*
Volley. *Volo.*
Voluble. *Volvo; ble.*
Volume. *Volvo.*
Voluntary. *Voluntas; ary.*
Volunteer. *Voluntas; eer.*
Voluptuary. *Voluptas; ary.*
Voluptuous. *Voluptas; ous.*
Voracity. *Voro; ity,* (state of being voracious.)
Voracious. *Voro; acious.*
Votary. *Votum; ary.*
Vote. *Votum.*
Voyage. *Via.*
Vulgarism. *Vulgus; ar, ism.*
Vulgarity. *Vulgus; ar, ity.*
Vulnerable. *Vulneris; able.*
Vulture. *Vultur.*
Vulturine. *Vultur; ine.*

Xylobalsamum, (Gr.) *Xylon, Balsamon.*
Xylography, (Gr.) *Xylon, Grapho; y.*
Xylophagous, (Gr.) *Xylon, Phago; ous.*

Zeal, (Gr.) *Zelos.*
Zealous, (Gr.) *Zelos; ous.*
Zephyr, (Gr.) *Zephyros.*
Zodiac, (Gr.) *Zoon; ac.*
Zone, (Gr.) *Zone.*
Zoography, (Gr.) *Zoon; Grapho, y.*
Zoolite, (Gr.) *Zoon, Lithos.*
Zoological, (Gr.) *Zoon, Logos; ical.*
Zoophyte, (Gr.) *Zoon, Phyton.*
Zootomy, (Gr.) *Zoon, Tomos; y.*

THE END.

CPSIA information can be obtained
at www.ICGtesting.com
Printed in the USA
BVHW042318120321
602295BV00005B/354